Finance Constraints and the Theory of Money
Selected Papers

This is a volume in
ECONOMIC THEORY, ECONOMETRICS, AND
MATHEMATICAL ECONOMICS
A Series of Monographs and Textbooks

Consulting Editor: Karl Shell, *Cornell University*

A complete list of titles in this series appears at the end of this volume.

Finance Constraints and the Theory of Money

Selected Papers

S. C. Tsiang
Chung-Hua Institution for Economic Research
Taipei, Taiwan

Edited by
Meir Kohn
Department of Economics
Dartmouth College
Hanover, New Hampshire

With contributions by
John Hicks, David Laidler, and Alan Stockman

ACADEMIC PRESS, INC.
Harcourt Brace Jovanovich, Publishers
Boston   San Diego   New York
Berkeley   London   Sydney
Tokyo   Toronto

ACADEMIC PRESS, INC.
1250 Sixth Avenue, San Diego, CA 92101

United Kingdom Edition published by
ACADEMIC PRESS INC. (LONDON) LTD.
24–28 Oval Road, London NW1 7DX

Library of Congress Cataloging-in-Publication Data

Tsiang, Sho-chieh.
  Finance constraints and the theory of money: selected papers/S. C. Tsiang; edited by
Meir Kohn: with contributions by Sir John Hicks, David Laidler, and Alan Stockman.
    p.   cm. – (Economic theory, econometrics, and mathematical economics)
  Bibliography: p.
  Includes index.
  ISBN 0-12-701720-8.   ISBN 0-12-701721-6 (pbk.)
  1. Money.   I. Kohn, Meir G.   II. Hicks, John Richard, Sir, Date–.   III. Laidler,
David E. W.   IV. Stockman, Alan C.   V. Title.
VI. Series.
HG221T79 1989   88-30264
332.4′01–dc19
                                                                                      CIP

Printed in the United States of America
89 90 91 92   9 8 7 6 5 4 3 2 1

Contents

v

Section II

Section III

Section IV

Section V

Preface

Following the Keynesian Revolution, and largely because of it, the theory of money underwent a long period of confusion and controversy, out of which it is only now beginning to emerge.

The focus of the *General Theory* was on macroeconomic coordination failure and the resulting unemployment; money and interest were of only secondary concern. However, because the existing theory of money and interest (call it the loanable funds theory) proved inconsistent with Keynes' income-expenditure mechanism—the key to his new concept of "unemployment equilibrium"—Keynes was forced to invent a new theory (the liquidity preference theory) that *was* consistent with it. It is increasingly recognized today that whatever the merits of Keynes' macroeconomics (and here, too, of course, opinions differ), his liquidity preference theory of money has proven to be a mistake.

The liquidity preference theory has undergone many incarnations, from the early Keynesian models of Hicks and of others, through Patinkin's Walrasian version and Tobin's portfolio-balance theory, to Wallace's overlapping-generations model. All of these versions have followed Keynes in viewing money essentially as an asset, as a store of value, and in viewing the theory of money as a branch of the theory of portfolio choice.

This Keynesian theory of money breaks with a centuries-old tradition that has understood money primarily in terms of its function as a medium of exchange. That tradition, to which almost every monetary theorist before Keynes adhered, could be characterized as a "flow" approach to money in contrast with the "stock" approach of Keynes and his followers.

This volume gathers together the work of one of the most cogent critics of the Keynesian stock approach to money in all its forms and one of the foremost champions of the flow approach—S. C. Tsiang.

Tsiang's criticism of the liquidity preference theory began with his "Note on Speculation and Income Stability," published in 1943 and reprinted here as Chapter 2. In it, he challenged the Keynesian account of how the speculative demand for money can transform investment shocks into fluctuations in spending. He showed that any attempt to make the story logically consistent leads back inexorably to the flow approach, and, in particular, to the Wicksellian mechanism of monetary accommodation by the banking system.

The clear implication is that the Keynesian income-expenditure theory should be combined not with a liquidity preference theory of money and interest but with a loanable funds theory à la Robertson. Tsiang attempts this in his "Liquidity Preference and Loanable Funds Theories, Multiplier and Velocity Analysis" (1956; Chapter 3). In "The Role of Money in Trade Balance Stability" (1961; Chapter 4), Tsiang takes the same approach to bringing money into Meade's theory of the balance of payments, in a paper that proven to be an influential precursor of the monetary approach to the balance of payments.

These points of theory are far from academic; they have profound implications for the conduct of policy. In "Fashions and Misconceptions in Monetary Theory and Their Influences on Financial and Banking Practices" (1979; Chapter 5), Tsiang draws on his experience at the IMF and as an economic adviser to the Nationalist government on Taiwan to show how Keynesian policies (low interest rates, inflation, and over-valued currencies) have proved to be a disaster for developing countries and how Taiwan's spectacular economic progress owes much to its Robertsonian monetary policy.

These papers make up Section I of the collection.

Section II takes up another strand in Tsiang's work, his criticism of the Walrasian version of Keynesian monetary theory that has its roots in the work of Lange and Patinkin. In some respects, Tsiang's "Walras' Law, Say's Law and Liquidity Preference in General Equilibrium Analysis" (1966; Chapter 6) goes beyond the better known critiques of Patinkin by Hahn and Clower. Like Clower, Tsiang develops the idea of a constraint involving the medium of exchange–in addition to the usual budget constraint–as a way of giving money a distinctive role in a general equilibrium model. But unlike Clower's static "cash-in-advance constraint", Tsiang's "finance constraint" is fully dynamic and integrates borrowing and lending (so that money is not the only asset) as well as banks and money creation.

The chief application of Walrasian monetary theory (to be distinguished, of course, from the monetary theory of Walras), and in particular of the reliance on Walras' Law, has been in the monetary approach to the balance of payments. This application is discussed in Chapters 7, 8 and 9.

Tsiang has also been a consistent critic of yet another version of the Keynesian stock approach–Tobin's portfolio balance theory of money. This is the subject of Section III. In "The Rationale of the Mean-Standard Deviation Analysis" (1972; Chapter 10), Tsiang argues for the validity in general, as an approximation, of this type of portfolio theory, but he also argues that it is inappropriate as a basis for the demand for money; money is a "dominated asset" in terms of portfolio theory, so the demand for it must rest on other motives. In "The Diffusion of Reserves and the Money Supply Multiplier" (1978; Chapter 11), he therefore replaces the standard theory of the money supply multiplier, based on the portfolio demand for cash and various types of deposit, with a theory built on money flows and turnover rates. Tsiang's critique of Tobin is summarized in Chapter 12.

Section IV is devoted to Tsiang's critique of Friedman. In Chapter 13, he argues that Friedman's "theoretical framework" is essentially Keynesian. The alternative to Keynes is not Friedman but Robertson. Chapter 14 attacks Friedman's notion of the "optimum supply of money" as being based on a fallacy of composition. What is best for the individual, in terms of the return to money as a store of value, is not best for society as a whole, considering money's social role as a medium of exchange.

The collected papers are preceded by a newly written introduction (Chapter 1) in which Tsiang provides a valuable perspective on the development of his ideas. It also provides a fascinating look at the tribulations to be endured by anyone critical of the fashion of the day in economic theory.

The volume concludes, in Section V, with three appreciative essays by distinguished monetary theorists. The first, by Sir John Hicks, is a reply to Tsiang's criticism of the liquidity preference theory. Hicks, of course, is one of the principal architects of that theory, as well as being, in recent years, one of its most forceful critics. The second, by David Laidler, puts both Tsiang's criticism and the theory he criticizes into the historical perspective of the development of monetary thought. The third, by Alan Stockman, surveys the application of the sort of monetary theory advocated by Tsiang in recent work in international economics. The work surveyed by Stockman is part of a broader resurgence of interest in the flow approach in its modern guise of the finance-constraint or cash-in-advance approach to money.

Meir Kohn

Acknowledgements

I wish to express my gratitude to Professor Meir Kohn whose persuasion and energetic help made the publication of this collection possible; to Sir John Hicks, and Professors David Laidler and Alan Stockman for gracing this book with their essays; to Dr. Chi-ping Mo for his help in correcting the galley proof; to Miss Yu-mei Wu for ungrudingly undertaking all the onerous secretarial work for the book; and lastly but above all, to my wife, Hsi-Tsin for her encouragement all these years and for suffering and bearing quietly my reticence and remoteness during my work.

My thanks are also due to *Economica*, the *Economic Journal*, the *American Economic Review*, John Wiley & Sons, Inc., the *International Economic Review*, the MIT Press Journals, the *Journal of Money, Credit and Banking*, Clarenden Press, Oxford University Press, *Zeitschrift für die gesamte Staatswissenschaft*, Physica-Verlag, the Institute of Economics, Academia Sinica, and the National Taiwan University for granting me permission to reproduce my articles under their copyrights.

S.C. Tsiang

CHAPTER **1**

Introduction

S. C. Tsiang

1. Background to the Development of My Thinking on Monetary Theory

This volume is a collection of a number of my papers on monetary theory written over a period that spans from 1943 to the present. I should perhaps beg indulgence for the inclusion of the earliest one, written when I was still a graduate student at the London School of Economics (then evacuated to Cambridge because of World War II). However, that paper shows quite clearly the origins of the line of thought that I followed almost unswervingly throughout my later work.

At the time that paper was written, Keynesian economics had already achieved a position of predominance, particularly in Cambridge, where even Professor Pigou, the venerable successor to Marshall, was then undergoing a gradual process of conversion and assimilation to Keynesian ideas. The younger LSE faculty (e.g. Lerner, Kaldor, and others) were gradually being won over by the Keynesian revolution and one by one joining the Keynesian camp even before the evacuation to Cambridge. However, the more senior LSE faculty, notably Hayek, Robbins, and Robertson, remained skeptical and critical of Keynes.

It was certainly a very exciting time for us young students. We were

Finance Constraints and the Theory of Money
ISBN 0-12-701720-8
ISBN 0-12-701721-6 (pbk)

1

free while in Cambridge to attend the lectures of teachers of both schools. To hear the traditional Marshallian theory and that of the Austrian School expounded by Robertson and Hayek and then to hear the same theories mercilessly attacked and ridiculed by Mrs. Robinson and others was a very thrilling experience. It could not help but generate on our part a cautious and critical attitude towards the whole controversy.

Traditionally, the interest rate had been thought of as the price that established equilibrium in the market for loans, which in turn had been analyzed in terms of the demand and supply of flows of funds. But Keynes' revolutionary new theory now insisted that the chief components of the demand and supply of loanable funds, investment and savings respectively, were either equal to one another by definition or always automatically brought into equality by a timeless multiplier process. It would therefore be meaningless to treat them as independent and opposite forces on the sides of demand and supply. Keynes suggested instead, as the only sensible alternative, that the interest rate be regarded as the price paid for the advantage of holding money, the most liquid asset, in place of other, less liquid assets (or alternatively the compensation received for foregoing this liquidity). Thus he claimed that the interest rate should be regarded as being determined by the demand schedule for holding money and the stock of money in existence. Although the key Keynesian assertion that savings and investment are automatically equal had been demonstrated by Robertson to be a deceptive fallacy once the proper time sequence of the supply and demand for funds in the money market had been considered, the stock approach to monetary theory seemed to have taken root firmly on both sides of the Atlantic.

2. Why I Objected to the Stock Approach from the Start

From the very beginning I was greatly puzzled by the Keynesian view that a stock equilibrium approach was needed to understand the circulation of money and to explain why that circulation should sometimes swell up and sometimes ebb down. Indeed, I often wondered why an equilibrium between the voluntary demand to hold money and the total stock of money in existence should not lead to a cessation of the circular flow of money altogether. Since money is constantly flowing, it has always seemed to me, ever since my days as a student, that the

Wicksell-Robertson flow approach is more natural than Keynes' new-fangled stock approach in explaining fluctuations in money flows.

My doubts about the Keynesian stock approach were brought to a head by my reading of Nicholas (later Lord) Kaldor's celebrated 1939 article "Speculation and Income Stability." Kaldor's main thesis was that purchases of securities on the securities market by bull speculators, in the face of a rise in the demand for funds, would prevent the price of securities from falling sufficiently or even make it rise instead. This would create an excess demand for investable funds on the part of investors, above the supply of savings, which would have to be met by the speculators themselves. He claimed that this type of speculative purchase of securities would have an expansionary multiplier effect, and its converse, the speculative sale of securities by bear speculators, would have a contractionary multiplier effect.

In his analysis of the securities market, Kaldor employed the traditional flow approach in which savings and investment are treated as flows of the supply and demand for investable funds. His analysis showed how speculators could impede the proper functioning of this market and create a situation of excess demand or excess supply. He also pointed out quite clearly that speculators do not normally maintain a large supply of idle speculative balances on which they can draw when they buy securities; nor do they normally put the proceeds of their speculative sales of securities into such idle balances. Instead, they usually go to the short-term money market (usually through their agents, the stockbrokers) to raise the funds they need, and put the extra cash they acquire from their sales into short-term assets, or else use it to pay off their outstanding short-term debts (in particular, margin debts to their brokers). This naturally gives rise to the crucial questions of what would happen to the funds so transferred by the speculators to the short-term market and how the funds they transferred from the short-term to the long-term market, would be supplied by the former.

In discussing these crucial questions in relation to the short-term money market, Kaldor abandoned the traditional flow approach, in favor of the then fashionable Keynesian approach that envisages the money market as operating in terms of the total stock demand for money and the total stock supply. The short-term rate of interest is thus supposed to be determined by the total stock of money and by the aggregate demand for money, which in turn is supposed to depend only on the level of income and on the interest rate. Since the activities of speculators in the long-term securities market have no immediate impact on the level of income or on the stock of money, they are regarded as also having no immediate effect on the short-term interest rate. Kaldor concludes, therefore, that speculators, by bringing about an excess of investment over savings (or an excess of savings over investment) in the securities market would directly set off an expansionary (or contractionary) multiplier process. The role of speculators in transferring excess demand or supply from the securities market to the money market is thus completely lost.

Even though Kaldor's article was widely acclaimed at the time and apparently enjoyed the approval of Keynes himself, I made bold to point out in my 1943 critique that there is inherent in the stock approach to analysis of the money market this tendency to overlook flows, and I supported my argument with statistics on the U.S. during the great boom of the 1920s and the stock market crash of 1929.

Those statistics clearly showed that the great speculative fever on the New York Stock Exchange led to very heavy borrowings on the part of speculators buying on margin. These borrowings were reflected in steady increases in the volume of brokers' loans; in the U.S., brokers generally accommodated their customers' demand for funds in the first instance, passing on this demand to the short-term money market in the form of brokers' loans. These borrowings by proxy in the short-term money market on the part of speculators certainly had an impact on that market. The borrowings were closely paralleled by corresponding increases in the supply of bank money as the demand for brokers' loans was largely accommodated by banks. This accommodation was supported by the monetary authorities who were anxious not to let the short-term rate of interest fluctuate too much. From January 1923 to May 1928, the monthly average rate on stock exchange call loans never rose above 5.7%, while total brokers' loans outstanding expanded from $1,860m at the end of 1922 to $4,640m at the end of March 1928 (an increase of $2,780m).[1] This enormous increase in the demand for loans by brokers was clearly accommodated to a very large extent by an expansion in the supply of bank money, since over the same period the demand deposits of all member banks also increased rapidly from $15,728m at the end of 1922 to $18,227m at the end of March 1928 (an increase of $2,499m). Thus, this is a clear case of a Wicksellian cumulative expansion perpetrated in the name of stabilizing the short-term interest rate and of maintaining so-called orderly conditions in the money market.

It was only after June 1928 that the short-term rate was allowed to rise to 6.32% and then further to 8.86% in December the same year. In

1929, a serious effort seems to have been made to check the expansion of the money supply; while the volume of brokers' loans continued to increase from $6,440m at the end of 1928 to $8,525m on October 4th, 1929, demand deposits of member banks not only did not rise but actually fell somewhat from $21,167m in December 1928 to $19,426m on October 4th 1929.

After October 4th, speculative selling became an avalanche, and brokers' loans, which reflected speculators' purchases on margin, dropped precipitously from $8,525m on October 4th, 1929, to $4,110m at the end of December that year, a drop of $4,415m in less than three months. Apparently, the monetary authorities tried at first to keep the money supply from falling, letting the short-term interest rate bear the brunt. Thus the average short-term rate tumbled from 8.62% during the month of September to 4.88% during December, while the demand deposits of member banks actually rose slightly to $20,543m at the end of December from $19,426m in October, despite a drop in the volume of brokers' loans of $4.4 billion during the same period. After the end of the year, however, the monetary authorities seem to have given up the fight and let member bank demand deposits drop together with the further drop in brokers' loans. Thus, by the end of 1931 member bank demand deposits had dropped $4,790m below their level at the end of 1929 to $15,753m, paralleling the $3,395m drop in brokers' loans from $4,110m at the end of the preceding year to a mere $715m then.

It is obvious, therefore, that the transfer by speculators of the excess demand (or excess supply) of funds from the stock market to the money market in the real world does have a tremendous impact on the latter, and the so-called multiplier effect of speculation in the capital market alleged by Kaldor depends very much on how the excess demand (or excess supply) of funds will be financed (or absorbed) in the money market. However, Kaldor, who adopted a flow analysis with respect to the capital market but switched to a Keynesian stock analysis in dealing with the money market, totally overlooked the effects of these transferred flows, because the stock approach has an inherent difficulty in dealing with flows.

3. My First Attempt to Criticize the Liquidity Preference Theory Making Use of Keynes' Own Post-General Theory Concessions

When I came to the United States in 1949 to work for the International Monetary Fund, I found that the liquidity preference theory of the rate of interest and the stock approach to the analysis of the money market had already been firmly accepted by the majority of American academic economists. Loanable funds theory and the traditional flow approach had come to be regarded as decisively refuted by Keynes and his followers and consequently had been banished from most textbooks and classrooms in the United States.

My own early analysis of speculation in the U.S. stock market in the 1920s and my later empirical work at the IMF[2] convinced me that the loanable funds approach was the more reliable and accurate method of analysis and that the newly fashionable liquidity preference approach had an inherent tendency to neglect important flow effects, often leading to incorrect conclusions. As a result, I ventured to challenge the prevailing orthodoxy by writing an article pointing out the common mistakes committed by practically all liquidity preference theorists in overlooking the flow elements of the demand and supply of money.

In that article, I pointed out that liquidity preference theory would become identical with loanable funds theory if (1) the flow elements of the transactions demand for money (Keynes' finance demand for liquidity) were fully taken into account and if (2) the adjustments in the stock demand to hold money in response to changes in the interest rate and other parameters could be assumed to be instantaneous. In practice, however, the flow nature of the transactions demand for money was persistently neglected by economists using the liquidity preference theory—Keynes himself, as well as Kaldor and other Keynesians. And although I too, like most Keynesians, assumed that adjustments in the stock demand for money could be regarded as being close enough to instantaneous, in actual fact, lags in response are inevitable, as well as rational in view of the costs of transactions and decisions. Full adjustment of the stock demand for money to the stock supply and to the ruling rate of interest cannot be completed instantaneously. Indeed, in a rapidly changing world, adjustments in stock demand may never be completed before the variables determining that demand, and the stock supply, have changed again.

Indeed, the first public critic of this article, G. Ackley (September 1957), actually used this noninstantaneous adjustment argument as a valid criticism of my attempt to reconcile the liquidity preference and loanable funds theories. Professor Ackley did not, however, seem to realize that while this argument does not affect the validity of the loanable funds theory, it does invalidate the claim of the liquidity preference theory that equilibrium between the stock demand and supply of money determines the rate of interest at every moment of time. If equilibrium between the stock demand and supply of money cannot be attained at every moment or even for most of the time in a rapidly changing world, how can it determine the interest rate at every moment as claimed by the liquidity preference theory?

My article was accepted for publication by a conservative managing editor of the *American Economic Review* who perhaps shared my views and so published it as the leading article in that issue. Soon after its publication, I was pleasantly surprised to receive letters of appreciation from some very eminent, though mostly conservative, economists, such as D. H. Robertson himself (then still teaching at Cambridge), Jacob Viner (then at Princeton), Fritz Machlup (then at Johns Hopkins), H. G. Johnson (then at Manchester), Lawrence Seltzer, Lowell Harris, Hla Myint, Murray Kemp, and others. This naturally gave me much needed encouragement.

Professor Robertson's letter was particularly touching. It began, "I have just read your recent article in the *A.E.R.* with great interest and appreciation. So far as I can judge, it really clears these matters up completely. . ." and concluded, "Again many compliments, and—if I may be so egotistical—warm thanks for the rigorous demonstration that I have not been talking utter rot all these years."

I also received a letter of a different sort from Professor A. H. Hansen of Harvard, who rebuked me for treating income (actually disposable income) as a given predetermined variable, as he insisted that it must be determined jointly with the interest rate as in the Keynesian model. I answered that, since we obviously cannot start our analysis from a day that has no yesterday, all that happened yesterday must be taken as given. Thus, income received yesterday and disposable today should always be treated as predetermined, while income to be earned today should indeed be regarded as determined today together with today's interest rate. It was this failure to distinguish sharply between the incomes of different dates that caused many of the confusions in Keynes' theory. I never received a reply from Professor Hansen, so I never learned what kind of reaction he had to my unrepentant attitude, nor what he finally thought of my article.

4. My Encounter with "Walras' Law"

A much more serious criticism came two years later from Professor Patinkin in his article "Liquidity Preference and Loanable Funds: Stock and Flow Analysis" (*Economica*, November 1958). His argument was based on what O. Lange termed the "Walras Law" in his 1942 article "Say's Law: Restatement and Criticism." Lange in turn probably picked up the idea from Hicks' demonstration of the equivalence between loanable funds and liquidity preference theories in his *Value and Capital*.

I was never really satisfied with this demonstration by Hicks, nor was I happy with the attempt along similar lines by W. Feller and H. M. Somers (which was also based on "Walras' Law"). In my 1956 article, however, I was able only to point out how unconvincing the proof of equivalence on the basis of Walras' axiom was, but not to pinpoint exactly why Walras' Law should not be applied to monetary theory or exactly what went wrong in Hicks' and Patinkin's ostensibly very neat and logical arguments. The reading of the latter's 1958 article, however, further convinced me that something must definitely be wrong with this line of reasoning.

Although Patinkin showed that, by what he called Walras' Law, the loanable funds theory was totally equivalent to the liquidity preference theory, in the very same article he claimed that in a dynamic analysis the loanable funds theory and the liquidity preference theory could, on certain occasions, indicate that the interest rate would move in opposite directions. If, on the basis of Walras' Law, both the loanable funds theory and the liquidity preference theory are logically correct, how could they yield diametrically opposite results on certain occasions? This puzzling question could not help but convince me further that something must have gone wrong somewhere with this line of argument.

5. An Enlightenment or a Confusion?

I decided, therefore, to go back beyond the writings of Hicks and Patinkin to check the original work of Walras and Keynes in search of clues to the solution of this puzzle. First, I checked whether there were any references to Walras in Keynes. I found the only one in the *General Theory* to consist of a claim that Walras was strictly in the classical tradition in asserting that "the rate of interest is fixed at the point where saving, which represents the supply of new capital, is equal to the demand for it". (*General Theory*, p. 177). Obviously, Walras' general equilibrium approach and the "Walras' Law" were quite alien to Keynes.

Futhermore, some of Keynes' elaborations of his theory one year after the publication of the *General Theory* convinced me that the

Keynesian line of thinking was incompatible with Patinkin's interpretation of Walras' Law and with his understanding of the liquidity preference theory. In answer to criticism by Ohlin and others, Keynes had admitted in June 1937 that saying that the rate of interest depends on the demand and supply of money "may be misleading, because it obscures the answer to the question, demand for money in terms of what?" The correct answer to this question had been suggested by Keynes in the preceding sentence of the same paragraph: "the liquidity preference theory of the rate of interest which I have set forth in my *General Theory* . . . makes the rate of interest depend on the present supply of money and the demand schedule for a present claim on money in terms of a deferred claim on money." That is, the demand for money for the purpose of Keynes' liquidity preference theory is supposed to consist only of the demand for money in terms of deferred claims on money. The demand for money in terms of other commodities— peanuts, labor services, etc.—are not to be considered at all.

However, Patinkin, in his interpretation of Walrasian general equilibrium, included all the excess demands for money, including those in terms of peanuts, labor services, etc., in his concept of the total excess demand for money. This potpourri total demand for money is to be brought into equality with the aggregate stock of money, and the market that is to bring this about is called the money market. Actually, in the real world, there is no market in which this potpourri demand for money plays any role at all. Furthermore, there is no logical reason why such a potpourri demand for money, together with the stock of money, should determine the interest rate in particular rather than any other price. The confusion which Keynes had feared and warned against in his 1937 note was indeed fully realized in Patinkin.

Thus, it was important to see whether the interpretation of Lange and Patinkin of the liquidity preference theory, based on what they called Walras' Law, had any foundation in Walras' own theory of money. I turned, therefore, to Walras himself to see how he defined the demand for money proper—the *encaisse désirée* rather than the demand for the *numeraire* commodity—and especially whether he too tried to derive it by aggregation of the excess demands for all other goods.

I was relieved to find that Walras never used "Walras' Law" in his monetary theory. Indeed, in his theories of exchange, production, and general equilibrium, money as a medium of exchange made no appearance; the omniscient, superhuman auctioneer obviated any need for it. It was only in Part VI of his book, *Theory of Circulation and Money*, that he tried to make amends for this lack of a circulating medium. He did this by introducing the arbitrary assumption that the preliminary *tâtonnement* conducted by the auctioneer merely determined relative prices (or prices in terms of an arbitrary *numeraire*) and the quantities to be supplied and demanded of all goods; the actual deliveries and transfers of goods, however, did not take place automatically at the close of the auction but only later against payments in actual money, the required means of payment. He further posited that actual payments and transfers of goods were to be made at fixed dates, which were not the same for different goods. To ensure the availability of those goods an individual wished to buy before he could receive payments for the goods he had sold, each individual would desire to keep in his possession a cash balance equal in value to all or some of the goods he wished to purchase. In Walras' own words (Jaffe's translation) "the value of all or part of the final products and perpetual net income which the parties to the exchange wish to purchase, and which they desire to keep in their possession in the form of cash or money savings, constitutes their desired cash-balance (*encaisse désirée*)" (Walras, p. 321).

Thus what Walras called the *encaisse désirée* is, like the demand for money for transactions purposes or Keynes' demand for finance, a function of planned expenditures. The aggregate *encaisse désirée* is then to be brought into equality with the existing stock of money in a secondary *tâtonnement* that determines the price level in terms of money. There is nowhere in Walras any suggestion that the demand and supply of money would determine the interest rate, which in Walras' scheme is already determined in the preliminary *tâtonnement* as the price of perpetual streams of income (i.e. the price of consol-like bonds) (see Walras, Part V).

Walras' monetary theory is, therefore, essentially the same as the quantity theory of Fisher or Marshall, and, like theirs, Walras' theory differs from one based on "Walras' Law"; the latter would interpret any purchase of goods as an act of supplying money, not as the basis for a demand for money (Lange, 1942, p. 50; Patinkin, 1949, p. 6 and 1965, p. 35). Thus Walras' own concept of the demand for money (like those of Fisher, Marshall, and Keynes) contrasts sharply with the one Lange and Patinkin derive from what they called Walras' Law. This seems to have escaped the notice of many economists who have never read Walras themselves, but have nonetheless learned to invoke Walras' Law routinely in their monetary analysis.

If the monetary theory of Walras is totally different from the theory that Lange and Patinkin developed on the basis of what they called Walras' Law, surely this is not Walras' fault but their own. They mistakenly understood the preliminary *tâtonnement* of Walras to refer to transactions in the real world, incorrectly presuming that an individual's demand for any good must be what he intends to carry away from the market after all the auctioneering and transactions are concluded. They failed to realize that in a money-using economy a major part of the demand for money—i.e., the demand for transactions balances or the demand for finance—arises prior to transactions. Formulating the demand for money in terms of "Walras' Law" (which is actually no more that the aggregate budget constraint for the preliminary *tâtonnement*) leaves out this transactions demand, while incorrectly including temporary passive receipts of cash as a part of the intentional demand for money.

6. Challenging an "Axiom"—Sheer Madness?

In light of these problems I decided to write a paper criticizing the application of "Walras' Law" to monetary theory. I was promptly warned by well-meaning friends that it was extremely unwise to do so because Walras' Law was quickly becoming accepted in economics as an axiom, and anyone who attacked an axiom would likely be regarded as either a crackpot or, at the least, muddleheaded. Nevertheless, I persisted and submitted the finished paper to the *AER*. The managing editor at the time bluntly rejected it, saying that, although his reader (whom I later found out to be Professor Paul Davidson) had recommended its publication, he had to exercise his prerogative to overrule the recommendation because he personally thought the paper was "absurd."

After trying another major American journal without success, I came to the conclusion that Walras' Law was too firmly entrenched in the mainstream of American economic thinking and that editors of American economics journals were too conformist to allow the publication of my attack on it. I decided, therefore, to seek publication abroad where conformism was less strong. My first try was the *International Economic Review*, which is partly edited by Japanese economists, and luckily it was accepted there with little fuss. But publication had already been held up for several years by the rebuffs the paper had encountered in the U.S.

7. The Confusing Influence of Walras' Law on the Theory of International Finance

"Walras' Law, Say's Law and Liquidity Preference in General Equilibrium Analysis" hardly created a ripple in the mainstream of American economics, which flowed on smugly as ever. Moreover, the application of Walras' Law was being further extended to open economies and hence to balance of payments theory and exchange rate theory. Here, the application of Walras' Law ruled out, by its very nature, consideration of the pretrade demand for transactions balances of both domestic and foreign money. When this type of analysis was combined with the prevalent stock approach to money and assets, it was little wonder that flow considerations, such as the influence of savings and investments on the domestic money market and of exports and imports on the foreign exchange market, tended to be left out of consideration.

As a consequence, we had a crop of new balance of payments theories and exchange rate theories that made the stock demand and supply of money the sole forces determining the balance of payments— or the exchange rate, if the latter was perfectly flexible. Since the demand and supply of money had previously been said by neoclassical economists such as Fisher, Marshall, Walras, Wicksell, and Friedman to determine the price level, and by Keynes and his followers to determine the interest rate, one was naturally rather bewildered to be told now that this same equilibrium condition for a single market could be called upon to determine yet even more variables. The source of confusion here is again precisely the one that Keynes had warned about a year after the publication of his *General Theory*: "the demand for money in terms of what?" By now, the answer had become thoroughly confounded.

Unfortunately, with the sloppy way of thinking induced by Lange's and Patinkin's interpretation of Walras' Law, economists had ceased to ask themselves this question. By assuming that all prices save one are determined in their own markets, and then applying "Walras' Law," the potpourri supply and demand for money can be said to determine any price "left over," be it the price of peanuts or the exchange rate. Thus, we obtain a convenient "monetary approach" as an alternative way to determine the price of any good, whenever we find it difficult to specify its own supply and demand functions.

Since I have grave doubts whether the so-called demand for money derived from "Walras' Law" has any economic meaning, I do not believe that there is any validity to this convenient alternative. Specifically, I do not believe that the demand and supply of money can be used as a short cut to explain the balance of payments.

8. Another Attempt to Buck a New Academic Fashion

When I visited Nuffield College, Oxford, during a sabbatical in 1976–77, I was invited to attend the annual conference of the International Economics Study Group of the United Kingdom, held at Sussex University in September 1976, and to present a paper. I decided to take the opportunity to express my dissenting views on the new monetary approach to the balance of payments. The paper, entitled "The Monetary Theoretic Foundation of the Modern Monetary Approach to the Balance of Payments," created a stir, but it was difficult to tell whether the reaction was predominantly positive or negative.

After the conference, the local organizer told me that, as in previous years, the proceedings of the conference, to include all papers presented, would be published by Macmillan. However, this year, since the founder of the International Economics Study Group was now in Chicago, he would have to send the papers and proceedings to him first for his general approval and editing.

A month or so later, the local organizer, a junior fellow at Nuffield at that time, told me rather sheepishly that the founder of the group had written back from Chicago that this year's proceedings were not to be published at all, and that he would let each contributor do whatever he liked with his own paper.

I knew immediately which paper had offended him. Apparently, the academic potentate in Chicago, who had issued this instruction, had not had the gall to exclude the offending paper alone, so he had resorted to denying publication to the whole volume of papers and proceedings. I felt extremely sorry for the other contributors.

I realized that the academic atmosphere in the United States was still very intolerant towards any critical discussion of Walras' Law, so that if I tried to publish the paper there, it would most likely receive a series of time-wasting rebuffs. I decided, therefore, to try to publish it in England rather than in the United States, because it seemed to me that English economists showed much more tolerance towards dissenting opinions than their American colleagues. As I was then visiting Nuffield, I submitted it to *Oxford Economic Papers*, which had a number of Nuffield economists on its editorial board. It was quickly accepted and published in the following year (1977) as the leading article in the November issue. This indicated to me that my thesis had some sympathetic support in England at least, even though in the United States it would have been regarded at that time by many journal editors as an unpublishable heresy, and would have been looked upon by some academics with something approaching odium theologicum.[3]

9. My Skepticism about Portfolio Balance as the Basis for Monetary Theory

In my criticism of the theory of liquidity preference and of Patinkin's interpretation of Walras' Law, I noticed that both shared a common feature—their emphasis on the portfolio demand for money, the demand for money to hold, rather than the demand for money to use or to spend. The theoretical justification, shared by both, for such a demand for money to hold was the one originally suggested by Hicks in his seminal article of 1935—the balance between the risk and expected returns of holding various assets. This principle was later elaborated further by Tobin, Markowitz, and Hicks himself and became accepted as an integral part of mainstream monetary theory. I have myself always objected to an exclusive reliance on this portfolio allocation argument to explain the demand for money, as I think it neglects the importance of the demand for money to spend—the demand for transactions balances or Keynes' rediscovered finance demand for liquidity.

In the later 1960s, mean-variance portfolio balance theory had come under a different kind of attack by K. Borch and M. Feldstein. This attack had forced Tobin to concede that the theory is applicable only if either the investor's utility function is quadratic or if the uncertain investment outcomes faced by the investor are normally distributed. However, acknowledging that at least one of these two conditions is necessary for the application of E-S analysis is equivalent to admitting that E-S analysis is practically useless. On the one hand, a quadratic specification is generally recognized as being unsuitable for a utility function: it not only limits its range of applicability, but, even within this range, it has the highly implausible implication of increasing absolute risk-aversion, which both Kenneth Arrow and John Hicks have denounced as absurd. On the other hand, the assumption of a normal distribution for investment outcomes is obviously unrealistic: stocks of limited-liability corporations would surely have a skewed distribution, since their prices cannot possibly fall below zero, and progressive taxation, stop-loss hedging, and other factors are all calculated to turn otherwise more or less symmetric distributions into negatively or positively skewed ones. Hence, this concession of Tobin's amounted to an acknowledgement that the mean-variance analysis of portfolio allocation might as well be abandoned. Tobin, of course, did not intend to go that far, but he offered no way to salvage mean-variance analysis. In fact, he seemed to show little concern for the threat this posed to the validity of the modern theory of money which had been built on a foundation of mean-variance analysis.

In the June 1972 *AER*, I published a paper, "The Rationale of the Mean-Standard Deviation Analysis, Skewness Preference, and the Demand for Money," which was ostensibly an attempt to rescue mean-variance analysis by demonstrating that it might still be an adequate approximation for analyzing the behavior of small risk takers—i.e., cautious investors who normally assume rather small risks relative to their total wealth. For major risk takers—i.e., entrepreneurs who regularly risk a major proportion of their total wealth—it would have to be supplemented by consideration of higher moments or abandoned altogether. As such a defense, it was promptly accepted by the editor. The real thrust of the paper, however, lay in its final section, "Implications for the Theory of the Demand for Money." There it was shown that E-S analysis, first suggested by Hicks in his seminal 1935 paper and later developed by Tobin (1958) and Hicks himself (1962, 1967), is not really capable of explaining a rational asset demand for cash balances as part of an investment portfolio. The reason for this conclusion, which should not have pleased supporters of the modern portfolio balance approach to the theory of money, is that when E-S indifference curves are derived from any acceptable utility function, they must have a positive slope of less than 45 degrees. This implies that so long as there is an asset the expected yield of which is larger than the standard deviation of this yield, such an asset will dominate the holding of cash in excess of transactions and precautionary balances. Since there must exist a host of such assets—e.g., savings deposits and treasury bills—E-S analysis is really quite incapable of doing what liquidity preference theorists have expected of it.[4]

Soon after the publication of this paper, I received a letter from Prof. Gerhard Tintner, then at the University of Southern California, which began with the sentences, "I have just read your article in the *AER* with great interest. As far as I am concerned, it finally cleared up the whole matter completely. . ." It reminded me of the nice letter that I had received from the late Sir Dennis Robertson after the publication of my 1956 article. Once again I experienced the joy of hearing some echoes of my own cries in the wilderness.

Several months later the editor of the *AER* sent me an assortment of comments on my article by K. Borch, G. O. Bierwag, and H. Levy for comments and replies. These comments, however, were all concerned with some technical problems to do with E-S indifference curves, which I think I solved and answered to my own satisfaction in my reply (*AER*, June 1974). Rather disappointingly, there were no comments on, nor responses to, the main thrust of my article, the assertion that E-S analysis is insufficient to explain the holding of cash balances as an investment. The liquidity preference school of monetary theory seemed to take no heed of my criticism and has remained oblivious to it right up to the present.

10. A Second Attempt to Challenge the Supremacy of the Liquidity Preference Theory

Disappointed with the total lack of response from the liquidity preference theorists, I decided to marshall all my critical arguments against the modern stock or portfolio approach to monetary theory and combine them into a single open frontal attack. The result was "Stock or Portfolio Approach to Monetary Theory and the Neo-Keynesian School of James Tobin."

I chose Professor Tobin as the target of my challenge because I thought him to be the most prominent and generally recognized leader of the school, at least in the United States. I hoped very much to elicit some reaction in the form of a formal reply from him, which could be taken as representing the whole school. I sent a copy of the unpublished manuscript to Tobin first and told him that if he thought that I had misrepresented his views anywhere, I would be ready to change or delete the misrepresentations immediately. He did not, however, reply.

I had also sent copies to Professor Machlup and to Lord Robbins for their comments and advice. Machlup, who in past years had given me much encouragement and kindly advice, replied that although he agreed with me on most of the points I raised, he would advise me to speak less harshly of Tobin because most editors would probably not dare to publish any harsh criticism of his work and incur his displeasure. Lord Robbins, however, with his bitter memories of the low interest rate policy pushed through by Hugh Dalton and other Keynesian economists in England, was of the opinion that no criticism could be too harsh.

I had my own gripes against the Keynesians in that they generally advised developing countries to keep the interest rate low, even if it meant increasing the money supply and imposing bureaucratic credit rationing, thus leading to constant inflationary pressure and wasteful allocation of the very scarce capital available in those countries.[5] I had a sentence in my paper on Tobin to the effect: "This deeply ingrained penchant for increasing the money supply and lowering the interest rate is, indeed, as the late Sir Dennis Robertson put it, 'the canker at the heart of the Keynesian theory'; and the Keynesian faithful in the United States have surely been seeing to it that it would come to roost in their own country as in Great Britain." Machlup suggested that I delete this sentence so as not to infuriate Tobin and other Keynesian readers, but I decided to let it remain because of my deep conviction that the Keynesians were responsible for no small share of the world's postwar economic problems.

Unfortunately, Machlup turned out to be a much better judge of the intellectual tolerance of American editors than Lord Robbins or myself. Moreover, just at that time, in 1981, Tobin was awarded the Nobel Prize for economics. No journal of economics in the United States would risk incurring the displeasure of the new Nobel laureate, of course. The paper thus became unpublishable in the United States for the time being.

In the spring of 1982, however, I received an invitation to give a series of lectures on monetary theory at the Institute for Advanced Studies in Vienna. I used this paper as my inaugural lecture there, and when I left I gave it to them to publish in their recently founded journal, the *IHS-Journal* (where IHS stands for Institut für Höhere Studien). It came out at the end of the same year in volume 6, issue 3 of that journal. Since that journal does not seem as yet to enjoy a wide circulation in the United States and elsewhere, many readers may see the paper for the first time in this collection.

11. An Attempt to Formulate a Money Market Model for an Open Economy and to Trace Out the Interrelation between the Money Market and the Foreign Exchange Market

Having thus given vent to my protests against Keynesian monetary theory and against the Patinkinesque interpretation of Walras' Law and its various applications, I now felt obliged to provide some positive suggestions on how the money market equilibrium condition should properly be formulated, in an open as well as in a closed economy. In particular, can the money market equilibrium condition formulated for a closed economy be applied as it is to an open economy, something done unquestioningly by many prominent proponents of the monetary approach to the balance of payments? In addition, can the equilibrium condition for the foreign exchange market be regarded as subsumed in the equilibrium condition for the domestic money market, so that the latter may be said to determine the exchange rate as well?

When in the fall of 1984 I was invited by Keio University in Japan to give a course of lectures on monetary theory, I tried to tackle these problems. Nothing of publishable form resulted at that time. However, the following year, the Chung-Hua Institution for Economic Research, which I now direct, decided to co-sponsor, together with the Institute of Economics, Academia Sinica, an international symposium on monetary theory, to be held January 3–8, 1986, with special emphasis on the role of the "finance constraint." I decided to take this opportunity to put down clearly my ideas on these questions and to invite critical discussion at this symposium. The result was the paper "The Flow Formulation of the Money Market Equilibrium for an Open Economy and the Determination of the Exchange Rate," which is also included in this collection.

This paper points out clearly why the prevailing stock formulation of the equilibrium conditions in the domestic money market and the foreign exchange market are inadequate, and why these two markets are two distinct and separate markets even though they are interconnected through the finance constraint (rather than through "Walras' Law"). When the two conditions are formulated separately, it can be seen that in an open economy it is still correct to say that the demand for loanable funds and the supply of loanable funds determine the domestic interest rate. However, the demand for loanable funds should now include not only the demand for funds to finance domestic investment and net hoarding but also the demand for funds to finance the planned increases in exports and imports and the net private purchase of foreign exchange assets. Moreover, equilibrium in the domestic money market in an open economy no longer necessarily implies, nor is implied by, the equality of the aggregate demand and supply of money as Keynes originally maintained for closed economies. In an open economy the increase in money supply is no longer entirely devoted to the purchase of bonds (or deferred claims on domestic money) as it is in a closed economy. Part of it may be directed by banks towards the foreign exchange market. It is only when the foreign exchange market is known to be in equilibrium that we can say that equality of the supply and demand for money implies domestic money market equilibrium and vice versa. Notice, however, that the interconnection between these two markets is not found through the application of "Walras' Law" but through the application of the finance constraint.

It would seem, then, that the monetarists are not, after all, so wrong in saying that if equilibrium in the domestic money market is always achieved instantaneously, then this equilibrium may be said to determine the exchange rate. The demand and supply of money equations in an open economy, however, should include several flow items—exports and imports, as well as domestic investment and consumption—that are usually not included by either liquidity preference theorists or monetarists in their formulation of the stock demand for money.

Note too, that equilibrium of the supply and demand for money has already been preempted by liquidity preference theorists to determine the domestic interest rate. As pointed out above, this is legitimate for an open economy only if we assume that the foreign exchange market is already in equilibrium. If after determining the domestic interest rate in this manner, we then try to determine the exchange rate with the same money supply and demand equations, assuming the domestic money market already to be in equilibrium, we would seem to be arguing in circles.

The paper also makes clear that it is incorrect to say that equilibrium in the money market necessarily implies equilibrium in the commodity markets and/or in the foreign exchange market as the Patinkin school of monetary theory has taught a generation of economists.

12. Inadequacy of the Portfolio Approach as the Basis for a Theory of the Supply of Money

My dissatisfaction with the timeless portfolio equilibrium approach is not confined to its application to the theory of the demand for money but also relates to its application to the theory of the supply of money, where it has also become the dominant approach. The current theory of the supply of money commonly assumes that, very quickly, through an unexplained process, high-powered money injected by the Central Bank

will be distributed among individual portfolio holders as they simultaneously adjust other assets and liabilities to restore full portfolio
equilibrium. This type of theory is obviously concerned only with final
portfolio equilibrium, and not at all with how this final equilibrium will
be reached. Nor is it concerned with how the supposedly given parameters of the so-called money supply multiplier are to be jointly
determined by the independent portfolio decisions of a vast multitude of
portfolio holders.

I therefore wrote a paper trying to show that the last two questions
can be addressed more conveniently using a flow approach rather than
the prevalent stock approach. With a flow approach, it is always the
flow demand and flow supply of money that are relied upon to explain
the interest rate as well as the dynamic process of expansion of income
and money circulation. The diffusion of an injection of high-powered
money throughout the economy and the subsequent steps of bank credit
expansion can then be studied conveniently in the context of the active
circulation of money.

My paper, eventually entitled "The Diffusion of Reserves and the
Money Supply Multiplier," proposed, therefore, a flow approach using a
modified Markov chain to study the stochastic diffusion of an injection
of reserves. It was shown that the traditional timeless version of the
money supply multiplier was valid only in the limit as an ergodic state of
the diffusion process. It could not be reached instantaneously or even
within a very short period of time.

The parameters of the traditional money supply multiplier, considered
fixed and determined by the public's desire to hold monetary assets in
given fixed proportions, were now shown to be the result not only of
portfolio choice decisions but also of expenditure decisions and of
various technical or frictional time lags in the transfer of the medium of
exchange from one recipient to another. This becomes clear once one
recognizes that money in general does not lie about in stagnant pools to
be consciously allocated into different portfolios, but rather it exists in a
continuous circular flow, in which its various successive temporary
resting places are rarely the result of deliberate portfolio decisions. The
vast bulk of the total supply of money does not lie in the portfolios of
different economic units but is found rather "on the wing" in various
channels of circulation.

Unfortunately, this paper too was rejected successively by two American journals. Disgusted with the conformist attitude of American
editors, and to avoid wasting more time, I decided to resubmit it abroad

to the *Economic Journal* of the United Kingdom, in which I had had an article published as early as 1944,[6] when Keynes was still the editor and I a mere graduate student. The paper was promptly accepted without major changes and published in the following year (June 1978). After its publication, I gave a reprint to Professor John S. Chipman of Minnesota who had written his thesis at Johns Hopkins in 1951 on the matrix multiplier, applying a similar Markov chain process. He told me that he was really surprised that no other monetary theorist had tried this approach before although there was an obvious call for it.

A decade now having passed since its publication, we should be able to judge the new approach that I proposed against the prevalent timeless portfolio allocation approach. I therefore include it in this volume so that a wider audience can make up its mind after reading it for itself.

13. Confirmation of My Belief in the Superiority of the Wicksell-Robertson Flow Approach Through My Empirical Work at the IMF and My Advisory Work in Taiwan, R.O.C.

All of these theoretical papers represent my protests against the prevalent theories of the day. They should not, however, be taken as mere academic quibbles carried on for argument's sake by a cranky curmudgeon. These protests arose out of a genuine conviction that the academic fashions and misconceptions that I criticized would surely lead, or had already led, to misunderstandings of actual events and to misguided policies that would do considerable harm to the countries that adopted them. Since my career included periods of practical research in international finance at the IMF, as well as work as an economic advisor to the government in Taiwan, Republic of China, I had many opportunities to observe how a wrong theoretical framework in the minds of economists could misguide and bias their interpretation of historical events, and how wrong theories and misinterpretations of facts could in turn lead to harmful policies.

I had observed and discussed a number of such misinterpretations of history while working at the IMF. See, for example, my papers, "The 1951 Improvement in the Danish Balance of Payments" (April 1953), "The Experiment with a Flexible Exchange System: The Case of Peru, 1950–1954" (February 1957), and "Fluctuating Exchange Rates in Countries with Relatively Stable Economies: Some European Experiences after World War I" (October 1959). (Not included in this volume.)

The improvement in the Danish balance of payments in 1951 was considered quite remarkable at the time for the speed and apparent ease with which Denmark recovered from a huge deficit in the previous year at a time when other major countries, like the U.K. and France, regarded their deficits vis-à-vis the U.S. as well-nigh incurable. My report on this problem, which was published later in the *IMF Staff Papers* of April 1953, attributed the quick improvement in the Danish balance of payments to the monetary policy of the Danish National Bank, which had allowed the payments deficits of the preceding year to bring about a concomitant contraction of the domestic money supply in the manner of the classical gold standard. This type of effect tended to be overlooked by my Keynesian colleagues, who generally regarded changes in the money supply as being a matter of little concern because the elasticity of the demand for money was always supposed to be high enough to obliterate any effect of a change in the money supply.

A different assignment led me to study Peru's experiment with a flexible exchange rate during 1950–54. This sort of policy was then regarded as being extremely risky, since it was expected to lead inevitably to destabilizing speculation. It turned out, however, that for the first three years, the fluctuating rate of the Peruvian sol was quite stable, and it was only in 1953 that the sol depreciated sharply (by 28%) because the world price of Peruvian exports slumped while domestic costs and prices rose as the result of a domestic inflation. Nevertheless, even then there was no sign of the sort of destabilizing speculative activity then believed to be inevitable.

Incidentally, this study (later published in *IMF Staff Papers*, February 1957) also revealed that Peru's money supply had had a remarkably strong effect on national income and hence on the demand for imports. This finding apparently made such a strong impression on my senior colleague, Dr. J. J. Polak, that he abandoned his former Keynesian views (witness his earlier paper, "Balance of Payments Problems of Countries Reconstructing with the Help of Foreign Loans," *Q.J.E.*, February 1943, written when he was with the economic research department of the former League of Nations) and turned towards a monetary approach to payments problems long before the latter approach had been made popular by Friedman and other Chicago economists (see his later work at the IMF—e.g., Polak, "Monetary Analysis of Income Formation and Payments Problems," *IMF Staff Papers*, November 1957, and Polak and Lorette Boissonneault, "Monetary Analysis of Income and Imports and Its Statistical Application," *IMF Staff Papers*, April 1960). Indeed, Polak could legitimately be said to be a forerunner of the modern monetary approach to balance of payments problems.

These encounters with new factual evidence further convinced me that changes in the money supply, and its interest elasticity, had far greater effect on the economy than Keynesian economists realized, and that the so-called inevitable instability associated with flexible exchange rates was usually the result of an inability of the country concerned to control its own money supply. To confirm this, I did another empirical study on the interwar experience with floating exchange rates in European countries. That study demonstrated that in countries that managed to restrain their money supply from overexpansion, fluctuations in the floating rates were generally quite moderate, indeed, more moderate than the fluctuations in the purchasing power parities of the relevant currencies, calculated on the basis of a comparison of wholesale prices. The sharp and cumulative depreciation of the franc in 1926, which used to be much cited as an example of the inevitable instability of a floating exchange rate, was really due to a virtually infinitely elastic money supply. The latter was a result of having a large volume of floating bonds (bons) issued and redeemable at any time at a fixed interest rate of 6%. Thus, the instability of the French franc was simply a case of a Wicksellian cumulative expansion generated by pegging the interest rate.

Economists brought up in the Keynesian tradition, however, usually fail to see any problem with pegging the interest rate, regarding it, rather, as the norm for monetary policy, a norm which J. E. Meade in his *Balance of Payments* actually dignified with the title of "Keynesian neutral monetary policy" (Meade, 1951). They tend, therefore, to blame the collapse of the franc on the "inevitable instability of the floating exchange rate" rather than on such a monetary policy. However, to an economist trained in the Wicksell–Robertson flow approach, it is easy to see the potential dangers of letting the money supply be infinitely elastic at a pegged rate of interest. This episode is, therefore, one more illustration of how bad economic theory can bias our understanding and interpretation of actual events in the real world. Incidentally, the paper in question provides empirical confirmation of my theory of foreign exchange speculation published in the previous year. ("A Theory of Foreign Exchange Speculation under a Floating Exchange System," *Journal of Political Economy*, vol. 66, Oct. 1958).

When I began as an adviser to the government of the Republic of

China on Taiwan in 1954, I found that the development of the country had been greatly hampered by misconceptions about economic development and monetary stability that were attributable to the new Keynesian economics which was then in fashion. I often felt obliged to make recommendations that were just the opposite of those derived from the prevailing theory of development, and to fight the criticism of economists trained in the Keynesian tradition. To record this experience of exasperation, I wrote "Fashions and Misconceptions in Monetary Theory and Their Influences on Financial and Banking Policies," which was published in *Zeitschrift für die gesamte Staatswissenschaft* and which also appears in this volume.

This volume as a whole, therefore, represents the evolution and development of my thinking on monetary theory and the ways in which I have sought to apply it to practical problems. What I have said in the past cannot be unsaid, and what I have done cannot be undone. Like everyone else, I must wait humbly and patiently for judgement at the bar of history.

Notes

1. The statistical data used here are taken from the Board of Governors, F.R.S., *Banking and Monetary Statistics, 1941–1970*, Wash. D.C., 1976. They may differ slightly from the old data I used in my 1943 paper, but the differences are unlikely to change the substance of my arguments.
2. See below pp. 31–35.
3. Some American economists, however, obviously held different opinions. For instance, I received a letter dated April 14, 1978, from Professor Fritz Machlup after I sent him a reprint of my article in the *OEP*, in which he wrote, "I have read the article from the first word to the last, and found myself in agreement with you on almost all the points that you made. In addition, I enjoyed the lucidity of your exposition. You are one of the few economists who can write English. . ." A nice compliment for one whose mother tongue is not English.
4. Incidentally, it was shown in this paper that a risk-averse investor would necessarily have a preference for positive skewness in the distribution of investment outcomes; this is not necessarily a trait of inveterate gamblers as Dr. Markowitz seemed to think.
5. *Vide infra*, p. 35.
6. "Professor Pigou on the Relative Movement of Real Wages and Employment," *Economic Journal*, 54 (December 1944), pp. 325–65.

Section I

Section 1

CHAPTER 2

A Note on Speculation and Income Stability

S. C. Tsiang

1.

In the October, 1939, issue of the *Review of Economic Studies* Mr. Kaldor has attempted to demonstrate in a brilliant article entitled "Speculation and Economic Stability" that the instability of our economic system can be attributed to speculation in stocks of commodities and particularly in stocks of securities. It is stated that when the current demand for any commodity, or for securities (in which case the current demand constitutes the current savings in the orthodox sense), increases and the speculators, by selling existing stocks of commodity or securities, prevent the relevant price from rising to the necessary extent to restore the balance between the current demand and supply, the level of income will decline until the flows of current demand and supply are once more equated by the decline of income. Conversely, if when the current demand falls, or the current supply increases, the speculators, by buying the current supply to add to their stocks, prevent the price from falling to the necessary extent so as to balance the current supply and demand, the level of income will tend to rise until the equilibrium between the flows of current supply and demand is restored again by the rise in the level of income. For, to quote Mr. Kaldor, "an increase in speculative stocks of any commodity implies an increase of investment in that commodity, or to use Mr. Hawtrey's expression, a release of cash by the market. (Conversely a reduction of stocks implies an absorption of cash). Unless this increase is simultaneously compensated by a decrease in the amount of stocks held in other commodities, it must imply a corresponding change in the level of investment for the system as a whole."[1]

Economists who have been incorrigibly inculcated with the orthodox way of thinking will, however, be prompted to go on to ask, will the reduction of speculative stocks necessarily imply an absorption of cash, or conversely an increase in speculative stocks a release of cash? In other words, will the speculators who have sold part of their stocks retain the proceeds in idle cash, or will not they invest them almost immediately in other assets? If they buy and add to their stocks, will they have a large balance of idle cash and release cash therefrom as they buy? If Mr. Kaldor had followed Lord Keynes in assuming that the speculators in the security market generally hold part of their wealth in the form of a speculative balance of idle cash which, though bringing in no monetary return, yet yields the same satisfaction at the margin as other income-yielding assets in the form of safety and convenience, then everything would be easy to understand. If an increase in the flow of current savings to the security market tends to depress the rate of interest (i.e., to raise the prices of bonds), the speculators, who somehow expect that the high prices will not last and anticipate them to fall back again thus involving them in a capital loss, will then substitute cash for securities. The cash embodying the flow of current savings offered to the security market will be partly absorbed into the speculative balances of the speculators. In the case where the stocks of ordinary commodities are the object of speculative selling, there is no reason to expect that the speculators will add the entire proceeds to their idle balances; for the interest rate which is supposed to determine the size of speculative balance will not be directly affected. If, however, the proceeds are transferred to the loan market and tend to lower the rate of interest, then again part of the cash proceeds will be absorbed into the speculative balances.

Mr. Kaldor, however, has explicitly rejected the idea that in normal circumstances the speculators hold large balances of idle cash and substitute cash for securities or vice versa as they speculate on the long-term capital market. For his theory of speculation in the capital market is based on the recent theory of the relationship between the long-term and short-term rates of interest as developed by Mr. Kalecki, Professor Hicks and Mr. Kaldor himself. According to them the current long rate must equal the average of the current short rate and the expected future short rates over the period of currency of the long-term bond concerned, plus or minus a certain premium to allow for the speculator's risk due to uncertainty of their expectations according as they are buyers or sellers of the stock of bonds.[2] If the current demand for investment "finance funds" and the current supply of loanable funds at the long-term capital market tend to make the current long rate diverge from the average of the current short rate and the speculators' expected future short rates discounted for uncertainty (discounted positively when the speculators intend to sell long-term securities, discounted negatively, i.e., risk premium will be added to the expected future rates, if they intend to buy additional stocks of bonds), the speculators will think it profitable to substitute short-term bills for long-term bonds or vice versa, even though the present short rate may have fallen or risen relatively to current long rate. The kind of speculation in the capital market as envisaged by Mr. Kaldor is therefore essentially an arbitrage operation between the short-term money market and the long-term capital market. Short-term bills which include savings deposits, call loans, etc., on the other hand are rightly considered as not subject to speculation, for the lifetime of short-term bills is too short for the capital values of bills to be appreciably affected by a change in short rate and big changes in the short rate are not expected in such short period.[3] It is only when the short-term rate of interest is lowered to such extent as not even to compensate the negligible risk attached to short-term assets and the inconvenience as compared with cash that idle cash will be held instead of short-term assets.[4] Therefore, speculation on the long-term capital market means substitutions between long-term securities and short-term bills. To quote Mr. Kaldor's own words, "there is no reason to expect, in normal circumstances at any rate, that the substitution (when speculators sell bonds) will be in favour of cash. 'Idle balances'—i.e., that part of short-term holdings which the owner does not require for transaction purposes—can be kept in forms such as savings deposits, which offer the same advantages as cash (as far as the preservation of capital value is concerned) and yield a return in addition."[5]

Now if the speculators in the stock exchange do not in normal circumstances keep idle speculative balances of cash, it is obvious that the stock market itself does not absorb or release cash, unless we contend that larger turnover on the stock exchange may tie up more cash there for transaction purposes. This latter contention, however, is of minor practical importance, for it is well known that the turnover on the stock exchange is chiefly effected by clearing arrangements and very little cash is required,[6] and it is certainly not what Mr. Kaldor meant by the absorption or release of cash due to speculation. What happens when speculators on the stock exchange sell their stocks of old securities is that they will immediately transfer the proceeds to the short-term money market and invest there in short-term assets. If the cash proceeds are to be absorbed they must be absorbed in the last resort by the short-term money market.

This argument on somewhat *a priori* grounds in perfectly in accord with the findings of Professor Machlup's penetrating and realistic investigation of the actual working of the stock market.[7] There Professor Machlup has shown that when the speculators sell their stocks of old securities thus absorbing part of the inflow of liquid funds into the capital market, they will generally use the proceeds either to pay off their margin debts with their brokers, or, if they have no margin debt to pay off, simply leave them on their brokerage deposits with the brokers, or they may withdraw the proceeds and lend at call on the money market. Call loans are generally regarded as just as liquid as cash and yield in addition a profitable return. If they leave the proceeds with the brokers or repay their margin debts, the brokers will not keep the money in idle cash either. For the transactions on the stock exchange are affected entirely by clearings, and consequently there is little need for the brokers to keep a large cash balance. In practice the brokers generally keep a very small fraction of their customers' brokerage deposits with them in balances of cash (i.e., demand deposits with the banks) and even a smaller fraction of their turnover. Once their cash balances exceed the minimum, they will immediately use them to repay their vast amount of outstanding debts or to a much smaller extent to grant short loans. In either case, that part of the inflow of the liquid funds into the capital market absorbed by the speculative sellers is transferred to the short-term money market.[8] Similarly when the flows of the demand for loanable funds for industrial purposes and the supply of loanable funds out of disposable income tend to raise the long-term rate beyond what the speculators believe to be the safe level, the speculators who buy additional securities to increase their holdings of stocks will not have the idle cash balances to release. What happens in practice is that the bullish speculators will give orders to their brokers to buy additional stocks with their brokerage deposits at their brokers, or, if they have exhausted their brokerage deposits, by incurring new "margin debts" with their brokers. The brokers, who, as we have observed, do not as a rule keep more than a minimum fraction of their customers' brokerage deposits with them in balances of demand deposits, will have to pay the sellers of securities, who wish to withdraw the monies to finance real investments, by borrowing new loans from the banks or other lenders in the money market, or by calling in their call loans. Thus the excess of the outflow of loanable funds over the inflow of savings on the long-term capital market must be raised by the speculators or their brokers from the short-term money market and transferred to the long-term market. In other words, part of the current demand for loanable funds on the long-term market is transferred by the speculators to the short-term market.

The function of speculation in securities is therefore merely to arbitrage between the long-term capital market and the money market. This arbitrage operation by itself certainly does not necessarily bring about instability in money income. It may disturb the equilibrium between the inflow and outflow of liquid funds on the long-term capital market, but if it sets up an opposite disequilibrium between the inflow and outflow on the money market to the same extent, there need not be any change in the stream of money expenditure. Similarly when speculators in other commodity markets sell their stocks, they will normally likewise transfer the proceeds to the money market and invest them for the time being in the more liquid types of short-term assets, e.g., call loans. And when the speculators add to their stocks they will have to raise the cash from the money market either by calling in their loans or by fresh borrowing.[9] It is therefore clear that speculation on the stock exchange, in bonds as well as in shares, or indeed in any other commodity market, and the variations in the size of speculative stocks do not provide the whole explanation of the instability of money income. Speculation in the stock exchange merely transfers, so to speak, the whole burden of adjusting savings and investment to the money market. It is the money market which is responsible in the last resort for the release or absorption of cash and which is, therefore, in that sense the source of instability.

That Mr. Kaldor should have overlooked that the ultimate mechanism which produces instability of money income is the short-term money market is, I believe, largely because of the method of approach he has adopted in dealing with the short-term rate of interest. Although he successfully combines a loanable fund approach (a flow analysis) with an analysis of speculation in stocks with regard to the long-term capital market, he reverts abruptly to a supply and demand for money approach and pushes the flows of loanable funds entirely into the background in respect of the short-term money market. According to him, the short-term rate "is not dependent on expectation at all (or only to a very minor extent) but only on the current demand for cash balances (for transaction purposes) and the current supply." And he depicts the nature of the equilibrium in the short-term interest market by the accompanying diagram, where the quantity of cash (i.e., bank notes and demand deposits; savings deposits are excluded, being re- garded as a kind of short-term bill) is measured along OX, the short-term interest rate along OY.

> "DD and SS stand for the demand and supply of money respectively. The demand curve is drawn on the assumption that the volume of money transaction (i.e., the level of income) is given. This demand curve is inelastic since the marginal yield of money declines rapidly with an increase in the proportion of the stock to turnover. Below a certain point (g) the demand curve becomes elastic, however, since the holding of short-term assets other than money is always connected with some risk (and perhaps inconvenience), and individuals will not invest short-term if the short-term rate is lower than the necessary compensation for this."[10]

The short-term interest rate is determined by the intersection of these two curves.

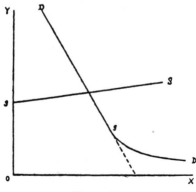

Figure 2.1.

Although it has been repeatedly demonstrated by Professor Hicks that the loanable fund approach and the demand and supply of money approach are but two alternative ways of saying the same thing,[11] the above procedure is misleading, however, in one respect. For it will be seen that there is no unique and definite demand schedule for money, even if we start from a given level of income. The demand for cash is in fact neither independent of the inducement to invest nor of the desire to save. For an increase in the desire to borrow for investment implies an increase in demand for cash as investment finance fund in the first instance, and an increase in the desire to save involves an increase in the willingness to part with cash out of disposable income.[12] The demand schedule for money is therefore not an independent function even with a given level of income. It will be shifted about by changes in investment borrowings and in savings before the level of income has as yet changed. To assume that a definite demand curve for money can be drawn, given the level of income, is therefore strictly speaking illegitimate and may prove rather misleading.[13] This will become amply evident when we return to our problem in hand. For if we follow Mr. Kaldor in assuming that the demand curve for cash is given, given the level of income, we shall be unable to see the immediate repercussion of speculation in the long-term capital market, or in any other commodity market, on the short-term money market. Indeed this kind of approach leads Mr. Kaldor to say that "a change in the long-term rate (either the current or the expected rate) cannot react back on the short-term rate except perhaps indirectly by causing a change in the level of income and hence in the demand for cash."[14] This is nothing but a restatement of the Keynesian doctrine that saving and investment have no direct effect on the rate of interest except indirectly through the level of income. Only it is now supposed to have a limited application to the short-term rate of interest only. This, however, is also untenable. For, as we have observed above, the selling of old securities by the speculators in the long term capital market implies that part of the flow of cash offered to the capital market will be transferred to the short-term money market; this certainly will have a direct effect on the equilibrium of the short-term money market. In other words, the demand curve for cash will be displaced bodily to the left because of the speculative selling of old securities on the stock exchange, although the income level has not as yet fallen to a new level. Indeed the level of income need not fall, if the cash or liquid funds transferred by the speculators to the money market get invested in real goods without appreciable delay through the mechanism of the short-term rate of interest.

How the mechanism of money market actually works and why it should fail to adjust the inflow of funds to the outflow can only be clearly observed with the help of a loanable fund approach of the Robertsonian type. We shall therefore attempt to describe the nature of the determination of the short-term interest rate in terms of loanable funds in order to bring out in strong relief the impact of speculation on the money market. In order to make the task of exposition at all manageable, we shall make certain simplifying assumptions. We assume after Professor Robertson that there is a period of time, a "day," which is so short that all active money is exchanged against commodities and services (excluding securities) only once during the day, and the money received in payment for commodities and services on a given day cannot be allocated to any further use during the course of the same day.[15] In other words, the transaction velocity of active money is one in a day; the transaction velocity of active money being assumed to be the same everywhere, so as to avoid the difficulties of averaging and of deciding which piece of money is active or idle, and also to avoid the complication that changes in the disposition of money receipts between the different lines of expenditure may involve changes in the average transaction velocity of money. Money stock (i.e., cash) which is not required to finance the expenditure during the day will be invested on short-term assets (e.g., savings deposits, Treasury Bills, call loans, etc.) unless the short-term rate of interest has fallen so low that it does not even compensate the risk and trouble involved. The transaction velocity of active money may certainly change over time due to changes in business confidence and in the usage of money substitutes, such as book credits and commercial bills, but in the short period such as the "day" it is assumed to be independent of the influence of the rate of interest. Financial transactions, viz., the exchange of money against securities and the transference of funds from the long-term capital market to the money market, however, are assumed to take no appreciable time.

The nature of the equilibrium of the short-term money market can then be shown by the accompanying diagram. Let DD be the demand to borrow, at the money market, liquid funds (i.e., money) which the industry will actually expend during the same day. Let SS represent the supply of liquid funds (embodied in money of course) to the money market on the same day. It consists of that part of the gross savings which is offered to the money market out of the money receipts of the previous day which become disposable only today (including therefore

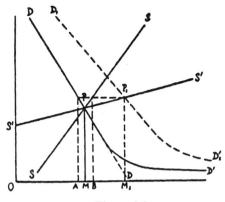

Figure 2.2.

depreciation allowances and liquidated capital). To this we must add the possible relending of the liquid funds raised from the long-term capital market, for people who have raised all the funds necessary to finance their whole investment projects, the construction periods of which may spread over a number of days, will find it profitable to retain only that part of the liquid funds that is necessary to finance their expenditures today and to relend the rest to the money market only to withdraw therefrom day by day the funds that will be needed for the expenditure of each future day. When the borrowing on the long-term capital market is equal to the gross savings that have flowed into the capital market and the demand and supply for short-term funds at the money market as defined above are also equal, then the stream of money expenditure is at equilibrium, without tendency either to rise or to decline. When the short rate falls very low, there will be further demand for liquid funds which people will like to hold as idle balances in preference to short-term securities. This will make the demand curve for liquid funds very elastic and asymptotic to the X axis at its lower end. We have so far excluded from our SS curve the supply of additional bank money. In fact, however, the banks can always supplement the inflow of liquid funds into the money market by creating new bank credits or reduce the supply of liquid funds by cancelling part of the cash flowing into the money market; a fact which has been recognised by economists, e.g., Thornton, Ricardo, and Joplin, since the times of the Bullionist and the Currency Controversies. The supply of bank money has a dominant influence on the short-term rate of interest because of its great elasticity except at the top of boom.[16] Taking the potential expansion and contraction of bank credit into consideration, we get the aggregate supply curve of loanable funds $S'S'$ which is normally very elastic. The horizontal distances between this curve and the SS curve measure the amounts of bank money which the banks are prepared to create or to cancel in the course of the day concerned at the various short-term interest rates. The short rate will therefore be determined by the intersection of the $S'S'$ and the DD' curves. If the SS curve also runs through the point of intersection of these two curves, the banks are merely renewing loans and maintaining the existing amount of money, and the stream of money expenditure will remain stable.

Now suppose owing to some technical inventions, the inducement for long-term investment has improved. The demand to borrow loanable funds to finance investment expenditures will therefore rise. If the entrepreneurs are seeking to finance their additional investment by short-term funds (with the hope of repaying them by floating long-term bonds or shares later on), this will directly be reflected in a shift of DD' to the right. But we shall assume that the entrepreneurs will go to the long-term capital market for the finance funds of their long-term investment projects. The demand for loanable funds or the supply of new securities on the capital market will then be increased. If the speculators in the capital market succeed in preventing the long-term interest rate from rising by taking up the additional supply of securities, the excess of the demand for investment finance fund over the inflow of gross savings on the capital market will have to be provided by the speculators, who, as we have seen above, will raise it chiefly through their brokers from the short-term money market. Thus the additional demand for investment finance funds is transferred by the speculators from the capital market to the money market, and the DD' curve will be shifted to the right just as if the entrepreneurs had attempted to raise the "finance" from the money market in the first instance.[17] If the short rate is allowed to rise to the point where the new demand curve D_1D_1' intersects the SS curve, the stream of money expenditures will not rise in spite of some increase in investment and speculation on the capital market. However, as the supply of bank credit is elastic, the short rate will only rise to the point where D_1D_1' cuts the $S'S'$ curve. Thus short-term lending will exceed the flow of savings into the money market, and the excess BM_1 will be provided by the creation of new bank money, which will be transferred to the capital market by the speculators to finance the extra investment expenditures, and consequently the stream of money expenditures will increase.

Similarly when there is an exhaustion of investment opportunities and the speculators attempt to peg the long rate by selling old securities, the proceeds will be immediately transferred to the money market. This can be represented by a shift of the SS and the $S'S'$ curve to the right (or alternatively a shift of the DD curve to the left), and the inflexibility of the short rate or the elasticity of bank credit will ensure that part of the liquid funds absorbed by the speculators and transferred to the money market will be cancelled. Thus in normal circumstances the elasticity of bank credit appears to be the chief explanation of the instability of the money stream although the banks merely play a passive part. Hoarding of idle balance comes into force on an important scale only when the banks have allowed the rate of interest to fall to a very low level.

The essence of speculation in the stock exchange is therefore that it shifts the burden of adjusting investment to the supply of savings from the long-term capital market, where the rate of interest is comparatively more effective in regulating the flows of investment and savings, to the money market where the short-term rate of interest, even when it is not arbitrarily fixed by the banking system, is quite impotent in regulating the industrial demand for loanable funds and the supply of savings. It is important because the industrial demand for short-term loans, which are used chiefly to finance investment in working capital and stocks, is very inelastic in relation to the short rates, as has been shown by Oxford inquiries,[18] and the supply of savings is likely to be even less responsive to the short rate. Although it is always possible to stop expansion by letting the short rate rise to whatever extent required, when there is an exhaustion of investment opportunities and the bearish speculators transfer the vast excess of savings over investment at the capital market to the money market, the banks will not be able to lower the short rate infinitely to stimulate a corresponding increase in short-term investment; for when the short rate falls to a very low level, hoarding of idle cash will set in and make further reduction impossible. It remains true, however, for normal times, when banks are supposed to keep the short rate at a more or less conventional level and there is no serious change in the transaction demand for cash due to changes in business habits and confidence apart from changes in the volume of transaction, that speculation in long-term securities (or in any other commodities) leads to fluctuations in activities chiefly through indirectly inducing the banks to create additional bank credit or to cancel existing money.

Thus the modern discussion on liquidity preference and speculation seems to lead us back to the age-old doctrine of the early classical economists, e.g., Thornton, Ricardo and Joplin, that the explanation of income instability is the divergence between some sort of natural rate of interest and the rate charged by the banks and the consequent expansion or cancellation of bank credit. What we have discussed above appears to justify their preoccupation with the short rate as arbitrarily fixed by the banking system, which is shared by Wicksell,[19] Professor Robertson and the modern Austrian School. For as we have seen above the inefficacy of the long-term capital market brings about fluctuations in activities only indirectly through its repercussion on the money market and only in so far as the latter is also ineffective.[20] It is when the money market has proved to be a broken reed, that our hopes for the automatic self-adjustment of our economic system have to be abandoned.

2.

In this section we shall make a simple attempt to examine the effect of speculation in the stock market on the volume of bank credit and the level of trade activity in the light of American statistics. If our theoretical analysis is more or less in conformity with the realistic situation, we shall expect to find some correlation between the net speculative buying or selling of securities and the expansion or contraction of bank credits and the ups and downs of business activity.[21] Of course very close correlation cannot be expected, for speculation on the stock exchange is not the only factor that affects the level of activities and the amount of circulating money. Other factors, e.g., the balance of trade, the granting of credits by banks directly to industry to finance investments, government deficit spending, etc., may reinforce or offset the effect of speculation on the capital market. In our present investigation, however, we shall make no attempt to eliminate the effects of these other factors. If in spite of the interference of other factors some correlation can be detected between the variations of speculative stockholdings and the level of activities and the amount of bank credit outstanding, the result will be at least of suggestive value.

It has been pointed out by Dr. Eiteman that the net amounts of speculative buying or selling of securities, which reflect the excesses (positive or negative) of the outflow of liquid funds into the industry from the stock market over the inflow of current disposable income thereinto, can be gauged to some extent by the variations of the volume of brokers' loans.[22] For the variation of brokers' borrowings depends on the difference between the payments in by customers who have bought shares (plus dividends received on securities held for the customers) and the withdrawals by customers who have sold shares (or are collecting dividends). Provided that the speculators always speculate on "margin" through their brokers, and do not go directly to the money market or banks for funds to finance their purchases, or in the case of selling, withdraw the proceeds from the brokers in order to transfer them to the money market on their own account, instead of leaving the proceeds with the brokers in repayment of the margin debts, the variations of brokers' loans would give us indication of the variations of the speculative stocks on the stock market. For the selling of bearish speculators, who use the proceeds to repay their margin debts to the brokers, will enable the brokers to discharge their own debts to the money market and the banks to the same extent, and the buying of the bullish speculators who buy on new margin debts, will oblige the brokers to borrow new loans to pay for their customers' purchases. The increase or decrease of the total brokers' loans will therefore indicate whether the speculators as a whole are adding to or diminishing their holdings.[23] The proviso which has to be made above, viz., that the speculators always raise their liquid funds from the money market and banks or return the proceeds of their sales to the money market and banks through the agency of the brokers, is perhaps not altogether a very unrealistic one, in view of the prevailing practice of the speculators (the professional ones at least) to speculate on margin.[24] Therefore the variations in brokers' loans may perhaps provide us a rough indication of the inflationary or deflationary effects of speculation on the stock market.

If, however, the speculators do sometimes borrow funds directly from the money market or mobilise their own savings deposits when they buy securities, the increase in brokers' loans may no doubt underestimate the inflationary effect of their speculative buying. On the other hand, if the speculators on selling their securities withdraw the proceeds from the brokers and use them to pay off their own short-term debts, or to grant loans to the money market or to buy short-term bills the deflationary effect of their selling will not be reflected in a decline in brokers' loans. Furthermore, if when the opinions of the speculators are divided, the bullish speculators raise their funds directly from the money market (e.g., by borrowing new short-term loans, or selling the bills in their possession, or mobilising their savings deposits) to buy from the bears who use the proceeds, however, to pay off their margin debts thus enabling their brokers to repay their own outstanding debts, brokers' loans will decrease, although there is no net speculative selling of securities. In other words, brokers' loans may decline without there being any absorption of current savings by the speculators. On the other hand, if the bullish speculators buy on margin from the bears, who withdraw the proceeds, however, from the brokers in order to invest on short-term assets on their own account (i.e., to repay their short-term debts, or to lend out on call loans, or to put the money on bills or savings deposits), brokers' loans will rise although no net speculative buying of securities has occurred. In this way, brokers' loans may rise without there being any excess of outflow of funds into industry from the stock market over the inflow of current income into the stock market.

Considerations similar to those given above led Professor Machlup to the rather extreme conclusion that the variations or brokers' loans can tell us absolutely nothing. [25] Whether or not these possibilities are in fact important enough to vitiate the variations of brokers' loans even as a rough indication of the excesses (positive or negative) of investment borrowings over the inflow of current savings on the capital market, i.e., whether the assumption that speculators generally buy and sell on "margin" and do not go indirectly to the money market or banks for funds or for investing the sale proceeds is realistic enough as a first approximation, cannot be judged *a priori*. In our present study we shall tentatively employ the monthly figures of brokers' loans as an index of the variations of speculative stocks on the capital market. If the variations of brokers' loans are found to correlate to some extent with the fluctuations of activities and the volume of bank credit, there will be then a *prima facie* case for Dr. Eiteman's interpretation of the significance of brokers' loans.

In the following chart we shall compare the monthly variations of brokers' loans by New York City banks ("for account of banks" and "total") with the variations of net demand deposits of the reporting member banks in the leading cities and the index of industrial production. The limitations of our statistics are at once obvious.

1. Brokers' loans by New York City banks may not be representative of brokers' loans for the country as a whole. Loans to brokers outside New York City have to be neglected for lack of monthly figures. Furthermore brokers' borrowings from other sources than banks and the money loaned out by brokers on the money market other than to other brokers or their clients have also to be

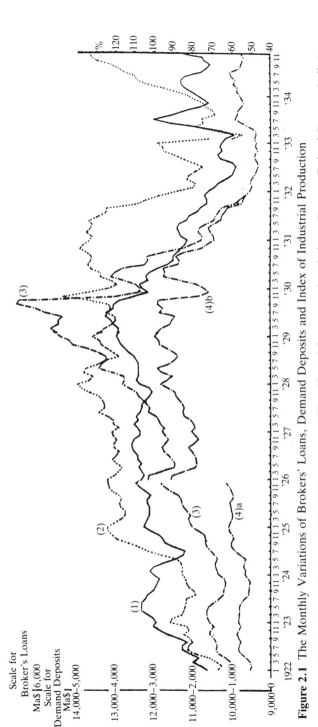

Figure 2.1 The Monthly Variations of Brokers' Loans, Demand Deposits and Index of Industrial Production

1. Index of industrial production, 1923–1925 average = 100, adjusted for seasonal variations. Source: *Federal Reserve Bulletin.*
2. Demand deposits, 1922–1930, net demand deposits of weekly reporting member banks in leading cities, monthly averages of weekly figures. Source: *Federal Reserve Bulletin.* 1931–1934, figures for weeks ending Wednesday nearest end of month. Source: *Royal Economic Society Memorandum.*
3. 1922–25, Brokers' Loans (on Call and on Time) by reporting member banks in N.Y. City, total. 1926–1934, Loans to Brokers and Dealers (on Call and on Time) secured by stocks and bonds, made by reporting member banks in N.Y. City, total (monthly averages of weekly figures). Source: *Federal Reserve Bulletin.*
4. (*a*) 1922–25, Brokers' loans by N.Y. City member banks for own account; (*b*) 1926–1934, Brokers' loans by N.Y. City member banks for account of banks.

neglected for lack of adequate statistics. Fortunately these are very small as compared with brokers' loans from banks.

2. The demand deposits of the weekly reporting member banks in leading cities may not be representative of the total amount of the demand deposits and currency of the whole country.

3. As is clear from our theoretical discussion, the excess of investment borrowing over the supply of current savings at the capital market affects in the first instance the aggregate private money outlay. The relation between the money expenditure and the physical output, however, may be disturbed by changes in prices and costs.

Nevertheless, our statistics seem to reveal some interesting correlations between the fluctuations of brokers' loans and the fluctuations of demand deposits and output, which cannot be dismissed as mere coincidence, and which appear to render some support to our argument.

There is a quite noticeable degree of synchronisation between the variations of brokers' loans and the variations of demand deposits from the beginning of our chart up to the first half of 1924. The sharp rise of demand deposits during the latter half of that year, which was probably due to the open market operation by banks and to the import of gold, and the subsequent fall in the opening months of 1925 are, however, quite out of proportion with the changes in brokers' loans. During 1925 and 1926 the relation between these two series is not very definite. From the end of 1926, however, the fluctuations of brokers' loans and demand deposits synchronised to a remarkable extent. Although since 1928 the brokers' loans total began to rise to an unprecedented height leaving brokers' loans "for account of banks" and the demand deposits behind the two latter still maintained a remarkably close correlation up to September, 1929.

The lack of correlation between brokers' loans and demand deposits since the October of 1929 was probably due to the special conditions of the crisis and the special monetary measures adopted by the authority, which entirely overwhelmed the relation between brokers' loans and demand deposits as we should expect from our previous argument. For instance, the sharp rise of demand deposits in October and November was no doubt brought about by the distress borrowing at the collapse of the stock market boom and the desperate effort of the member banks to come to the aid of the stock market. And the fact that demand deposits remained at a high level until September, 1931, after the drastic decline of production and the wholesale liquidation of brokers' loans was probably because the risk of default of short-term assets had increased so much that people fled to cash and demand deposits until even deposits came to be distrusted, as again before the banking crisis in the beginning of 1933.

A positive correlation between the index of industrial production and brokers' loans is also observable for some periods in our chart. During 1922 and 1923, the fluctuations of the index of production seemed to correspond with the variations in brokers' loans. But the sharp decline of production in the middle of 1924 was not sufficiently accounted for by the slight dip in brokers' loans. One explanation for this is that the recession was chiefly brought about by disinvestment in inventories which were generally financed not by stock market credit but mostly by short-term credits. Moreover the index of physical output might have exaggerated the decline in money expenditure, for the national income in terms of money was actually higher in 1924 than in 1923. The rising trend of brokers' loans undoubtedly contributed to the recovery of production in the second half of 1924 and in 1925. In 1926 the relation was not very clear and the recession of 1927 was not reflected in brokers' loans, which were rising during that year. Since October, 1927, however, the index of production seemed to follow the lead of brokers' loans total and resumed its rise, reaching a peak in June, 1929, three months behind the peak of brokers' loans in March, 1929.

The rise of the index of production together with brokers' loans total, relatively to demand deposits, indicates that part of the speculative buying of securities, which conduced to the rise of activity, was financed not by additional bank credit but by a speeding up of the velocity of circulation of demand deposits. This was probably because after the long period of prosperity of the twenties, business men became more confident in outlook, so that money substitutes, e.g., book credits, commercial bills, etc., were used and circulated to a greater extent and consequently less money was required for a given volume of transaction. It might also be partly due to the fact that the very high short-term rate of interest prevailing then might have induced business men to keep less cash in our strict sense for precautionary purposes, thus making more cash available to the stock market. The explanation that this might have been the result of the dishoarding of speculative balances by the speculators is, however, out of question, for, as we have seen, speculators do not as a rule keep idle balances in demand deposits.

The resumption of the spectacular rise of brokers' loans total from

July to September, however, seemed to have hardly any effect on production, suggesting that the speculative spirit of the bulls had so completely run wild that the bears sold their holdings but, in order to take advantage of the very high rate on call loans, relent the proceeds to brokers who used them in turn to finance the purchases of their bullish clients. In this way brokers' loans soared up possibly without there having been any real afflux of funds out of the stock market. And consequently industrial production was hardly affected.

The sharp decline of production set in only in November when brokers' loans were drastically liquidated, and the short-lived recovery of production early in 1930 seemed to coincide with the revival in brokers' loans. After that the downward trend of output seemed to correspond with the similar trend of brokers' loans.

In conclusion, we may say that our chart, crude as it is, seems to reveal, for certain periods at least, some interesting correlations between the variations of brokers' loans (which we have taken as a rough indication of the discrepancies between investment demand for funds and the current supply of savings at the stock market), the demand deposits and the index of production. It appears to afford some factual support to our contention that in normal circumstances, speculation in securities on the capital market brings about fluctuations in income and activity mainly by shifting from the capital market to the money market the excess demand or supply of liquid funds which the banking system meets by expanding credit or absorbs through credit cancellation as the case may be.

Notes

1. Kaldor, *loc. cit.,* p. 17.
2. Mr. Kaldor originally held the view that the current long rate must equal the average of the expected future short rates plus a positive premium for risk due to uncertainty. However, in view of his later opinion in a symposium on the theory of the forward market, the above modified version will probably be his view now. (Cf. N. Kaldor, "A Note on The Theory of Forward Market," *Review of Economic Studies,* Vol. VII, pp. 196–201.)
3. N. Kaldor, *Speculation and Economic Stability*, p. 13, footnote 2.
4. *Ibid.,* p. 14, footnote 1.
5. *Ibid.,* p. 13, footnote 2.
6. Cf. Keynes, *A Treatise on Money*, Vol. I, p. 249, 2nd paragraph. Also F. Machlup, *Stock Market Credit and Capital Formation*, Chap. VI.
7. Machlup, *The Stock Market Credit and Capital Formation*, Chaps. VI, VII and VIII.

8. It is very interesting to note that this is in fact Lord Keynes' opinion in his *Treatise*. For according to that book, the bears will either put the proceeds of their sales on the savings deposits or else use the "bear funds" to buy Treasury Bills and to grant loans to the money market and the stock exchange. (See Keynes, *A Treatise on Money*, p. 252.)

9. Speculation in foreign exchange may constitute an exceptional case, if the "speculator," or rather the price-stabiliser, is the monetary authority or an exchange equalisation fund which does keep large funds of idle cash. In such cases when they sell foreign exchanges, cash is directly absorbed or cancelled, and when they buy foreign exchanges cash is directly released without passing through the mechanism of money market.

10. *Loc. cit.,* p. 14, footnote 1.

11. J. R. Hicks, "Mr. Keynes' General Theory of Employment," *Economic Journal*, June, 1936. Also Hicks, *Value and Capital*, Chap. XII.

12. That any borrowing for investment implies a preliminary demand for finance funds and thus must have a direct influence on the rate of interest before any change in income has yet occurred is admitted by Lord Keynes. (Cf. Keynes, "The Alternative Theories of the Rate of Interest," *Economic Journal*, 1937.) It is, however, not yet generally recognized that a change in the propensity to save would likewise involve a change in the demand for money, although it is quite obvious with Professor Robertson's terminology. An increase in the propensity to save implies a decrease in the public's planned consumption in the coming period. Less cash will therefore be kept to finance consumption, and more cash out of disposable incomes, i.e., incomes of the preceding period received in cash will be offered to the security and money markets.

13. This point perhaps deserves a little more emphasis than a mere *obiter dictum* in this note. For it reveals the logical weakness of the Keynesian doctrine which treats the demand for money as an independent function of the rate of interest and the level of income, independent of the marginal efficiency of investment and the propensity to save; whereas the two latter functions are supposed to affect the rate of interest only indirectly through their effect on the income level. The fact, however, is that both these functions have a direct effect on the demand for money and so on the rate of interest. It should also be noted that Professor Hicks' and Lange's attempts to reconcile the Keynesian theory with the classical theory appeared to have overlooked this point, in so far as they regarded the liquidity preference function (in its broad sense) as independent of the savings and investment functions. This assumption inevitably led them to the Keynesian conclusion that savings and investment affect the rate of interest only indirectly through their effect on the level of income. (See Hicks, "Mr. Keynes and the Classics," *Econometrica*, 1937, and Lange, "The Rate of Interest and The Optimum Propensity to Consume," *Economica*, 1938.)

14. *loc. cit.,* p. 13 footnote 2.

15. I am inclined to think that it is more convenient to take as the minimum period of lag the circulation period of money against the total commodity turnover than the circulation period of money against real income.

16. According to Mr. Kaldor, the elasticity of the supply of money in a modern banking system is ensured partly by the open market operations of the central bank, partly by the commercial banks not maintaining a strict reserve ratio in the face of fluctuations in the demand for loans, and partly it is a consequence of the fact that under present banking practices a switch-over from current deposits to savings deposits automatically reduces the amount of deposit money in existence, and vice versa (Kaldor, *loc. cit.,* p. 14, footnote 1.)

17. It is possible that not all the extra funds borrowed on the long term capital market will be needed to finance expenditures during the day. Consequently part of the funds will flow back to the money market and thus shift the *SS* curve to the right. However, the relending of the extra funds borrowed on the capital market will always fall short of the amount borrowed by the fund needed to finance investment expenditures today. Therefore *SS* will always be shifted less to the right than *DD*. For the sake of simplicity, we assume that *SS* is not shifted, but *DD* is displaced to the right by the amount which the entrepreneurs retain to finance their investment expenditures during today.

    The transference of the demand for liquid funds to the money market, i.e., the speculators' demand for short loans may be to some extent a function of the short rate that will be established on the money market. Its elasticity depends on the extent to which speculators' expectation of long rate will be affected by the rise of the current short rate and whether the rising cost of short loans may or may not deter the speculators from holding additional stocks of securities.

18. See P. W. S. Andrews, "An Inquiry into The Effects of The Rate of Interest," and R. S. Sayers, "Businessmen and The Terms of Borrowings," *Oxford Economic Papers*, III.

19. Although Wicksell mentioned explicitly at some places that it was the long rate that should be equated to the natural rate (see *Lectures on Political Economy,* Vol. II, p. 191), he accounted for the inflexibility of the money rate of interest by the arbitrariness of the rate charged by the banks and the elasticity of bank credit.

20. There seems therefore to be little ground for the apprehension, as expressed by Dr. Lachmann, that inelastic expectations with regard to the long-term interest rate would vitiate the Wicksellian doctrine that booms and slumps are engineered by banks fixing the money rate of interest below or above its natural level. (See L. M. Lachmann, "The Rôle of Expectations in Economics as a Social Science," *Economica,* Feb., 1943, p. 23.)

21. The term speculative selling of long-term securities, as it is employed in our theoretical discussion, means the selling of securities not for the purpose of financing investment or consumption expenditures, but for the purpose of transforming the capital into more liquid types of assets. And the term speculative, buying means in our sense the purchase of securities not with the current disposable income (gross) but with the accumulated liquid capital or borrowed capital.

22. Wilford J. Eiteman, "The Economics of Brokers' Loans," *American Economic Review*, 1932, also "The Economic Significance of Brokers' Loans," *Journal of Political Economy*, 1932.

23. Lord Keynes, therefore, appears to have been misled by false scent when he maintained that "an increase (in the volume of brokers' loans) meant that the rise of security prices had gone still further beyond the point at which it would be just enough to offset the bullishness of average sentiment, in the sense that it had led to an increase in the 'bear' position." (*Treatise,* Vol. I, p. 251.) On the contrary, as pointed out by Dr. Eiteman and as we shall see from our statistics, the increase in brokers' loans during the prosperous years of the twenties appeared to imply that the rise of security prices was not sufficient to check the average bullish sentiment, so that the speculators as a whole were adding to their holdings and had to borrow on the short-term loan market through their brokers to pay for the purchases. It was in fact the first of the four types of speculative markets enumerated by Lord Keynes. (*Ibid.,* pp. 252–3.)

24. The speculators may no doubt use their current incomes (e.g., dividends on their holdings of securities) to buy securities or to put up their margins. However, in so far as they purchase securities with current incomes, their purchases are not speculative buying in our present definition of the term. Speculators' current incomes paid in to reduce their margin debts may be considered as current savings flowing into the stock market. They tend to diminish brokers' loans outstanding unless offset by other speculative stock market. They tend to diminish brokers' loans outstanding unless offset by other speculative buying of securities on margin.

25. See Machlup, *op. cit.,* Chap., VII, especially pp. 123–128.

CHAPTER **3**

Liquidity Preference and Loanable Funds Theories, Multiplier and Velocity Analyses: A Synthesis

S. C. Tsiang[*]

The great polemics of the thirties between the proponents of liquidity preference and loanable funds theories of interest have flared up again recently.[1] Nevertheless, no general agreement seems to have been reached on the two main issues: (1) Are the two theories the same? (2) If they are not the same, which theory is correct?

It is the purpose of the first two parts of this paper to show that the two theories are indeed identical in the sense that the two sets of demand and supply functions, i.e., the demand for and the supply of loanable funds, and the demand for money to hold and the stock of money in existence—would determine the same rate of interest in all circumstances, if both sets of demand and supply functions are formulated correctly in the *ex ante* sense.

In the third part, we shall show that the reconciliation between the loanable funds and liquidity preference theories of interest provides also a key for the reconciliation of the multiplier and velocity analyses of income expansion.

Finance Constraints and the Theory of Money
ISBN 0-12-701720-8
ISBN 0-12-701721-6 (pbk)

Reprinted with permission from *American Economic Review*, American Economic Association, Vol. XLVI, 4 (September 1956), pp. 539–564.

1. Previous Attempts to Reconcile the Two Theories

To the knowledge of the author, there have been published in English four attempts to prove that the two theories are identical. These are the contributions of Lerner, Hicks and Fellner and Somers, and Swan.[2]

1. Abba Lerner's proof of the equivalence of the liquidity preference and loanable funds theories was achieved only at the expense of total distortion of the latter. For to establish the identity of the two theories, he interpreted the two main components of the demand and supply of loanable funds, viz., savings and investment, in the *ex post* sense in which they are always identical. This made nonsense of the loanable funds theory in which savings and investment must be defined in the *ex ante* sense.

2. A more subtle and sophisticated proof of the identity of the two theories is that of J. R. Hicks. In his *Value and Capital*,[3] he demonstrates that according to Walras' Law, the demand for everything including money is necessarily equal, or rather identical, to the supply of everything including money; for the effective demand for (or purchase of) one thing necessarily implies the supply of something else in exchange for it. If in the goods and services market demand and supply are equated through their respective prices, then the equality of the demand for and the supply of capital assets (securities) would necessarily imply the equality of the demand for and the supply of money. In other words, in the solution of the general equilibrium system of all the prices and the rate of interest, we shall always have a redundant demand and supply equation which necessarily follows from all the rest. If we choose to eliminate the demand and supply equation for money, we shall have the loanable funds theory of interest. If we choose to eliminate the demand and supply equation for securities (or loans), we shall have the liquidity preference theory of interest. In either case, the same interest rate would be determined in the solution of the general equilibrium system.

Although this argument appears to be logically correct, it is not fully convincing. Indeed, as Hicks himself has observed, "the argument merely enables us to eliminate *one* out of the $n + 1$ equations; it does not matter in the least which equation we choose to eliminate."[4] This readily elicited the quip that if we eliminated neither the money equation nor the equation for securities (or loans) but the demand and supply equation for peanuts what then?[5] Are we then to have a loanable funds theory of interest and a liquidity preference theory of peanut prices? Or rather a liquidity preference theory of interest and a loanable funds theory of peanut prices? Hicks gives us no enlightenment on this point. In any case, he gives us no adequate explanation why in a general equilibrium system of $n + 1$ equations, either the demand and supply of loanable funds or the demand and supply for money should be singled out to be "matched" with the determination of the interest rate, while none of the demands and supplies of other commodities and services have ever been credited with such a direct influence upon it.[6] Surely there must be more to the interrelation between the demand and supply for loanable funds and the demand and supply for money than that they are merely two of the Walrasian system of $n + 1$ simultaneous equations, any one of which can be eliminated as otiose. To prove convincingly that the two theories are in fact the same, we must demonstrate that the decision on the part of any economic subject, be it a firm or an individual, to demand or supply loanable funds necessarily involves a corresponding decision to hold or part with money.

3. The fundamental shortcoming of establishing the equivalence of the two theories on the basis of Walras' Law becomes clear when this line of argument is further elaborated by Fellner and Somers and presented in precise diagrammatic form. In their joint article,[7] they have attempted to demonstrate that the two theories are identical and would always lead to one and the same rate of interest; and they conclude that the rate of interest equates demand and supply of cash only in the sense in which the price of shoes can be also be said to perform this function if all other prices are given.[8]

Their argument is also based upon the Walrasian axiom that during any period of time the total "demand" for money is identical with the aggregate supply of all goods and services including "claims" (securities in Hick's terminology) exchanged for money, plus the demand to retain one's own money (the reservation demand); and conversely that the total "supply" of money is identical with the aggregate demand in terms of money for all goods and services including "claims" plus one's own money "supplied" to oneself by not spending.[9]

Thus it is demonstrated that the total demand and supply for money (interpreted in their fashion) will always be equated at the same rate of interest as would the demand and supply for "claims"; for the other two components of the total demand for money are alleged to be equal respectively to the corresponding components of the total supply of money at all rates of interest.[10] It is then concluded that the demand and supply for claims are the natural determinants of the rate of interest and that the total demand and supply for money may be said to determine the rate of interest only when other prices have already equated the demands and supplies for all other commodities and services.

This procedure of proof is in fact merely an elaboration of Hicks' line of argument, the inadequacies of which are now made amply clear.

First, their definitions of the demand and supply of money derived from Walras' Law are quite different from those implicit in the liquidity preference theory. Total supply of money in their terminology is simply total money expenditures on goods and services as well as on the purchases of "claims" plus the amount of money held unspent. This total of the so-called "supply of money", the main components of which are flows over time, does not necessarily equal the total stock of money in existence (which is the usual meaning of the supply of money in the liquidity preference theory), unless the period of time over which the flows of money expenditures are measured is so defined as to make them equal. Similarly, the total demand for money in their nomenclature is simply the sum total of the flows of goods and services and securities sold during a period of undefined length plus the amount of money held unspent. Again this definition of the demand for money is totally alien to the liquidity preference theory where the demand for money is defined as the demand to hold one's wealth in the form of stocks of money. Fellner and Somers made no attempt whatever to reconcile the usual Keynesian definitions of the demand and supply of money in the stock sense with their own definitions in the flow sense.

More fundamentally, we may call the demand and supply of money under their definitions the *ex post* demand and supply for money; for the demand and supply of money under their special definitions are derived from Walras' Law, which is really nothing but the truism that the effective demand for any good implies the supply of something else in exchange for it, and conversely the supply of any good implies the demand for something else in exchange for it. On this ground, Fellner and Somers have so defined the demand for money that any sales of goods and services must automatically be treated as a demand for money as such, regardless of how the economic subject concerned would choose to allocate these money receipts if he had time to do so. This reminds one of the *ex post* definitions of savings according to which a supplier of goods and services, who has just effected a sale but who has not yet had time to allocate the proceeds to any particular use, is said to have saved the proceeds. Now according to Fellner and Somers, he is said to have demanded the proceeds as a cash balance!

In adopting the Walrasian *ex post* definitions for the demand and supply of money, which render them identical except for the components consisting of the demand and supply of securities (claims), Fellner and Somers are in fact just as unfair to the liquidity preference theory as Lerner, in adopting the Keynesian *ex post* definitions of savings and investment in his reconciliation of the two theories, is to the loanable funds theory.[11]

Secondly, the assertion that the demand for money arising from the sales of goods and services is always matched by the supply of money arising from the purchases of goods and services, and hence has no influence upon the rate of interest, seems to be tantamount to saying that the volume of transactions and the level of income could have no influence upon the rate of interest through increasing the demand for money for transaction purposes. Indeed it is hard to see how the demand for money for transaction purposes is taken into account in their definitions of the demand and supply of money.

4. Another reconciliation of the liquidity preference and loanable funds theories was attempted by Swan.[12] He started with Lerner's diagrammatic exposition of the loanable funds theory (Figure 1), which shows the total demand for loanable funds as the sum of investment (the I schedule) plus net "hoarding" (the L schedule) and the supply of loanable funds as the sum of savings (the S schedule) plus net increase in money supply (the M schedule).[13] Then, like Lerner, he regards the fact that L and M schedules intersect at a different rate of interest from that represented by the point of intersection of the $I + L$ and $S + M$ curves as indicative of the conflict between the loanable funds and liquidity preference theories. He then proceeds to resolve this conflict by arguing without much explanation that (a) the excess of *ex ante* savings over *ex post* savings as well as (b) the excess of *ex post* investment over *ex ante* investment constitute some sort of "imaginary liquidity," which though imaginary can nevertheless satisfy actual demand for cash balances. When these two components of "imaginary liquidity" are added together the two *ex post* magnitudes (*ex post* savings and *ex post* investment) luckily cancel out as they are identical. Thus the total "imaginary liquidity" is equal to the excess of *ex ante* savings over *ex ante* investment. This amount of "imaginary liquidity" would be just enough to satisfy the excess of "hoarding" over the increase in the quantity of money; since at the equilibrium rate of interest, $S + M = I + L$, hence, $S - I = L - M$.[14] "The original

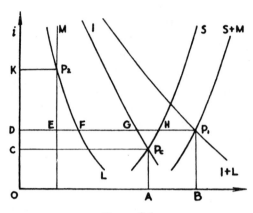

Figure 3.1.

Keynesian formulation of the liquidity preference theory, in which the supply of liquidity is identified with the actual quantity of money, is equivalent to the loanable funds theory only when saving and investment *ex ante* are equal and there is no 'imaginary money' to complicate the analysis."[15]

This is much ado about something quite imaginary. For Haberler was certainly quite right in attaching no significance to the intersection of the L and M curves in Lerner's diagram. If $L + I$ is to represent the total demand for loanable funds, L must be interpreted as the net demand for additional idle balances.[16] If it is interpreted, as by Lerner and apparently by Swan too, in the sense of the increase in demand to hold money in general, then the $I + L$ curve would make no sense, and certainly could not be said to represent the total demand for loanable funds as understood by the loanable funds theorists.[17] The diagram merely shows that when *ex ante* savings exceed *ex ante* investment by the amount GH at the equilibrium rate of interest, that much money would be transferred from the active balances into the idle balances, the increase of which is shown here to exceed the increase in the quantity of money by $EF = GH$.[18] There is nothing imaginary about the money thus transferred.

Nor would the above diagram indicate any conflict between the loanable funds theory which it purports to depict and the liquidity preference theory which is not depicted there at all. If the L curve must be interpreted as the demand for additional idle balances to conform to the loanable funds theory, then the L curve cannot at the same time be interpreted to represent the increase in total demand for money (liquidity preference), including both active and idle balances, as the demand for money should be interpreted under the liquidity preference theory. By the same token, this diagram cannot be manipulated to prove that these two theories are compatible and equivalent either.

2. A Synthesis of the Two Theories

To give a convincing demonstration of the equivalence of the two theories, we must explain how the decision of any economic subject on how much to borrow or to lend necessarily implies a corresponding decision to hold money for one purpose or another. This is not difficult to do if we merely follow closely D. H. Robertson's formulation of the loanable funds theory.

Loanable funds are flows over time. Their magnitude cannot be measured unless we define the period over which these flows are to be measured. It is convenient, following Robertson, to divide time into "days," "which are so short that the income [or sales proceeds] which a man [or a firm] receives on a given day cannot be allocated during its course to any particular use."[19] Furthermore, although Robertson himself did not specifically make this assumption, it will greatly clarify the analysis if we assume further, this time after Hicks,[20] that all contracts on the loan market are concluded at the very beginning of each day, and during the rest of the day people merely carry out their plans for spending (consumption and investment) with either their own money or borrowed money. There would be only one rate of interest for each "day" to be determined at the beginning of the day. In this way, we shall be enabled to analyze the dynamic process of changes in income, interest rate, etc., into a series of "cinematographic" pictures of short-term equilibria at small intervals of time. Net savings available to the loan market at the beginning of a day are defined as the difference between the net income of the previous day and consumption expenditure planned for the day. Similarly gross saving is defined as the difference between the gross income (net income plus "disentanglings" of past savings released from embodiment in fixed capital or working capital) of the previous day and planned consumption of the current day.

At the opening of each day (or rather at the end of the previous day) all disposable incomes, gross or net, are embodied in money; for these incomes received during the previous day cannot be disposed of until the coming day.[21] Thus, at the opening of each day, each economic subject starts with a stock of money equal to his gross income received during the previous day plus his stock of idle cash, i.e., money which he did not allocate either to any spending or to lending (purchase of securities) during the previous day. For the community as a whole, the day is opened with a stock of money equal to the aggregate gross income of the community during the previous day plus the aggregate amount of idle cash balances—and this total stock is necessarily equal to the total amount of money in existence at the end of the previous day.

Since a day is defined as so short that income or sales proceeds received during the day cannot be used to meet expenditures during the same day, all expenditures, whether consumption or investment, planned for the day must require funds equal in amount to these planned expenditures to be set aside at the beginning of the day. It is in this sense that, in accordance with the loanable funds theory, planned investment expenditures for the current day give rise to demands for loanable funds. Keynes in his reply to criticism also admitted that "an investment *decision* (Prof. Ohlin's investment *ex ante*) may sometimes involve a temporary demand for money before it is carried out," and that "planned investment—i.e. investment *ex ante*—may have to secure its 'financial provision' before the investment takes place; that is to say, before the corresponding saving has taken place."[22]

From what we have said about the length of our "days," it should be clear that the requirement for such "financial provision" is not peculiar to planned investment expenditures but applies to all expenditures. And we must contend that Keynes was confused in adding after his concession as to the demand for "finance," almost as a second thought, that this demand for "finance" is "quite distinct from the demand for active balances which will arise as a result of the investment activity while it is going on" (presumably by which he meant the transaction demand for money *proper*). These requirements for "finance" for all planned expenditures actually constitute the whole transaction demand for money for the "day." There will be no further demand for transaction balances when the planned expenditures are carried out; for the economic subject concerned will only part with the "finance funds" accumulated at the beginning of the day as he executes his expenditure plan. The money that he will receive during the day from sales of goods and services, however, is merely the temporary embodiment of his gross income which will not become disposable until the next day. These money receipts during the later part of the day cannot be regarded in any sense as his demand for transaction balances to carry out his current transactions.[23] In any case, since we have assumed that the contracts on the loan market are concluded at the very beginning of the day, it is only the requirements for funds at the beginning of the day to finance all planned expenditures during the day that would influence the rate of interest, not the ensuing receipts of money embodying the incomes of the day which are not disposable until the next day.

Now that the confusion about "finance" and transaction demand for money, which we have shown to be really the same thing, has been cleared up, it is easy to show that the loanable funds and the liquidity preference theroies really say the same thing in different terminology. According to the loanable funds theory, the supply of loanable funds to the loan market at the beginning of each day is equal to the sum of (1) current planned savings, defined as the net income of the preceding day minus the planned consumption of the current day; (2) "disentanglings" or disinvestment of either fixed or working capital during the previous day; (3) "net dishoardings," i.e., the net decrease in idle money which it is planned to withhold from both spending and purchases of claims as compared with the idle money thus held during the previous day (this, of course may be negative); and (4) net additional credit creation. The demand for loanable funds on the loan market is for (1) funds destined for net investment expenditure; (2) funds destined for expenditure on the maintenance or replacement of fixed or working capital.[24]

The rate of interest is the mechanism through which the demand for loanable funds is equated to the supply of loanable funds, i.e., through which the consumption and investment plans and the demand for idle balances are made consistent with each other. Since (1) and (2) of the supply of loanable funds and (1) and (2) of the demand for loanable funds may be summed up, respectively, as planned gross savings and planned gross investment expenditures, the equation for the determination of the rate of interest according to the loanable funds theory may be simplified as

Planned current gross savings

   + net decrease in the demand for idle money

   + net creation of new money

$$= \text{current planned gross investment.} \quad (1)$$

Furthermore, since planned gross savings are defined as gross income of the preceding period minus planned consumption of the current period and the decrease in the demand for idle money is equal to the idle money of the preceding period minus the demand for idle money in the current period, the above equation can be rewritten as

Gross income of the previous day − current planned consumption

+ idle money of the previous day

− the current demand for idle money

+ net creation of new money

$$= \text{current planned gross investment.} \quad (2)$$

Moreover, since as explained above, gross income of the previous period plus the idle money of the previous period equal the total stock of money existing at the end of the previous period, this equation can be further written as

Existing stock of money + net creation of new money

= current planned consumption + current planned gross investment

$$+ \text{current demand for idle money.} \quad (3)$$

Again, as explained above, since planned consumption and investment give rise to demands for "financial provision" of equal amount (which we have shown to be the real meaning of the transaction demand for money), we may further rewrite the loanable funds equation as

Existing stock of money + net creation of new money

= current demand for "finance"

(or current transaction demand for money)

$$+ \text{current demand for idle money.} \quad (4)$$

Thus the equation for the demand and supply of loanable funds is shown to be exactly equivalent to the equation for the demand and supply of money. The key to this transformation is the understanding that, in a slice of time so short as a Robertsonian day, the demand for "finance" funds must be equal to the planned expenditures during the day. There is no need to resort to the far fetched reasoning based upon the Walrasian general equilibrium system, where any offer of goods and services for sale must be treated automatically as a demand for money balances as such, regardless of how the economic subject concerned would allocate his money receipts if allowed time to do so.

In order to express the components of the above equations in schedules or functions, we shall demonstate the exact equivalence of the two theories by means of a diagram (Figure 2) showing equation (2). In Figure 2, OA and AB on the horizontal axis are the amounts of gross income and idle money, respectively, of the previous day. These magnitudes are given data for the current day. Suppose that, given the amount of disposable income, planned consumption for the current day is a decreasing function of the current rate of interest (measured along the vertical axis) as depicted by the C curve. Suppose the current demand for idle money is also a decreasing function of the interest rate as represented by the horizontal distances between the C curve and the $C + H$ curve. Thus by definition, the horizontal distances between the $C + H$ curve and the vertical line through B give the supply of loanable funds of the nonbanking sector at different rates of interest. This supply becomes negative when the $C + H$ curve passes to the right of the perpendicular through B. If the supply of additional new money by the banking system may also be regarded as a function of the rate of interest (an increasing one) as the banks are probably more willing to stretch their reserve ratios when the returns on loans are high, this may be represented as curve M, the horizontal distances between which and the perpendicular through B measure the amounts of new money that would be created at various rates of interest. When the M curve is to the left of the line through B, there will be a disappearance of existing money into the banking system instead of creation of new money. Thus the supply schedule of loanable funds for the whole community is

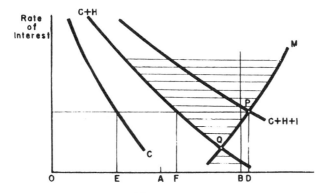

Figure 3.2.

represented by the horizontal distances between the $C + H$ curve and the M curve. The supply becomes negative when the rate of interest falls below the point of intersection of the $C + H$ curve and the M curve (viz., point Q).

The demand for loanable funds on the left-hand side of equation (2) consists of the current planned gross investment which we shall assume to be a decreasing function of the current rate of interest, given the disposable income received during the preceding day and the stock of capital equipment in existence. The schedule for planned investment may be represented by the horizontal distances between the $C + H + I$ curve and the $C + H$ curve.

The current rate of interest will then be determined at point P, the intersection of the $C + H + I$ curve and the M curve; for at that point the horizontal distance between the $C + H + I$ curve and the $C + H$ curve, i.e., the demand for loanable funds, is equated to the horizontal distance between the $C + H$ curve and the M curve, i.e., the supply of loanable funds.

Now exactly the same diagram may be used to illustrate the determination of the interest rate according to the liquidity preference theory. For the $C + H + I$ curve relative to the vertical axis is nothing but the aggregate demand curve for money consisting of the demand for "finance" for planned consumption and investment (i.e., the current transaction demand for money) and the demand for idle money (for speculative and precautionary purposes), viz., the right-hand side of equations (3) and (4). $OA + AB$ is the total stock of money existing at the end of the previous day and BD the amount of additional money that is induced by the current rate of interest PD. Thus at the equilibrium rate of interest PD, the aggregate demand for money is equal to the total stock of money including the new addition to money supply. Thus the liquidity preference and loanable funds theories are indeed two different ways of saying the same thing, leading in all conceivable circumstances to the same result. The perfect agreement between the two theories is found to exist because the *ex ante* decisions to supply loanable funds to the market necessarily imply corresponding decisions (also *ex ante*) as to the funds required to finance one's own consumption and one's own demand for idle money, while the decisions to take loanable funds off the market necessarily imply corresponding decisions as to the requirements for funds to finance investment expenditures.

Not all the practical and policy issues arising out of the old controversy, however, are mere issues of terminology. For Keynes and his followers were often confused about the nature of the transaction demand for money (or "finance"), and this confusion led them to make unwarranted assertions about the effects of increased thrift and increased productivity of investment (marginal efficiency of investment). For instance, it was a common assertion on the part of proponents of the liquidity preference theory that an increase in thrift or an increase in the marginal efficiency of investment would have no direct effect upon the rate of interest, and that the ultimate effect of either type of change upon the interest rate would come about only indirectly through the effect on the level of income, which would contract or expand, as the case might be, as a result of the multiplier process regarded as operating independently of the money market. This early naïveté of the Keynesians can easily be shown to have been based on erroneous analysis.

An increase in thrift (or a decrease in the propensity to consume) would shift the planned consumption curve C to the left. Given the demand schedule for idle money, the $C + H$ curve would also shift to the left. Thus, in the terminology of the loanable funds theory, the supply of loanable funds would be increased. If the planned investment schedule were unchanged, the rate of interest would fall. In the terminology of the liquidity preference theory, the total demand for money $(C + H + I)$ curve would be shifted to the left because of a decrease in the demand for "finance" for planned consumption expenditures. Again the rate of interest would fall. And this would happen before the new consumption and investment expenditure plans were executed, i.e., before the fall in income had taken place. It is not just a matter of the assumption about the elasticity of the demand for idle money. Similarly the marginal efficiency of investment can be shown to have a direct effect upon the rate of interest before the rise in income takes place. Thus our reconciliation of the two theories really points to a victory of the loanable funds theory on practical issues.

3. Static and Dynamic Theories of Interest

If the two theories are equivalent under all circumstances, why is it that the liquidity preference theory has come to be looked upon as a comparative static theory, whereas the loanable funds theory is regarded as a dynamic theory at least by the adherents of the latter?[25] It is submitted here that again it is the confusion on the part of liquidity preference theorists about the transaction demand for money which obscures the dynamic nature of the liquidity preference theory and lends it the appearance of a static theory. On the other hand, the way in which the demand and supply equation is formulated by the loanable funds theory necessarily brings out in strong relief the dynamic process of change over time.

To demonstrate this thesis, we shall restate our equations for the demand and supply of loanable funds and the demand and supply of money in symbols.
Let

$$C_t = C(Y_{t-1}, r_t) \tag{5}$$

$$I_t = I(Y_{t-1}, r_t) \tag{6}$$

$$Mi_t = Mi(r_t) \tag{7}$$

$$M_t = M(R_t, r_t) \tag{8}$$

where C_t, current consumption, is expressed as a function of gross income of the previous period Y_{t-1} and the current rate of interest r_t; I_t, current gross investment, as a function of gross income of previous period and the current rate of interest; Mi_t, the current demand for idle balances, a function of the current interest rate; and M_t the current supply of money, a function of current bank reserves R_t and the current interest rate. The subscripts t and $t - 1$ refer to the periods concerned. Then equation (1) above, which expresses the equality of the demand and supply of loanable funds, may be written as

$$(Y_{t-1} - C_t) - \frac{dMi}{dr} \Delta r_t + \frac{\partial M}{\partial R} \Delta R_t + \frac{\partial M}{\partial r} \Delta r_t = I_t \tag{9}$$

where Δr_t is defined as $(r_t - r_{t-1})$ and ΔR_t as $(R_t - R_{t-1})$. Since $I_t + C_t = Y_t$, gross income of the current period,[26]

$$Y_t - Y_{t-1} = \frac{\partial M}{\partial R} \Delta R_t + \frac{\partial M}{\partial r} \Delta r_t - \frac{dMi}{dr} \Delta r_t. \tag{9'}$$

This plainly indicates the dependence of the present on the past. Not only are current consumption and investment dependent upon the income of the preceding period, but net hoarding and net increase in the money supply are stated to depend upon the change in the current rate of interest and the change in bank reserves as compared with the previous period. This equation also provides a direct link between the change in income and changes in the interest rate and the money supply; for the expansion (or contraction) of income flow (which is identified with the discrepancy between *ex ante* investment and *ex ante* savings in the Robertsonian sense) is stated to be achieved only through a decrease (or an increase) in the demand for idle balances and/or an increase (or a decrease) in the total money supply, which are partly induced by the current interest rate.

Equations (5) to (9) inclusive plus the identity $C_t + I_t = Y_t$ are sufficient to determine the six variables C_t, I_t, Y_t, Mi_t, M_t and r_t; given Y_{t-1}, the income of the previous period, and R_t, which we here treat as an exogenous variable. There is no room for another independent liquidity preference equation of the general form $M_t = L(Y_t, r_t)$, which would make the system overdetermined. Therefore, if both theories are correct, the liquidity preference equation and the loanable funds equation cannot be independent but must be mutually implied, as we have shown above. That is, when we add Mi_{t-1} to both sides of equation (9), the equation for the demand and supply of loanable funds, then after some shifting of terms and substituting Y_t for $(C_t + I_t)$, we obtain

$$Y_{t-1} + Mi_{t-1} + \frac{\partial M}{\partial R} \Delta R_t + \frac{\partial M}{\partial r} \Delta r_t = Y_t + Mi_{t-1} + \frac{dMi}{dr} \Delta r_t,$$

which, as explained above (pp. 57–58), implies:[27]

$$M_t = Y_t + Mi(r_t). \tag{10}$$

This is the liquidity preference equation, equation (4) above, rewritten in symbols showing the aggregate demand for money as a function of the current income and the rate of interest.

Equation (10) may appear to have the advantage of greater simplicity over equation (9) above, which fact probably accounts for the great attraction of the Keynesian theory of interest. If, however, Y_t is understood as income realised in the current period, as it is generally understood by most Keynesians, the dynamic nature of the money market mechanism is entirely obscured. It provides no obvious link between the past and the present. It appears to define only the equilibrium relationship between money supply, income and interest rate, but not to be concerned with the changes of these variables over time.

This difference, however, is only apparent. If the two theories are really equivalent, one cannot be a dynamic theory while the other remains a static one. If we understand Y_t as the sum of planned current consumption and investment, which are themselves functions of Y_{t-1}, then the dynamic nature of the liquidity preference equation becomes clear; for then equation (10) rewritten in the form of

$$M_t = C(Y_{t-1}, r_t) + I(Y_{t-1}, r_t) + Mi(r_t) \tag{11}$$

would clearly indicate the dependence of the present upon the past.[28]

Indeed, the demand for money in general, i.e., the righthand side of equation (11) can be expressed as a function of the income received in the previous period and the current rate of interest,[29] i.e., as $L(Y_{t-1}, r_t)$, where

$$\frac{\partial L_t}{\partial Y_{t-1}} = \frac{\partial C_t}{\partial Y_{t-1}} + \frac{\partial I_t}{\partial Y_{t-1}} \tag{12}$$

and

$$\frac{\partial L_t}{\partial r_t} = \frac{\partial C_t}{\partial r_t} + \frac{\partial I_t}{\partial r_t} + \frac{dMi_t}{dr_t}. \tag{13}$$

In other words, the liquidity preference function is neither independent of the consumption function nor of the investment function but is a sort of composite function of the consumption and investment functions and the function of the demand for inactive balances. All the disagreements between the loanable funds and liquidity preference theories on practical issues seem to arise from the failure on the part of liquidity preference theorists themselves to perceive the dependence of the aggregate liquidity preference (or demand for money) function upon the consumption and investment functions.

Furthermore, the beguiling simplicity of the demand and supply of money equation (10) tends to mislead the liquidity preference theorists into overlooking the relation between income changes and changes in the interest rate and money supply from period to period, which is so clearly shown by the loanable funds equation that it cannot possibly be neglected.[30] Neglect of this link led many early Keynesian economists to think that the multiplier process of income expansion operates independently of the money-market mechanism and regardless of what happens to the money supply. From what has been said above, it should be clear that in every step of the evolution of the multiplier process, changes in the interest rate and/or money supply are necessarily involved.

4. Reappraisal of the Multiplier and Velocity Analysis

Our understanding of the link between income changes and changes in the money supply and interest rate should enable us to reappraise the multiplier approach and the traditional velocity approach to the problem of income expansion and to achieve a reconciliation between the two.

More than ten years ago, Samuelson spoke of the unsuccessful attempts to reconcile the multiplier analysis and the velocity approach as either "trivial" or "founded upon error."[31] Even today it seems that the only points of agreement between the two approaches are perhaps that the velocity of circulation of active money is substantially constant under normal circumstances[32] and that the period of time for which the income velocity of active money is unity should be taken as "the income propagation period" or "multiplier time period" in the multiplier analysis.[33]

The period over which the total net income is equal to the total active money is necessarily longer than the period over which the total gross income (or gross expenditure) is equal to the total active money, viz., the period which we have chosen to identify with our "day" in order to accommodate Robertson's definition of the demand and supply of loanable funds which includes disinvestment of working as well as fixed capital as part of the supply of, and replacement as part of the demand for, loanable funds. To use instead the longer income-propagation period as our unit period would not make any difference to our argument above; for there would still be a one-to-one equivalence between the demand for transaction balances (or the demand for loanable funds) and the expenditures on consumption and investment (the latter taken *net* in the present case).

For the convenience of exposition of the multiplier theory, let us assume that consumption and investment (net) in money terms may be approximated by the two following linear functions, respectively,

$$C_t = cY_{t-1} - c'r_t + C_a \tag{14}$$

$$I_t = iY_{t-1} - i'r_t + I_a \tag{15}$$

where Y is net money income, r the rate of interest, C_a and I_a the autonomous elements, and the t-subscripts of the variables indicate the period concerned. Furthermore, we shall assume that the demand for idle balances Mi and the supply of money M may also be expressed as the following linear functions:

$$Mi_t = Mi_a - \beta r_t \tag{16}$$

$$M_t = R_t + \gamma R_{t-1} + sr_t \tag{17}$$

where Mi_a is the autonomous element in the demand for idle money; R, the reserve money created by the central bank (i.e., deposits at the central bank and currency); and γ, the inverse of the normal reserve ratio of commercial banks. The expansion of commercial bank credit following an increase in reserve money is supposed to lag one period behind the increase in reserve money. Given the reserves, the supply of money by commercial banks is supposed to be an increasing function of the current rate of interest.

The rate of interest r_t, as shown above, may be regarded as determined either by the demand and supply of loanable funds or the demand and supply of money. As the equation of the demand and supply of loanable funds brings out the dynamic process of changes more clearly than the demand and supply of money equation, we shall use the former to determine the rate of interest r_t. Thus

$$Y_{t-1} - C_t - \Delta Mi_t + \Delta M_t = I_t.$$

Hence

$$Y_t - Y_{t-1} = \Delta M_t - \Delta Mi_t$$

or

$$\Delta Y_t = \gamma \Delta R_{t-1} + \Delta R_t + (s + \beta)\Delta r_t. \tag{18}$$

That is, the change in income would necessarily equal the sum of the increment in money supply plus dishoarding.

In a period of income equilibrium, however, $Y_t = Y_{t-1}$ and there should be no change in money supply (in particular there should be no change in reserve money). Then ΔY, ΔR and Δr would all be zero.[34] Suppose we start from such an equilibrium period (let it be Period 0). Then

$$Y_0 = I_a + C_a + (i + c)Y_0 - (i' + c')r_0. \tag{19}$$

Starting from such an equilibrium, let us assume that the flow of investment is supplemented by a constant injection of A each period, say by deficit spending of the government. The early enthusiasts for multiplier theory would claim that, whether these injections were financed by creations of additional money or by borrowings that involve no increase in the money supply, money income would expand in much the same way to a new higher level determined by the multiplier and stay there.[35] The crude quantity theorists, on the other hand, would expect that the aggregate income would remain substantially unchanged, in spite of the government's deficit spending, if the financing of the deficits involved no increase in the money supply. If the deficits were financed by a steady creation of new money, they would expect the money income to increase also steadily without limit instead of approaching the level set by the multiplier. These conflicting expectations can easily be resolved as the results of different assumptions about the demand functions for idle money, both of which may be approximations of certain particular historical and geographical circumstances.

Let us first suppose that the constant stream of additional autonomous expenditure A is financed by government borrowing involving no increase in reserve money. In Period 1, the equilibrium on the money market (the equality between the demand for and the supply of loanable funds) signifies

$$A + I_1 = Y_0 - C_1 - \Delta Mi_1 + \Delta M_1. \tag{20}$$

Substituting (14), (15), (16), (17) and (19) in (20), while keeping $\Delta R_t = 0$, we have

$$A = [(i' + c') + (\beta + s)]\Delta r_1,$$

$$\therefore \Delta r_1 = \frac{A}{(i' + c') + (\beta + s)}. \tag{21}$$

That is, in period 1, the rate of interest would rise by

$$\frac{A}{(c' + i') + (\beta + s)}.$$

Then

$$\Delta Y_1 = A - (c' + i')\Delta r_1,$$

$$= \frac{\beta + s}{(c' + i') + (\beta + s)} A. \tag{22}$$

By repeated substitution we could indeed find out how the rate of interest and income would change from period to period and whether they would approach respectively to new equilibrium levels. However, this would be a tedious process. Instead, we may find the answer by solving the following difference equation. From the definition of Y_t and the consumption and investment functions given in (14) and (15), we may write

$$Y_t = (i + c)Y_{t-1} - (i' + c')r_t + (C_a + I_a + A).$$

Then

$$\Delta Y_t = Y_t - Y_{t-1} = (i + c)\Delta Y_{t-1} - (i' + c')\Delta r_t. \tag{23}$$

But from (18), when ΔR is always assumed to be zero, we get

$$\Delta r_t = \frac{1}{\beta + s} \Delta Y_t.$$

Substituting this in (23), we get

$$\left[1 + \frac{i' + c'}{\beta + s} \right] \Delta Y_t - (i + c)\Delta Y_{t-1} = 0. \tag{24}$$

The general solution for ΔY_t is

$$\Delta Y_t = \Delta Y_1 \left[\frac{i + c}{1 + \dfrac{i' + c'}{\beta + s}} \right]^{t-1}$$

$$= \frac{(\beta + s)A}{(c' + i') + (\beta + s)} \left[\frac{i + c}{1 + \dfrac{i' + c'}{\beta + s}} \right]^{t-1}. \tag{25}$$

Income will approach asymptotically to a new level only when ΔY_t tapers off to zero, i.e., when

$$\frac{i + c}{1 + \dfrac{i' + c'}{\beta + s}} < 1,$$

or

$$1 + \frac{i' + c'}{\beta + s} - i - c > 0. \tag{26}$$

If this condition holds, income will gradually reach a new equilibrium Y_e, and

$$Y_e - Y_0 = \sum_1^\infty \Delta Y_t = \frac{A}{1 - (i + c) + \dfrac{i' + c'}{\beta + s}}. \tag{27}$$

This gives us a mulitplier formula that is generalized to include the effects of induced changes in the rate of interest, assuming there is no change in reserve money (central bank credit and currency).

The early Keynesians were of the opinion that β and s, the interest elasticities of demand for idle money and of supply of money by commercial banks, respectively, are infinitely large, so that $i' + c'/\beta + s$ is negligibly small. Thus, they could claim that the multiplier process is independent of the money market and the multiplier is determined solely by the propensity to spend (the propensities to consume and to invest).

The crude quantity theorists, on the other hand, believe that β, the interest elasticity of demand for idle money, is very small if not zero. If the monetary authorities not only did not allow reserve money to increase but also took effective measures to offset the induced increase in bank money by the commercial banks so that s is also zero, then $i' + c'/\beta + s$ becomes infinitely large. The multiplier then is infinitely small. In other words, in spite of the constant additional autonomous spending by the government, the effect upon money income would be quite negligible, so long as the government spendings were financed without involving any increase in money supply.

Thus, the conflicting views of the multiplier theorists and the crude quantity theorists are merely the result of the two opposite extreme assumptions they have respectively made. In times of deep depression when the rate of interest has already fallen to a minimum level where the rate of return on securities barely covers the bother and risk of investing money in them, such as at the time the *General Theory* appeared, the assumption of an infinitely elastic demand for money (with respect to the interest rate) may indeed be a good approximation to reality. However, when a high level of employment has been sustained for many years and the interest rate has continued to be well above that minimum (particularly in a backward country where the practice of holding large and highly volatile speculative balances has never been of any importance), the interest elasticity of demand for idle money may be quite small and not far from the assumption of the crude quantity theorists.

It must be admitted that, in the present case, so long as $\beta > 0$, the multiplier principle is at least qualitatively correct, viz., that with a constant injection of autonomous expenditures, even though it involves no increase in money supply at all, income will expand to a new equilibrium. However, the multiplier may be very much smaller than might be expected on the basis of income-coefficients (propensities) of spending alone. Furthermore, income may still reach a stable equilibrium, even if the sum of the propensities to consume and to invest is equal to or greater than unity, so long as the quantity of money is kept constant.

Next let us assume that the constant stream of additional autonomous expenditure is financed by constant creation of additional reserve money by the central bank, or by whoever has the right to issue currency. Then in Period 1, the equilibrium on the money market (the equality between the demand and supply of loanable funds) implies

$$A + I_1 = Y_0 - C_1 - \Delta Mi_1 + \Delta M_1.$$

Upon substituting (14), (15), (16), (17) and (19) into this equation, while letting $\Delta R_1 = A$, this can be reduced to

$$A - i'\Delta r_1 = c'\Delta r_1 + (\beta + s)\Delta r_1 + A,$$

$$\therefore \Delta r_1 = 0 \tag{28}$$

and

$$\Delta Y_1 = Y_1 - Y_0 = A - (c' + i')\Delta r_1$$

$$= A. \tag{29}$$

That is to say, in the first period, there would be no change in the rate of interest and the increase in income would be simply equal to the additional autonomous expenditure. In later periods, however, the rate of interest would probably fall, given the investment function, since the successive increases in reserve money are not only themselves cumulative, but each increase would lead to a multiple expansion of commercial bank credit.[36] This may be shown by a more general approach.

From (18) we have

$$\Delta Y_t = (\beta + s)\Delta r_t + \gamma \Delta R_{t-1} + \Delta R_t.$$

As it is assumed that, from Period 1 onwards, the reserve money is increased in each period by a constant A, therefore $\Delta R_{t-1} = \Delta R_t = A$, from $t = 2$ onwards. Hence

$$\Delta Y_t = (\beta + s)\Delta r_t + (1 + \gamma)A$$

and

$$\Delta r_t = \frac{\Delta Y_t - (1 + \gamma)A}{\beta + s}. \tag{30}$$

On the other hand, from the definitions for Y_t and Y_{t-1}, we get

$$\Delta Y_t = Y_t - Y_{t-1} = (i + c)\Delta Y_{t-1} - (i' + c')\Delta r_t$$

$$= (i + c)\Delta Y_{t-1} - \frac{(i' + c')}{(\beta + s)}[\Delta Y_t - (1 + \gamma)A],$$

$$\therefore \left[1 + \frac{i' + c'}{\beta + s}\right]\Delta Y_t - (i + c)\Delta Y_{t-1} = \frac{(1 + \gamma)(i' + c')}{\beta + s}A. \tag{31}$$

The solution of (31) for ΔY_t is of the following form:

$$\Delta Y_t = \Delta Y_E + K \left\{ \frac{i + c}{1 + \dfrac{i' + c'}{\beta + s}} \right\}^{t-1}, \tag{32}$$

where

$$\Delta Y_E = \frac{A(1 + \gamma)(i' + c')}{\beta + s} \cdot \frac{1}{1 - (i + c) + \dfrac{i' + c'}{\beta + s}}, \tag{33}$$

and

$$K = \Delta Y_1 - \Delta Y_E$$

$$= A - \Delta Y_E, \tag{34}$$

ΔY_1 being equal to A as shown by (29).

This solution for ΔY_t is radically different from the previous one obtained for ΔY_t in (25) under the assumption that the additional autonomous expenditures are financed by borrowing involving no increase in reserve money. For there if

$$\frac{i + c}{1 + \dfrac{i' + c'}{\beta + s}} < 1,$$

ΔY_t would approach zero as t approached infinity. Here even if

$$\frac{i + c}{1 + \dfrac{i' + c'}{\beta + s}} < 1,$$

ΔY_t would never approach zero, but would approach a constant increment ΔY_E. That is to say, money income would never reach a new equilibrium level, but would keep on increasing without limit, except under the extreme assumption that β and/or s are infinitely large.[37] Only under this extreme assumption will it be found that $\Delta Y_E = 0$, $\Delta Y_t = A(i + c)^{t-1}$, and that the usual multiplier formula, $Y_E - Y_0 = A/1 - (i + c)$ holds. So long as β and s are finite, however, ΔY_t would never taper off to zero and there can be no finite multiplier, even if the propensity to consume plus the propensity to invest $(c + i)$ is well below unity. In this case, it is the crude quantity theory (velocity approach) that is at least qualitatively correct, even though its extreme assumption that $\beta = 0$ may not be strictly true.

As we have seen above, Y_t would go on increasing and the rate of increase would approach ΔY_E, which is a constant multiple of A, the interjection of reserve money per period by the government, viz.,

$$\Delta Y_E = \frac{(1 + \gamma)(i' + c')}{(\beta + s) + (i' + c') - (i + c)(\beta + s)} A.$$

It is not difficult to see the connection between this multiple and the velocity of circulation. If $\beta = 0$, as is assumed in the crude quantity theory, and if A is the entire net creation of new money per period so that there is no further interest-induced creation of money nor further expansion of credit on the basis of A, then, with β, s and γ all equal to zero, $\Delta Y_t = \Delta Y_E = A$.

That is to say, the increase in income per period from the very beginning of inflation is simply equal to the injection of additional money supply into the flow of expenditures per period, the velocity of active balances being assumed to be equal to one in our unit period. Certainly, this prediction would not be quantitatively exact, if the interest elasticity of demand for money were not in fact zero, but it is at least qualitatively in the right direction so long as the elasticity concerned is not infinity and especially when it is not far from zero. Since the science of economics cannot yet be said to have reached the stage where quantitatively exact predictions can be made (particularly in the case of underdeveloped countries where statistical data are not sufficiently available to set up elaborate econometric models), it is important that we should at least be enabled to make qualitatively correct predictions.

Thus in considering the effect of inflationary financing of development investment, the multiplier principle, which neglects the supply of money and the money-market mechanism, can be dangerously misleading. This is evidenced by the fact that not a few competent economists have expressed the opinion that inflation brought about by deficit financing of investment for economic development (which, in underdeveloped countries, practically always means financing with the creation of new money) is "self-destructive," because the stream of deficit financing would only raise the level of money income to a new level according to the multiplier principle, whereas output of real goods would rise continuously without limit, even though at a slower pace, with the annual formation of additional productive capital.[38] This view, is, however, misleading, because, as we have shown above, so long as the additional investments are financed by constant creation of new money, income would not come to an equilibrium at a new level but would also go on rising. It would seem to be advisable, at least in the case of underdeveloped countries, to shun the multiplier principle and rely instead upon the more primitive rule of thumb of a marginal velocity of circulation, which would at least provide us a qualitatively correct estimate of income expansion on the basis of the increases in money supply.

Notes

* The author is an economist of the International Monetary Fund. He wishes to acknowledge his debt to T. C. Liu for checking the mathematics for him and for discussions on many points in this paper.

1. *E.g.*, L. R. Klein, *The Keynesian Revolution* (New York, 1949), pp. 117–23; W. Fellner and H. M. Somers, "Note on 'Stocks' and 'Flows' in Monetary Interest Theory," *Rev. Econ. Stat.*, May 1949, XXXI, 145–46; L. R. Klein, "Stock and Flow Analysis in Economics," *Econometrica*, July 1950, XVIII, 236–41; Karl Brunner on the same topic, *ibid.*, pp. 247–51; Replies by Fellner and Somers to Klein and Brunner, *ibid.*, pp. 242–45; H. G. Johnson, "Some Cambridge Controversies in Monetary Theory," *Rev. Econ. Stud.*, 1951–52, XIX(2), 90–105; D. H. Robertson, "Comments on Mr. Johnson's Note," *ibid.*, pp. 105–11; and F. H. Hahn, "The Rate of Interest and General Equilibrium Analysis," *Econ. Jour.*, March 1955, LXV, 52–66.

2. A. P. Lerner, "Alternative Formulations of the Theory of Interest." *Econ. Jour.*, June 1938, XLVIII, 211–30; J. R. Hicks, *Value and Capital* (Oxford, 1939), Ch. XII, pp. 153–162; W. Fellner and H. M. Somers, "Alternative Monetary Approaches to Interest Theory," *Rev. Econ. Stat.*, Feb. 1941, XXIII, 43–48; T. W. Swan, "Some Notes on The Interest Controversy," *Econ. Record,* Dec. 1941, XVII, 153–65.

3. Hicks, *op. cit.*, pp. 153–62.

4. *Ibid.*, p. 158.

5. Allegedly from Lerner. See Klein, *The Keynesian Revolution, op. cit.*, p. 118.

6. Hicks, *op. cit.*, p. 161.

7. "Alternative Monetary Approaches to Interest Theory," *loc. cit.*, pp. 43–48.

8. *Ibid.*, p. 48.

9. *Ibid.*, p. 45.

10. *Ibid.*, pp. 45–46.

11. Lerner, by defining savings and investment in the *ex post* sense, in which they are identical even as schedules, was able to contend that they are completely otiose in the determination of the interest rate, a sort of "sleeping partner in the firm." (*Op. cit.*, pp. 215–21). Now Fellner and Somers, by defining the demand and supply of money arising from the

purchases and sales of goods and services and from the retention of idle balances in the *ex post* sense, in which they are identical as schedules, are also able to argue that these demands and supplies of money are in turn completely otiose. The nemesis of *ex post* definitions seems to have befallen their initiators!

12. *Op. cit.*, pp. 153–65.
13. Lerner, *op. cit.*, Figure 1, p. 213.
14. Swan, *op. cit.*, pp. 158–63.
15. *Ibid.*, p. 163.
16. Haberler, *Prosperity and Depression,* 3rd ed. (New York, 1946), pp. 184–87 and pp. 200–02.
17. See pp. 55–57.
18. Cf. Haberler, *op. cit.*, p. 187. Although Haberler believed that the loanable funds and liquidity preference theories are but alternative ways of expressing the same thing, he too, like Robertson, made no attempt to demonstate formally that the two theories would always lead to one and the same rate of interest. He contented himself merely with showing that under various specific situations, the two theories would lead us to expect the rate of interest to move in the same direction (*ibid.,* pp. 211–18).
19. *Essays in Monetary Theory* (London, 1940), p. 65. The insertions in brackets are my own.
20. *Value and Capital, op. cit.,* pp. 122–23. Only Hicks calls his period a "week."
21. This statement appears to involve the assumption that all sales are effected in cash transactions. In reality, it is likely that part of the total sales during any period would be effected against credit. This kind of complication, however, does not change the substance of our argument; for we can always consider sales against credit as actually consisting of two separate steps; first a granting of loan by the seller to the purchaser and then a sale against cash. To include the supply and demand for such loans as are implied in sales on credit into the aggregate supply and demand for loanable funds would not change the equilibrium on the money market, because the same amount would be added to both the demand and the supply sides of the loanable funds equation.

    "Disentanglements" of past savings would also be temporarily embodied in money at the end of each period, as they must constitute part of the gross sales proceeds.
22. "Alternative Theories of the Rate of Interest," *Econ. Jour.,* June 1937, XLVII, 246.
23. Contrast with Fellner and Somers' definition of the demand for money on the basis of Walras' Law. See above pp. 541–43.
24. *Cf.* D. H. Robertson, "Mr. Keynes and the Rate of Interest," *Essays in Monetary Theory, op. cit.,* pp. 2–3.
25. See Johnson, "Some Cambridge Controversies in Monetary Theory," *op. cit.,* esp. pp. 90–92.
26. Since our period is defined as such a short slice of time that income received during a given period cannot be allocated within the same period to any

particular use, it is reasonable to assume that expenditure plans for a given period, once decided upon at the beginning of the period concerned, would not be revised during the course of the same period. (See pp. 55–56.) Therefore $Y_t \equiv I_t + C_t$, may be regarded as both the *ex ante* and the *ex post* income of the current period.

27. Incidentally, our repeated demonstration of the exact equivalence of the loanable funds equation and the liquidity preference equation should also serve to show that the "flow approach" represented by the loanable funds theory and the "stock approach" represented by the liquidity preference theory are not so fundamentally different as L. R. Klein and Karl Brunner appear to believe. (See Klein, *The Keynesian Revolution, op. cit.,* pp. 122–23, and "Stock and Flow Analysis in Economics," and Brunner on the same subject, *loc. cit.,* pp. 236–41 and pp. 247–51, respectively.) We have in fact shown above that the loanable funds equation, equations (9), which define a "flow" equilibrium, can be easily transformed into the liquidity preference equation, equation (10), which defines a "stock" equilibrium.

28. See Johnson, *op. cit.,* p. 91; "one could 'dynamise' the liquidity preference theory, for example, by making the amount of money held to satisfy the transaction demand for money in one period a function of the income received in the previous period."

29. Of all the expositors of the liquidity preference theory, Franco Modigliani alone has expressed the liquidity preference theory in this dynamic form. He did not, however, explain why he adopted this functional form, nor did he seem to be aware, like all other expositors of the liquidity preference theory, notably Hicks and Lange, of the dependence of the liquidity preference function upon the investment and consumption functions. See his "Liquidity Preference and the Theory of Interest and Money," *Econometrica,* Jan. 1944, XII, 45–88, reprinted in *Readings in Monetary Theory* (Philadelphia, 1951), pp. 186–239, esp. pp. 206–08. See also Hicks, "Mr. Keynes and the 'Classics'; A Suggested Interpretation," *Econometrica,* 1937, V, 147–59, and Lange, "The Rate of Interest and the Optimum Propensity to Consume," *Economica,* Feb. 1938, V, n.s., 12–32.

30. Although this link as shown by equation (9) can be easily derived also from equation (10), the demand and supply of money equation, by taking the first differences of both sides.

31. "Fiscal Policy and Income Determination," *Quart. Jour. Econ.,* Aug. 1942, LVI, esp. 601–05. Nor does the recent attempt by Vera Lutz to "marry" the two approaches strike the author as very successful. (See V. Lutz, "Multiplier and Velocity Analysis: A Marriage," *Economica,* Feb. 1955, XXII, n.s., 29–44.)

32. See, for instance, J. M. Keynes, *General Theory,* p. 201; Richard Goodwin, "The Multiplier," *The New Economics,* ed. S. E. Harris (New York, 1947), p. 488.

33. See F. Machlup, "Period Analysis and Multiplier Theory," collected in *Readings in Business Cycle Theory* (Philadelphia, 1944), pp. 203–34, esp. pp. 208–14, and Goodwin, *op. cit.,* pp. 487–88.

34. When $Y_t = Y_{t-1}$, savings in the Robertsonian sense are necessarily equal to

investment, and the converse is also true. For savings are defined as $Y_{t-1} - C_t$. If $Y_{t-1} = Y_t = C_t + I_t$, then $Y_{t-1} - C_t = I_t$.

35. See, for instance, Samuelson, *op. cit.,* pp. 590–95.
36. In a violent price inflation, the rate of interest would generally be found to rise with the increase in money supply. This is because when rises in prices generate expectations of futher and further rises in prices, the investment function is continuously shifted bodily upwards. Such rapid upshifts of the investment function would force up the rate of interest in spite of the constant increase in money supply. It is, however, very difficult to allow for such shifts of the investment function in a multiplier analysis. They are implicitly assumed away here. We are, therefore, dealing with a special case particularly favorable to the application of the multiplier analysis. Our criticism, therefore, is not to be dismissed on the basis that we have made unfavorable implicit assumptions.
37. In this paper, we are dealing with a closed economy only, but the above analysis can be easily extended to an open economy. The above analysis however, would indicate that the so-called "leakage" due to imports would radically differ from the "leakage" due to savings; for additional imports under an inflexible exchange rate system would automatically lead to an equal reduction in reserve money whereas induced savings would not.
38. See for instance W. Arthur Lewis, "Economic Development with Unlimited Supplies of Labour," *The Manchester School,* May 1954, XXII, esp. 162–65, and p. 190.

CHAPTER 4

The Role of Money in Trade-Balance Stability: Synthesis of the Elasticity and Absorption Approaches

S. C. Tsiang*

The spirited controversy between S. S. Alexander and Fritz Machlup[1] on the relative merits of the relative prices (or elasticities) and aggregate spending (absorption) approaches to the problem of determining the effect of devaluation appears to have ended, for the time being, in a rather disappointing anticlimax. After having witnessed the mutual accusation of the rival approaches as consisting of implicit theorizing based upon purely definitional tautologies[2] one feels somewhat let down by the compromise which Alexander now proposes[3] that the result obtained by the traditional elasticities approach may be treated as the "initial" (or primary) effect of a devaluation to which a sort of "multiplier" (normally less than unity), computed from the propensities to hoard, to import, etc., is to be applied to yield the final effect of the devaluation.

The extension of the elasticity approach by a superimposition of a multiplier analysis in this manner is essentially the same as what A. J. Brown had already done in 1942.[4] Indeed, it was already indicated by J.

Finance Constraints and the Theory of Money
ISBN 0-12-701720-8
ISBN 0-12-701721-6 (pbk)

Reprinted with permission from *American Economic Review*, American Economic Association, Vol. VI, 5 (December 1961), pp. 912–936.

Robinson[5] in her pioneering article on the foreign exchanges first published in 1937.

The superimposition of a multiplier upon the elasticities solution of the effect of a devaluation usually glosses over the following difficulty: Unless the supplies of exportable and domestic goods in both countries concerned are all infinitely elastic, so that prices in both countries (except prices of imports) will remain constant, the multiplier effect of the initial change in the trade balance will bring about further changes in relative prices, and hence further substitution between imports and domestically produced goods in both countries. Thus if the conventional elasticities solution is treated as a sort of multiplicand, to which a multiplier (or a damping coefficient) is to be applied to obtain the final effect, then the multiplier itself should again involve the relevant elasticities that are in the multiplicand. There can be no neat dichotomy of the final effect of a devaluation into a part that consists of the elasticities solution and another that consists of the multiplier (or absorption) solution. The total effect of a devaluation must be analyzed in a comprehensive system in which changes in incomes, prices and outputs are all taken into consideration. In fact, even before Alexander raised the outcry against the elasticities approach and proposed the substitution of the absorption approach, a number of attempts had already been made to analyze the effect of a devaluation with more or less comprehensive mathematical systems that allow for both income and price changes, notably those by Meade, Harberger, Laursen and Metzler, and Stuvel.[6] If the controversy between the relative-prices and aggregate-spending approaches merely leads to a synthesis which had already been worked out before the controversy, what then has been gained by the debate?

If anything of enduring value has come out of Alexander's proposal of the absorption approach, it is the fact that the simple identity:

$$
\begin{array}{ccccc}
B & \equiv & Y & - & A \\
\text{Trade} & & \text{National} & & \text{Absorption} \\
\text{Balance} & & \text{Income} & & \text{or National} \\
& & & & \text{Expenditure}
\end{array}
$$

which he pushed to the forefront in the analysis of the effect of a devaluation, has brought out in strong relief a fundamental fact, viz., that a negative trade balance necessarily implies national expenditure in excess of national income. This obvious truth was underscored by

Machlup[7] who therefore emphasized the role played by credit creation in sustaining the excess expenditure in the case of a trade deficit (a negative B) and concluded that "nothing can be said about the effects of a devaluation unless exact specifications are made regarding the supply of money and credit." The highlighting of the monetary implications of a balance-of-payments deficit or surplus was also stressed by Johnson[8] as the major contribution of the absorption approach. More recently, Michaely, in an attempt to reconcile the relative-prices and absorption approaches under the assumption of full employment, also naturally resorted to the "real balance effect" of devaluation-induced price changes with the money supply kept constant.[9] Thus as a by-product of Alexander's attack on the elasticities approach, the much neglected role played by the supply of money and credit in working out the effect of a devaluation and the stability of the trade balance is once more being recognized.[10]

The rediscovery of the significance of monetary factors, however, has not yet been reflected in the formulae and mathematical models for the analysis of the effect of a devaluation on the balance of trade. Not only did the conventional elasticities formulae of the effect of devaluation take no account of the monetary factors (since implicitly they generally assume a constant money income), but in the various attempts to combine the elasticities approach with a multplier analysis (e.g., those of Brown and Allen, and even in most of the more or less comprehensive models of Harberger, Laursen and Metzler, Stuvel, and Jones),[11] the role of money and credit was also totally disregarded. In a quite recent attempt to marry the elasticity and the absorption approaches, Brems also did not include either the money supply or the rate of interest in his otherwise rather complicated mathematical model.[12] Even Alexander himself tends to neglect the role of money; for in his discussion of the multplier process engendered by the initial change in the trade balance, a process supposed to be determined by the propensities to hoard and to spend on imports and exportables, the monetary mechanism of income expansion was never brought in at all. It was only in his discussion of the cash balance effects at full employment that the money supply was briefly mentioned.[13]

In this respect, Meade's model for the analysis of the balance of payments stands out as a splendid exception; for he alone included the money supply and the rate of interest as variables in his model and always clearly stated the specific assumptions he made about monetary and fiscal policies. Unfortunately, however, Meade worked out the solution for the effect of a devaluation from his model only under the assumption of either a so-called "Keynesian neutral economy" or that of a monetary policy that ensures "internal balance." Under the "neutral economy" assumption, the monetary authorities are supposed to keep the supply of money infinitely elastic at a constant interest rate, so that the supply of money will passively adapt itself to whatever the demand for money might be at the constant interest rate.[14] This in effect obliterates all possible influences the supply of money and the interest rate might have on his solution for the effect of a devaluation. On the other hand, the assumption of a monetary policy that ensures "internal balance" (i.e., a constant level of employment),[15] coupled with the assumptions that money wage rates are exogenously given and that prices always equal marginal labour cost, in effect implies that money income is somehow effectively kept constant, provided money wage rates remain constant. This again eliminates all the positive influences the money supply and the interest rate might exert on the effect of a devaluation, as they are assumed to adjust themselves passively to the requirements of the policy objective of maintaining money income constant.[16]

The purpose of this paper is to demonstrate the crucial role that could be played by monetary factors and thus to show in a more comprehensive way how relative prices and income-expenditure adjustments combine to determine the effect of a devaluation. To avoid further proliferation of models, each with the idiosyncracies of its creator fully displayed in the choice of variables and notation system, I shall adopt Meade's simplified two-country, two-commodity model, which seems by far the most economically sound, and shall only make a slight modification to make good an omission (viz., that of the effect of changes in the terms of trade on aggregate expenditure) which has been much discussed since Harberger, Laursen and Metzler pointed out its possible significance. I shall also trim his model of all nonessential policy variables, such as tariff rates and various shift variables, which he adopted to represent controlled or uncontrolled shifts in various functional relationships, so as to make the system intelligible to the reader without overtaxing his perseverance.[17]

1. The Model

We shall adopt Meade's notation throughout so as to facilitate comparison between his results and ours. In Meade's notation, a subscript a refers to country A and a subscript b to country B. The subscript ab for a term indicates that it is the sum of a corresponding A-term and B-term (e.g., $\pi_{ab} = \pi_a + \pi_b$). Capital italic letters refer to total quantities; small italic letters to small increments (or differentials) of those qualities; and a bar over a term means a price corresponding to that term. The small Greek letters stand for functional relationships between the differentials (i.e., either partial derivatives or elasticities obtained from such partial derivatives). Thus,

Q_a = A's product.

$\bar{Q}_a$ = the price of A's product, which is put equal to 1 at the initial position by using the appropriate unit for Q_a.

H_a = volume of employment in country A.

$\bar{H}_a$ = the money wage rate in country A, which is put equal to 1 at the initial position by choosing the appropriate unit for H_a.

I_a = the physical volume of A's imports, which constitute B's exports.

D_a = domestic expenditures in A in terms of domestic currency.

R_a = the rate of interest in A.

M_a = the amount of money in A.

The corresponding terms for country B with the subscript b are similarly defined.

E = the rate of exchange expressed as the number of units of A's currency per unit of B's currency, which is again put equal to 1 at the initial position by choosing the appropriate unit for B's currency.

T = the balance of trade, i.e., the net excess of A's receipts from exports valued in A's currency.

It is assumed that at the initial position

$$I_a \bar{Q}_b E = I_b \bar{Q}_a = I_a = I_b = I.$$

The differentials of these terms are represented by the corresponding small italic letters with the same subscripts, thus $dQ_a = q_a$, $d\bar{Q}_a = \bar{q}_a$, etc.

Meade's system as simplified for our purpose may be represented by the following system of equations in differentials. First, we have a pair of identities for the increments in domestic expenditures for the two countries,

$$d_a \equiv q_a - i_b + i_a + (Q_a - I)\bar{q}_a + I\bar{q}_b + Ie, \qquad (1)$$

$$d_b \equiv q_b - i_a + i_b + (Q_b - I)\bar{q}_b + I\bar{q}_a - Ie, \qquad (2)$$

which are obtained by differentiating the following definitional expenditure identities:

$$D_a \equiv \bar{Q}_a(Q_a - I_b) + \bar{Q}_b EI_a,$$

$$D_b \equiv \bar{Q}_b(Q_b - I_a) + \bar{Q}_a \frac{1}{E} I_b.$$

Next Meade gives us the two domestic expenditure functions in differentials:

$$d_a = (1 - \lambda_a)q_a - \rho_a r_a + D_a \bar{q}_a, \qquad (3)$$

$$d_b = (1 - \lambda_b)q_b - \rho_b r_b + D_b \bar{q}_b, \qquad (4)$$

where $(1 - \lambda_a)$ and $(1 - \lambda_b)$ are the partial derivatives of domestic expenditures with respect to domestic money incomes, and hence λ_a and λ_b are the marginal propensities to hoard, and ρ_a and ρ_b are the partial derivatives of domestic expenditures with respect to the interest rate in the two countries, respectively. The terms $D_a \bar{q}_a$ and $D_b \bar{q}_b$ are introduced to indicate that these expenditures functions are "real functions" in the sense that domestic expenditure in real terms is a function of real income, so that a change in the general price level would bring about a proportionate change in money expenditures. Here for the sake of simplicity, Meade has taken the change in the price level of domestic products to represent the change in the general price level so that the effect of a change in the terms of trade on the price level and on the level of aggregate domestic expenditures is neglected.[18]

However, the effect upon domestic expenditure of a change in the terms of trade produced by a devaluation has been emphasized by both Harberger and Laursen and Metzler[19] as having the effect of making the stability condition for the exchange rate more stringent. To assume away with Meade the effect of the terms of trade on domestic expenditure would, therefore, seem to gloss over a potentially significant factor. In fact, Meade has been strongly criticized by H. G. Johnson for this omission.[20] Actually, Meade could have allowed for the effect of a change in the terms of trade on domestic expenditure without making the aggregate expenditure functions too complicated to handle. For if we assume with Meade that the relationship between domestic expenditure and its determinants is a "real" and not a "money" relationship and that there is no money illusion (so that the money expenditure function is homogeneous of degree 1 in money income and all prices, including prices of imports), then the two equations for changes in aggregate expenditures, taking into consideration the effect of the terms of trade, would be no more complicated than

$$d_a = (1 - \lambda_a)q_a - \rho_a r_a + D_a \bar{q}_a - \lambda_a I(\bar{q}_a - \bar{q}_b - e) \quad (3a)$$

and

$$d_b = (1 - \lambda_b)q_b - \rho_b r_b + D_b \bar{q}_b - \lambda_b I(\bar{q}_b - \bar{q}_a + e).[21]$$

$$(4a)$$

In view of the lively controversy over the possible effect of a change in the terms of trade upon aggregate domestic expenditure,[22] I shall try to derive (3a) and (4a) in the most unsophisticated and least controversial way. Let us suppose that in the absence of money illusion and dynamic price expectations, domestic expenditure in real terms is a function of domestic real income and the interest rate, i.e.,

$$\frac{D_a}{P_a} = D_a \left\{ \frac{Q_a \bar{Q}_a}{P_a}, R_a \right\} \quad (5)$$

where P_a is the general price level in country A, defined as

$$P_a = \frac{D_a - I_a}{D_a} \cdot \bar{Q}_a + \frac{I_a}{D_a} \cdot \bar{Q}_b E, \quad (6)$$

which is equal to 1 at the initial position, since $\bar{Q}_a = \bar{Q}_b = E = 1$. Equation (5) indicates that domestic money expenditure is homogeneous of degree 1 in money income and all prices.[23]

Differentiating (5) and (6) and substituting, we get

$$d_a - (D_a - I)\bar{q}_a - I(\bar{q}_b + e)$$

$$= (1 - \lambda_a)\left[q_a + Q_a \bar{q}_a - \frac{Q_a(D_a - I)}{D_a} \bar{q}_a - \frac{Q_a I}{D_a}(\bar{q}_b + e) \right] - \rho_a r_a.$$

Since at the initial position $Q_a = D_a$, therefore,

$$d_a = (1 - \lambda_a)q_a + D_a\bar{q}_a - \lambda_a I(\bar{q}_a - \bar{q}_b - e) - \rho_a r_a.$$

By a similar procedure, (4a) may be obtained.[24] Equations (3a) and (4a) clearly indicate that the partial derivative of domestic expenditure with respect to a change in the terms of trade (an improvement is here to be treated as a positive change and a worsening a negative change) is equal to minus the marginal propensity to hoard times the initial amount of imports of the country concerned (i.e., $-\lambda_a I$ or $-\lambda_b I$).[25]

The two import functions are written by Meade in differentials as follows: For country A,

$$i_a = \pi_a d_a + [-(Q_a - I)\pi_a + I\varepsilon_a]\bar{q}_a - I(\pi_a + \varepsilon_a)(\bar{q}_b + e) \quad (7)$$

$$= \pi_a d_a - \pi_a Q_a \bar{q}_a + I(\pi_a + \varepsilon_a)(\bar{q}_a - \bar{q}_b - e)$$

where π_a is A's propensity to import defined with reference to A's aggretate national expenditure instead of national income; ε_a is what he calls "the expenditure compensated price elasticity of demand for imports in A" (or in other words, the elasticity of the pure substitution effect on A's import demand with respect to the relative price ratio between domestic products and imports); and hence $-(Q_a - I)\pi_a\bar{q}_a$ and $-I\pi_a(\bar{q}_b + e)$ are the familiar Slutsky-Hicksian income effect on A's demand for imports of a change in the price of A's domestic products and a change in A's import prices, respectively, and $I\varepsilon_a(\bar{q}_a - \bar{q}_b - e)$ the pure substitution effect on A's import demand of the change in the relative price ratio in A between domestic products and imports.[26]

Similarly, for country B, we have

$$i_b = \pi_b d_b - \pi_b Q_b \bar{q}_b + I(\pi_b + \varepsilon_b)(\bar{q}_b - \bar{q}_a + e). \quad (8)$$

The income effect components of the effect on import demand of a change in domestic prices or import prices perhaps require a little further explanation. Since Meade has defined π_a as the partial derivative of imports with respect to domestic expenditure instead of national income, it might be thought that in formulating these import functions, Meade has not been consistent with his definition of the propensity to import. For it might be questioned that if π_a (or π_b) is defined as the marginal propensity to import with reference to aggregate money expenditures, should not the income effect on the demand for imports of a change in, say, domestic prices be written as $-(Q_a - I)\pi_a(1 - \lambda_a)\bar{q}_a$, since out of the equivalent implicit increase in money income only $(1 - \lambda_a)$ part of it will result in new expenditure and only π_a times the new expenditure concerned will be on additional imports? This inconsistency, however, is only apparent; for if the decrease in domestic prices should result in a net decrease in aggregate money expenditure (a net hoarding) equal to $\lambda_a(Q_a - I)$, its effect on import demand is already taken care of by the term $\pi_a d_a$. When aggregate money expenditure is included as a separate determining variable of import demand, therefore, we may assume, in formulating the income effect of a change in domestic prices (or in import prices), that all the implicit increase in income will be spent or that all the implicit decrease in income will be borne by a cut in expenditure.

Meade's definition of the propensity to import with reference to aggregate expenditure must be regarded as an improvement over the conventional one which related the demand for imports to domestic national income. For the demand for imports, in so far as they are finished products, as is tacitly assumed in this model, is clearly primarily a function of total expenditure and, hence, is correlated with national income only at one remove (i.e., through the correlation between income and expenditure). Since in the present model the relationship between income and expenditure is subject to the influence of both the interest rate and the terms of trade, the relationship between income and demand for imports may also be expected to change under the influences of these factors. Such influences on the functional relationship between income and import demand can only be taken into account when the propensity to import is defined as Meade did, i.e., with respect to expenditures instead of income.

Next we shall adopt Meade's equations for the changes in domestic prices simplified by the assumption of constant money wages, viz.

$$\bar{q}_a = \frac{1}{\eta_a} \frac{q_a}{Q_a} \tag{9}$$

$$\bar{q}_b = \frac{1}{\eta_b} \frac{q_b}{Q_b} \tag{10}$$

where η_a and η_b are the elasticities of supply of A and B's products, respectively, in terms of real labor cost (i.e., in terms of wage units).[27]

When full employment is reached, the expressions on the right-hand side of (9) and (10) would automatically become indeterminate forms, with q and η both approaching zero, and thus would leave it entirely to the other equations of the system to determine the changes in domestic prices with no change in domestic products (i.e., a zero q).

We shall also simplify the demand-for-money equations in Meade's model by getting rid of the assumed link between money supply and gold or foreign exchange reserves, as there is hardly any country that mechanically follows this rule of the gold standard game. Thus we shall simply state that

$$m_a = \xi_a(q_a + Q_a\bar{q}_a) - \zeta_a r_a \tag{13}$$

$$m_b = \xi_b(q_b + Q_b\bar{q}_b) - \zeta_b r_b \tag{14}$$

where ξ_a and ξ_b are redefined, as distinct from Meade's own usage, as the partial derivatives of the demand for money with respect to money income in countries A and B, respectively, and ζ_a and ζ_b are redefined as the partial derivatives of their demand for money with respect to domestic interest rates, respectively.

Finally, the balance-of-trade equation in differentials and in terms of A's currency may be stated as

$$t = i_b - i_a + I\bar{q}_a - I(\bar{q}_b + e). \tag{15}$$

The eleven equations (1), (2), (3), (4), or alternatively (3a) and (4a) as we have amended them, (7)–(10) and (13)–(15) should normally be sufficient to determine the eleven variables, d_a, d_b, $\bar{q}_a$, $\bar{q}_b$, i_a, i_b, r_a, r_b, and t. The variables m_a, m_b and e will be treated as exogenous policy variables. In particular, when we want to examine the effect of a devaluation on the trade balance, we shall determine the value of t in terms of e and the parameters when all the other dependent variables have adjusted to the new situation.[28]

2. Effect of a Devaluation

Internal Balance Assumed

As pointed out above, the effect of a devaluation was examined by Meade only under the assumption of either a Keynesian neutral monetary policy or a monetary policy that assures internal balance. The assumption of a monetary policy that ensures internal balance for both countries concerned implies that q_a and q_b are both zero. With the additional assumption that money wages are given, $\bar{q}_a$ and $\bar{q}_b$ may also be taken as zero. Thus equations (9) and (10) may be dropped and the rest of the equations greatly simplified. The solution for t/e obtained from equations (1), (2), (7), (8) and (15) is

$$\frac{t}{e} = \frac{dT}{dE} = \frac{(\pi_{ab} + \varepsilon_{ab} - 1)I}{1 - \pi_a - \pi_b} \tag{16}$$

where

$$\pi_{ab} = \pi_a + \pi_b \quad \text{and} \quad \varepsilon_{ab} = \varepsilon_a + \varepsilon_b.^{29}$$

The solution is different from the Marshall-Lerner formula in that it has a denominator of $1 - \pi_a - \pi_b$. This is solely due to the fact that the propensities to import are defined here with respect to aggregate expenditures instead of incomes, so that the effect on the demand for imports of changes in aggregate expenditures cannot be excluded even though incomes in both countries are, by assumption, kept constant.[30]

For stability of the exchange rate, it is necessary that t/e should be positive, i.e., that a devaluation should bring about an improvement in the balance of trade. Since the denominator $(1 - \pi_a - \pi_b)$ can normally be assumed to be positive, the stability-condition for the exchange rate is the same as that implied in the Marshall-Lerner formula, viz., that the sum of the elasticities of demand for imports in both countries (including both the income effect and the substitution effect) should be greater than unity.

Also note that under Meade's assumption of internal balance, the introduction of the terms-of-trade effect on aggregate expediture would make no difference at all in the effect of a devaluation on the trade balance. In other words, substituting (3a) and (4a) for (3) and (4) in the above system of 9 equations would yield exactly the same solution for t/e as (16). This is because the additional effect on expenditure of a change in the terms of trade would be automatically compensated by monetary policy which is assumed to offset any tendency of deviation from full employment.[31]

Under such an implicit assumption of internal balance, the influence of monetary factors is not observable at all from the equation for the effect of a devaluation, because changes in monetary factors are assumed to happen implicitly. It is therefore rather uninteresting for the study of the role played by monetary factors.

Keynesian Neutral Monetary Policy

The alternative policy assumption made by Meade is that of a neutral policy combination, under which, in addition to the assumed absence of direct government efforts to influence imports, exports and domestic expenditures by commercial and fiscal policies, the domestic rate of interest is specifically assumed to be kept constant by the monetary authorities by maintaining the supply of money and credit infinitely elastic at the existing rate of interest. According to Meade, this neutral monetary policy is the type generally assumed in "what may be called Keynesian analysis." Indeed, it is tacitly taken for granted by all economists who apply the multiplier analysis to international trade without any explicit mention of monetary factors at all.

To distinguish this type of neutral monetary policy from the more orthodox type of neutral money policy, we shall call the former the Keynesian neutral monetary policy. The latter will be called the orthodox neutral monetary policy, which, in the absence of long-run growth of population and real productive capacity of the economy, may be described simply as the monetary policy that keeps the money supply of the economy constant.

When Keynesian neutral monetary policy is assumed for both countries A and B, r_a and r_b are *ex hypothesi* zero and equations for the demand for money, i.e., (13) and (14), can be omitted altogether in the solution for the change in the balance of trade t. Using Meade's own domestic expenditure functions, i.e., (3) and (4), together with the other seven equations (1), (2), (7)–(10), and (15), the result obtained is

$$\frac{t}{e} = \frac{dT}{dE} = \frac{\lambda_a \lambda_b (\pi_{ab} + \varepsilon_{ab} - 1)I}{\Delta_1}, \tag{17}$$

where

$$\Delta_1 = \lambda_a \lambda_b \left\{ 1 + \frac{\pi_a(1 - \lambda_a)}{\lambda_a} + \frac{\pi_b(1 - \lambda_b)}{\lambda_b} \right.$$
$$\left. + (\pi_{ab} + \varepsilon_{ab} - 1)\left(\frac{\Pi_a}{\lambda_a \eta_a} + \frac{\Pi_b}{\lambda_b \eta_b} \right) \right\}, \tag{18}$$

and Π_a and Π_b are the proportions of national expenditures (hence of national incomes, since with initial balance assumed to be zero, national incomes and expeditures are identical) initially spent on imports in countries A and B, respectively.[32]

Again the stability of the exchange rate requires that $t/e > 0$. However, since it is by no means unlikely that either one or both of the two propensities to hoard (i.e., λ_a and λ_b) should be negative, we need to be more specific about this stability condition. For it has been pointed out by Samuelson that for an equation system such as the nine equations (1)–(4), (7)–(10) and (15), to be dynamically stable, it is necessary that Δ_1 (which is the determinant of the system with the sign reversed) be positive too.[33] Since it is impossible for the exchange rate to be stable when the whole system is dynamically unstable, we must conclude that it is necessary, for the stability of the exchange rate, that both (17) and (18) be positive.[34] This is what Samuelson calls "the correspondence principle" which enables us to narrow down the necessary stability conditions in comparative static analysis with dynamic stability requirements.

We shall leave for later discussion the more complicated cases where one or both of λ_a and λ_b might be negative, and for the time being concern ourselves with the simple case where they are both positive. As long as λ_a and λ_b are both positive, (17) and (18) will both be positive when $(\pi_{ab} + \varepsilon_{ab} - 1) > 0$. In other words, the critical value for the sum of the elasticities of demand for imports in the two countries concerned is 1 in this Keynesian case of variable income, just as in the classical case of constant money incomes. The only difference is that the effect of devaluation will be much dampened by the changes in incomes and prices in both countries.

The Terms-of-Trade Effect

Let us now allow for the terms-of-trade effect upon aggregate expenditures by substituting equations (3a) and (4a) for (3) and (4) in the above system of nine equations. The solution for t/e then becomes

$$\frac{t}{e} = \frac{dT}{dE} = \frac{\lambda_a \lambda_b (\varepsilon_{ab} - 1)I}{\Delta_2} \tag{19}$$

where

$$\Delta_2 = \lambda_a \lambda_b \left\{ \left[1 + \frac{\pi_a(1 - \lambda_a)}{\lambda_a} + \frac{\pi_b(1 - \lambda_b)}{\lambda_b} \right] \left(1 + \frac{\Pi_a}{\eta_a} + \frac{\Pi_b}{\eta_b} \right) + (\varepsilon_{ab} - 1) \left(\frac{\Pi_a}{\lambda_a \eta_a} + \frac{\Pi_b}{\lambda_b \eta_b} \right) \right\}.^{35} \tag{20}$$

Again Samuleson's correspondence principle would require that for the stability of the exchange market it is necessary that both (19) and (20) be greater than zero.

Again assuming for the time being that λ_a and λ_b are both positive the crucial stability condition is now $(\varepsilon_{ab} - 1) > 0$, i.e., the sum of the components of the pure substitution effect alone in the two elasticities of demand for imports must be greater than 1.

A comparison of (17) and (19) therefore confirms the findings of Harberger as well as Laursen and Metzler that when the effects of the terms of trade on aggregate expenditures are taken into consideration, the stability condition for the exchange rate becomes more stringent. The crucial stability condition implied in (19), when λ_a and λ_b are both assumed to be positive, i.e., $(\varepsilon_{ab} - 1) > 0$, although apparently much simpler, is in fact identical to the stability conditions obtained by Harberger and Laursen and Metzler.[36] This simpler form, however shows more clearly the true magnitude of this bugbear, which, according to Laursen and Metzler, might require the crucial value of the sum of the two elasticities of demand for imports to "exceed unity by a considerable amount."[37] Equation (19) clearly shows that the result of allowing for the terms-of-trade effect on aggregate expenditures is merely to cancel out the components of the income effect in the crucial sum of the two elasticities of demand for imports. If the proportion of the national income spent on imports is high so that the terms-of-trade effect on expenditure may be expected to be of some significance, so also would be the income effect component in the elasticity of demand for imports which offsets it. Conversely, if the income effect component in the elasticity of import demand is negligible, then the terms-of-trade effect upon aggregate expenditure, that is supposed to cause difficulty, would also be of negligible significance. Therefore, the existence of the terms-of-trade effect upon aggregate expenditure is not likely to make the stability condition of the exchange rate so dangerously stringent as was at first suggested.

Instability of the Keynesian Neutral Monetary Policy

This observation about the significance of the terms-of-trade effect upon aggregate expenditure, however, is rather a digression from our main purpose in this paper, which is to achieve a synthesis of the elasticity and the absorption approaches and to highlight the role played by monetary factors. More pertinent to the main purpose of this paper are the following facts about the effect of a devaluation, as may be observed from (17) and (18) or (19) and (20).

1. It is impossible to dichotomize the effect of a devaluation into two clear-cut components, viz. a relative-price effect and an absorption or multiplier effect which constitutes a damping coefficient to the former; for as soon as we abandon the usual assumption of constant costs and prices of domestic products in both countries, the multiplier process would again involve changes in relative prices and hence the relative-price effect on the trade balance.[38] It is quite naive, therefore, to claim

that the absorption approach is a superior new tool that could supersede entirely the relative-price approach.

2. The absorption approach is right in the case of a Keynesian neutral monetary policy in pointing out that unless there is a positive propensity to hoard in both countries, the balance of trade is unlikely to be stable even if the sum of the elasticities of demand for imports of the two countries is greater than 1. For if one of the propensities to hoard is negative while the sum of the elasticities of demand for imports is greater than 1, then (17) or (19) cannot be positive, when the necessary condition for the dynamic stability of the system is satisfied, i.e., when Δ_1 or $\Delta_2 > 0$.

If one of the propensities to hoard is zero, t/e would be zero, which implies that the effect of a devaluation would be zero. If both λ_a and λ_b are negative, it might seem that it is not impossible for both (17) and (18), or (19) and (20), to be positive as required for stability, and hence for the exchange rate to be stable, provided the absolute values of the negative λ_a and λ_b are large enough relatively to π_a and π_b, respectively, and η_a and η_b are also large. This is, however, illusory; for it must be remembered that Δ_1 (or Δ_2) > 0 is only a necessary condition for the dynamic stability of the system. By direct economic reasoning, it can be shown that there can be no stability for the system if the marginal propensities to spend in both countries are greater than 1. For with marginal propensities to spend greater than 1 and the supplies of money infinitely elastic at constant interest rates as assumed under the Keynesian neutral monetary policy, both countries would be unstable in isolation. It is therefore impossible that the two countries would become stable when joined together in mutual trade, since there is no possibility for the instability of the one being compensated by the stability of the other.[39]

In the actual state of affairs, it is not at all unlikely that the marginal propensity to hoard, in the sense of 1 minus the marginal propensity to spend (on both investment and consumption), should be zero or negative. Thus it would appear that the stability of the exchange rate and the balance to trade is frequently in a very precarious state, even if the sum of the elasticities of demand for imports is well above 1.

We shall soon see, however, that only under the Keynesian neutral monetary policy that eliminates all the stabilizing influences of monetary factors is the stability of the exchange rate so precarious. Under a different monetary policy, say, the orthodox neutral monetary policy, would not be necessary at all for the stability of the exchange rate and the dynamic system that the propensity to hoard of either country be greater than zero.

3. Furthermore, even if the sum of the elasticities of demand for imports is well above 1 and the marginal propensities to hoard of both countries are greater than zero, the exchange rate would at best be in a sort of "indifferent" or "neutral" equilibrium under the Keynesian neutral monetary policy, as soon as full employment is reached in the devaluing country. For when full employment is reached in country A, η_a approaches 0 as a limit and equations (17) and (19) would also approach zero as a limit, i.e.,

$$\frac{dT}{dE} = \frac{t}{e} \to 0, \quad \text{as } \eta_a \to 0;$$

for Δ_1 and $\Delta_2 \to \infty$, as $\eta_a \to 0$. In other words, the effect of devaluation on the balance of trade would be zero.[40] Thus if a freely fluctuating exchange rate system is adopted in a country with full employment and a Keynesian neutral monetary policy, any slight chance imbalance in trade could cause violent depreciation of the currency as the exchange rate would be entirely indeterminate.[41]

4. So far we have abstracted from money-wage changes due to trade union pressure and speculative capital movements. We have reached the conclusion that a full-employment economy with a Keynesian neutral monetary policy would imply instability in the balance of trade and the exchange rate without taking into consideration the possibilities of a wage-price spiral and a destabilizing speculative capital movement.

When these possibilities are taken into consideration, the instability implied in the Keynesian monetary policy will certainly be aggravated. I have shown elsewhere[42] that the Keynesian monetary policy—i.e., the pegging of the interest rate at a fixed level with an infinitely elastic supply of money—provides precisely the monetary condition that is most conducive to the generation of a cumulative (self-aggravating) speculative capital movement; and that the instability of the French franc due to speculative capital flights in the twenties, a case which has been much cited as the evidence of the inherent instability of a floating exchange rate system, was really made possible and stimulated by the French monetary policy at the time of pegging the interest rate on the large amount of floating debt then in existence and being issued. Those economists with a Keynesian inclination, who decry the traditional reliance on exchange rate adjustment to restore the balance of payments, often forget that one of the chief reasons why devaluation may fail to improve the balance of trade, particularly in the postwar world of full or overfull employment, is precisely the monetary policy which they either take for granted or are actively advocating.

Orthodox Neutral Money Policy

That monetary factors can play a vital stabilizing role in the exchange market can be clearly shown by substituting the orthodox neutral money policy as defined above for the Keynesian neutral monetary policy. Under the assumption of an orthodox neutral money policy, changes in money supply, i.e., m_a and m_b, may be put equal to zero, whereas interest rates would be permitted to change freely. The effect of a devaluation can then be obtained by solving the system of 11 equations, consisting either of (1)–(4), (7)–(10), and (13)–(15) or (1), (2), (3a), (4a), (7)–(10) and (13)–(15), for t in terms of e after putting m_a and m_b equal to zero.

The result obtained with the first set of equations, i.e., the set of equations that do not allow for the terms-of-trade effect on aggregate expenditures, is

$$\frac{t}{e} = \frac{dT}{dE} = \frac{\alpha\beta(\pi_{ab} + \varepsilon_{ab} - 1)I}{\Delta_3} \tag{22}$$

where

$$\Delta_3 = \alpha\beta\left\{1 + \frac{\pi_a(1 - \alpha)}{\alpha} + \frac{\pi_b(1 - \beta)}{\beta}\right.$$
$$\left. + (\pi_{ab} + \varepsilon_{ab} - 1)\left(\frac{\Pi_a}{\alpha\eta_a} + \frac{\Pi_b}{\beta\eta_b}\right)\right\} \tag{23}$$

$$\alpha = \lambda_a + \left(1 + \frac{1}{\eta_a}\right)\frac{\rho_a\xi_a}{\zeta_a} \tag{24}$$

and

$$\beta = \lambda_b + \left(1 + \frac{1}{\eta_b}\right)\frac{\rho_b\xi_b}{\zeta_b}. \tag{25}$$[43]

Equations (22) and (23) are of exactly the same form as (17) and (18) respectively; the only difference is that in (22) and (23) α and β are substituted for λ_a and λ_b of (17) and (18). The terms α or β may be regarded as consisting of two components: First, there is the usual marginal propensity to hoard directly induced by real-income changes (viz., λ_a or λ_b, respectively). Secondly, we have the interest-induced marginal propensity to hoard brought about by changes in the interest rate resulting from changes in the demand for transaction balances in connection with changes in money income, viz.,

$$\left(1 + \frac{1}{\eta_a}\right) \frac{\rho_a \xi_a}{\zeta_a} \text{ or } \left(1 + \frac{1}{\eta_b}\right) \frac{\rho_b \xi_b}{\zeta_b},$$

respectively. As long as the interest-elasticity of the demand for money is not infinitely large (in absolute value) and the interest elasticity of aggregate expenditure is not zero, the interest-induced marginal propensity to hoard is always positive. Moreover, if there is a practical limit to the velocity of circulation of money, ζ_a or ζ_b would approach zero as the limit of the velocity of circulation is gradually approached.

Thus unless we start from a position deep down in the liquidity trap, the second component is bound eventually to overwhelm the first, regardless of whether the latter is positive or negative. The danger of instability due to a negative propensity to hoard (or a greater than unity propensity to spend), which is after all quite a normal phenomenon, will, therefore, be quite under control if an orthodox neutral monetary policy is adopted instead of Keynesian neutral monetary policy.

Furthermore, and what is more important for the current world, full employment at home need not imply instability in the balance of trade and the exchange rate. For when full employment is reached in country A, and hence η_a approaches zero, t/e would not approach zero as under the Keynesian neutral monetary policy. For equations (22)–(25) indicate that, as $\eta_a \to 0$,

$$\frac{t}{e} \to \frac{(\pi_{ab} + \varepsilon_{ab} - 1)I}{1 - \pi_a + \dfrac{\pi_b(1 - \beta)}{\beta} + (\pi_{ab} + \varepsilon_{ab} - 1)\left(\dfrac{\Pi_a \zeta_a}{\rho_a \xi_a} + \dfrac{\Pi_b}{\beta \eta_b}\right)} \tag{26}$$

since

$$\alpha = \lambda_a + \left(1 + \frac{1}{\eta_a}\right)\frac{\rho_a \xi_a}{\zeta_a} \to \infty, \quad \alpha \eta_a \to \frac{\rho_a \xi_a}{\zeta_a}, \text{ as } \eta_a \to 0.$$

The limit for t/e as $\eta_a \to 0$ will be greater than zero as long as the primary stability condition $\pi_{ab} + \varepsilon_{ab} > 1$ is fulfilled. Thus full employment at home and a marginal propensity to spend equal to or greater than 1 are no threat to the stability of the balance of trade and the exchange rate under an orthodox neutral money policy.[44]

The introduction of the effect of terms-of-trade changes on aggregate expenditures would make no difference to the substance of the above conclusions. In addition it may be shown that the significance for exchange rate stability of the terms-of-trade effect on expenditure is less under an orthodox neutral money policy than under a Keynesian monetary policy. For by substituting equations (3a) and (4a) for (3) and (4) in the system and putting m_a and m_b equal to zero as before, we get

$$\frac{t}{e} = \frac{\alpha\beta\left(\pi_{ab} + \varepsilon_{ab} - 1 - \dfrac{\lambda_a \pi_a}{\alpha} - \dfrac{\lambda_b \pi_b}{\beta}\right)I}{\Delta_4} \tag{27}$$

where

$$\Delta_4 = \alpha\beta\Bigg\{1 + \frac{\pi_a(1 - \alpha)}{\alpha} + \frac{\pi_b(1 - \beta)}{\beta}$$

$$+ \left[\pi_{ab} + \varepsilon_{ab} - 1 + \lambda_a(1 - \pi_{ab}) - \frac{\pi_b(\lambda_a - \lambda_b)}{\beta}\right]\frac{\Pi_a}{\alpha\eta_a} \tag{28}$$

$$+ \left[\pi_{ab} + \varepsilon_{ab} - 1 + \lambda_b(1 - \pi_{ab}) - \frac{\pi_b(\lambda_b - \lambda_a)}{\alpha}\right]\frac{\Pi_b}{\beta\eta_b}\Bigg\}.{}_{45}$$

Comparison of equation (27) with (22) again indicates that, as pointed out by Harberger, and Laursen and Metzler, if λ_a and λ_b are positive so that a worsening of the terms of trade has a stimulating effect on the aggregate spending of the country concerned, the terms-of-trade effect upon aggregate expenditure would make the stability condition for the exchange rate more stringent. On the other hand, comparison of (27) with (19) shows that the significance for exchange stability of the terms-of-trade effect on expenditure is clearly reduced under an orthodox neutral monetary policy. For whereas under the Keynesian neutral monetary policy the effect of the terms-of-trade changes on expenditure would exactly cancel out the income-effect components of the elasticities of demand for imports, thus making the stability condition $\varepsilon_{ab} > 1$, under an orthodox neutral money policy it will normally fall short of doing this. Given that α and β are both positive, which is practically always ensured under such a monetary policy, the crucial stability condition for the balance of trade is now

$$\left(\pi_{ab} + \varepsilon_{ab} - 1 - \frac{\lambda_a \pi_a}{\alpha} - \frac{\lambda_b \pi_b}{\beta}\right) > 0. \tag{29}$$

Since α and β are normally greater than λ_a and λ_b, respectively, the influence of the terms-of-trade effect on expenditure will not be big enough to offset completely the income-effect components in the elasticities of import demands. Thus the terms-of-trade effect on expenditure appears to be a much exaggerated bugbear in the eyes of elasticity pessimists.

It also can be shown that under an orthodox neutral money policy full employment at home will cause no difficulty to exchange rate stability even if the terms-of-trade effect on expenditure is allowed for. For as $\eta_a \to 0$, equation (27) becomes

$$\frac{t}{e} \to \frac{\left(\pi_{ab} + \varepsilon_{ab} - 1 - \frac{\lambda_b \pi_b}{\beta}\right)I}{\Delta_5}, \tag{30}$$

where

$$\Delta_5 = 1 - \pi_a + \frac{\pi_b(1 - \beta)}{\beta}$$

$$+ \left[\pi_{ab} + \varepsilon_{ab} - 1 + \lambda_a(1 - \pi_{ab}) - \frac{\pi_b(\lambda_a - \lambda_b)}{\beta}\right] \frac{\Pi_a \zeta_a}{\rho_a \xi_a}$$

$$+ \left[\pi_{ab} + \varepsilon_{ab} - 1 + \lambda_b(1 - \pi_{ab})\right] \frac{\Pi_b}{\beta \eta_b}. \tag{31}$$

When λ_a is positive, the stability condition implied in (30), i.e.,

$$\left(\pi_{ab} + \varepsilon_{ab} - 1 - \frac{\lambda_b \pi_b}{\beta}\right) > 0,$$

is certainly fulfilled, when that implied in (27) is fulfilled.

When $\lambda_a < 0$, it implies that the terms-of-trade effect on expenditure in country A will give a boost to, instead of detracting from, the stability of the balance of trade. Equation (30) would then merely indicate that when full employment at home is attained, this possible boost to stability would disappear. In any case, the stability condition

$$\left(\pi_{ab} + \varepsilon_{ab} - 1 - \frac{\lambda_b \pi_b}{\beta}\right) > 0$$

is not substantially different from the traditional Marshall-Lerner stability condition of $(\pi_{ab} + \varepsilon_{ab} - 1) > 0$.[46]

3. Concluding Remarks

We conclude that the absorption approach to the analysis of the effects of devaluation has contributed to our understanding of the problem only in emphasizing the fundamental facts that a positive trade balance implies the presence of hoarding (nonspending) of incomes or credit contraction and that a negative trade balance implies the presence of dishoarding or credit expansion, and that a more comprehensive analysis, including in particular an analysis of the effect on income and expenditure, is needed than is implied in the classical elasticity approach. As an independent analytical tool, in substitution for the traditional elasticity approach, however, it is quite inadequate; for we have shown that not only is the primary effect of a devaluation determined by the elasticities, but the secondary damping factor also depends on the relevant elasticities, once domestic prices are recognized as liable to change with the changes in income.

The significance of monetary factors, the role of which is clearly indicated by the fundamental identity of the absorption approach, is however entirely obliterated by the usual assumption of constant interest rates supported by infinitely elastic supply of or demand for money with respect to the interest rate, an assumption explicitly or implicitly made in practically all modern Keynesian analyses. Such a monetary assumption, however, would imply instability in the exchange rate as soon as full employment is reached at home, even without allowing for the destabilizing influence of speculative capital movements and the possibility of a wage-price spiral. To take for granted such a monetary policy may have been justified in the deep depression years of the thirties, but it is hardly appropriate in the current world of prosperity and high-level employment.

It is high time that we abandoned this ubiquitous underlying assumption in our aggregate analysis lest we should scare ourselves out of our own wits in "discovering" dangerous instability lurking everywhere in our economy (notably for example, the supposed razor-edge instability of our growth path) and thus clamor for more and more government controls on our economic life.

Notes

*The author is professor of economics at the University of Rochester. He is indebted to T. C. Liu and E. Zabel for discussion at different stages of the preparation of this paper, and to Fritz Machlup, J. J. Polak, J. M. Fleming, and R. A. Mundell for reading the manuscript and making a number of valuable suggestions.
1. Alexander [1952] and [1959], and Machlup [1955] and [1956].
2. Machlup [1955], pp. 268-71, and Alexander [1959], pp. 22-24.

3. Alexander [1959], pp. 26–34.
4. See [6, esp. pp. 64–66]; also Allen [3].
5. Robinson [1949], esp. p. 93.
6. Meade [1951], Harberger [1950], Laursen and Metzler [1950], and Stuvel [1951].
7. Machlup [1955].
8. Johnson [1958].
9. Michaely [1960].
10. Monetary factors were certainly not overlooked by classical economists, who regarded the contraction or expansion of the money supply under the gold standard as the automatic mechanism for the adjustment of the balance of payments. It is with the advent of the "new economics" and the breakdown of the gold standard that monetary factors came to be disregarded in the discussion of the balance of trade and devaluation.
11. Brown [1942], Allen [1956], Harberger [1950], Laursen and Metzler [1950], Stuvel [1951], Jones [1960]. Harberger, in his review article [8, esp. pp. 858–59], strongly criticized Stuvel for not even mentioning the amount of money or the rate of interest in his analysis, nor stating what kind of monetary or fiscal policy he assumes. Harberger also admitted that he himself committed the same omission in his own earlier attempt at model construction.
12. Brems [1957].
13. Alexander [1959], p. 33.
14. Meade [1951], pp. 31, 49.
15. Meade [1951], p. 33, pp. 56–57.
16. Meade [1951], pp. 68–72; Table 4, p. 150.
17. The popularity of Meade's excellent work has suffered a great deal from the overcomplicated model and its formidable list of variables, which he presented at the very beginning of his book, but which he himself abandoned later as too cumbersome to yield any definite result. Even Alexander complained that Meade's model is "unintelligible to any but the most dogged readers" [2. p. 24].
18. In effect, (3) and (4) are derived by differentiating aggregate expenditure functions of the type:

$$D_a = D_a\{Q_a \bar{Q}_a, \bar{Q}_a, R_a\} \tag{i}$$

which is supposed to be homogeneous of degree 1 in $Q_a \bar{Q}_a$ and $\bar{Q}_a$. By Euler's Theorem,

$$D_a = \frac{\partial D_a}{\partial(Q_a \bar{Q}_a)} \cdot Q_a \bar{Q}_a + \frac{\partial D_a}{\partial \bar{Q}_a} \bar{Q}_a$$

$$= (1 - \lambda_a)Q_a + \frac{\partial D_a}{\partial \bar{Q}_a} \tag{ii}$$

$$\therefore \frac{\partial D_a}{\partial \bar{Q}_a} = D_a - (1 - \lambda_a)Q_a.$$

Substitute (ii) in the differentiation of (i), we get:

$$d_a = (1 - \lambda_a)q_a + D_a\bar{q}_a - \rho_a r_a.$$

Alternatively, (3) and (4) may be regarded as derived from expenditure functions of the form:

$$\frac{D_a}{\bar{Q}_a} = D_a^* \left\{ \frac{Q_a\bar{Q}_a}{\bar{Q}_a}, R_a \right\}, \tag{iii}$$

which, upon differentiation, yields directly the same result.

19. Harberger [1950], pp. 50–55, and Laursen and Metzler [1950], pp. 295–97.
20. Johnson [1951], pp. 816–18 and 830–32.
21. This was first pointed out to me by T. C. Liu of Cornell University.
22. See, for example, [25] [21] [17] and [11]. Although Laursen and Metzler have specifically discussed the effect of a change in the exchange rate upon domestic money expenditure, including investment as well as consumption, later participants in this discussion have concentrated exclusively on the effect upon consumption expenditure to the total neglect of the effect upon investment expenditure, as if the latter may be assumed to be fixed in money terms with a change in import prices. Actually, under the assumptions of no money illusion and no dynamic price expectations, there is as much reason to assume money expenditure on investment to be homogeneous of degree 1 in all prices and money income as to assume the same for money expenditure on consumption.
23. The money balances effect (or the Pigou effect) of a proportionate rise in money income and all prices may preclude the homogeneity of the money expenditure function. However, an increase in the relative scarcity of cash balances implies a rise in the marginal convenience yield of money balances and hence would lead to a rise in the interest rate, which is included as another determining variable of the expenditure function. The Pigou effect of a proportionate rise in all prices is therefore taken care of in the term $\rho_a r_a$, and hence would not interfere with the homogeneity of the expenditure function in money income and all prices, exclusive of the interest rate.
24. A crucial assumption here is that $Q_a\bar{Q}_a = Q_a = D_a$ and $Q_b\bar{Q}_b = Q_b = D_b$ at the initial position which is implied in the assumption that trade is initially balanced.
25. This result agrees fully with those obtained by Harberger and Jones. Harberger, in whose model there is no investment, has shown that the effect of the terms of trade (an adverse change is treated as a positive change) is equal to the propensity to save times the initial amount of imports [7, pp. 52–53]. Jones, by a more general and elegant method, has shown that the partial derivative of consumption expenditure with respect to a rise in import prices is equal to: (1 minus the ratio of the marginal propensity to consume to the average propensity to consume) times the initial amount of imports [11, pp. 78–79]. Substituting total expenditure and the propensity to spend for consumption expenditure and the propensity to consume, respectively, and taking into account the assumption that in our model the average propensity to spend is 1 in the initial position (trade being initially balanced), their results can be readily converted to ours.

26. The Slutzky-Hicksian way of splitting off the income effect of a price change presumes that the effect on real income of a change in the price of a commodity, with money income fixed, is equal to the initial volume of that commodity purchased times the change in its price. In his criticism of Harberger, however, Spraos has rightly pointed out that in so far as there is a part of income which is neither spent on domestic products nor on imports, the loss in real income out of a fixed money income implied by, say, a rise in import prices is greater than the initial amount of imports consumed times the rise in import prices; for the loss in real value of the part of income that was initially not spent must also be compensated. Otherwise the demand function would imply some degree of money-illusion. In the present case, however, it is assumed that trade was initially balanced so that all income msut have been spent initially either on imports or on domestic products. Hence, as Spraos himself has conceded, his objection would not apply to the present case [21, p. 144, esp. fn. 4].

Meade's import demand equations, i.e., (7) and (8), certainly cannot be accused of implying the presence of money illusion, because it can be shown that the partial derivatives of the demand for imports in these two equations satisfy Eulers' theorem for a homogeneous equation of degree zero in all the determining variables; for from, say, equation (7) we have

$$\frac{\partial I_a}{\partial D_a} = \pi_a; \quad \frac{\partial I_a}{\partial \bar{Q}_a} = [-(Q_a - I)\pi_a + I\varepsilon_a]$$

and

$$\frac{\partial I_a}{\partial(\bar{Q}_b E)} = -I(\pi_a + \varepsilon_a).$$

Thus

$$\pi_a D_a + [-(Q_a - I)\pi_a + I\varepsilon_a]\bar{Q}_a - I(\pi_a + \varepsilon_a)\bar{Q}_b E = 0,$$

since at the initial position $\bar{Q}_a = \bar{Q}_b = E = 1$, and $D_a = Q_a$.

27. These are derived from the condition that the prices of domestic products in both countries must equal the marginal costs of those products, i.e.,

$$\bar{Q}_a = \bar{H}_a \frac{h_a}{q_a}, \tag{11}$$

$$\bar{Q}_b = \bar{H}_b \frac{h_b}{q_b}. \tag{12}$$

Differentiating (11), we get:

$$\bar{q}_a = \bar{H}_a d\left(\frac{h_a}{q_a}\right) + \frac{h_a}{q_a} \bar{h}_a = d\left(\frac{h_a}{q_a}\right)$$

since $\bar{H}_a$ is assumed constant and put equal to 1 at the initial position. By definition,

$$\eta_a = \frac{\dfrac{h_a}{q_a}}{Q_a} \frac{q_a}{d\left(\dfrac{h_a}{q_a}\right)}.$$

By (11), however, $\bar{Q}_a$ and $\bar{H}_a$ are put equal to 1, h_a/q_a must also equal 1;

$$\therefore \bar{q}_a = d\left(\frac{h_a}{q_a}\right) = \frac{1}{\eta_a}\frac{q_a}{Q_a}.$$

The derivation of (10) is exactly the same.

28. It should be noted that substituting (15) into (1) and (2) in turn, we get

$$t = q_a + Q_a\bar{q}_a - d_a \tag{1'}$$

$$t = d_b - (q_b + Q_b\bar{q}_b). \tag{2'}$$

Furthermore, by substituting (3) into (1') and (4) into (2'), we get

$$t = \lambda_a q_a + \rho_a r_a \tag{3'}$$

$$t = -\lambda_b q_b - \rho_b r_b \tag{4'}$$

and similarly, by substituting (3a) into (1') and (4a) into (2') we get

$$t = \lambda_a q_a + \rho_a r_a + \lambda_a I(\bar{q}_a - \bar{q}_b - e) \tag{3'a}$$

$$t = -\lambda_b q_b - \rho_b r_b - \lambda_b I(\bar{q}_b - \bar{q}_a + e). \tag{4'a}$$

These equations facilitate the solution of t in terms of e, i.e., the ascertainment of the effect of a small devaluation on the trade balance, which we shall presently proceed to do.

(1') and (2') indicate that the change in the trade balance must be equal to the change in the gap between national product and expenditure (absorption). (3') and (4'), or (3'a) and (4'a), further tell us that the improvement in the trade balance must equal the increase in hoardings, which are either income-induced, or interest-induced, or terms-of-trade-induced–the last mentioned item being shown only in (3'a) and (4'a). These equations, however, provide only partial solutions for the effect of devaluation on the trade balance; for q_a, q_b, r_a, r_b, $\bar{q}_a$ and $\bar{q}_b$ will all be affected by e, and the total effect on t will depend on how they in their turn are affected. This is, however, as far as the absorption approach can carry us. To obtain a full solution for the effect of a devaluation, the elasticity approach must be called in.

29. From (1') and (2') in footnote 28 above, we can see directly that, when internal balance is maintained in both countries,

$$t = -d_a = d_b.$$

Substitute this result into (7), (8) and (15), we get the result (16).

30. It can be shown that when the propensities to import of both A and B are defined with respect to their respective money incomes, as is usually done, so that the import demand functions may be written as

$$i_a = \pi_a^* q_a + I(\pi_a^* + \varepsilon_a)(\bar{q}_a - \bar{q}_b - e) \tag{7a}$$

and

$$i_b = \pi_b^* q_b + I(\pi_b^* + \varepsilon_b)(\bar{q}_b - \bar{q}_a - e), \tag{8a}$$

the denominator would disappear.

31. In fact the solution (16) for t/e can be derived without reference to equations (3) and (4). The substitution of (3a) and (4a) for (3) and (4), respectively, merely affects the monetary changes that will be required for the maintenance of internal balance.

32. The method of solution is simply successive substitution to eliminate all other variables than t and e. While the order in which these other variables are eliminated is quite immaterial, the particular procedure used was first to reduce the variables $\bar{q}$'s, d's and i's to expressions in terms of the q's only, and then, making use of equations (3') and (4') in footnote 28, to solve for the q's. Then t can be readily solved as $t = \lambda_a q_a$, using (3') in footnote 28 and assuming $r_a = 0$.

33. The number of equations being odd in this case, it is a necessary condition, for all the eigenvalues of the matrix of the system to be negative, that the determinant of the system be negative also [19] [20]. For an excellent lucid exposition of this principle, see also Baumol [4, pp. 373–78].

34. This point was glossed over by Meade, who, after canceling out $\lambda_a \lambda_b$ from both the numerator and the denominator, observed that the denominator (with $\lambda_a \lambda_b$ canceled out) "is certainly positive if $\varepsilon_{ab} + \pi_{ab} > 1$, which we shall assume normally to be the case" [15, p. 50]. This point appears also to have been overlooked by Stuvel who, after obtaining a similar expression for the effect of a devaluation on the balance of payments, asserted that it is only the sign of the whole expression that matters for stability, regardless of the sign of the denominator. See [22, Ch. 4, esp. Math. App., pp. 233–35].

35. The method of solution adopted here is again successive elimination, and the particular procedure is first to reduce the $\bar{q}$'s, d's, and i's to expressions in terms of the q's only and then solve for the q's. The solution for t can then be obtained from those for q_a and q_b.

36. Harberger's stability condition is:

$$(\eta_1 + \eta_2) > (1 + c_1 + c_2),$$

where η_1 and η_2, the two elasticities of demand for imports, correspond to our $(\pi_a + \varepsilon_a)$ and $(\pi_b + \varepsilon_b)$, respectively; and c_1 and c_2, the two propensities to import, correspond to our π_a and π_b, respectively. Thus his condition can be easily converted to our form, viz. $(\varepsilon_{ab} - 1) > 0$ [7, p. 53, esp. fn. 13].

Laursen and Metzler's condition is given in the form

$$\{(1 - w_1)(1 - w_2)v_1(\eta_1 + \eta_2 - 1) - s_1 m_1(1 - w_2) - s_2 m_2(1 - w_1)\}$$
$$> 0,$$

where w_1 and w_2 are the propensities to spend, and hence $(1 - w_1)$ and $(1 - w_2)$ correspond to our λ_a and λ_b; v_1, the initial volume of imports (assumed to be the same for both countries), corresponds to our I; η_1 and η_2 to our $(\pi_a + \varepsilon_a)$ and $(\pi_b + \varepsilon_b)$, respectively; m_1 and m_2 to our π_a and π_b, respectively; and s_1 and s_2 are partial derivatives of the aggregate expenditures with respect to the exchange rate for the two countries, respectively. In our notation, $s_1 = \partial D_a/\partial E$ and $s_2 = \partial D_b/\partial(1/E)$, which, according to equations (3a) and (4a) above, are respectively equal to $\lambda_a I$

and $\lambda_b I$. Thus written in our notation, Laursen and Metzler's condition becomes

$$\{\lambda_a\lambda_b I(\pi_{ab} + \varepsilon_{ab} - 1) - \lambda_a I \pi_a \lambda_b - \lambda_b I \pi_b \lambda_a\} = \lambda_a\lambda_b I(\varepsilon_{ab} - 1) > 0,$$

which is exactly the same as implied in equation (19).

37. Laursen and Metzler [1950], p. 296.

38. If we make the usual simplifying assumption that the elasticities of supply of products of A and B are both infinite, i.e., $\eta_a = \eta_b = \infty$, so that prices of domestic products will remain constant, then (19), for instance, can be simplified to

$$\frac{t}{e} = \frac{\lambda_a\lambda_b(\varepsilon_{ab} - 1)I}{\lambda_a\lambda_b + \pi_a(1 - \lambda_a)\lambda_b + \pi_b(1 - \lambda_b)\lambda_b}. \tag{21}$$

In this case, it is indeed permissible to say that the relative-price effect determines the initial change in trade balance to which a damping coefficient, determined by propensities to hoard and import is to be applied. Too often, however, analyses of the effect of a devaluation stop with such simple cases.

39. There seems to be a possibility that, if one of the propensities to hoard is negative and at the same time the sum of the elasticities of demand for imports is smaller than its critical value, the necessary condition for the stability of the dynamic system as well as the exchange rate might be satisfied. I am not sure, however, whether the sufficient condition for dynamic stability can be satisfied by such a combination since I have not worked out fully the sufficient condition for dynamic stability. Futhermore it seems that in such cases, the relative speed of price and income adjustments will have to be taken into consideration.

40. The fact that the other country is fully employed is not a menace to the stability of the trade balance and exchange rate for a devaluing country. For under full employment, the elasticity of aggregate supply is likely to take on different values according to the direction in which aggregate demand is changing. The elasticity of aggregate supply is zero when confronted with an increase in aggregate demand, but it is not likely to be zero when confronted with a decrease in aggregate demand, particularly when money wages in the country concerned are rigid. Since the aggregate demand for the products of the country whose currency has relatively appreciated is likely to fall, the relevant elasticity of supply of its products is not likely to be zero, even when it is enjoying full employment.

41. So far we have assumed a balanced trade position as the starting point. It has been pointed out by A. O. Hirschman that if there is a trade deficit to start with, the necessary and sufficient condition for a devaluation to improve the balance of trade becomes easier to fulfill [9]. However, in a sense, the condition for $dT/dE > 0$, assuming no initial trade deficit, is still the basic stability condition; for if $dT/dE > 0$ only when there is an initial trade deficit, but < 0 when there is no initial deficit, then the country concerned may use devaluation to improve its balance of trade to some extent when it has an initial trade deficit, but it cannot use devaluation to

eliminate its deficit; for when its deficit gets smaller, further devaluation may begin to have an adverse effect on its trade balance. If $dT/dE > 0$ when there is an initial deficit, but equals 0 when trade is balanced, then theoretically it is not impossible for the country eventually to eliminate its initial trade deficit by keeping on devaluing its currency. But once the trade deficit is eliminated, the momentum of devaluation may carry it further and further for then the exchange rate becomes indeterminate (being in an indifferent equilibrium).

42. Tsiang [1958] and [1959].

43. The procedure adopted here is again to reduce the $\bar{q}$'s, r's, d's and i's to expressions in terms of the q's only and then solve for q_a and q_b. The solution for t is then obtained from those for q_a and q_b.

44. I have shown elsewhere [23, pp. 410–12] that so long as the interest elasticity of supply of money is zero (as is implied by the orthodox neutral monetary policy) and the interest elasticity of demand for money is fairly small, as it would be when the prevailing interest rate is well above the minimum set by the liquidity trap, it is highly unlikely that the speculative demand for foreign exchange will be unstable or self-aggravating.

45. The procedure adopted here is similar to the one used in the preceding case.

46. In fact a comparison of (22) and (23) with (17) and (18), or of (27) and (28) with (19) and (20), shows that the dampening influence of income variation on the effect of a devaluation is generally reduced by the adoption of an orthodox, instead of a Keynesian, neutral monetary policy.

   In the extreme case, where the interest elasticity of demand for money is zero in both countries (i.e., $\zeta_a = \zeta_b = 0$, which implies that the velocities of circulation of money are constant in both countries), α and β would approach infinity. Then (22), (26), (27) and (30) would all become the same as (16); i.e.,

$$\frac{t}{e} = \frac{(\pi_{ab} + \varepsilon_{ab} - 1)I}{1 - \pi_a - \pi_b},$$

which is the solution we obtained under the assumption of internal balance in both countries (see above p. 923).

   Thus the neglect of the dampening influence of income variation by the neoclassical economists is probably due partly to their customary assumption of zero interest elasticity of demand for money (or constant velocity of circulation of money). Alexander's characterization of the neoclassical elasticity approach as pure tautological theorizing is, therefore, quite unjustified.

References

1. S. S. Alexander, "Effects of a Devaluation on a Trade Balance," Internat. Mon. Fund *Staff Papers*, Apr. 1952, **2**, 263–78.
2. S. S. Alexander, "Effects of a Devaluation: A Simplified Synthesis of

Elasticities and Absorption Approaches," *Am. Econ. Rev.*, Mar. 1959, **49**, 23–42.

3. W. R. Allen, "A Note on the Money Income Effect of Devaluation," *Kyklos*, 1956, **9**, 372–80.

4. W. J. Baumol, *Economic Dynamics*, 2nd ed. New York 1959.

5. H. Brems, "Devaluation, A Marriage of the Elasticity and Absorption Approaches," *Econ. Jour.*, Mar. 1957,**67**, 49–64.

6. A. J. Brown, "Trade Balances and Exchange Stability," *Oxford Econ. Papers*, No. 6, Apr. 1942, 57–75.

7. A. C. Harberger, "Currency Depreciation, Income and the Balance of Trade," *Jour. Pol. Econ.*, Feb, 1950, **58**, 47–60.

8. A. C. Harberger, "Pitfalls in Mathematical Model Building," *Am. Econ. Rev.*, Dec. 1952, **42**, 856–65.

9. A. O. Hirschman, "Devaluation and Trade Balance—A Note," *Rev. Econ. Stat.*, Feb. 1949, **31**, 50–53.

10. H. G. Johnson, "Towards a General Theory of the Balance of Payments," *International Trade and Economic Growth*, London 1958, Ch. 6.

10A. H. G. Johnson, "The Taxonomic Approach to Economic Policy," *Econ. Jour.*, Dec. 1951, **61**, 812–32.

11. R. W. Jones, "Depreciation and the Dampening Effect of Income Changes," *Rev. Econ. Stat.*, Feb, 1960, **42**, 74–80.

12. S. Laursen and L. A. Metzler, "Flexible Exchange Rates and the Theory of Employment," *Rev. Econ. Stat.*, Nov. 1950, **32**, 281–99.

13. F. Machlup, "Relative Prices and Aggregate Spending in the Analysis of Devaluation," *Am. Econ. Rev.*, June 1955, **45**, 255–78.

14. F. Machlup, "The Terms of Trade Effects of Devaluation upon Real Income and the Balance of Trade," *Kyklos*, 1956, **9**(4), 417–52.

15. J. E. Meade, *The Balance of Payments, Mathematical Supplement.* London 1951.

16. M. Michaely, "Relative Prices and Income Absorption Approaches to Devaluation: A Partial Reconciliation," *Am. Econ. Rev.*, Mar. 1960, **50**, 144–47.

17. I. F. Pearce, "A Note on Mr. Spraos' Paper," *Economica*, May 1955, N.S. **22**, 147–51.

18. J. Robinson, "The Foreign Exchanges." *Essays in the Theory of Employment*, New York 1937, Pt. III, Ch. 1, reprinted in *Readings in the Theory of International Trade*, ed. H. S. Ellis and L. T. Metzler, Philadelphia 1949, pp. 83–103.

19. P. A. Samuelson, "The Stability of Equilibrium: Comparative Statics and Dynamics," *Econometrica*, Apr. 1941, **9**, 97–120.

20. P. A. Samuelson, *Foundations of Economic Analysis.* Cambridge 1947.

21. J. Spraos, "Consumers; Behaviour and the Conditions for Exchange Stability," *Economica*, May 1955, N.S. **22**, 137–47.

22. G. Stuvel, *The Exchange Stability Problem.* Oxford 1951.

23. S. C. Tsiang, "A Theory of Foreign Exchange Speculation under a Floating Exchange System," *Jour. Pol. Econ.*, Oct. 1958, **66**, 399–418.

24. S. C. Tsiang, "Floating Exchange Rate System in Countries with Relatively Stable Economies: Some European Experience After World War I," Internat. Mon. Fund *Staff Papers,* Oct. 1959, **7**, 244–73.

25. W. H. White, "The Employment-Insulating Advantages of Flexible Exchange Rates: A Comment on Professors Laursen and Metzler," *Rev. Econ. Stat.,* May 1954, **36**, 225–28.

CHAPTER 5

Fashions and Misconceptions in Monetary Theory and Their Influences on Financial and Banking Policies*

S. C. Tsiang

Keynes had once written that "the ideas of economists and political philosophers, both when they are right and when they are wrong, are more powerful than is commonly understood. . . . Practical men, who believe themselves to be quite exempt from any intellectual influences, are usually the slaves of some defunct economists."[1] This may seem to overglorify us economists a little bit, but there is considerable element of truth in it. Moreover, it appears that economic ideas that are wrong and bad are unfortunately much more likely to prevail in economic policies than good and sound ones, partly because bad ideas are generally more comforting and pleasing to listen to than good ones, and partly because generally long lags are needed for academic ideas to seep into the heads of practical men in authority, so that, when at last their influences are felt in practical policies, they are likely to be badly out of date and place. Thus, there seems to be a sort of Gresham's Law operating: bad ideas tend to chase out sound ideas in economic policies.

Indeed, Keynes is said to have complained privately to one of his

Finance Constraints and the Theory of Money
ISBN 0-12-701720-8
ISBN 0-12-701721-6 (pbk)

Reprinted with permission from Zeitschrift für die gesamte Staatswissenschaft/Journal of Institutional and Theoretical Economics, Vol. 135, 4 (December 1979), pp. 583–604.

friends, Prof. Colin Clark, in the late thirties that his ideas were not likely to be acceptable to the policy-makers while they are still timely and appropriate, whereas when they are taken for granted even in the exchequers of remote countries, they would probably have become hoplessly out of· date and harmful. Unfortunately this alleged grumble turned out to be highly prophetic. In the deep depression years of the thirties, Keynes was laboring hard to persuade the policy makers to expand public and private spending and to discourage saving. To convince the men in authority and his fellow economists, he put forward the theory that saving is entirely passively determined by the amount of investment (the multiplier theory). An autonomous increase in the propensity of saving (i.e., in the thriftiness of the public) would only cause a recession and is, therefore, antisocial instead of being beneficial. The rate of interest is entirely determined by the liquidity preference of the public and the supply of liquidity. Saving has no direct effect on the interest rate, nor has the interest rate any effect on the amount of saving forthcoming. To stimulate investment and, hence, the prosperity and growth of the economy, the only sensible interest policy then is a low interest policy.

After the war, this type of monetary theory has indeed become the accepted orthodoxy even in the remote countries of the world. If the men in authority there are still innocent of the new economics, at least the foreign aid officials to those countries would try to enlighten them in this fashion. This new fashion in monetary theory makes the traditional view that banks and other financial intermediaries are the mediators between savers and investors sound utterly silly. If saving would always be automatically generated by investment, why should there be any need for financial intermediaries to collect scattered savings of the public to finance investment?[2] Thus, according to the new monetary theory, the function of banks and other financial intermediaries is said to be the provision of liquidity, i.e., highly liquid assets,[3] such as currency, demand deposits and other deposits. There is supposed to be no sharp dividing line between them. Since saving is said to be independent of the interest rate nor is the interest rate in any direct way influenced by saving, the interest rate can allegedly be set at any level by the monetary authorities to stimulate investment and, hence, the growth of the economy, so long as it is above the minimum level at which the liquidity preference becomes infinitely elastic. Money supply in the narrow sense of the sum of the supplies of currency and demand deposits is regarded as not a meaningful concept. What is regarded as significant is rather the so-called "total liquidity of the economy," viz., some nebulous concept of weighted aggregate of all the liquid assets in the economy.

Furthermore, since the appropriate expansion of the aggregate effective demand is a sacrosanct objective, inflationary consequences are generally blamed upon cost-push. Since interest obligations are also an element of costs on the part of producers, a rise in interest rate is thus regarded as an inflationary factor by itself, just as a rise, say, in wage rate.

Such prevailing academic views in monetary theory gradually permeated into the minds of the monetary authorities in remote countries, and, as Keynes reputedly had predicted, their influences proved to be harmful rather than beneficial; for the theories advocated by Keynes to sell his anti-depression expansionary policy were hardly suitable for the postwar inflationary situation, particularly in developing countries, where more rapid accumulation of capital is vital and the scarcity of domestic savings is the chief obstacle to their economic growth.

As a consequence of these prevailing views in monetary theory, the banking policy in a typical developing country in the early postwar years tended to be as follows. Typically the monetary authorities in a developing country would impose arbitrary control over the interest rates charged and offered by banks, and keep them at such a low level in the face of inflation that, allowing for the rate of price increase, the real rate becomes close to zero or, as in many cases, even negative. The result is, of course, that current savings of the public would gradually cease to flow into the banking system. People would either be discouraged from saving altogether, or put their savings on the hoardings of real goods, precious metals, real estates, or foreign currencies, which are all non-productive kinds of investment. The accumulation of real productive capital for the development of the country is thus severely reduced.

Moreover, although the monetary authorities may succeed in holding the interest rates charged by banks at an extraordinary low level, they could never fully satisfy the enormous demand that would surely develop for such cheap credit on the part of business without inflating the economy to a hopeless extent. There must be a severe credit rationing on the part of banks, which would imply arbitrary discretion, inefficiency and corruption. The genuine demand for credit on the part of producers that could not be satisfied by the arbitrary credit rationing at banks would have to seek supplementary supply of loans at the black market, or unorganized money market, where the allowance for price inflation, the extra risks involved, and the fundamental scarcity of savings would combine to push the interest rate to a very high level, indeed, much higher than what the equilibrium rate at banks would have been, had the authorities let the banks and the organized money market find it out by competition.

By the traditional criterion, we can surely say that under such conditions banks had failed miserably in discharging their primary function of collecting the savings from the public for the financing of productive investment. Under the new banking theory, however, banks' function is supposed to be the provision of liquidity. In an inflationary situation, who can accuse the banks as having failed to supply enough liquidity to the economy? If so, that can surely be remedied quickly with the help of the central bank and the printing press!

Such banking policy is, indeed, the curse of developing countries, which effectively hamstrings their effort to develop quickly, as it not only drastically reduces the available supply of non-inflationary investible funds for the financing of investment, but would also cause the available supply to be allocated very inefficiently. Nor are the developing countries its only victims; for as early as 1951, D. H. Robertson, the arch critic of Keynes, already declared that "this is, indeed, I think, the canker at the heart of the Keynesian theory of interest – a canker which has since (if cankers can so act) abundantly come home to roost,"[4]

As I pointed out above, however, the folly of such banking policy is obscured by the Keynesian liquidity preference theory of interest and its erroneous views about saving and investment. The foolishness of such policy would become very obvious, if we analyze the problem by means of the Robertsonian loanable funds approach. This is not the appropriate place to settle the issues between loanable funds and liquidity preference theories of interest. I shall merely refer the interested, and especially the skeptical, audience to two articles of mine[5] in which I have demonstrated that when the liquidity preference theory is corrected for the neglect of what Keynes called the "finance demand for liquidity," which he admitted that he should not have overlooked in the *General Theory*,[6] it would in effect come to the same thing as the loanable funds theory as formulated by Robertson. I shall ask you simply to bear with me when I use the loanable funds apparatus here, as it can portray much better the social function of the banking system as the intermediary between the suppliers of savings and the demanders for finance for investments.

In the accompanying diagram (Figure 1), let DD' be the demand curve for loanable funds on the part of investors, and SS' be the supply curve of ex ante savings of the public (in the Robertsonian sense of the surplus of disposable income over planned consumption) flowing into the banking system. In a developing country where currency and demand deposits bear no interest rate while savings and time deposits carry substantial nominal interest, and checking on savings and time deposits is utterly unheard of, the inflow of ex ante savings into the banks may be fairly adequately represented by the increment of the latter deposits at all banks. We shall not draw other possible components of the supply of loanable funds into our diagram, such as increases (or decreases as a minus item) in money supply (i.e., currency and demand deposits) and dishoarding (or hoarding as a minus term) of money. We exclude the increase in money supply as an additional source of supply of financing for investment because it has undesirable inflationary effects and thus should be consciously avoided. As to hoardings or dishoardings (i.e., increases or decreases of idle speculative cash balances), we regard them as of negligible importance in a

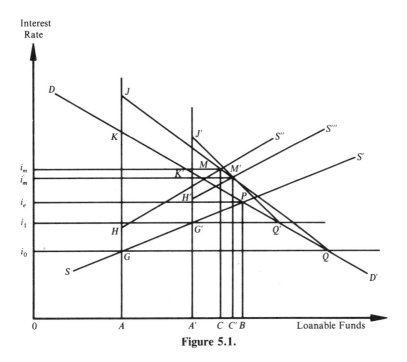

Figure 5.1.

developing country with a history of inflation, where the nominal interests on savings and time deposits are likely to be substantial even with government control, and where, in the unorganized money market beyond the control of monetary authorities, the nominal rate would be even higher.

Suppose that the rate of interest on savings and time deposits (which for convenience shall be treated as a single category) is controlled by the authorities at i_0, which is substantially below the equilibrium rate of interest that would equate the demand for loanable funds on the part of investment on the one hand and the supply of ex ante savings through banks on the other hand. The flow of savings into the banks per period of time would be only OA. There is thus a huge excess demand for loanable funds at banks, if banks' lending rates are not much higher than i_0. If the monetary authorities are sensible enough to exclude the use of the expansion of money supply to fill up the gap, strict credit rationing must be imposed to hold demand down to the available supply. There is thus a large amount of unsatisfied demand that spills over to the unorganized money market.

If credit rationing is conducted in a perfectly efficient way so that only those investment demands that yield the highest returns (i.e., only those with a marginal yield higher than AK) are satisfied by the available supply, then the spill-over demand to the money market outside the banking system will simply be the portion of the demand curve below K. With discretionary allocation by bureaucrats, however, this is rather unlikely to happen. Inevitably, some investment demands with an expected marginal yield little higher than i_0, or AG, might get allotted their full or partial requests for funds, whereas some demands with expected yields higher than AK may be denied satisfaction. In this case, the spill-over demand curve for loanable funds on the money market outside the banking system, with the vertical line through AK as its zero axis, will be a partially tilted version of the original demand curve below K, viz, something like JQ, which, however, must coincide with the original demand curve at Q, since when the curb money market rate coincides with the interest rate charged at the banks, the combined demands for funds in the two markets must be what the aggregate demand curve indicates.

The spill-over supply of loanable funds to the unorganized money market will not be just the untapped portion of the original supply curve either, because the unorganized money market does not have big intermediaries with established reputation to help the lenders spread risks, and, furthermore, in countries where the authorities impose a legal ceiling on interest rates on the basis of an anti-usury law, loan contracts made at the uncontrolled money market rates are often denied legal enforcement. Therefore, a considerable risk premium must be added to the original supply curve of loanable funds to the banking system, so that the supply curve of loanable funds to the unorganized money market will be a curve like HS'', higher than the original supply curve. The risk premium required is presumably an increasing function of the supply to the unorganized money market, as marginal risk aversion generally tends to rise with the amount of risk taken. Thus, the rate of interest there will be determined at M, the intersection of the spill-over demand and supply curves, which obviously can be very much higher than i_0, and even higher than the equilibrium rate i_e also.

This depicts fairly accurately the actual situation of the banking system and the curb money market in most developing countries with government control of the interest rates charged by banks. Under such circumstances, it is important to observe that the marginal cost of investible funds to most producers is not i_0 (or rather the lending rates of banks based upon it), but the curb money market rate i_m or CM. For with strict credit rationing on the part of banks in order to make the insufficient supply of loanable funds go around, no borrowers, except a few privileged public enterprises, are likely to have their full demands satisfied at the banks' lending rate. Most borrowers will have to resort to the uncontrolled money market for their marginal credit requirements for investment and pay the ruling market rate.

Confronted with such a situation, if the monetary authorities should raise the controlled rate on deposits from i_0, say, to i_1, which we presume to be still lower than the equilibrium rate, i_e, the flow of savings attracted into the banking system could be increased from OA to OA'. Again, if the banking system devotes the increased inflow of savings to finance the most productive of the demand for funds, the new spill-over demand curve for funds on the curb money market will simply be the demand curve below K', i.e., the portion of aggregate demand curve to the right of the vertical line through A'. If, as is more likely to happen, the banking system should fail to lend the increased supply of loanable funds to the most productive investment demands, then again the spill-over demand curve would be tilted upward from the original demand curve, say, to start from a point J' above K', but must converge to the original demand curve at Q' where the latter cuts the horizontal line drawn from i_1, the new rate charged by banks.

The new spill-over supply curve in the curb money market would start from H' above G' on the original supply curve of loanable funds and run toward S'''. It would lie throughout its whole length below HS'', the spill-over supply curve of funds on the curb market before the rise of the banks' rate, because of the principle of increasing risk premium stated above.

Thus, barring very extreme and unlikely happenings, e.g., that the second spill-over demand curve for funds $J'Q'$ should be tilted upward from the original demand curve DD' to a much greater extent than the first one, i.e., JQ, the new rate of interest on the curb market will generally be lower than the original one, i.e., $C'M' = i'_m < CM = i_m$, and the aggregate supply of non-inflationary investible funds is likely to be increased, i.e., $OC' > OC$.

The scale of operations of the curb money market would indeed be reduced from AC to $A'C'$, but nevertheless, the total amount of investments that can be financed with non-inflationary funds is likely to be increased (from OC to OC'). Furthermore, since the gap between the interest rates of the banking system and of the outside money market is bound to be reduced, the allocation of investible funds would be more efficient, as the higher lending rate of the banks would rule out many low yield projects, that were only marginally profitable at the former low rate, and would also force those favored investors to seek faster rates of turnover for their investment.

It is quite wrong, therefore, to say, as a large number of economists seemed to believe, that such a rise in the controlled interest rate of the banking system would contribute to cost-push inflation.[7] For the true relevant marginal cost of investible funds to most entrepreneurs would be more likely to fall, from CM to $C'M'$, than to rise. Besides, there would be the beneficial effects on total output of larger aggregate supply of noninflationary investible funds available for the expansion of productive capacity, and more efficient allocation of available investible funds.

Many Keynesian econmists were brought up to think that any increase in investment, however financed, is inflationary. We are of the opinion, however, that an increase in investment financed by genuine increase in savings (i.e., a reduction in planned consumption), or by a switching from hoardings of commodities, precious metals, or foreign currencies, will not inflate the effective demand to any significant extent. On the contrary the increase in productive capacity resulting from the increased investment activities, particularly when the latter are confined to those with very high rate of returns and quick turnover by the high real rate of interest would instead be an anti-inflationary force in the longer run (see Tsiang [1949]).

It is a great pity that under the prevailing influence of Keynesian economics so many developing countries, in spite of their great shortage of capital and savings, should indulge in the wrong policy of keeping the interest rate of their domestic banking system down at the conventional level of developed countries with more stable prices, under the mistaken idea that this is necessary for checking cost-push inflation or for stimulating real investment. Actually, such an enforced low interest rate policy would either add fuel to domestic inflation by creating an enormous excess demand for bank credits from inflationary sources, or would slow down real capital formation at home by discouraging the inflow of savings into organized financial intermediaries, or both at the same time.

If any of you should be skeptical about the above theoretical conclusion, let me quote you as an illustration the experience of Taiwan, where the above suggested interest rate policy has been tried on a limited extent since 1950 and where I have been involved personally in an advisory capacity. Taiwan today has been deservedly regarded as a shining model of a developing country that has succeeded in developing itself. From 1951 to 1977, in a period of 26 years, the gross domestic products in real terms had grown by 7.9 folds (see Table 1). Real income per capita had nearly trebled during the same period. The growth of her foreign trade is even more remarkable. From 1951 to 1977, her exports in terms of U.S. dollars had increased from $93 millions to $9,494 millions, an increase of more than a hundred fold (see Table 2).

These achievements certainly did not come about effortlessly. In the early postwar years, Taiwan was still recovering from the ravages of World War II, and had, at the same time, to accommodate and provide for the large influx of over a million soldiers and civilian refugees from the Mainland China – a sudden addition of approximately one sixth to the original population. On top of the real difficulties, Taiwan was at that time following a totally misguided economic policy. Like most developing countries then, Taiwan was suffering from a rampant inflation. The theory of inflation as understood by the persons in authority was predominantly the popular cost-push theory. To combat inflation, a host of controls on prices, costs, interest rates, exchange rates and trade were imposed in the vain hope of holding down prices, instead of making a real effort to curb the expansion of effective demand. These controls misdirected the allocation of available resources and stifled private incentives and initiatives in industrial development.

Table 1 Gross Domestic Products of Taiwan at Current Prices and at Constant 1971 Prices (in millions of NT$'s)

	At Current Prices	(chain index)	At Constant 1971 Prices	(chain index)
1951	12,322		52,146	
1952	17,251	140.00	57,809	110.86
1953	22,992	133.28	62,593	108.28
1954	25,229	109.73	68,032	108.69
1955	30,091	119.27	73,277	107.71
1956	34,550	114.82	77,162	105.30
1957	40,346	116.78	82,561	107.00
1958	45,006	111.55	87,221	105.64
1959	51,967	115.47	93,302	106.97
1960	62,814	120.87	98,528	105.60
1961	70,363	112.02	105,048	106.62
1962	77,578	110.25	112,744	107.33
1963	87,853	113.24	122,387	108.55
1964	102,872	117.10	136,354	111.41
1965	113,732	110.56	150,696	110.52
1966	126,667	111.37	162,348	107.73
1967	146,091	115.33	179,003	110.26
1968	171,375	117.31	195,106	109.00
1969	195,819	114.26	211,588	108.45
1970	226,840	115.84	234,573	110.86
1971	261,558	115.31	261,558	111.50
1972	307,293	117.49	292,625	111.88
1973	388,699	126.49	327,698	111.99
1974	524,655	134.98	329,697	100.61
1975	560,027	106.74	339,863	103.08
1976	651,464^P	116.33	387,708^P	114.08
1977	745,640^P	113.70	410,118^P	107.97

^{P} indicates preliminary.

Source: "National Income of the Republic of China", Directorate-General of Budgets, Accounts and Statistics, Executive Yuan.

Among the most injudicious and injurious controls is the one on nominal interest rates of the banking system, which kept the nominal interest rates of the banks so low in the face of rapid inflation, that it turned the real rates of interest offered and charged by banks into negative. Savings quite naturally stopped flowing into the banking system, and banks, therefore, could lend only by creating new money, which further aggravated the inflation. This kind of controlled low interest policy, superimposed on huge budget deficits, kept inflation progressing at an ever increasing speed. From 1948 to 1949, wholesale prices in Taiwan actually increased thirty five times in a single year.

Table 2 Merchandise Trade of Taiwan (in U.S.$ millions)

	Exports	Average Annual Rate of Growth	Imports	Average Annual Rate of Growth	Trade Balance
1951	93.1		142.5		−49.4
1952	119.5		208.3		−88.8
1953	128.6		192.9		−62.3
1954	95.9		204.9		−109.0
1955	127.1		184.7		−57.6
1956	124.1		222.1		−98.0
1957	148.3	5.8%	244.7	8.7%	−96.4
1958	155.8		273.5		−117.7
1959	156.9		263.9		−107.0
1960	164.0		286.5		−122.5
1961	195.2		330.3		−135.1
1962	218.2		328.0		−109.8
1963	333.7		373.3		−39.6
1964	434.5		395.4		39.1
1965	450.8	24.5%	517.2	16.9%	−66.4
1966	542.7		545.6		−2.9
1967	653.7		728.1		−74.4
1968	816.3		888.8		−72.5
1969	1081.4		1093.0		−11.6
1970	1468.6		1363.4		105.2
1971	2047.2		1754.6		292.6
1972	2979.3	30.6%	2331.9	29.4%	647.4
1073	4475.9		3709.9		766.0
1074	5592.0		6403.9		−811.9
1975	5304.1		5558.6		−254.5
1976	8035.5		7245.0		546.7
1977	9493.9		8279.2		1214.7

Source: Taiwan Financial Statistics Monthly, The Central Bank of China.

In June 1949, a monetary reform that introduced a new currency, known as the New Taiwan Yuan (NT$ in abbreviation), was carried out, but without any fundamental changes in monetary and fiscal policies to support it. In spite of this bogus monetary reform, prices soon resumed their upward climb after a short pause. Already in the second half of 1949, prices again rose by no less than 82%, followed by another 34% in the first three months of 1950. Realizing that a mere change in the name and denomination of the currency is no cure for inflation, the authorities made a determined effort to curb the expansion of money supply by a remarkable high nominal interest policy. In March 1950, a special system of savings deposits, called the Preferential Interest Rate Savings Deposits, was introduced by the Bank of Taiwan, which offered an extraordinary nominal interest rate of 7% per month for one-month savings deposits. When compounded monthly this came to 125% per annum. The new high rate was hoped to be attractive enough to domestic savers in the face of a price inflation of 34% per quarter in the first quarter of the year.

This measure was a sort of compromise response to the urging by some economists, including myself, to adopt a system of price-index-escalated savings certificates to attract private savings into banks to provide for the finance of vital investments, which hitherto banks had to supply out of monetary expansion. To the monetary authorities, however, to commit themselves to escalate the interest rate on the basis of price index appeared to involve unfathomable risks. They would rather have this high nominal interest deposit scheme. The truth is, however, that unlike the price-index-escalated savings certificates, this high nominal interest deposit scheme obviously carried the risk of turning its own interest rate into an unbearable burden by its very success. This explained why at first this preferential interest rate was offered only on one-month savings deposits. Obviously, the Bank of Taiwan felt the need to keep its freedom to alter the nominal rate from month to month as the rate of inflation slowed down.

The impact of the introduction of these savings deposits was indeed very prompt and successful. Total time and savings deposits including the new PIR deposits in the whole banking system quickly rose from a meager NT$6 millions or barely 1.7% of the contemporary money supply (currency + demand deposits) at the end of March, 1950, to NT$28 millions at the end of June of the same year, which was appoximately equal to 7% of the total money supply at that time. What is even more remarkable was the fact that price inflation was very rapidly brought to a halt. Although during the first quarter of 1950 the rate of price inflation had been as high as 10.3 per cent per month, from April to the end of June wholesale prices in Taiwan increased only by 0.4 percent per month. Indeed, in the month of June it actually declined a little. This stabilization of prices happened before the propitious turn of fortune in favor of Taiwan, viz., the resumption of U.S. Aid to Free China in July 1950 after the outbreak of the Korean War, which, as you remember, began on June 25, 1950.

Partly encouraged by the immediate success of the new deposit scheme as well as by the resumption of the U.S. Aid, and partly fearing quite naturally that the 125% per annum interest rate would be intolerable with stable prices, the government sharply cut the interest rate payable on one-month deposits in July by half to 3.5% per month and again in October to only 3.0%.

The public, taken quite aback by the abrupt reversal of the government's high interest policy so soon after its inauguration, reacted by stopping the flow of their savings into the banking system and even started to withdraw their deposits. By the end of December the same year, total savings and time deposits dropped absolutely by NT$10 million from NT$36 millions or 6.1% of the current money supply at the end of September to only NT$26 million or only 4.5% of the current money supply. Thus, in spite of the resumption of U.S. Aid to Taiwan and President Truman's announcement that Taiwan would be under the protection of the U.S. 7th Fleet, prices resumed their rapid rise from August, 1950, until in Feb. 1951, they were 65% higher than in July 1950, when the cut in interest rate was announced.

Alarmed by the prospect of a renewed rampant inflation, the monetary authorities were obliged to raise the monthly rate on one-month deposits from 3% to 4.2% (equivalent to a yearly rate of 64%). Apparently the public was then appeased and the flow of savings into the banking system resumed at such a spectacular pace that by the end of March 1952 total savings and time deposits had already reached NT$271 million, or 31.2% of the contemporary money supply, and at the end of September that year, they further rose to NT$541 million or 56.4% of the contemporary money supply. Prices were once more completely stabilized. (See Tables 3(a) and 3(b)).

Thenceforth, the monetary authorities gingerly lowered the interest rate step by step, whenever they felt that the stability of prices warranted it. Owing to the lack of a free money market, these successive downward adjustments were guided only by the subjective feelings of the monetary authorities with respect to the general expectation of future price inflation. Not infrequently they would overestimate the public's confidence in price stability and their willingness to supply savings to the banking system, and would thus make too precipitous cuts in interest rate that would send prices on the upward climb again. However, when the interest rate was raised again, prices would again be stabilized and the upward trend of the savings and time deposits would be resumed.

One incident is particularly worth noting here. In 1972 and 1973, the worldwide inflation gave Taiwan two successive big trade surpluses,

Table 3(a) Money Supply; Savings, Time and PIR Deposits; Interest Rates; and Wholesale Prices 1950–54

End of Period	Money Supply	Savings, Time & PIR Deposits[1] (in millions of N.T. $'s)	Col. (2) as % of Col. (1)	Monthly Interest Rate on One-Month PIR Deposits	Monthly Rate of Price Inflation During the Quarter Just Ended
1950 Mar	348	6	1.7%	7.00 (effective)	10.3%
Jun	401	28	7.0%	7.00 (from Mar 25)	0.4%
Sept	595	36	6.1%	3.50 (from July 1)	6.0%
Dec	584	26	4.5%	3.00 (from Oct 1)	5.4%
1951 Mar	732	30	4.1%	4.20 (from Mar 26)	4.8%
Jun	942	59	6.3%	4.20	3.9%
Sept	687	164	23.9%	4.20	1.8%
Dec	940	163	17.3%	4.20	3.9%
1952 Mar	867	271	31.2%	4.20	2.6%
Jun	942	494	52.4%	3.80 (from Apr 29) 3.30 (from Jun 2)	−1.0%
Sept	959	541	56.4%	3.00 (from July 7) 2.40 (from Sept 8)	−0.4%
Dec	1336	467	34.9%	2.00 (from Nov 30)	0
1953 Mar	1074	499	46.5%	2.00	1.5%
Jun	1198	640	53.4%	2.00	1.4%
Sept	1292	671	51.9%	1.50 (from July 16)	1.6%
Dec	1683	599	35.6%	1.20 (from Oct 10)	0.5%
1954 Mar	1622	667	41.1%	1.20	0
Jun	1809	747	41.3%	1.20	−1.4%
Sept	1923	782	40.6%	1.00 (from July 1)	−0.6%
Dec	2128	765	35.9%	1.00	1.3%
1955 Mar	2300	816	35.5%	1.00	2.7%

[1] Preferential Interest Rate Deposits Scheme was phased out in March 1955. Afterwards the former PIR deposits were merged into ordinarily savings deposits and the name was abolished.
Sources: Taiwan Financial Statistics Monthly, The Central Bank of China, and *Taiwan Commodity Prices Statistics Monthly*, Bureau of Accounting and Statistics, Taiwan Provincial Government.

amounting to U.S.$647 millions and U.S.$766 millions, respectively, and caused the money supply (currency plus demand deposits) to increase by 34.6% and 47.0% in those two years, respectively. As a result, prices started to rise, after a long period of stability, first by 7.3% in 1972 and then shot up by a further 40.3% in 1973. This evoked the specter of inflation, which was still fresh in the memory of the public in Taiwan. The annual rate of increase of savings and time deposits dropped from 40% in 1971 to 21.5% in 1973. If no quick action was taken, the rate of

Table 3(b) Money Supply, Savings and Time Deposits, Interest Rate and Wholesale Prices 1955–1977

End of Period	Money Supply	Savings & Time Deposits (in millions of NT $'s)	Col. (2) as % of Col. (1)	Interest Rate on One-Year Time Deposits % p.a.	Average Rate of Price Increase Over the Preceding Year %
1955	2,555	993	38.9	20.98	14.08
1956	3,161	1,006	31.8	23.87	12.71
1957	3,740	1,399	37.4	21.70	7.22
1958	5,041	2,464	48.9	21.70	1.39
1959	5,486	3,290	60.0	18.43	10.27
1960	6,037	4,536	75.1	18.43	14.51
1961	7,231	7,478	103.4	15.39	3.23
1962	7,832	9,368	119.6	14.19	3.04
1963	10,060.	12,228	121.6	12.68	6.46
1964	13,259	15,480	116.8	11.35	2.48
1965	14,695	18,161	123.6	11.35	-4.66
1966	17,004	23,629	139.0	10.56	1.47
1967	21,875	28,559	130.6	10.16	2.52
1968	24,649	32,166	130.5	10.16	1.99
1969	28,584	40,046	140.1	10.16	-0.24
1970	34,508	50,169	145.4	9.72	2.72
1971	40,914	70,241	171.7	9.25	0.02
1972	55,066	94,307	171.3	8.75	7.25
1973	80,938	114,543	141.5	11.00[1]	40.34
1974	86,617	157,638	182.0	13.50[1]	14.87
1975	109,303	201,808	184.6	12.00[1]	-0.60
1976	130,568	254,610	195.0	10.75	4.50
1977 July	141,487	307,632	217.4	9.50	4.08[2]
1978 Apr.	172,972	366,862	212.1	9.50	2.01[2]

Sources: Taiwan Financial Statistics Monthly, The Central Bank of China, and *Monthly Statistics of the Republic of China*, Directorate-General of Budget, Accounting and Statistics.

[1] The interest rate was first raised to 9.50% on July 26, 1973, then to 11.00% on October 24, 1973, and finally to 15.00% on January 27, 1974. On September 19, 1974, however, it was lowered to 14.00%; on December 13, 1974, to 13.50%; on February 22, 1975 to 12.75%; and on April 21, 1975, to 12.00%.

[2] Percentage price increase over July 1976.

increase could readily turn into a rate of decrease. The monetary authorities reacted by raising interest rates on time and savings deposits, e.g., the rate on one-year savings deposits was raised from 8.75% to 9.50% in July 1973, then to 11% in October the same year, and finally to 15% in January 1974, in the hope of arresting the declining tendency of the rate of increase of such deposits.

These efforts proved quite successful, for during 1974 savings and time deposits increased by as much as NT$43,095 millions or 37.6% over the balance at the end of the preceding year, as compared with the increase during 1973 of only NT20,236 Millions or 21.5%. This increment of NT$43.1 billions in savings and time deposits was equal to 49.8% of the total money supply (M_1) of the year 1974, out of which this sum would have to be transferred unless the banks restored the latter with their lending and investment operations. This anti-inflationary force was added to the huge trade deficit of U.S.$811.9 millions (equivalent to NT$30.9 billions) during 1974, which was partly deliberately created by the government through relaxing the restrictions on imports of luxury goods, including foreign automobiles, and encouraging the imports of raw materials and machinery, and partly caused by a worldwide recession in that year. These two hefty anti-inflationary forces were powerful enough to curb the rate of interest in money supply and to bring it down to only 7% during 1974. Price inflation was promptly reduced to 14.9% during 1974 in spite of the big jump in oil prices, and in 1975 the price level was completely stabilized. (See Table 3[b])

Thus the fact that the interest rates of time and savings deposits are necessary inducement to attract the public's savings into the banking system and constitute a significant anti-inflationary instrument was repeatedly and convincingly demonstrated by the experience of Taiwan. It has thus conclusively given the lie to the arguments of the cost-push inflation theorists against raising the officially controlled bank rates as an anti-inflationary measure.

Looking at its long run effects on the development of the economy it should be noted that the resumed and enlarged inflow of voluntary savings into the banking system provided exactly the needed noninflationary financing for the domestic investment stimulated by the concurrent exchange devaluation and trade liberalization, which opened up vast investment opportunities in the new export industries. This made possible the industrial take-off of Taiwan. On the other hand, as the economy of Taiwan took off into a spectacular growth in the 1960s, voluntary savings in turn got a big boost; for with a rapid growing gross national product and per capita income, saving becomes relatively painless and effortless because of the so-called ratchet effect in consumption. With this kind of snowball effect, Taiwan has been very rapidly turned from a country with a very low propensity to save into a country with one of the highest domestic saving propensities in the world. In 1952, the percentage of national income saved in Taiwan was only 5.2, which further declined to 3.2 in 1954. In 1963, however, the percentage saved had already risen to 13.2, surpassing the corresponding percentages in both the United Kingdom (9.8) and the United States (8.4). In 1973, the percentage saved in Taiwan had climbed to the outstanding level of 32.3, commensurate with that in Japan (31.1), leaving most developed as well as developing countries far behind (see Table 4).

It is this kind of high domestic propensity to save that enabled the country to invest a very high percentage of its national product on productive capital formation without undue inflation. Thus, gross capital

Table 4 Taiwan's Savings as Percentage of National Income (Compared with Several Other Selected Countries)

Period	China, Rep. of (Taiwan)	Japan	Belgium	Canada	Nether- lands	U.K.	U.S.
1952	5.2	24.1	8.6	15.9	18.2	6.4	10.4
1953	5.0	17.3	8.8	14.9	19.9	8.0	10.0
1954	3.2	18.2	8.1	10.6	20.5	8.0	8.9
1955	4.8	20.4	11.4	13.8	22.3	9.8	12.2
1956	4.7	25.5	13.4	16.8	19.3	10.4	12.8
1957	5.9	27.4	12.5	14.2	20.8	10.5	11.1
1958	5.0	24.2	12.4	11.5	20.8	9.9	8.2
1959	4.9	26.5	10.2	12.5	23.1	10.2	10.4
1960	7.5	27.7	10.2	7.8	22.6	10.9	8.1
1961	7.9	29.9	12.2	7.1	20.9	11.0	8.4
1962	7.5	28.4	13.1	10.1	19.0	9.4	9.0
1963	13.2	26.6	11.6	10.5	17.2	9.8	8.4
1964	15.7	25.2	15.5	11.8	19.8	11.2	9.8
1965	16.2	24.3	15.4	12.9	19.7	12.3	10.9
1966	19.6	24.7	15.1	14.2	19.0	11.5	10.3
1967	20.8	27.5	15.7	12.8	19.4	10.5	8.8
1968	21.3	29.4	14.7	12.4	20.7	11.3	9.0
1969	22.6	29.8	16.1	13.4	20.2	12.8	9.2
1970	24.1	31.3	18.7	11.4	19.8	12.9	6.9
1971	26.9	30.6	17.4	12.1	19.6	11.2	7.1
1972	29.1	30.4	17.5	13.1	20.1	9.6	8.0
1973	32.3	31.1	17.5	14.5	21.2	9.4	9.7
1974	29.3	27.3	18.0	15.2	19.3	7.4	6.8
1975	23.6	25.6	13.9	11.0	14.4	5.4	3.5

Sources: For Taiwan, the source is *Taiwan Statistical Data Book,* 1978; for other countries, the source is *Yearbook of National Accounts Statistics,* 1976, United Nations.

formation as a percentage of gross national expenditure in Taiwan increased from 14.4% in 1952 to 17.5% in 1963, which was already abreast with the United Kingdom and the United States. In 1974, the percentage for Taiwan had further risen to 35.4%, again comparable to that of Japan (37.9%), but surpassing all other industrial countries, including West Germany (26.4 in 1973 and 23.6 in 1974), the United Kingdom (20.7 in 1974) and the United States (19.3 in 1974). The last two countries, which persistently have the lowest percentages of savings as well as investment among the major developed countries, happen also to be the countries in which the Keynesian economics had enjoyed, at least until very recently, the most dominant position (see Table 5).

The experience of Taiwan also brought out the inadequacy of some other prevailing ideas in modern monetary and banking theory that are

Table 5 Gross Capital Formation as Percentage of Gross National Expenditure in Taiwan and Several other Selected Countries

Period	Rep. of China, (Taiwan)	Japan	Belgium	Canada	Germany, Rep. of	Netherlands	U.K.	U.S.
1952	14.4	27.8	14.9	23.7	23.8	18.6	13.2	17.1
1953	13.3	23.7	16.4	24.3	21.9	21.0	14.3	21.0
1954	14.8	26.4	15.9	21.3	24.0	24.9	13.7	16.6
1955	12.7	24.9	17.2	23.0	26.3	25.1	15.8	23.7
1956	15.0	28.4	19.1	27.8	25.4	26.6	15.7	23.2
1957	15.0	33.9	19.0	26.4	25.0	27.6	16.3	21.4
1958	16.3	28.1	17.1	23.5	24.3	23.6	15.6	20.1
1959	17.3	31.0	18.1	24.1	25.7	25.0	15.9	22.0
1960	18.6	34.2	18.9	21.2	29.4	27.7	17.3	17.7
1961	18.5	39.8	20.7	21.3	27.8	27.3	18.1	16.7
1962	17.6	35.8	20.9	22.2	27.4	25.8	16.8	17.8
1963	17.5	35.4	20.5	22.2	26.7	24.5	17.1	17.7
1964	19.2	36.1	23.4	23.3	28.5	27.6	20.0	17.8
1965	22.1	33.4	22.6	25.6	28.7	26.6	19.6	19.9
1966	23.0	34.1	23.3	26.4	26.8	26.8	19.2	19.9
1967	24.8	37.3	23.1	23.9	23.6	26.6	19.5	18.7
1968	25.7	38.3	22.2	22.8	26.1	27.4	19.9	18.8
1969	25.0	38.3	23.1	23.4	27.5	26.8	19.7	19.0
1970	26.0	39.8	24.6	21.5	29.1	27.7	19.7	17.5
1971	26.5	37.7	23.6	22.3	27.8	27.1	18.9	18.2
1972	25.3	37.5	22.5	22.4	27.1	25.1	18.5	18.9
1973	29.0	39.9	23.1	23.3	26.4	25.5	20.3	19.5
1974	35.4	37.8	24.9	25.1	23.6	24.6	20.7	19.3
1975	28.5	32.3	21.4	23.5	21.3	21.2	18.3	16.0

Sources: For Taiwan, the source is Taiwan Statistical Data Book, 1978; for other countries, the source is Yearbook of National Accounts Statistics, 1976, United Nations.

also gradually permeating into the central banks of the world. First of all, it may be observed (from Tables 3[a] and 3[b]) that as the economy of Taiwan took off into a spectacular growth in the 1960's, savings and time deposits at banks and other financial institutions also went into a steep climb. (See Tables 3[a] and 3[b].) From a start in 1950 of a mere NT$6 millions, or 1.7% of the contemporary money supply (M_1), they increased to NT$50.2 billions or 145.4% of the contemporary money supply in 1970. In the seventies they continued their rapid growth and in April 1978 reached NT$367 billions or 212% of the contemporary money supply.

This interesting phenomenon appears to defy explanation by the currently fashionable wealth (or portfolio) approach to the demand for money and other assets. For over the long run the interest rate on savings and time deposits have been steadily reduced with only a few brief interruptions since 1950, as the inflation was successfully curbed and as saving capacity of the economy increased over the years, yet the ratio of time and savings deposits to the money supply (M_1) continued to increase on a steep rising trend from less than 2% to 212%. This long run phenomenon is to be sharply distinguished from the short run observation that a change in the interest rate on savings and time deposits would definitely tend to change the rate of increase in these deposits in the same direction.[8] This seems to indicate that the money supply (M_1) and savings and time deposits (before the former is made interest bearing and the latter made checkable, as in the United States recently) are two quite different types of assets. The former is essentially a medium of exchange, the demand for which is determined chiefly by the volume of transactions to be carried out with its service as such.[9] The latter, in the case of developing countries like Taiwan at least, is essentially an instrument of savings or store of value, for which the demand increases with the annual savings of the public. There is no reason whatever that the two should increase in the same proportion in the long run even when the interest rates remain absolutely constant. Nor is there any reason to expect that savings and time deposits would bear any constant relationship with the level of income or expenditure either. From Table 1 and Tables 3(a) and 3(b), we may observe that the ratio of the year end balance of savings and time deposits to the money value of gross domestic products of the year was only 1.32% for 1951, but rose sharply to 7.22% in 1960, 22.12% in 1970 and 45.87% in 1977.

All this indicates that for a developing country, it is rather meaningless to lump currency plus demand deposits (M_1) together with savings and time deposits to form M_2, no matter whether we call this aggregate "money and quasimoney," or "total liquidity created by the banking system." Furthermore, if we should take it into our head to regulate quantitatively this aggregate as an alternative to M_1 as a target variable for monetary control, we would clearly impose an undesirable restraint on the primary function of the banks in collecting savings from the public to provide noninflationary financing for investment. For what official controllers of this monetary aggregate (M_2) could have correctly foreseen that savings and time deposits should have increased from 1.32% of the annual GDP in 1951 to 45.87% in 1977? And who could accurately determine the correct optimal relationship between total savings plus time deposits and the GDP or M_1? To hold the rate of increase of those deposits down, say, to the expected rate of growth of GDP would surely hamper the function of banks and other financial intermediaries to a very severe extent.

To be sure, I have so far been analyzing the problem with the actual situation of a developing economy like Taiwan in mind. A recent development in banking in the United States, however, has made my argument totally inapplicable there. I mean the recent practices of permitting checking on savings deposits and paying comparable interest rate on checking account deposits. These new practices have insidiously blurred or even eliminated the distinction between currency and demand deposits on the one hand and savings and time deposits on the other. The latter might be held for transactions purposes as well as the former. It is, therefore, quite ineffective to control the quantity of M_1 alone for the purpose of controlling total expenditures and inflation. On the other hand, however, if we are to control quantitatively M_2, i.e., the sum of M_1 and savings and time deposits together, we would obviously restrain the banking system from carrying out to the full extent its function of mediating between the savers and the investors, for the experience of Taiwan clearly demonstrates that there is no reason whatever to expect that the rate of accumulation of savings and time deposits should bear any fixed and predictable relation with the rate of increase of GDP or national expenditure. Thus we would be confronted with an insoluble dilemma: either our control of inflation would become totally ineffective, or the primary function of the banking system as financial intermediaries would be severely constrained. Most likely we would get both evils. Moreover, it is quite impossible to control the aggregate M_2 by manipulating the reserve base along, since its two components currently have widely different required reserve ratios. Any shift in the distribution between the two would permit vast changes in the total M_2

given the reserve base. Thus, this recent development in banking is, in my opinion at least, partly responsible for the difficulties in controlling inflation in the United States at present.

Is this new development in banking practices in the United States a definite advance which should be emulated by developing countries like Taiwan? I for one would strongly doubt it. I think this is another instance in which a misconception in monetary theory exerts its bad influences upon actual policy. In this instance, this misconception originates from the most prominent oponent to the Keynesian School, viz., Prof. Milton Friedman. Since 1959, he has been advocating the idea that since money is essentially costless for the society to produce, therefore, everybody's demand for money balances should be satisfied to the full. To achieve this purpose, he suggests that the opportunity cost of holding money balances should be reduced to zero to match the zero cost of creating money supply. Surprisingly, this idea was readily embraced by the leading Neo-Keynesian of the United States; presumably to a Keynesian the appeal to satiate the economy's demand for liquidity always has an attractive ring. Thus, the idea quickly permeates into the minds of practical men and brings about insidiously these changes in banking practices.

Already in 1968 I have warned against the hidden danger involved in this widely accepted idea and pointed out its theoretical flaws in a paper presented at the Conference on Money and Economic Growth, held at Brown University.[10] Again, it would not be appropriate for me to recapitulate here the theoretical argument in technical terms. In plain language, my argument is briefly as follows. Professor Friedman's claim of the huge welfare gain obtainable for the community from satiating everybody's demand for money balances involves a gross fallacy of composition; i.e., the arithmetic addition of the gains that might be expected by individuals do not make the aggregate gain for the community as a whole. The external effects of increasing everyone's money balances, or, alternatively, paying interest on everyone's money balances, must be considered. These external effects could be so harmful to the proper functioning of the economy as to outweigh the apparent individual gains.

This warning is now being partially borne out by recent development in the United States. The permission to draw checks on savings and time deposits is to some extent equivalent to paying the same interest rate on checking account deposits as Friedman advocated. If there is indeed no restriction at all on drawing checks on savings deposits, non-interest-earning demand deposits would surely disappear and be all transferred to savings and time deposits which can now be used as transactions balances. If the required reserves ratio of the latter kind of deposits is still much lower than the former, as they are now, the banks would get a false signal to expand their loans on the basis of excess reserves thus created. The result will be inflationary, because such a transfer of deposits for higher interest earning does not imply any savings. This is by no means only a transitional difficulty; for after such transfer or merging has been completed, additional voluntary savings flowing into the banks would simply take the form of a slowing down in the velocity of circulation of these deposits. The individual banks would receive no clear signal to expand or contract their loans to finance investment at all. If Friedman's idea is carried out one step further to make the interest rate on these deposits equal to those on bills or bonds, then the bill and bond market would also be destroyed; for who would bother to buy bills and bonds, if the money they use to make the purchase already carries the same rate of return? Thus, interest rates cannot be determined by the free purchases and sales of bills and bonds on the money markets. They would have to be arbitrarily fixed by the monetary authorities with the inevitably concomitant instability and inefficiency which Friedman abhors. Thus, this rather frivolous pet idea of Friedman appears to carry the seed for the destruction of the very type of economy favored by his whole philosophy.

It is a great pity that while Prof. Friedman's good ideas, such as that the rate of increase in money supply should be kept constant and commensurate with the rate of growth of real income, still fail to find wholehearted reception by the monetary authorities in the United States, his frivolous and ill-considered idea should be so readily adopted, in part at least, by the American banking system. Indeed, as I observed in the beginning, a sort of Gresham's Law seems to be operating in the reign of economic ideas also. It would be a supreme tragedy for an economist, if his good ideas are never accepted in his life time, when they are timely and appropriate, whereas his occasional frivolous idea would be quickly put into practice with predictable bad effects to his embarrassment.

Notes

*This is a revised version of a talk given at the First International Conference on the Financial Development of Latin America and the Caribbean, held February 26–28, 1979.

1. Keynes [1936], p. 383.
2. Keynes, in a post *General Theory* article, even argued that current consumption is just as effective as current saving in providing new finance for investment. See Keynes [1938], p. 322.
3. Or "Secondary Assets," as Gurley and Shaw [1960] chose to call them.
4. Robertson [1951], p. 212.
5. Tsiang [1956] and [1979]. The latter paper not only developed the proposition of the former in a more cogent form, but also demonstrated the superiority and usefulness of the loanable funds approach (or the revised liquidity preference theory) in comparison with Friedman's new theory of money income.
6. Keynes [1937], p. 667.
7. Unless it can be shown that the controlled interest rate somehow directly enters the official cost of living index (e.g., as mortgage interest cost) and such cost of living index forms the basis for wage determination. This, however, is not likely to be the case in most developing countries.
8. It is for the difficulty of separating this long run phenomenon from the short run effects of policy adjustments in the deposit rate of interest on account of collinearity and lags, that we did not resort to the usual regression analysis for the whole period under investigation (i.e., 1951–1977) to determine the causal relationship between the amount, or the rate of increase, of total savings and time deposits and the rates of interest on them. The long run trend of the steep climb of total savings and time deposits in spite of the fairly steady decline in the nominal interest on them, due to the slowing down of inflation and the increasing propensity to save of the public, would surely dominate the scene and result in a negative regression coefficient for the latter as a determining variable of the former.

   We have, therefore, chosen rather to examine each major adjustment in the deposit rate of interest, specifically adopted by the monetary authorities to cope with a specific crisis of sharply reduced inflow of savings into banks and excessive price inflation, and to trace out whether its effects had not been in the desired directions.
9. In Tsiang [1977], I have presented a simple estimate of the demand function for real money balances in Taiwan as below:

$$\ln m = 0.1037 + 0.8313 \ln y + 0.6965 \ln T/Y - 0.3219 \ln r$$

$$(2.888) \quad (0.2493) \qquad (0.2216) \qquad (0.1780)$$

$$(3.3349) \qquad (3.1430) \qquad (-1.8080)$$

$$R^2 = 0.9950, \; S^2 = 0.0036, \; D.W. = 1.8925$$

where m is the real money balances (currency plus demand deposits), y is the GDP in real terms, T/Y is the ratio of the volume of trade to GDP both in their nominal values, and r is the average market rate of interest. The explanatory variable T/Y was added on the ground that both export and import trade would increase the necessary volume of transactions given the GDP and, hence, the demand for transactions balances. As may be observed, the t value of the coefficient for this variable is almost as high as that for the variable y. Furthermore, the addition of the variable T/Y not only improves the coefficient of correlation as compared with a regression without the variable, but also greatly improves the Durbin-Watson statistic, i.e., increases it from a very unsatisfactory figure of 1.3796 to 1.8925 quite close to its ideal value 2.

10. Tsiang [1969]. See also Pesek [1979].

References

Gurley, J., and Shaw, E. S. [1960], *Money in a Theory of Finance,* Washington.

Keynes, J. M. [1936], *The General Theory of Employment, Interest and Money,* London.

Keynes, J. M. [1937], "The Ex Ante Theory of the Rate of Interest," *Economic Journal* **47**, 663–669.

Keynes, J. M. [1938], "D. H. Robertson on 'Mr. Keynes and Finance,' Comments," *Economic Journal* **48**, 318–322.

Pesek, B. [1979], "Modern Bank Deposits and the Theory of Optimum Undefined Money," in Ballabon, M. B., (ed.), *Economic Perspectives, an Annual Survey of Economics,* Chur – London – New York.

Robertson, D. H. [1951], "Some Notes in the Theory of Interest," in: *Money, Trade and Economic Growth, Essays in Honor of Professor J. H. William,* New York; reprinted in: D. H. Robertson, *Essays in Money and Interest,* Manchester 1966, pp. 203–222.

Tsiang, S. C. [1949], "Rehabilitation of Time Dimension of Investment in Macrodynamic Analysis," *Economica* N.S. **16**, 204–217.

Tsiang, S. C. [1956], "Liquidity Preference and Loanable Funds Theories of Interest, Multiplier and Velocity Analysis: A Synthesis," *American Economic Review* **46**, 539–564.

Tsiang, S. C. [1969], "A Critical Note on the Optimum Supply of Money," *Journal of Money, Credit and Banking* **1**, 266–280.

Tsiang, S. C. [1977], "The Monetary Theoretic Foundation of the Modern Monetary Approach to the Balance of Payments," *Oxford Economic Papers* **29**, 319–338.

Tsiang, S. C. [1980], "Keynes' Finance Demand for Liquidity, Robertson's Loanable Funds Theory and Friedman's Monetarism," *Quarterly Journal of Economics,* **94**, 467–491.

Section II

CHAPTER **6**

Walras' Law, Say's Law, and Liquidity Preference in General Equilibrium Analysis*

S. C. Tsiang [1]

1. Introduction

Ever since Hicks revived the Walrasian general equilibrium approach to the theory of money and interest in his attempt to reconcile the liquidity preference and loanable fund theories,[2] the accounting identity that the aggregate demand for all goods necessarily equals the aggregate supply of all goods—dubbed Walras' Law by Lange—has come to be accepted as a fundamental axiom for monetary economics as well as for barter economics. Theories and doctrines have been rejected on account of their incompatibility with the so-called Walras' Law. In particular, the liquidity preference theory is now condemned, notably by Patinkin and Johnson, because on the basis of Walras' Law it can be shown to lead to unreasonable results under certain dynamic situations.[3] The classical Say's Law is attacked anew, not on account of its naive optimistic view of the negligibility of hoardings and dishoardings, but on the alleged ground that under Walras' Law it would exclude money altogether from any influence on economic behavior and thus rule out any monetary theory.[4]

Finance Constraints and the Theory of Money
ISBN 0-12-701720-8
ISBN 0-12-701721-6 (pbk)

Reprinted with permission from the *International Economic Review*, Vol. VII, 3 (September 1966), pp. 329–345.

The purpose of this paper is to show that Walras' Law, as defined by Lange, does not apply to an economy where money as the necessary medium of exchange and generally accepted means of payments is demanded for transaction purposes.[5] It also attempts to show that a number of widely accepted modern doctrines have to be rejected as false deductions resulting from the indiscriminiate application of Walras' Law.

2. Alleged Dubiousness of Liquidity Preference Theory in the Light of Walras' Law

It has been contended by Patinkin that the liquidity preference theory of interest, in the very broad sense of the theory that seeks to explain the determination of the interest rate by the money supply and demand, is equivalent to the loanable funds theory only in an equilibrium situation. In a position of disequilibrium, the two types of interest theories are quite different, so much so that under certain circumstances they might even indicate that the rate of interest would move in the opposite direction.[6]

Patinkin's argument has as its starting point the so-called Walras' Law. If for the sake of simplicity we assume with Patinkin that there are only three homogeneous groups of goods, viz., commodities, bonds and money, Walras' Law may be represented as

$$C^d + B^d + M^d \equiv C^s + B^s + M^s \tag{1}$$

or

$$(M^d - M^s) \equiv (C^s - C^d) + (B^s - B^d)$$

when C^d, B^d and M^d are the demands for commodities, bonds and money, respectively, and C^s, B^s and M^s the supplies of these goods, respectively.

In a position of equilibrium, it is easy to show on the basis of Walras' Law that it is a matter of indifference whether we say that the rate of interest (or the price of bonds) is determined by the demand and supply of bonds, or that it is determined by the demand and supply of money. For when the demand and supply of commodities have been brought to equality by the prices of commodities, the equality of the supply and demand for bonds necessarily implies the equality of the supply and demand for money, and conversely. This much has been made familiar to us all by Hicks.[7]

Patinkin points out, however, that in a state of disequilibrium both $(M^d - M^s)$ and $(B^d - B^s)$ can be positive at the same time, provided $(C^s - C^d) > (B^d - B^s)$. In this case, the loanable funds theory would indicate that the rate of interest would be driven down by the excess demand for bonds, whereas the liquidity preference theory would indicate that the rate of interest would be forced up by the excess demand for money, regardless of the existence of an excess demand for bonds. Since the rate of interest is simply a different expression for the price of bonds, it is indeed difficult to understand why an excess demand for money should force up the interest rate or drive down the price of bonds when it is granted that there is an excess demand for bonds on the bond market.

This seems to suggest that, in a dynamic context, the liquidity preference approach is seriously amiss. In a previous article of the present author, however, it was argued that the liquidity preference in the broad sense, when properly formulated, should always lead to the same conclusions as the loanable funds theory, whether in a static analysis or in a dynamic analysis.[8] The cause of this difference in verdict on the validity of the liquidity preference theory lies entirely in the fact that I have rejected Walras' Law as inapplicable to the excess demand for money in the sense relevant to the determination of the interest rate,[9] whereas Patinkin, following Hicks and Lange, treated Walras' Law as the very basis for analyzing the demand for money in a general equilibrium framework.

3. Inapplicability of Walras' Law to the Excess Demand for Money

At bottom Walras' Law is merely the aggregation of all the individual "budget restraints" which stipulate that in an exchange economy, where stealing and robbing are ruled out, the effective demand of any individual for any goods implies a willingness on his part to supply something of equal market value in exchange.[10] This restraint is commonly written for the ith individual or firm in the form of

$$\sum_{j}^{n} p_j(X_{ij} - \bar{X}_{ij}) \equiv 0, \tag{2}$$

where $\bar{X}_{ij}$ represents the quantity of the jth good which the ith individual holds at the beginning of the period before any exchange has taken place, and X_{ij} the quantity of the jth good which he holds or will acquire at the end of the period after all the transactions are settled. If the nth good is regarded as money, and p_n is therefore always equal to 1, (3) may be rewritten as

$$(X_{in} - \bar{X}_{in}) \equiv \sum_{j}^{n-1} p_j(\bar{X}_{ij} - X_{ij}). \tag{3}$$

Aggregated over all individuals and firms, this becomes

$$\sum_{i} X_{in} - \sum_{i} \bar{X}_{in} \equiv \sum_{i} \sum_{j=1}^{n-1} p_j(\bar{X}_{ij} - X_{ij}) \tag{4}$$

which, if all the goods other than money can be grouped into two groups, commodities and bonds, is equivalent to (1) above, i.e.,

$$(M^d - M^s) \equiv M - M_0 \equiv (C^s - C^d) + (B^s - B^d). \tag{5}$$

It is implied in the above formulation of Walras' Law that the increase (or decrease) in the quantity of any good which an individual will possess at the end of the period after all the exchanges, as compared with the quantity of that good which he holds at the beginning of the period before the exchanges, i.e., $(X_{ij} - \bar{X}_{ij})$ is to be defined as his net demand for (or net supply of) that good. This definition of net demand is certainly logical in the case of most goods and services, the enjoyment or productive utilization of which normally begins *after* trading. It seems to have been taken for granted that the same definition of net demand applies to money (the nth good) as well. The difference between the amount of money which an individual will hold at the end of the period after all the exchanges are settled and his initial holding of money at the beginning of the period is thus defined as his net demand for (or, if negative, net supply of) money for that particular period, and $\sum_i (X_{in} - \bar{X}_{in}) \equiv M - M_0$ is defined as the net demand for money on the part of the whole community for the period.

Such a definition of the excess demand for money, however, is untenable in an important sense, and all the confusions that beset the application of Walrasian general equilibrium approach to monetary analysis seem to stem from it. For money, unlike other goods, is not merely wanted for its services or utilities as an asset to hold *after* all the transactions in the current period are settled, though this would be the case with the asset demand for money for which the function of money as a liquid store of value is the primary consideration. Money, however, is not merely a store of value, but also a necessary medium of exchange; money is demanded to finance the planned transactions yet to be carried out. This is what Keynes called the demand for "finance" which he regarded as some peculiar kind of demand for money, but which is really nothing but the transactions demand for money proper.

The nature of the transactions demand for money (or the demand for "finance") is best explained by the cost of asset transactions, emphasized by Hicks, Baumol and Tobin,[11] together with the lack of synchronization between payments and receipts. There is usually an overhead element in the cost of making an exchange of financial assets which does not vary proportionately to the amount of money involved, e.g., the minimum brokers' charge, the psychological cost of trouble and bother, etc., in addition to cost that varies in proportion to the amount of transaction involved. These costs of exchange would make the investment of cash in earning assets in very small amount, or for a very short period, quite uneconomical.

In a world, where receipts and expenditures are not synchronized and would be very costly for any individual to attempt to synchronize through his own effort, it is, therefore, not economical for any individual to keep his wealth all invested in income yielding assets and to meet every temporary excess of payments over receipts by selling some of such assets at the very instant money is needed, or to invest every temporary excess of receipts over payments in earning assets as soon as it occurs, even if there were no risk of capital losses and inevitable delay in asset liquidation.

Thus it is rational for each individual spending unit to keep a certain amount of cash balances sufficient to finance his planned expenditures at least for a short period ahead (which indeed need not be a rigidly fixed period) without having to rely upon the irregular and unpredictable cash receipts during the same short period.[12]

By the same token the temporary accumulation of irregular cash receipts from sales during such a short period, though *ex hypothesi* not immediately needed to finance the expenditures of the same period, the financing of them already having been taken care of, would not be invested *ad hoc* in interest-bearing assets as soon as they arise, but would be disposed of in a lump in connection with the new requirement for finance for the planned expenditures of the next such short period. For, apart from the fact that investing in small separate doses is uneconomical, unless the new decision is made about the requirement for finance during the next period, it is not known how much of the *ex post* accumulation of cash can be spared for investment in securities and for how long.[13]

It seems to me, therefore, more appropriate to designate the temporary accumulation of cash at the end of such a short period, i.e., $(X_{in} - \bar{X}_{in})$ in the budget identity of Walras' Law, as "the net acquisition of cash by trading" (a noncommittal term originally used by Hicks[14]) rather than to call it "the excess demand for money" in accordance with Lange and Patinkin.

Thus the identification of the "net acquisition of cash by trading" at the end of a given period with the "excess demand for money" for the period involves two kinds of difficulties. Firstly, the net acquisition of cash at the end of a period cannot possibly reflect the *pretrading* demand for transactions balances of the same period. Secondly, it would include all the temporary acceptances of money up to the end of the period which are only temporarily held pending rational allocation at the beginning of the next period, in accordance with the decision on expenditures planned for the next period. To designate all such temporary acceptances of money as the demand for money as such would surely make a travesty of any theory of money, whether it be the liquidity preference or the classical quantity theory. [15,16]

4. Budget Restraint Versus the Restraint of the Requirement for Finance

To take proper account of the pretrading demand for "finance" (or transactions balances), as determined by the current plans of expenditures, we must realize that this demand for "finance" constitutes another restraint upon each individual spending unit, apart from the so-called "budget restraint" (which, as pointed out above,[17] should really be called the "fair exchange restraint"). That is, under a given institutional set-up, in which I shall include the degrees of synchronization between receipts and payments and the costs of asset transactions, there is a practical minimum requirement for transactions balances in order to carry out a given volume of planned expenditures during a given period. This restraint is additional to the budget restraint, which merely stipulates that total purchases equal total sales (or that there should be no cheating or robbing in trading), but which imposes no restriction whatsoever on the amount of transactions that can be carried out in a given period with a given amount of money as the medium of exchange.

As explained above, the costs of asset transactions and the lack of synchronization between expenditures and receipts as well as the imperfect predictability as to their time patterns makes it sensible for any spending unit to hold a certain amount of transaction balances, enough to finance his planned expenditures for a certain period ahead. The amount of transaction balances demanded in relation to planned expenditures, or to put it another way, the period over which the planned expenditures are to be financed entirely by the initial provision of transaction balances, is by no means invariant for every individual, but is *prima facie* dependent upon the expected degree of synchronization between his receipts and expenditures and upon the relation between the cost of asset transactions and the rates of yield of assets alternative to money balances. However, there should be a practical minimal limit to this relationship under a realistic range of interest variations. This practical minimum may be treated as roughly constant in the absence of major institutional changes that affect the cost of asset transactions and payments-receipts synchronization. Thus we can most conveniently analyze the implication of the demand for transaction balances and the additional restraint on spending units which it implies by following the late Sir Dennis Robertson in choosing as the unit time period over which the practical minimal requirement for transaction balances is on the average equal to the planned expenditures of the spending units concerned.[18] When this is done, we can say that at the beginning of each such period each typical individual must acquire a minimum transaction balance equal to his planned expenditures on commodities before these expenditures are carried out. This implies that the inflow of money receipts from the sales of commodities and services during such a short period will not be needed to finance the expenditures of the same period. However, as explained above, they will not be invested in bonds immediately as they arise, but will be disposed of at the beginning of the next period in connection with the decision on the requirement for finance of that period.

This type of Robertsonian period analysis also implies that trading in financial assets will always take place at the very beginning of the period. For as soon as each individual makes his decision as to how much to spend during the coming period, he will know how much of his accumulated cash holding can be spared from his own requirement for finance, or how much further finance he must procure for his planned expenditures. It is to his interest that such adjustments of his cash holding should be carried out right at the beginning of the period.[19]

Thus the new restraint for a typical individual (say, the ith) may be written, under the simplifying assumption that all goods may be classified into three categories, viz., commodities, bonds and money, as

$$C_i^d + M_i^* \equiv M_{0i} + (B_i^s - B_i^d), \tag{6}$$

where C_i^d is the money value of planned purchases of commodities of the ith individual during the current period which, by our definition of the length of the period, is equal to his minimum requirement for transaction balances (or "finance"); M_{0i} his initial money holding accumulated up to the end of the preceding period; B_i^s and B_i^d his sales and purchases of bonds at the beginning of the period; M_i^* is the "supplementary" cash balance, which he may desire to hold for additional convenience and security in addition to the minimum necessary transaction balances and which is obviously a decreasing function of the yields of alternative assets.

Aggregated over all individuals, we obtain the additional aggregate restraint

$$C^d + M^* \equiv M_0 + (B^s - B^d),^{20} \tag{7}$$

which we may either call the "velocity of circulation restraint" or the "requirement for finance restraint."

When this restraint is substituted for the restraint represented by Walras' Law as the link between the money market and the commodity and bonds markets, we shall see that all the confusion about the liquidity preference theory of interest as well as the classical quantity theory of money resulting from the misinterpretation and misapplication of Walras' Law can be cleared up easily.

5. Budget Restraint of Banking Institutions and the Modified Form of Walras' Law

One more difficulty with the popular formulation of Walras' Law should be pointed out here. That is, Walras' Law, as it is stated in the form of (4) or (5), precludes any changes in the stock of money supply in any equilibrium situation, even in the sense of Walrasian market equilibrium of the shortest run. When both the commodity and the bond markets are cleared, i.e., when $\Sigma_i \Sigma_{j=1}^{n-1} p_j (\bar{X}_{ij} - X_{ij}) = 0$, the net acquisition of money by the community as a whole according to Walras' Law must necessarily be zero, i.e.,

$$\sum_i (X_{in} - \bar{X}_{in}) \equiv M - M_0 = 0.$$

This is patently unsatisfactory, as there is no reason at all why the commodity and bond markets cannot both be cleared when there is a net change in money supply by the monetary authorities.[21]

This difficulty arises from a failure to take into consideration in the formulation of Walras' Law the fact that the budget restraint, or more accurately the "fair exchange restraint," for monetary authorities and banks (which together we shall call the banking sector), that possess the power to create money by passing out their own demand liabilities, is quite different from that applicable to the nonbank public. To simplify our exposition, we shall make the assumption that the banking sector consists of pure financial institutions in the sense that they operate only in the bond and money markets but not in the commodity market.[22] The budget restraint for such a pure banking sector should then be written not in the usual form of

$$(B_b^d - B_b^s) \equiv (M_b^s - M_b^d),$$

but as

$$(B_b^d - B_b^s) \equiv \Delta M, \tag{8}$$

where ΔM is the net increase (or net decrease, if negative) in the stock of money supply in the hands of the public during the period concerned, and the subscript b refers to the banking sector; for an excess supply of money by the banking sector means a corresponding net creation of money by banks and an excess demand for money by the banking sector implies a corresponding net destruction of money by banks.

When Walras' Law is derived by the aggregation of all budget restraints including the anomalous one, i.e., identity (8), it becomes

$$(C^d - C^s) + (B^d - B^s) \equiv (M_p^s - M_p^d) + \Delta M \equiv M_0 + \Delta M - M, \tag{9}$$

where the subscript p refers to the nonbank public sector. Thus the attainment of market equilibrium in both the commodity and bond markets is quite compatible with a net increase or decrease in the total supply of money.

6. Absence of Conflict Between Liquidity Preference and Loanable Funds Theories of Interest

The combination of (8), the budget (fair exchange) restraint of the banking sector, and (7), the "requirement for finance restraint" of the nonbank sector (where B^s and B^d must now be understood as referring, respectively, to those of the nonbank sector only), gives us a new identity, viz.,

$$C^d + M^* \equiv M_0 + \Delta M + (B^s - B^d), \qquad (10)$$

where B^s and B^d represent as before the aggregate supply and demand for bonds, respectively, of both the non-bank and the banking sectors.

When this identity is recognized as the relevant restraint on the *ex ante* (pretrading) demand and supply for money, instead of Walras' Law, we shall see that the alleged conflict between the liquidity preference and loanable funds theories in certain cases of dynamic disequilibrium disappears altogether. For according to the loanable funds theory, the rate of interest is determined by the equilibrium between the demand and supply of bonds, i.e.,

$$B^s - B^d = 0. \qquad (11)$$

The liquidity preference theory on the other hand states that the rate of interest is determined by the equilibrium between the demand and supply of money. When the demand for money is interpreted in the *ex ante* (pretrading) sense to take proper account of what Keynes calls the demand for "finance" as well as the demand for money to hold as assets, the equilibrium condition of the money market should be written as

$$C^d + M^* = M_0 + \Delta M. \qquad (12)$$

It is easy to see that by virtue of identity (10) the two equilibrium conditions necessarily imply each other. Moreover, unlike Walras' Law, identity (10) would indicate the coincidence of the equilibrium between the demand and supply for bonds and that between the demand and supply for money, regardless of whether there is equilibrium in the commodity market; for the equivalence between (11) and (12) on the basis of (10) is not predicated in a way upon the equilibrium between the supply and demand for commodities, (i.e., $C^d = C^s$). Even in a situation of disequilibrium, an excess demand for bonds necessarily implies an equivalent excess supply of money and vice versa. It is, therefore, impossible for the two theories to give opposite indications as to the direction of movement of the interest rate. Thus the accusation by Patinkin and Johnson that the liquidity preference theory might give false indications as to the direction of movement of the interest rate under certain dynamic situations is really based on the false identification of the net acquisition of cash by trading in Walras' Law with the excess demand for money.[23]

7. The Equation for Money versus the Equation for Peanuts

It should be clear from what we have said above that Walras' Law is not to be interpreted to mean that the summation of the *ex ante* excess demands for all goods including money is identically equal to zero; for the term $\Sigma_i (X_{in} - \bar{X}_{in})$—the nth good being money in the accounting identity of Walras' Law (4) is not really the *ex ante* excess demand for money relevant for the determination of the equilibrium of the money market. It follows, therefore, that we cannot maintain, in order to determine the $n - 1$ prices of a general equilibrium system of n goods (including money, the price of which is identically equal to unity), that any $n - 1$ excess demand equations of the system will suffice by virtue of Walras' Law, and that it does not matter in the least whether it is the equation for money or bonds, or for that matter the equation for peanuts, that we choose to eliminate. Since Walras' Law does not include the relevant excess demand for money along with the excess demands for other goods, none of the excess demand equations can really be eliminated as redundant on its basis alone.

The only way to eliminate the one surplus equation is by virtue of identity (10)—or identity (7) when there is no change in money supply by the bank system. Identity (10) or (7), however, enable us to eliminate only either the equation for bonds or the equation for money, but none of the equations for commodities. Thus, an understanding of the true meaning of Walras' Law and the requirement for finance restraint would enable us to provide a more satisfactory answer to the thought provoking question posed by Lerner: "What if we eliminate the equation for peanuts?" Obviously, in that case the whole price system would still be indeterminate even if the equations for both bonds and money were kept; for the equilibrium of the excess demand for peanuts does not automatically follow from the equilibrium of all the other excess demand equations and the relevant *ex ante* excess demand equation for money. On the other hand, the equilibrium on the bond market and the interest rate can only be determined by the equality of the demand and supply of either bonds or money. After all, even in a general equilibrium analysis, one should expect that the demand and supply of money, the generally accepted means of payment, would have more to do with the determination of the interest rate than the demand and supply of peanuts which are not a means of payment at all. A peanut preference theory of interest rate, or a liquidity preference theory of peanut price, is after all impossible.

8. Say's Law and Walras' Law in a Monetary Economy

The introduction of the requirement for finance restraint and the relegation of Walras' Law to a secondary role would also help to clarify some misconceptions about the classical monetary theory.

The classical economists, as is well known, believe that money is normally not wanted for its own sake but in order to buy other goods with it. In other words, money itself does not enter the utility function. This belief leads to the famous Say's Law which asserts that people offer things for sale only because they want other goods in exchange. If they accept money for the goods they sell, it is not because they want the money for its own sake but because they desire to use the money at once to buy other goods with it. In this way, every supply of a good creates a demand for an equivalent amount of other goods. Lange, in his renowned article on Say's Law,[24] tried to give mathematical precision to this classical doctrine with the help of Walras' Law. The result, however, is utterly misleading and confusing. Identifying, quite falsely as we have seen, the net acquisition of cash by trading shown in the accounting identity of Walras' Law with the net demand for money for its own sake, he claims that Say's Law, by asserting that the net demand for money for its own sake is identically equal to zero, implies that the aggregate demand for all goods (other than money) is necessarily identical with the aggregate supply of all other goods, irrespective of the price level.[25] If this is the true assertion of Say's Law, then of course the price level would be entirely indeterminate in contradiction to the quantity theory of money which is also accepted by the classical economists in one form or another.

This formulation of Say's Law by Lange and Patinkin[25] has been as widely accepted as their interpretation of Walras' Law. Yet one cannot help thinking that the classical economists cannot be as stupid and inconsistent as Lange and Patinkin would have us believe. For it should be clear that when the classical economists say that money is not wanted for its own sake, they certainly do not mean that money will not be wanted even as the necessary medium of exchange, but merely that money is not wanted as an asset to hold. And when they say that money accepted for the sale of goods will be used *at once* to buy other goods, they certainly do not mean that there will be absolutely no time lag between the receipt of money and the spending of it, but that money receipts will be spent as quickly as the institutional set-up normally permits. Thus the assertion of Say's Law is quite compatible with the existence of the maximum velocity restraint for the individuals as well as for the community. All that was claimed under Say's Law about the demand for money is that money will not normally be held as an idle asset, i.e., that M^* in our maximum velocity restraint—identity (7) or (10) above—would normally be equal to zero, so that there would not be a liquidity trap for the effective demand for goods. This certainly does not imply that the maximum velocity restraint would have to be waived altogether, but would only mean that this restraint would take the form of

$$C^d \equiv M_0 + \Delta M + (B_p^s - B_p^d) \tag{13}$$

which means that there is a rigid relation between the planned expenditure and the requirement for money as means of payment (finance).[26] The equilibrium condition for the demand and supply of money is then simply

$$C^d = M_0 + \Delta M. \tag{14}$$

It is true that with this equilibrium condition in force, the aggregate demand for goods in physical units determined by the available quantity of money might be smaller than the aggregate supply of goods at too high a price level. That is, the aggregate demand for goods certainly would not equal the aggregate supply at all possible price levels. This possibility, however, did not seriously worry the classical economists because they believed that the price level was highly flexible, so that an excess supply would quickly bring about an appropriate fall in the price level to restore equilibrium between the aggregate demand and supply of goods.[27]

There is absolutely no need to worry about any inconsistency between the demand and supply equation for money (14) and Walras' Law. For (14) refers to the pretrading demand for finance, whereas the term misidentified as the excess demand for money in the accounting identity of Walras' Law is really the *ex post* net acquisition of cash by trading. In classical quantity theory as well as in modern liquidity preference theory, the demand for transactions balances must be understood as the *pretrading* demand for finance, not the *ex post* acquisition of cash by trading.[28]

Notes

*Manuscript received November 13, 1964, revised May 19, 1965.

1. This paper in its early stage benefited greatly from detailed comments of the late Sir Dennis Robertson, whose method of approach constitutes the key of

the following analysis. It is a matter of profound sadness to me that, in spite of his encouragement, I could not get the paper published before his death in 1963. Let this paper be my dedication to him, a great teacher and economist, whose sound common sense often provided the much needed check for latterday esoteric theoretical developments in monetary economics.

I am also indebted to Professors J. R. Hicks, F. Machlup and my colleagues at the University of Rochester, especially Professor Lionel McKenzie for helpful comments.

2. Hicks [1939] pp. 153–62.
3. Patinkin [1958] pp. 307–12 and Johnson [1961] p. 7.
4. Lange [1942], Patinkin [1948], Patinkin [1949], and Johnson [1961].
5. Recently Archibald and Lipsey [1, (16)] also maintain that Walras' Law does not hold for what they call the classical model. However, they have not provided any adequate theoretical explanation why Walras' Law should not hold.
6. Patinkin [1958] pp. 307–12.
7. Hicks [1939].
8. Tsiang [1956]. The same conclusion was reached by W. L. Smith using similar methods. [25].
9. Tsiang [1956] pp. 540–43.
10. The term "budget restraint" is in fact a misnomer; for it really has nothing to do with the concept of budgeting. Nor would it be appropriate to call it either the "income constraint" or the "wealth constraint," since obviously income is not the limit of expenditure, and wealth can be added to out of income or consumed. The most appropriate term for this restraint seems to be the "fair exchange constraint;" for in any fair exchange that rules out robbing and cheating the goods supplied in exchange for the goods demanded must have the same market value. This is all that is implied in the so-called budget constraint which should apply to capital as well as current transactions.

It is, therefore, quite groundless to contend that, whereas demands for commodities are subject to an income constraint, the demand for money is subject to a wealth constraint, an argument used by A. H. Meltzer to justify the so-called "wealth approach" to the demand for money. See [18, (231–32)].
11. Hicks [1935], Baumol [1952], and Tobin [1960].
12. Regular and predictable cash receipts, however, frequently constitute the convenient dividing points of such cash holding periods.
13. These considerations seem to indicate that for a dynamic analysis of the demand for money, it is more appropriate to adopt a Robertsonian period analysis rather than a continuous analysis where the demands for money as well as for other assets are supposed to be continuously adjusted, according to one's scale of preference. The theoretical basis for such a period analysis is not merely that money simply takes time to circulate, but that the cost of asset transactions makes it uneconomical to dispense with the holding of adequate transaction balances of money beforehand and to make the

decisions continuously of investing and disinvesting infinitely small amounts of money.

14. It is to be noted, however, that although Hicks persistently refrains from naming this term in the budget identity "the excess demand for money," yet in the end he concludes that "to say that the net acquisition of money by trading is zero, taken over the whole community, is the same as to say that the demand for money equals the supply of money" [13, (155–8)]. Could there be some ambivalence in his mind?

15. One glaring example of the confusion resulting from the false identification of the net acquisition of money by trading with the excess demand for money is that by all common sense an entrepreneur planning an increase in his investment expenditures would *pro tanto* have an increased demand for "finance" or transactions money; according to the definition of excess demand for money implied in this false identification, he must be said to have planned *ipso facto* an increased supply of money to the money market. No wonder it is easily shown on the basis of such an interpretation of Walras' Law that the liquidity preference theory can lead to very strange results.

16. Valvanis in an interesting article called the net acquisition of money by trading shown in Walras' Law the "mirror image excess-demand for money," which he points out to be totally different from the kind of demand for money shown in the quantity equation. However, he did not explain why this "mirror image excess-demand for money" is not relevant to the equilibrium of the money market [28, (354–57)].

17. See footnote 10.

18. That is to say, given the costs of asset transactions and payments-receipts synchronization, the demand for transaction cash balance of an individual may be regarded as a function $M_i(C_i^d, r)$ where C_i^d is his planned expenditure on commodities for a period of arbitrary length and r the current rate of interest on the only alternative asset. This function can be expanded according to Taylor's Theorem into

$$M_i(C_i^d, r) = M_i(C_i^d, r_0) + (r - r_0)\frac{\partial M_i}{\partial r} + \frac{(r - r_0)^2}{2!}\frac{\partial^2 M_i}{\partial r^2}$$
$$+ \frac{(r - r_0)^3}{3!}\frac{\partial^3 M_i}{\partial r^3} + \dots$$

The first term on the right-hand side is obviously independent of the current rate of interest. If we select for r_0 a rate of interest which is practically never exceeded in the economy during the period under study, say, 10 or 15 per cent per annum, then we may call the first term the "practical minimum requirement for finance." The rest of the terms of the Taylor's expansion may be grouped together with precautionary and asset demands for money and called the "supplementary demand for money" that are functions of interest rate.

It is implicitly assumed here that given r, the transaction demand for money is a linear function of planned expenditures. The investigations by Baumol [4], however, suggested that the transaction demand for cash might vary proportionately with the square root of planned expenditures. On the other hand, the more elaborate and realistic study by Tobin [26] indicates that, although the scale of expenditures would have an influence on the ratio of transaction balances demanded to the planned expenditures at a given interest rate, the influence is highly discontinuous [26, (245)]. Thus, for the short term variations of planned expenditures of an individual, we may assume that his demand for transaction balances varies proportionately with his planned expenditures, although major differences in the scales of expenditures between different individuals or firms might result in quite different practices in cash management.

19. Similar observations were made by Tobin [26, (244)]. This also provides an answer to the perennial criticism which I have been confronted with: viz., if expenditures on commodities and services (including physical assets) are supposed to require "finance" or "transactions balance" in advance, why is it not the same with purchases of bonds or financial securities in general? The answer is that, in general, purchases of financial securities with cash by an individual or a firm may be regarded as an attempt to reduce his (or its) excessive cash holding to the desired level in accordance with his (or its) prospective expenditures on commodities and services in the immediate future. Purchases of financial securities with cash are, therefore, the consequence of an estimated excess in cash holdings rather than the cause for an increase in demand for transaction balances. For the reason given above in the text, such transactions must be carried out at the very beginning of the decision period.

Exchange of one financial security for another can be regarded as a direct swap hardly involving any means of payments or medium of exchange (at least in a country with well developed financial markets), as transactions in securities are generally settled by clearings; only the net balances need to be settled with cash.

20. Identity (6) may indeed be written in a more general form as

$$M_i^d(C_i^d, r) \equiv M_{01} + (B_i^d - B_i^d). \tag{6'}$$

At first glance, putting the requirement for finance restraint in this form would seem to dispense with the definition of a unit time period so short that the practical minimum requirement for transaction balances is equal to the prospective expenditures of the spending unit concerned. However, if we choose an arbitrary long period for (6'), say, a month, or a year, it is difficult to see why the demand for money on the part of an individual, the left hand side of (6'), cannot be satisfied with his cash receipts from current sales of commodities and services, but must be met by his cash holding at the beginning of the period and cash receipts from net sales of bonds (net borrowing). Therefore, unless the period is chosen in the Robertsonian way as we did above, we cannot see clearly why an individual cash requirement restraint should be formulated either in the form of (6) or (6').

Readers might be interested in a comparison of the above formulation of the requirement for finance restraints for individuals (6) and for the community (7) with the so-called Cambridge money equation formulated in various forms by those economists who also recognize that the classical quantity theory imposes an additional restraint on aggregate transactions of the community in addition to the budget restraint. See, e.g. Hickman [11], Brunner [7], Valavanis [28] and Archibald and Lipsey [1].

21. In fact, as Hicks pointed out, since we are dealing with the temporary market equilibrium, "there is a sense in which current supplies and current demands are always equated in competitive conditions. Stocks may indeed be left in the shop unsold, but they are unsold because people prefer to take the chance of being able to sell them at a future date rather than cut prices in order to sell them now." [13, (131)]. It is quite inconceivable that such temporary clearing of all the markets is impossible whenever there is some change in money supply. Nevertheless, this difficulty was neglected by Hicks himself, who stated elsewhere that the net acquisition of cash by the community as a whole being zero is the equilibrium condition between the demand and supply for money. (*Ibid.*, 157.)

   This again is the case with Lange, who in his famous article on Say's Law writes $M = 0$ as the equilibrium condition for the money market and $M \equiv 0$ as Say's Law. [17, (52)].

   See however, A. C. Enthoven, [10, (314–15)], where the different nature of the budget identity of the government sector, as distinguished from that of the household and business sectors, is clearly pointed out.

22. If they do in fact operate to some extent on the commodity market, we shall assume that these operations are performed by their non-bank subsidiaries which obtain their funds by borrowing from "banks proper."

23. It is, however, an irony of history that the Keynsian liquidity preference theory has to be defended by a demonstration on the basis of the Robertsonian period analysis to show that it leads to identical results as the loanable funds theory.

24. Lange [1942].

25. Walras' Law states that

$$\sum_i \sum_{j=1} P_j(X_{ij} - \bar{X}_{ij}) \equiv 0.$$

Now according to Lange and his followers, Say's Law rules that

$$\sum_i (X_{in} - \bar{X}_{in}) \equiv 0$$

where X_n denotes money. Hence

$$\sum_i \sum_{j-1}^{n-1} P_j(X_{ij} - \bar{X}_{ij}) \equiv 0$$

irrespective of $[P_j]$.

26. Lange [1942] and Patinkin [1948] and [1949].

27. This monetary version of Say's Law (i.e., $M^* = 0$, so that there is no liquidity trap for effective demand) was held neither as an immutable law of nature nor as an inexorable logical identity, but merely as a normal way of life. For it was well recognized, especially by J. S. Mill, that in time of

waning commercial confidence, money may be in great demand as a store of value with the result that the aggregate money demand for commodities shrinks considerably. The stronger version of Say's Law, viz., that a supply of goods *necessarily* implies a demand for other goods of equal value, is well recognized as applicable only to a world of barter, where it is self-evident and in fact becomes the same thing as Walras' Law [19, (68–74)].

28. As Becker and Baumol pointed out, Say's Law, at least as it was understood among the English classical economists, claimed that "supply creates its own demand not despite the behavior of the price level, but because of it" [6, (360, 61)].

29. The first draft of this paper was originally written four years ago. Since then there have appeared a number of articles and discussions on the alleged inconsistency and indeterminacy of the classical monetary theory; viz., the so-called Patinkin controversy. See in particular Archibald and Lipsey [2], Ball and Bodkin [3], Baumol [5], Clower and Burstein [8], Clower [9]. Hahn [11], Kuenne [16], and Mishan [19] and [20]. None of these writers, however, seem to me have succeeded in resolving this confusing problem by explaining clearly that the so-called excess demand for money in the Walras' Law is something quite different from the demand for money in the Cambridge cash balance equation. This paper is, therefore, left substantially as it was originally written.

References

1. Archibald, G. C. and R. G. Lipsey, "Monetary and Value Theory: A Critique of Lange and Patinkin," *Review of Economic Studies*, XXIV (October, 1958), 1–22.
2. Archibald, G. C. and R. G. Lipsey, "Monetary and Value Theory: Further Comment," *Review of Economic Studies*, XXVIII (October, 1960), 50–6.
3. Ball, R. J. and R. Bodkin, "The Real Balance Effect and Orthodox Demand Theory: A Critique of Archibald and Lipsey," *Review of Economic Studies*, XXVIII (October, 1960), 44–9.
4. Baumol, W. J., "The Transactions Demand for Cash: An Inventory Theoretic Approach," *Quarterly Journal of Economics*, LXVI (November, 1952), 545–56.
5. Baumol, W. J., "Monetary and Value Theory: Comments," *Review of Economic Studies*, XXVIII (October, 1960), 29–31.
6. Becker, G. S. and W. J. Baumol, "The Classical Monetary Theory: The Outcome of Discussion," *Economica*, XIX (November, 1952), 355–76.
7. Brunner, K., "Inconsistency and Indeterminacy in Classical Economics," *Econometrica*, XIX (April, 1951), 152–73.
8. Clower, R. W. and M. L. Burstein, "On the Invariance of Demand for Cash and Other Assets," *Review of Economic Studies*, XXVIII (October, 1960), 32–6.
9. Clower, R. W., "Classical Monetary Theory Revisited," *Economica*, XXX (May 1963), 165–70.

10. Enthoven, A. C., "A Neo-Classical Model of Money, Debt and Economic Growth," Mathematical Appendix in *Money in A Theory of Finance,* by J. G. Gurley and E. S. Shaw, (Washington D.C.: Brookings Institution, 1960), 303–59.

11. Hahn, F. H., "The Patinkin Controversy," *Review of Economic Studies,* XXVIII (October, 1960), 37–43.

12. Hickman, W. B., "The Determinacy of Absolute Prices in Economic Theory," *Econometrica,* XVIII (January, 1950), 9–20.

13. Hicks, J. R., *Value and Capital,* (Oxford: Clarendon Press, 1939).

14. Hicks, J. R., "Suggestions for Simplifying The Theory of Money," *Economica,* II (February, 1935), 1–19; reprinted in *Readings in Monetary Theory,* eds. F. A. Lutz and L. W. Mints, Chapter 2, 13–32.

15. Johnson, H. G., "The General Theory after Twenty-five Years," *American Economic Review, Papers and Proceedings,* LI (May, 1961), 1–17.

16. Kuenne, R. E., "Say's Law and Walras' Law Once More: Comment," *Quarterly Journal of Economics,* LXXVIII (August, 1964), 479–87.

17. Lange, O., "Say's Law: Restatement and Criticism," *Studies in Mathematical Economics and Econometrics,* ed. O. Lange and F. E. McIntyre, T. O. Yntema (Chicago: University of Chicago Press, 1942), 49–68.

18. Meltzer, A. H., "The Demand for Money: The Evidence from the Time Series," *Journal of Political Economy,* LXXI (June, 1963), 219–46.

19. Mill, J. S., "Of the Influence of Consumption on Production," Essay II in *Essays on Some Unsettled Questions of Political Economy,* 2nd. ed., (London: Longmans, 1874).

20. Mishan, E. J., "Say's Law and Walras' Law Once More," *Quarterly Journal of Economics,* LXXVII (November, 1963), 617–25.

21. Mishan, E. J., "Reply," *Quarterly Journal of Economics,* LXXVIII (August, 1964), 484–88.

22. Patinkin, D., "Relative Prices, Say's Law and the Demand for Money," *Econometrica,* XVI (April, 1948), 135–54.

23. Patinkin, D., "The Indeterminacy of Absolute Prices in Classical Economic Theory," *Econometrica,* XVII (January, 1949). 1–27.

24. Patinkin, D., "Liquidity Preference and Loanable Funds: Stock and Flow Analysis," *Economica,* XXV (November, 1958), 300–18.

25. Smith, W. L., "Monetary Theories of the Rate of Interest: A Dynamic Analysis," *Review of Economics and Statistics,* XL (February, 1958), 15–21.

26. Tobin, J., "The Interest Elasticity of Transactions Demand for Cash," *Review of Economics and Statistics,* XXXVIII (August, 1956), 241–47.

27. Tsiang, S. C., "Liquidity Preference and Loanable Funds Theories, Multiplier and Velocity Analysis: A Synthesis," *American Economic Review,* XXXXVI (September, 1956), 539–64.

28. Valavanis, S., "A Denial of Patinkin's Contradiction," *Kyklos,* VIII Fase. 4, 1955, 351–68.

CHAPTER 7

The Monetary Theoretic Foundation of the Modern Monetary Approach to the Balance of Payments[1]

S. C. Tsiang

1. Introduction

The monetary approach to the balance of payments really began with Hume's "price-specie-flow mechanism," as most proponents of the modern version of this approach are quick to point out. In the heyday of the Keynesian Revolution, however, this mechanism had come to be regarded as inoperative, as the quantity of money itself was regarded by the prevailing monetary theory as a matter of no consequence. The balance of payments theory developed in those days naturally tended to neglect the influence of money supply. The elasticity approach that dominated the scene from the depression years to the early post-war days is primarily concerned with the effects of relative prices upon exports and imports under the assumption that domestic money wages and prices of nontraded goods somehow remain constant. The subsequent Keynesian extension of it merely superimposes a multiplier analysis upon the primary change in trade balance under the usual

Finance Constraints and the Theory of Money
ISBN 0-12-701720-8
ISBN 0-12-701721-6 (pbk)

"The Monetary Theoretic Foundation of the Modern Monetary Approach to the Balance of Payments," Oxford Economic Papers, Oxford University Press, Vol. XXIX, 3 (November 1977), pp. 319–338.

Keynesian assumptions of an infinitely elastic demand for or supply of money in addition to the assumption of constant wages and prices of domestic goods. Any possible effects of the money supply are effectively eliminated by these implicit assumptions.

During the post-war years of continuous inflationary pressure and high levels of employment in most countries, it became increasingly hard for any intelligent economist to continue to believe in the infinite interest elasticity of the demand or supply of money. Quite independently of the rise of the Chicago School of monetary theory, economists in general began to feel once again that perhaps money supply did matter after all in our monetary economy. Those who worked in the field of international finance, like the present author, could not help but perceive that money supply did play a vital role in determining the balance of payments. For instance, as early as 1952, the present author, then working at the International Monetary Fund, had pointed out that the remarkable improvement of the Danish balance of payments in 1951 after huge deficits was to a very large extent due to the conservative monetary policy of allowing the payments deficit to result in a contraction of its domestic money supply.[2] Again in a study of the Peruvian experiment with a floating exchange rate system, I pointed out that the volume of Peru's imports was remarkably closely correlated with the money supply of that country.[3] And in going over the experiences with floating exchange rate system in several European countries after the First World War, I noted that in countries that managed to keep their money supplies from expanding, the fluctuations of the floating rates were generally quite moderate, and that the sharp and cumulative depreciation of the franc in 1926, which used to be much cited as the example of the 'inevitable' instability of a floating exchange rate, was really due to the virtually infinitely elastic supply of money at a pegged interest rate then prevailing in France.[4] These empirical observations culminated in a theoretical article emphasizing the vital role played by money supply in the balance of trade.[5]

The new monetary approach that has come in vogue lately, therefore, is neither objectionable nor alien to me in its broad conclusions. Yet I have deep qualms about the attempt to formulate the new theory of the balance of payments in such a simple statement as that the balance of payments surplus (or deficit) is determined by the excess flow demand for (or supply of) money. My uneasiness is certainly not alleviated by the fact that among the proponents of this approach quite different versions of the demand for money function are espoused either for the exposition of the theory or for the application of the theory to particular problems.

Moreover, I also feel uncomfortable about the claim by the leading proponents of this approach that the Walras' Law relation between excess demands and supplies in various markets is the key to the analysis of the balance of payments;[6] for in my opinion the so-called Walras' Law is a much abused and highly tricky concept in monetary economics, which is more likely to confuse than to enlighten.[7]

My criticism, therefore, is not directed at the monetary approach to the balance of payments in the broad sense that the balance of payments is essentially a monetary phenomenon,[8] but only at the monetary theory that the modern exponents of this approach employ in their elaboration and application of this theory.

2. The Demand for Money Function

Firstly, what precisely is the excess flow demand for money? The proponents of the monetary approach to the balance of payments theory claim that the balance of payments surplus B can be formulated as

$$B = \pi[L(\ ) - M] \tag{1}$$

where $L(\ )$ is the demand function for money, M is the actual money supply, both in the stock sense, and π is the desired (usually assumed constant) speed of adjustment of the demand and supply to each other. This formulation does not mean very much, and has little predictive value, unless the demand function for money can be precisely specified and is known to be stable. Obviously, much depends on the demand function for money, yet there does not yet seem to be general agreement among the proponents of the monetary approach about its precise specification, even though everyone would assure us that, whatever it is, it is stable in the long run at least.

There are two basic types of demand function for money employed in the monetary theory of the balance of payments. Either nominal money balances are described as a function of real income, the interest rate, and the price level, or nominal money balances are treated as a function of the money value of total real wealth and the interest rate. Apparently, the choice of income or wealth as the chief argument of the demand function for money is treated as immaterial, and the actual decision to pick one or the other seems to depend mostly upon expediency in relation to the problem the author is tackling. If the author lays emphasis upon capital movements and portfolio equilibrium, the demand for money is described as a function of wealth and interest. On the other hand, if the author is dealing with the determination of the price level and the movements of trade in goods and services, the money demand function is presented as a function of income and interest rate. Since so much depends upon the money demand function, the casual way in which one specification of the function is picked in preference to the others does not inspire much confidence among the skeptics.

Let us first take the wealth version of the money demand function as employed by two prominent proponents of this approach, J. A. Frenkel and C. A. Rodriguez (1975). There the demand for money function is formulated as

$$m = l(\rho)P_k k, \ l'(\rho) < 0 \qquad (2)$$

where m is real money balances in terms of consumption goods, $l(\rho)$ the desired ratio of real money balances to the real value of capital, ρ the rate of interest, P_k the price of capital goods in terms of consumption goods, and k the stock of real capital goods.[9] That is to say, given ρ the interest rate, the demand for money balances would somehow be a constant proportion of the total value of the stock of capital goods (assets). The authors do not feel obliged to give any explanation of why this should be so.

Apparently, they think of money as just another store of value like capital goods (or the titles to them) for people to hold in their asset portfolios. For lack of any good reason to think otherwise, it is simply presumed that, if its relative yield does not change, it is held in constant proportion to the total when the size of the portfolio changes. This is, however, quite unsatisfactory as a portfolio theory, for it takes no account of the basic fact that money as a store of value produces no pecuniary yield. It would normally be completely dominated by other income-yielding assets, such as capital goods in this model, but for two very special characteristics of money; viz., it is firstly the only generally accepted medium of exchange, and, secondly, if the risk of inflation is abstracted from, money may be regarded as riskless as far as capital loss is concerned. On the latter ground, if people in the community have on the average constant relative risk aversion, the aggregate holdings of the riskless asset, money, can be expected to remain a constant proportion of total assets, provided that riskless money and risky capital goods are indeed the only assets available. Frenkel and Rodriguez, however, are apparently abstracting from all risks in their model. They cannot, therefore, invoke the convenient assumption of constant relative risk aversion to account for the tendency of asset holders to hold a constant proportion of wealth in the form of money. In fact, even if risks are introduced at a sufficiently realistic level to simulate the real world, where there are always assets of graduated shades of risks, it can easily be shown that money would still be dominated by other short-term assets with little risk but finite positive yields.[10]

The primary reason for which cash balances are held must be that money is the only generally accepted medium of exchange, a fact the proponents of the portfolio approach to the analysis of money demand tend to overlook. As a medium of exchange, however, money should obviously be demanded in proportion to the volume of transactions that require to be carried out with its service. It is difficult to see, then, why the money balances required to finance the expected volume of transactions should change in exact proportion to every change in the market value of the capital stock.

Frenkel and Rodriguez, however, feel no need to justify their postulated money demand function, but simply expect their readers to take it for granted, and proceed to operate on it mathematically to draw conclusions which they expect to hold from one balanced growth steady-state to another. Considering the fact that the transition from one balanced growth steady state to another after some disturbance might take over a century to be 90 per cent completed, skeptics like myself cannot help but remain sceptical about this form of modern elaboration and sophistication of the classical monetary approach to the balance of payments.[11]

Other equally prominent proponents of this approach, e.g. H. G. Johnson, however, would prefer the income version of the money demand function.[12] In his expository essay "The Monetary Approach to the Balance of Payments Theory," Johnson writes the demand function for money as

$$M_d = pf(y, i) \tag{3}$$

where M_d is nominal money balances demanded, y is real output (or income), i is the interest rate or the opportunity cost of holding money, and p is the international price level.[13] This is indeed a very widely accepted form of the money demand function, but strictly speaking it is also unsatisfactory. And its defects come out very clearly in the monetarists' application of it to balance of payments theory.

The basic difficulties with using income as the chief argument for the money demand function are as follows. If, as we have pointed out above, the property of being the only generally accepted medium of exchange is the basic function of money, then obviously the demand for its service should be directly related to the amount of expenditure that the public plan to make in a forthcoming period, rather than to the total income received or output produced. [14]

In a period of dynamic changes, aggregate planned expenditures need not be identical with total income received or produced. Indeed, the discrepancy between the two is the dynamic force making for changes in aggregate nominal incomes.

It is true that statistical measurement of *ex ante* magnitudes is hard to achieve, and in *ex post* statistics aggregate expeditures and aggregate incomes in a closed economy must be identical. In an open economy, however, where the balance of payments becomes a problem, aggregate expenditures can be different from aggregate incomes even in the *ex post* sense. For national expenditure, E, is usually defined as $E = C + I$, i.e. consumption plus investment, whereas total national income, Y, is defined as $Y = C + I + X - I_m$, i.e. consumption plus investment plus exports minus imports, the last two items only cancelling out under balanced trade.

Moreover, as far as the demand for domestic money is concerned, the expenditure that would give rise to requirements for transactions balances in domestic currency need not be just national expenditure, or the aggregate of the expenditures of domestic residents only. Expenditures of foreign residents or their agents in domestic markets equally give rise to demand for domestic money in so far as the expenditure in domestic markets must be carried out with domestic means of payment.

It might be objected that the fact that exports in many countries (particularly small developing ones) are frequently financed by foreign credits would surely invalidate the above argument. This is, however, clearly a misconception. The financing of exports by foreign credits should by no means be confused with the "finance" for purchase of labour services and commodities for export purposes in the sense the word "finance" was used by Keynes in his controversy with Ohlin and Robertson. [15] Exports financed in the usual sense by foreign credits still require in the final analysis domestic means of payments to make the necessary purchases on the domestic markets in order to assemble, to process, and to ship abroad. Typically an export firm, that has received a line of credit from abroad for a certain export contract, will immediately sell the foreign exchange to a bank, or on the domestic foreign exchange market, to obtain domestic currency for its transactions requirements on the domestic labour and goods markets. Of course, when the foreign credit covers a period longer than its optimal length of time, during which transactions-cum-precautionary cash balances are held, the firm will reinvest the excess cash proceeds from the sale of foreign exchange credit in domestic short-term liquid assets, for later conversion into cash again as the need for replenishment of its transactions balances arises. This is exactly the same way in which a firm producing entirely for domestic consumption will provide for its excess demand for transactions balances out of its borrowings from the domestic capital or money market. It is, therefore, quite obvious that exports create a demand for transactions cash balances even if they are financed by foreign credit.

On the other hand, it certainly cannot be argued by way of symmetry that imports eliminate the demand for transactions balances on the part of domestic residents to the extent of their domestic market value. For domestic consumers, their demand for transactions balances per unit of expenditure is the same whether their expenditure is on imported goods or on domestic goods. Moreover, imports generally create a whole series of intermediate transactions of their own that call for transactions cash balances from the time of unloading through wholesale distribution and retailing until they reach the hands of final consumers. Finally, the sales proceeds in domestic currency must be accumulated in some bank accounts in domestic currency for some minimum length of time to await conversion into foreign exchange for remittance to foreign suppliers, as such conversions and remittances, due to transactions costs, have to be done in instalments of fair size and, hence, at finite discrete intervals.

It is certainly not correct to assume that so long as national income (or wealth) remains the same, the aggregate volume of trade has no effect on the demand for money, which is what Johnson's (or Frenkel and Rodriguez's) demand for money function clearly implies. Or to put it in a slightly different way, it is not correct to assume that so long as trade remains balanced, the total volume of trade has no effect on the demand for money.

The incorrectness of such an assumption appears to be borne out by empirical studies of the demand for money in countries where the volume of trade has undergone rapid expansion in relation to the national income. For instance, in the case of the rapidly developing economy of Taiwan, with which I can claim some familiarity, the rate of increase in money supply during the past two decades has far exceeded the rate of increase of the real income of the island economy; the former being on the average approximately 20 percent per annum and the latter on the average 8–9 percent per annum. Yet the rate of price inflation was quite moderate (averaging around 3–4 percent per annum) until 1973, when the rate of increase of money supply was speeded up to 47 percent by a big trade surplus plus a substantial capital inflow. [16]

Regression of real money balances against real income and interest rate would inevitably yield an unreasonably high income elasticity of demand for money of more than 1.5. Using the statistics of the twenty years period from 1953 to 1972, the following regression equation has in fact been obtained,

$$\ln m = -8.3706 + 1.5441 \ln y - 0.0073 \ln r \qquad (4)$$

$$(0.8567) \quad (0.0905) \qquad (0.1556)$$

$$(17.0618) \qquad (-0.0469)$$

$$R^2 = 0.9928 \quad S^2 = 0.0048 \qquad \text{D.W.} = 1.3796.$$

where m is real money balances (currency plus demand deposits deflated by the GDP deflator), y is the real GDP, and r is the average market rate of interest. The first row of bracketed numbers under the estimated coefficients gives their respective standard errors, and the second row of such numbers gives their respective t values. [17] It would be clearly too farfetched to attempt to explain away such a high income elasticity as 1.54 by means of Professor Friedman's proposition that money is a luxury good and therefore should have an income elasticity greater than unity. Indeed, Friedman himself would probably never regard such a high income elasticity as plausible. Furthermore, although the degree of correlation is extremely high, partly because of the common upward trend, the Durbin–Watson statistic is quite unsatisfactory. This indicates that the systematic influence of some relevant factor left out in the regression equation must be contained in the residuals.

If we follow the *a priori* reasoning given above that the volume of trade also creates a demand for transactions balances in addition to income, a ready explanation of this phenomenon can be found in the fact that, during the past 20 years, there was a tremendous expansion in Taiwan's foreign trade relative to its national income. Exports and imports increased, respectively, from 12.7 percent and 22 percent of the national income in 1952 to 51.5 percent and 44.5 percent in 1972, and to 53.9 percent and 66.6 percent in 1974.[18]

When the influence of changes in the volume of trade relative to the national income is introduced into the regression equation for the demand for money balances, we obtain the following regression equation:

$$\ln m = 0.1037 + 0.8313 \ln y + 0.6965 \ln T/Y - 0.3219 \ln r \quad (4a)$$

$$(2.8882) \quad (0.2493) \quad (0.2216) \quad (0.1780)$$

$$(3.3349) \quad (3.1430) \quad (-1.8080)$$

$$R^2 = 0.9950 \quad S^2 = 0.0036 \quad \text{D.W.} = 1.8925.$$

where T/Y is the ratio of the volume of trade to GDP, both in current nominal values, and the other variables are defined as before.[19] It may be observed that, with the introduction of this additional variable, the estimated income elasticity of the demand for money is much closer to unity. In fact, it drops slightly below unity, but not significantly below in comparison with its standard error. The already very high degree of correlation is further improved and, what is more important, the Durbin–Watson statistic is significantly raised towards 2, its ideal value.

This strongly suggests that changes in the volume of trade relative to national income must have some infuence on the demand for money. If the demand for money function in an open economy should indeed be specified as

$$M_d = pf(E, X + Im, i) \quad (5)$$

then the assumption, which is regarded as the 'essential foundation' of the monetary approach,[20] viz., that the demand for money is a stable function of a few macroeconomic variables, would be at stake. For as a function of its true structural arguments, viz., E, X, Im, and i, the demand for money may indeed be a fairly stable function. Personally, I do believe it to be so. However, as a function of functions of income and interest rates, the indirect relationship may not be stable at all; for planned expenditures (especially the investment components among them) and the volume of trade (especially its export component) are not very stable as functions of domestic income and interest rates, but would obviously be subject to frequent exogenous disturbances. For instance, let us suppose that

$$E = E(y, i, \mu), \quad (6)$$

$$X = X(q, r, u), \tag{7}$$

$$Im = Im(y, q, r, \tau), \tag{8}$$

where q is the relative price ratio between domestic prices and foreign prices, r is the exchange rate, τ is the explicit or implicit import barrier due to tariff and other trade restrictions, and μ and u are the exogenous disturbance terms affecting the expenditure and export functions, respectively. Then substituting into, say, equation (5) we get

$$M_d = pf[E(y, i, \mu), X(q, r, u) + Im(y, q, r, \tau), i]$$

$$= pl(y, i, q, r, \tau, \mu, u). \tag{9}$$

Thus the demand for money, expressed as a function of y and i, as in Johnson (1973 and 1975), would be subject to the exogenous disturbances μ and u, which would make the excess demand for money very difficult to estimate and predict. Furthermore, it can no longer be claimed that the exchange rate r and the relative price ratio q have no lasting effects on the balance of payments merely on the ground that the latter is ultimately determined by the excess demand for money; for now we have shown that the demand for real balances itself is not independent of the influences of the exchange rate and relative prices, apart from the latter's effects on the price level and hence the supply of real balances.

The proponents of the new monetary approach would no doubt protest by appeal to statistical evidence which they claim to be overwhelmingly in favour of a stable functional relationship between the demand for money on the one side and income on the other side. Even interest rates are regarded as having only a minor influence on the demand for money in the long run. However, appeal to statistics without first clarifying the logical structural relationship is always inconclusive. The apparently fairly stable relationship between the demand for money and income could be the result of the fact that interest rates usually move to offset the influence of μ and u on the demand for money and income, as one would clearly expect to happen under any sensibly managed monetary policy. Furthermore, if these exogenous shifts are not offset by counter movements in interest rates calculated to offset them, then they would surely result in expansions or contractions in expenditure and the income stream. In *ex post* statistics of sufficiently long time units, wherein the dynamic changes that happened during the time unit tend to be telescoped together, we would only observe increases or decreases of money balances occurring more or less together with expansions or contractions of money income, which would serve to confirm the observer's belief in a stable functional relationship between the demand for money and income.[21]

The observed stability of the demand for money in relation to income is, therefore, no guarantee that the excess demand for money can be easily estimated for the prediction of the balance of payments. For the shifts in the *ex ante* demand for money function due to such exogenous disturbance factors as μ and u, or the movements of interest rates necessary to offset them, could obviously have considerable effects on the balance of payments, which could not be predicted at all from the presumed stable demand function for money.

Thus the modern monetary approach to the balance of payments appears at least to raise false hopes that the balance of payments surplus or deficit can be easily predicted because the excess demand for money is a stable function of a few macroeconomic variables, that are themselves easily predicted, e.g. real income or real wealth.

3. "Money to Spend" and "Money to Hold"

The fact that the overwhelmingly major part of the demand for money in the real world is for so-called transactions balances further points out a more fundamental weakness in the monetary theory that lies at the foundation of the modern monetary approach to the balance of payments. The demand for transactions balances is what Sir John Hicks and the late Sir Dennis Robertson would call the demand for "money to spend" as distinguished from the demand for "money to hold," which terms they would reserve for speculative or asset money balances and precautionary money balances.[22] Modern proponents of the monetary approach to the balance of payments, however, being mostly brought up on the so-called "portfolio approach" to the theory of money, are totally oblivious of this distinction, and treat transactions balances as well as asset money balances equally as "money to hold," and generally refer to any increase in the demand for money balances as "hoarding."

This unfortunate lack of discrimination has confused the modern monetarists into thinking that an increase (decrease) in the demand for transactions balances would, just like any increase (decrease) in the speculative or asset demand for money, necessarily imply the withholding of a corresponding amount of income from (the addition of a corresponding amount to) spending. And such withholdings of income from (additions to) spending are supposed to be the active cause of a balance of payments surplus (deficit).

If Marina v. M. Whitman's masterly survey of the monetary approach to the balance of payments,[23] which carries the awesome sponsorship of the departments .of State, Treasury, and Labour of the Government of the United States, and which has received the advice of two prominent authorities of the new approach, Rudiger Dornbush and Jacob A. Frenkel, among other distinguished economists, is to be relied upon as a fair representation of this approach, the theory goes as follows:

$$H = \pi(L - M) \tag{10}$$

i.e. hoarding H is defined as the addition to money balances induced by the stock excess demand for money. As defined above, π is the coefficient for the speed of adjustment. This hoarding is alternatively called the flow (excess?) demand for money.

$$py - Z = H \tag{11}$$

$$B = py - Z = H. \tag{12}$$

Hoarding is supposed to cause Z, desired nominal expenditure, to fall short of nominal income py, which leads to a corresponding balance of payments surplus B. And then

$$B = \dot{R} = \dot{M} \tag{13}$$

i.e. the balance of payments surplus leads to an increase in international reserves, which, assuming no sterilization of reserve inflows, increases the money supply. Thus the gap between the demand for money and the supply of money is filled up.

The definition of hoarding to include additions to both the transactions balances and the asset balances in this case is most unfortunate and misleading. For an increase in "money to spend" (i.e. transactions balances) cannot imply a withholding of money from spending out of income received, as these money balances *ex definitione* are meant to be spent. It is only the increase in the demand for money to hold that could imply a corresponding reduction in spending.[24]

One simple example will clarify the distinction and illustrate the confusion into which we are likely to fall when it is overlooked. Suppose we have a person with a monthly income of £100, who spends £80 of it over the month in an even stream and stashes the other £20 away in a shoe box, there being no other asset available for him to hold. At the beginning of this month, when he makes his decisions on spending, saving, and portfolio allocation, his demand for money at that particular moment is £20 for "money to hold" (i.e. asset balance) and £80 for "money to spend" (i.e. transactions balance). Looked at as an average over the month, his demand for money is £20 for asset balance and only £40 as transactions balance. Now let us suppose that, in the next month, he decides to spend the whole of his income, which remains at £100. At the beginning of the next month, his total demand for money at that point of time rises to £120: the £20 demand for money to hold is carried over from last month; but his demand for money to spend has increased from £80 to £100. Looked at as an average over the month, his demand for money has also increased when compared with that of the last month, though only by £10 from £60 to £70. Yet in spite of the increase in his demand for money no matter how we measure it, with his income remaining the same, his spending on goods has increased by £20 during the month, much to the confusion of those brought up to think in terms of the so-called Walras' Law and to treat the demands for transactions balances and asset balances with no distinction.

Readers of the article by Keynes quoted above should also have noticed that an increase in what he calls the "finance" demand for liquidity on the part of entrepreneurs certainly implies an increase in planned investment expenditure on their part. As I have pointed out in an earlier article,[25] the demand for "finance" is nothing but the demand for money to spend (or transactions balance), which Keynes would rather call the "active demand for liquidity" in contrast with the "inactive demand for liquidity," which correponds to what we call here the demand for money to hold.[26]

In the current real world, where on account of the high interest rates prevailing, money balances held certainly consist predominantly of transactions balances (i.e. money to spend), it is very odd indeed to hear the monetarists saying that an excess demand for money would actually lead to a shortfall of spending compared with income, which in turn would bring about a surplus in the balance of trade. An excess demand for money to spend generally implies an attempt to spend more than one's income. For in a modern monetary economy, incomes are normally received embodied in the form of money (so are sales receipts of firms). There is therefore no need for any person (or firm) to seek additional "money to spend" unless he (or it) intends to spend more than his income (or its receipts). For the community as a whole, an excess of the aggregate demand for "money to spend" over the total money supply is a sure indication that the community as a whole intends to spend (i.e. to consume and invest) more than its aggregate income. Strange indeed that modern monetarists should regard it as the sufficient condition for a failure to spend the entire income and, hence, as an explanation for a balance of trade surplus! Indeed, the ghost of Oscar Lange appears still to haunt the Chicago School long after he has gone physically.[27]

Nor can the attempt to explain the balance of payments by the excess demand for money be salvaged by introducing the capital account into the picture. An excess demand for money over the supply of money would normally tend to push up the rate of interest. If, as the proponents of the new monetary approach assume, the rate of interest is rigidly fixed at the international level by the perfect mobility of capital, this would lead to an equal amount of capital inflow or surplus on the capital account. So a surplus in the balance of payments is indeed brought about by an excess demand for money.

However, this cannot be the end of the story, if the excess demand for money is for spending (i.e. for transactions purposes). The resulting increase in money supply (even if we assume that there is strictly no multiple creation of money on the basis of the increase in international reserves) would surely result in an excess of expenditure over income and, hence, an excess demand for commodities, because the increase in money supply from abroad has now enabled the intention to spend more than income to be carried out. If again we assume with the new monetary approach that there is a single world market for goods with perfect commodity arbitrage between countries, this would then lead to an equal deficit on the trade account, which would offset the capital account surplus and bring the money supply down to its former level. So the ultimate result of an excess demand for money may only be a ripple in the balance of payments which quickly returns to equilibrium.

This is not a strange result at all; it is what the classical theory would teach us to expect. The inflow of financial capital leads to an equal net inflow of goods. The intention of the community to spend more than its income is fulfilled in actually purchasing more goods than it produces, at the cost, of course, of incurring some additional interest burden. If everything works out perfectly, i.e. if the financial capital inflow is exactly matched by a commodity import surplus, and only if so, money supply need not change at all. In the next period, if the domestic community still intends to spend more than its income, and, hence, again has an excess demand for "money to spend" over its money supply, and the domestic banking system is unwilling or unable to accommodate it, this process will be repeated, until at last the marginal cost of the additional interest burden exactly balances the marginal benefit of having more resources available than produced at home at zero rate of foreign borrowing.

If there is no such thing as a single world market for goods with perfect commodity arbitrage between countries, which is certainly more likely to be the fact, then things are much more complicated. The excess of expenditure over income, or the excess demand for goods, will partly be dissipated in pushing up prices on the domestic market and only partly result in an import surplus. How the impetus of the excess demand for goods will be split between causing a rise in domestic prices and bringing about an import surplus demands upon such familiar concepts as the elasticity of demand for imports with respect to their relative price ratio and the propensity to import, which the proponents of the new monetary approach would dismiss as unimportant, but without which the problem is really insoluble.

Anyway, this is not what the proponents of the modern monetary approach to the balance of payments would have us to expect. They would rather claim that the flow excess demand for money would somehow generate an overall balance of payments surplus of equal amount, which could either be a surplus on the capital account, or a surplus on the trade account, or a mixture of the two in any proportion. The overall balance of payments surplus would bring about an increase in international reserves, which would increase the domestic money supply to fill the gap between the demand for and the supply of money. And general equilibrium could thus be restored.

Obviously this can be true if the flow excess demand for money is entirely for adding to the asset demand for money, i.e. "the money to hold." Otherwise, to satisfy the excess demand for money with an increase in the supply, whether domestically or internationally generated, will always bring about an expansion in aggregate expenditure, which must have further repercussions on the balance of trade. What will happen in the end when there is no such thing as a single world market for goods cannot be predicted at all easily from the initial excess demand for money.

4. The Walras' Law Relation

By now many of you will probably be impatient to interrupt me by asking: "Have you not taken leave of Walras' Law somewhere in your argument?" The answer is "Yes, surely and wittingly." In my opinion, the so-called Walras' Law, as interpreted by Lange and Patinkin, certainly qualifies as the biggest red herring that has ever been drawn across the trails of monetary research in the past thirty years.

As should be clear from Walras' own discussion of the *tâtonnement* process, Walras' Law applies strictly only to simultaneous settlement of all the exchange transactions on all markets at a single set of prices. Under such strict conditions, the constaint that, for every participant in the exchange process, the value of goods he receives must be identically equal to the value of goods he offers in exchange for them can be expected to imply the so-called Walras' Law relation. If, however, all the transactions are not settled simultaneously, but are concluded at different points of time and not necessarily at the same set of prices, and if there may be a lot of trading back and forth in the same goods by the same person possibly at different prices, then it is no longer certain that the total value of the net amounts of different goods taken off the markets by any given participant over a fairly long period is necessarily equal to the total value of the net amounts of goods he supplies to the markets during the same period. The valuation of the cumulative net demand for, or supply of, any good over the period becomes a serious problem. The basic constraint that serves as the logical foundation of Walras' Law (commonly known as the budget constraint) cannot be stated simply as being that the net excess demands of each individual unit for all the goods traded, each valued at their respective current market prices, must sum up to zero. Walras' Law, if it can still be claimed to hold at all, simply degenerates into an accounting identity, namely, that the two sides of a double entry ledger must always add up to the same total. This can hardly be interpreted as a law that rules that the value of excess demand for one good (say, money) must equal the aggregate value of the excess supplies of all other goods. For this reason alone, we should be extremely wary of applying the so-called Walras' Law to cumulative accounts over a fairly long period.

More fundamentally, the demand for money as a behavioural function of other macroeconmic variables is particularly unsuitable to be fitted into the Walras' Law relation. Under the Walrasian scheme, it is the money balance which one is left with after all the transactions have been concluded and settled that is counted as one's "demand" for money. However, money being by definition the generally accepted medium of exchange, and sometimes the legal tender which one is legally obliged to accept, such temporary acceptances of money in exchange for other things, pending rational disposition later, are quite passive and irregular, and certainly do not conform to any stable behavioural function.

The rational demand for transactions balances, which monetary theorists try to formulate into a demand function for money, generally refers either to the average holding of money over the income period of an individual, or, more correctly in my opinion, to the planned holding of money at the very beginning of each spending period of an agent when he has not yet entered the markets for his planned purchases of that period (i.e. Keynes' finance demand for liquidity). Neither of these concepts can be fitted into the Walras' Law relation at all; for under the Walrasian scheme we are compelled to regard the amount of any good one is left with after all the transactions have been settled as one's "demand" for that good.

The simple numerical example we gave above can be used to demonstrate this much overlooked fact. In our example above, the person in the first month earns £100 by selling his labour service, and spends £80 of it on commodities. By the budget constraint as employed in the Walrasian scheme of analysis, he must be said to have a flow demand for money of £20. In the second month, he continues to earn £100 but spends the whole amount. By the budget constraint, he must be said to have a net flow demand for money of zero. Yet using the conventional measure of the demand for money as an average over the month, we have seen that the stock demand for money in the first month is £60: £20 for the asset balance and £40 for the transactions balance. In the second month, the stock demand for money similarly measured is £70: again £20 for the asset balance but £50 for the transactions balance. If the flow demand for money is defined as the increase in the stock demand per unit of time, then there is clearly a flow demand for money of £10 in the second month by this count, in contradiction to the budget constraint. This example clearly demonstrates that the Walrasian scheme of dealing with the demand for money completely leaves out the demand for money to be used as the medium of exchange during the process of transactions, as it only regards the amount of any good one is left with *after* the transactions as one's demand for that good.

Thus in applying indiscriminately the so-called Walras' Law relation to the excess demand for or supply of money, we either claim an equality between it and something else, which does not really hold, or we falsely identify something, which is obviously not the rational demand for money based on a behavioural function, as the demand for money.[28]

Finally, one should also bear in mind the invalidity of Walras' Law in a disequilibrium situation as pointed out by Clower (1965). In his 1965 article, he pointed out that when there is an excess supply of labour service (i.e. unemployment), it cannot be taken for granted that the excess supply of labour service necessarily implies an excess demand for other goods on the part of the unemployed as Walras' Law would lead one to believe. This kind of implicit excess demand for other goods might be "effective" and taken into account by the Walrasian imaginary auctioneer who coordinates all demand and supply functions to seek a simultaneous equilibrium solution. In the real world, however, where there is, of course, no such superhuman auctioneer, and where money is used as a necessary medium of exchange, the implicit excess demand for goods on the part of the unemployed simply does not become "effective," unless they can manage to sell their service for money first. Otherwise, their implicit excess demand for other goods is not registered at all by the price mechanism, as it is supposed to be in the mind of the all-observing Walrasian auctioneer.

We might add here that we cannot infer from Walras' Law that the excess supply of labour on the part of the unemployed implies a corresponding excess demand for money on their part. Again such alleged implicit excess demand for money is not effective in the harsh real world, because of the lack of credit-worthiness on the part of the unemployed. It is not registered in the money market and cannot exert any influence at all on the rate of interest. Thus the real world, which uses money as the medium of exchange, is indeed quite different from Walras' imaginary world with an all-observing auctioneer who solves simultaneously all the demand and supply equations for the equilibrium set of prices, though the vast number of economists who regularly invoke Walras' Law in their theorizing and prediction seem to be totally oblivious of the fact. To talk glibly that the excess supply of one thing necessarily implies a corresponding excess demand for all other things on the ground of Walras' Law is likely to lead to gross errors in the kind of real world we are living in.

It is indeed amazing that in spite of all its logical weaknesses, the so-called Walras' Law should have enjoyed the status of a basic axiom in monetary theory for so many years. If the modern monetary approach to the balance of payments claims Walras' Law as its theoretical foundation, then it is built upon shaky ground indeed. As often happens in the history of the development of economic science, attempts to derive facile and sweeping conclusions from simple accounting identities end up in something either false or trivial. The sweeping proposition of the modern monetary approach to the balance of payments theory that the over-all balance of payments surplus (or deficit) must be equal to the flow excess demand for (or supply of) money, derived as it is from the so-called Walras' Law, which, in a non-*tâtonnement* world, is nothing more than the accounting identity of a double-entry ledger, may well be the latest example of this general rule.

Notes

1. This is a revised version of a paper read at the International Economics Study Group Conference at Sussex University, September 1976, and again at the Money Study Group Seminar at the London School of Economics, October 1976.
2. Tsiang (1953).
3. Tsiang (1957).
4. Tsiang (1959).
5. Tsiang (1961).
6. J. A. Frenkel and H. G. Johnson (1976).
7. My own view on Walras' Law has been set out previously in Tsiang (1966).
8. Indeed, in a barter economy it would be impossible to have a balance of payments surplus or deficit.
9. Frenkel and Rodriguez (1975), p. 676, equation (7).
10. See Tsiang (1972).
11. R. Sato (1963).
12. H. G. Johnson (1973) and (1975).
13. Johnson (1973), p. 215.
14. Tsiang (1956) and (1968).
15. Keynes (1937).
16. See *Taiwan Statistical Data Book,* 1976.
17. C. N. Chen and J. H. Hsu (1974), p. 6. Rates of price increase with various lags have been tried as proxies for the expected rate of price inflation in this regression equation, but without any success. The regression coefficients obtained for these rates of price increase are not statistically significant. See also F. C. Liu (1970), ch. 3, in which, by using the statistics of the period 1949–68, he obtained an estimated income elasticity of the demand for money in Taiwan of 1.481.
18. *Taiwan Statistical Data Book,* 1976.
19. C. N. Chen and J. H. Hsu (1974), p. 7.
20. Frenkel and Johnson (1976), p. 25.
21. By the same token, the apparent insensitivity of the demand for money to changes in the interest rate offsetting the exogenous disturbances μ and u should not lead us to believe that the interest rate really has no significant influence on the demand for money. As may be seen from equation (9), the effect of the interest rate on the demand for money operates in two ways; first, we have the direct influence pf_i, which may well be quite negligible,

and secondly, there is the indirect influence $pf_E E_i$, which is by no means negligible, but which might be obliterated to a considerable extent by the opposite influences of μ and u, which the changes in i were meant to offset.

22. See, e.g. Hicks (1967), pp. 14–16 and p. 37, and Robertson (1946) ch. 1, p. 12.

Some economists, e.g. Pesek and Saving (1967), would strongly object to the distinction between "money to spend" and "money to hold" on the grounds that they are inseparable. It is perhaps necessary, therefore, for us to point out that the conceptual distinction between these two kinds of demand for money does not presume that there are two separate functions for them as, for instance, Keynes formulated them in his *General Theory*— i.e. as $L_1(Y)$ and $L_2(r)$, respectively.

Suppose we can all agree tentatively that the demand for money is an inseparable function such as

(i) $M_t^d = L(E_t, i_t, \hat{p}_t, \ldots)$,

where $\hat{p}_t$ is the expected rate of price inflation, which might be expected to influence the demand for money as a cost of holding money, like the interest rate i. Nevertheless, for comparison with the preceding period $t - 1$, this function can always be expanded into

(ia) $M_t^d = L(E_t, i_{t-1}, \hat{p}_{t-1}, \ldots) + L_i(i_t - i_{t-1}) + L_{\hat{p}}(\hat{p}_t - \hat{p}_{t-1}) +$

+ higher order terms in differentials and derivatives.

Thus comparing (ia) with the demand for money of the preceding period, i.e.,

(ii) $M_{t-1}^d = L(E_{t-1}, i_{t-1}, \hat{p}_{t-1}, \ldots)$

which, assuming that L is linear in E, can be rewritten as

(iia) $M_{t-1}^d = k(i_{t-1}, \hat{p}_{t-1}, \ldots)E_{t-1} + \bar{L}(i_{t-1}, \hat{p}_{t-1}, \ldots)$,

we can obtain by subtraction, after rewriting the first term on the right hand side of (ia) in the same manner,

(iii) $\Delta M_t^d = k(i_{t-1}, \hat{p}_{t-1}, \ldots)(E_t - E_{t-1}) + L_i \Delta i_t + L_{\hat{p}} \Delta \hat{p}_t + \ldots$

+ higher order terms in differentials and derivatives.

This equation would enable us to say, in spite of the inseparability of the money demand function, that the increase (or decrease) in the demand for money consists of two parts: first, an increase (or decrease) in the demand for money to spend (i.e. the first term on the right-hand side), and secondly, an increase (or decrease) in the demand for money to hold (the rest of the terms on the right-hand side).

The fastidiousness of Pesek and Saving about the inseparability of the transactions demand and the asset demand for money, therefore, appears to me rather out of place and unnecessary.

23. M. Whitman (1975), esp. pp. 495–502.

24. If, in equation (iii) of n. 2 pp. 328–9 above, we substituted Y_{t-1} for E_{t-1} on the ground that, if equilibrium in the money market had been established in the past period, then the final expenditure plans would have been carried out and thus have become income received, it would be at once obvious that an increase in the demand for money to spend (i.e. a positive first term on the right-hand side of equation (iii)) must imply an excess of current planned expenditure in excess of income received. It is plainly ridiculous to say that an increase in demand for money for this purpose must imply a corresponding withholding of money from spending out of income received.

25. Tsiang (1956), esp. p. 547.

26. Keynes (1937), esp. p. 668.

27. Oscar Lange who first coined the term "Walras' Law" and its current interpretation (1942) would probably denounce the "demand for money to spend" as a contradiction in terms. For according to his interpretation of Walras' system of equations, any purchase of goods with money is an act of supplying money to the market. Thus the term "demand for money to spend" is as self-contradictory as the demand for money to supply money, which must imply no net demand for money. In his Walrasian scheme of general equilibrium, therefore, the net demand for money consists only of the demand for money to hold.

   Such interpretation of Walras' Law amounts to a total denial of the basic function of money as the necessary medium of exchange. In actual fact, to spend money to buy goods is the normal way to make use of the essential function of money as the medium of exchange. It is not just an act to get rid of an excess supply of money.

   Lange's interpretation of the demand for money under the so-called Walras' Law is passed on to Patinkin, who declares that "the demand for money per unit of time is identically equal to the aggregate money value of all good supplied during the period. . . . A corresponding statement holds for the supply of money" (1949, p. 6) and again in his well-known book (1965, p. 35) that "the amount of excess demand for money equals the aggregate value of the amounts of excess supplies of commodities." Obviously, Lange–Patinkin's intepretation of Walras' Law and their definition of the demand for money have been handed down to the Chicago monetarists. We have more to say about Walras' Law in the next section.

28. A fuller discussion of this difficulty with Walras' Law is presented in Tsiang (1966). Somewhat similar views are presented in Clower (1967).

   Recently, D. K. Foley (1975) has also joined the ranks of disbelievers in "Walras' Law" in declaring that it does not apply to the demand and supply of money in the liquidity preference theory, because he has recognized, on the basis of Keynes' later emphasis on the "finance" demand for liquidity (Keynes, 1937), that the demand for money (or liquidity) is a "beginning-of-period" concept.

   Foley, however, argues that the loanable funds theory, being concerned with the "end of period equilibrium" (*sic*!), is still subject to Walras' Law. In view of the usual emphasis on "ex ante" analysis by loanable funds theorists, this is certainly a most astonishing statement. Foley's 1975 article indicates that he has never consulted any of the writings of D. H. Roberston, the chief exponent of the lonable funds theory, in preparing that article. This might be the reason for such a rash judgement. Any person who has read Robertson's 1939 lectures "Mr. Keynes and the Rate of Interest" and the present author's 1956 *AER* paper, and yet still insists that the loanable funds theory is concerned with what Foley calls the end-of-period equilibrium, must have had a very biased previous education indeed.

References

1. Chen, Chau-Nan, and Hsu, Jih-Ho, *Taiwan's Money Supply and Prices,* Economic Planning Council, Executive Yuan, Republic of China, memorandum **84**, Taipei, June 1974.
2. Clower, R. W., "The Keynesian Counterrevolution: A Theoretical Appraisal," F. H. Hahn and F. Brechling (eds.), *The Theory of Interest Rates,* Macmillan, 1965, ch. 5, pp. 103–25.
3. Clower, R. W., "Reconsideration of the Microformulations of Monetary Theory," *Western Economic Journal,* vol. 6, Mar. 1967, pp. 1–9.
4. Economic Planning Council, Executive Yuan, Republic of China, *Taiwan Statistical Data Book,* 1976.
5. Foley, D. K., "On Two Specifications of Asset Equilibrium on Macroeconomic Models," *Journal of Political Economy,* Apr. 1975, pp. 303–24.
6. Frenkel, J. A., and Johnson, H. G., "The Monetary Approach to the Balance of Payments: Essential Concepts and Historical Origins," in Frenkel and Johnson (eds.), *The Monetary Approach to the Balance-of-Payments,* Allen & Unwin, 1976, ch. 1, pp. 21–45.
7. Frenkel, J. A. and Rodriguez, C. A., "Portfolio Equilibrium and the Balance of Payments: A Monetary Approach," *American Economic Review,* vol. 65, Sept. 1975, pp. 674–88.
8. Hicks, Sir John, *Critical Essays in Monetary Theory,* Oxford, 1967.
9. Johnson, H. G., "The Monetary Approach to the Balance-of-Payments Theory," M. B. Connolly and A. K. Swoboda (eds.), *International Trade and Money—The Geneva Essays,* 1973, pp. 206–25.
10. Johnson, H. G., "The Monetary Approach to the Balance of Payments Theory: A Diagrammatic Analysis," *The Manchester School of Economics and Social Studies,* Sept. 1975, pp. 220–74.
11. Keynes, J. M., "The Ex-ante Theory of the Rate of Interest," *Economic Journal,* vol. 47, Dec. 1937, pp. 663–9.
12. Lange, Oscar, "Say's Law: A Restatement and Criticism," *Studies in Mathematical Economics and Econometrics,* University of Chicago Press, 1942.
13. Liu, Fu-Chi, *Essays on Monetary Development in Taiwan,* Taipei, Taiwan, 1970.
14. Patinkin, Don, "The Indeterminacy of Asbolute Prices in Classical Economics Theory," *Econometrica,* vol. 17, Jan. 1949, pp. 1–27.
15. Patinkin, Don, *Money, Interest and Prices,* 2nd ed., Harper & Row, 1965.

16. Pesek, B. P., and Saving, T., "The Demand for Money: Some Post Keynesian confusions," *Money, Wealth and Economic Theory,* Macmillan, 1967, ch. 14, pp. 323–31.

17. Robertson, D. H., *Essays in Monetary Theory,* Staples, 1946.

18. Sato, Ryuzo, "Fiscal Policy in a Neoclassical Growth Model: An Analysis of Time Required for Equilibrating Adjustment," *Review of Economic Studies,* vol. 30, Feb. 1963, pp. 16–23.

19. Tsiang, S. C., "The 1951 Improvement in the Danish Balance of Payments," *IMF Staff Papers,* vol. 3, 1953, pp. 155–70.

20. Tsiang, S. C., "Liquidity Preference and Loanable Funds Theories, Multiplier and Velocity Analyses: A Synthesis," *American Economic Review,* vol. 46, 1956, pp. 539–64.

21. Tsiang, S. C., "An Experiment with a Flexible Exchange Rate System: The Case of Peru, 1950–54," *IMF Staff Papers,* vol. 5, 1957, pp. 449–76.

22. Tsiang, S. C., "Floating Exchange Rate System in Countries with Relatively Stable Economies: Some European Experiences After World War I," ibid., vol. 7, 1959, pp. 244–73.

23. Tsiang, S. C., "The Role of Money in Trade Balance Stability," *American Economic Review,* vol. 51, 1961, pp. 912–36.

24. Tsiang, S. C., "Walras' Law, Say's Law, and Liquidity Preference in General Equilibrium Analysis," *International Economic Review,* vol. 7, Sept. 1966, pp. 329–45.

25. Tsiang, S. C., "The Precautionary Demand for Money: An Inventory Theoretical Approach," *Journal of Political Economy,* vol. 76, January and February 1969, pp. 99–117.

26. Tsiang, S. C., "The Rationale of the Mean-Standard-Deviation Analysis, Skewness Preference and the Demand for Money," *American Economic Review,* vol. 62, June 1972, pp. 354–71.

27. Whitman, Marina v. N., "Global Monetarism and the Monetary Approach to the Balance of Payments," *Brookings Papers,* Mar. 1975, pp. 491–555.

CHAPTER **8**

The Total Inadequacy of "Keynesian" Balance of Payments Theory, or Rather that of "Walras' Law"?*

S. C. Tsiang

In a sweeping article that appeared in the Sept. 1978 issue of *American Economic Review*, E. A. Kuska condemned as logically inconsistent practically the whole literature on the balance of payments theory that appeared in the postwar period, except those works that embrace the new Chicago monetary approach. A host of economists, including J. E. Meade, J. M. Fleming, J. Vanek, R. A. Mundell, A. Kruger, E. Sohmen, R. W. Jones, J. Niehans, R. N. Cooper, and myself, have been the victims of his criticism. Even some of his distinguished fellow members of the Chicago School of Monetary Approach, e.g., H. G. Johnson, R. A. Mundell, A. K. Swoboda and R. Dornbush, either in their moments of unwariness, or before their total conversion to the "new truth," came under his relentless censure.

Readers will no doubt ask: "How come that so many prominent economists have been guilty of apparent logical inconsistencies without themselves realizing what they were doing?" Indeed, as Kuska himself exclaimed, "It will be an interesting topic in the history of economic

Reprinted with permission from *Economic Essays*, National Taiwan University, Vol. XIII (June 1985).

analysis to attempt to explain how international monetary economics was able to develop along these lines for such an extended period of time."[1]

As one who had only recently raised certain objections to the modern monetary approach to the balance of payments theory.[2] I think I can offer a straightforward explanation to this question. In a single sentence, the explanation lies in the fact that while Kuska and his fellow proponents of the monetary approach hold that the so-called Walras' Law is strictly applicable to all transactions in or out of equilibrium, the economists attacked by him have, consciously or unconsciously, rejected the so-called Walras' Law as inapplicable to the real world.

As early as 1966, I had published an article entitled "Walras' Law, Say's Law and Liquidity Preference in General Equilibrium Analysis," denouncing the so-called Walras' Law as interpreted by 0. Lange and D. Patinkin.[3] In my 1977 criticism of the modern monetary approach to the balance of payments theory, I pointed out that the identification of the balance of payments surplus (or deficit) with the excess demand for (or supply of) money is the fortuitous result of the misapplication to the real world of the so-called Walras' Law, which I described as "the biggest red herring that has ever been drawn across the trail of monetary research in the past thirty years."[4]

Now Kuska's article serves as an excellent illustration demonstrating how Walras' Law could befuddle one's thinking on monetary theory. So let us see what kind of arguments he was marshalling for his attack on the Keynesian theory. His attack starts with the widely used IS-LM model, viz.,

$$Y = C + I \tag{1}$$

$$C = C(Y, r) \tag{2}$$

$$I = I(r) \tag{3}$$

$$M = L(Y, r) \tag{4}$$

where equation (1) is said to be the condition for equilibrium on the commodity market, and equation (4) is the equilibrium condition for the money market. Equations (2) and (3) are the behavioral functions for aggregate consumption and investment. He then says that while Walras' Law permits the suppression of the equilibrium condition for the remaining goods, viz., bonds, it perforce implies that the implicit demand function for bonds must take a most implausible form. For the aggregate budget constraint, according to Lange and Patinkin's interpretation of Walras' Law, implies that the excess demands for commodities, bonds, and money, respectively, must add up to zero in or out of equilibrium, i.e.,

$$[C + I - Y] + [L(Y, r) - M] + 1/r[H(\ ) - A] = 0 \qquad (5)$$

where $H(\ )$ is the demand function for bonds, A is the supply of bonds and $1/r$ the price of bonds. This implies that

$$H(\ ) = r[Y - C - I] + r[M - L(Y, r)] + A$$

$$= \bar{H}(Y, r) + A + rM \qquad (6)$$

where $\bar{H}(Y, r)$ is an expression in Y and r, summarizing all the terms in Y and r in equation (6), (presumably, except the term rM). This allegedly inevitable implication is said to be most implausible, because "firstly any exogenous increase in the quantity of bonds will be willingly held (demanded) no matter what the values of the level of income, the rate of interest and the quantity of money;" "secondly, any increase in money stock is, for any given level of income, the stock of bonds and the rate of interest, *entirely used to purchase bonds.*" (Sic!)[5] Such implausible implications are alleged to be totally unnoticed by the innumerable users of the popular IS-LM model.

Next, turning to the two country model, he uses the same approach to show that the aggregate budget constraint for each country (or the so-called Walras' Law) implies that the overall balance of payments must equal the domestic excess demand for money, which implication is now regarded as the basic tenet of the modern monetary approach to the balance of payments theory. Thus, since most earlier economists have assumed in their models for the balance of payments analysis that the equilibrium in the domestic monetary market is achieved at all times, it is claimed that they have thereby implied that the balance of payments must be zero at all times also. It is, therefore, logically inconsistent to use such models to explain the existence or the variations of the balance of payments deficit or surplus.[6]

Furthermore, as in most Keynesian type of two-country models the equations for bonds for both countries are usually suppressed together, he contends that this is suppressing one equation too many and would result in indeterminancy of the system, because Walras' Law permits the omission of only one market clearing condition.[7]

These are very serious charges. If the economists he criticizes were totally unaware of such alleged logical inconsistencies in their theoretical structures, they should, indeed, be condemned as unworthy. But to be fair, Kuska and his fellow monetarists should also question themselves whether the so-called Walras' Law, which turns so many theoretical models into such travesties, is not itself at fault. They should at least take a look at the arguments given by those who explicitly object to such applications of Walras' Law, why the so-called Walras' Law might be totally irrelevant to the real world.

In Tsiang (1966), I already objected strongly to the application of Walras' Law to monetary theory and macroanalysis in general. Again in 1977, I pointed out specifically that it is invalid to apply this pseudo law to the balance of payments analysis as it is commonly done by the modern monetary approach. As these papers, as well as others by Clowers, etc.,[8] appear to have totally escaped Kuska's attention, and as already a whole generation of economists have been (and more are still being) indoctrinated with this pseudo law as a basic axiom of economics, it is high time that we take a look at the source of this law and its logical foundation.

Walras' Law, as interpreted and formulated by its principal exponents, Lange and Patinkin,[9] is an illegitimate extension of the budget constraints in Walras' grandiose scheme for the simultaneous determination of prices and quantities of commodities through the fictitious process of *tâtonnement* by a superhuman auctioneer. Walras himself never formulated such a law, and, as we shall presently see, he would be the first one to object to its application to the supply and demand for money. The simultaneous settlement of the demand and supply equations for all goods through the effort of an auctioneer is only an expedient theoretical device of his to avoid the indeterminancy of the final equilibrium that would result from the indeterminable paths of trading at nonequilibrium prices before final equilibrium is approached.[10] It is certainly not meant to be a faithful description of the real world. At best, it is a crude first attempt to simulate the real world.

When all transactions, buying and selling, or demands and supplies, are settled simultaneously at a single set of equilibrium prices, it naturally follows that the aggregate demand of every one who participates in trading must equal his aggregate supply for all goods traded, including the commodity chosen as numeraire and used as the means of settling the discrepancies. When the amount of numeraire, which traders receive, or pay out, to settle the clearing discrepancies of their transactions is falsely identified as their demands for, or supplies of, money, we get the so-called Walras' Law as taught at first by Lange and Patinkin at Chicago and subsequently spread throughout the United States, that the demand for money is identically equal to the net aggregate excess supply of all other goods.

The Walrasian scheme of simultaneous clearing of all transactions with numeraire money used only for settling the final clearing discrepancies, however, is a gross distortion of the real world, where money is needed as the medium of exchange and not all transactions are cleared and settled simultaneously. In the real world, no economic entity, firm or household, enjoys perfect synchronization between all his purchases and sales. Indeed, one of the functions of money is to enable economic entities to separate the purchases of goods they need from the sales of goods they produce or have in surplus, so that purchases and sales can be done independently, each at their own appropriate times and in their appropriate quantities. In order to carry out his purchase plans at the most convenient moments, it is necessary to have money, the necessary medium of exchange (or means of payment) on hand. Thus, there is a transactions demand for money (or what Keynes in 1937 chose to call the "finance demand for liquidity")[11] prior to the consummation of any act of purchases. And only those demands for goods that are backed by the holding of adequate means of payments (or generally accepted substitutes for it) are "effective" in the real world.

This kind of transactions demand (or "finance demand") for money will be totally left out when one follows the above Walrasian simulation. When all transactions are settled simultaneously, there will be no need for transactions balances at all, so long as one does not intend to spend beyond one's income, or proceeds from one's simultaneous sales of goods and securities. Furthermore, under the Walrasian scheme, it is the amount of the numeraire, which one is left with after the transactions have been settled, that is to be counted as one's "demand" for that numeraire. In the real world, however, where money is not just a numeraire but, by definition, the generally accepted means of payment and frequently the legal tender of the country which one is obliged to accept for the settlement of debts, such temporary acceptances of money in exchange for other goods sold, pending rational disposition later, are quite passive and irregular, and certainly do not conform to any stable behavioral function worthy of the name of a demand function for money.

The rational demand for transactions balances, which traditional monetary theorists tried to formulate into a demand function, generally refers either to the average holding of money of an economic entity over a given period, or more meaningfully in my opinion, to the planned holding of money at the beginning of each expenditure decision period before he has yet entered the market for commodities (i.e., Keynes' finance demand for liquidity). Neither of these demand functions for money can be fitted into the Walras' Law relation at all; for under the Walrasian scheme we are compelled to regard the amount of any good one is left with after all the transactions have been settled as one's "demand" for that good, be it money or any other commodity. The pretrading demand for transactions balances (or finance) is totally excluded.[12] Therefore, I said in my 1977 paper: "In applying indiscriminately the so-called Walras' Law relation to the excess demand for or supply of money, we either claim an equality between it and something else, which does not really hold, or we falsely identify as the demand for money something, which is obviously not the rational demand for money.[13]

In fact, Walras himself would probably be the first one to deny the validity of this pseudo law ironically named after him. For he had obviously realized that his theoretical construct of perfect synchronized transactions through the arbitration of a superhuman auctioneer would eliminate all demands for money as transactions balances. He soon set about to remedy this in Part VI of the definitive edition of his *Elements* under the heading of "Theory of Circulation and Money." *The preliminary tâtonnement,* that is supposed to determine the relative prices and quantities supplied of goods and services, is supposed to be conducted by means of "tickets" ("bons") only.[14] The actual purchases and transfers of goods and services, however, will begin later against payments in real money, the generally accepted means of payments. Here, apparently, he just posited that the payments for services and the payments for products are to be made in money *at fixed dates,* which presumably are not identical with each other. Therefore, to ensure the availability of those products or services he wishes to purchase before he can receive payments for his sales of services or products, each individual would desire to keep in his possession a cash balance equal in value to all or part of the goods which he wishes to purchase.[15] In Walras' own expression, "the value of all or part of the final products and perpetual net income which the parties to the exchange *wish to purchase,* and which they desire to keep in their possession in the form of cash or money savings, constitutes their desired cash-balance (*encaisse désirée*)."[16]

The phrase "which the parties to the exchange *wish to purchase*" should be particularly noted, for it indicates that what Walras calls the *encaisse désirée* consists mainly of the demand for transactions balance, or the finance demand for liquidity, which depends upon the amount of purchases of other products that the individual concerned intends to make shortly. This should be contrasted with Lange and Patinkin's definition of the demand for money derived from their misinterpretation of Walras. Apparently they regard the preliminary *tâtonnement* of Walras as covering all the transactions in the real world. Thus, on the basis of the budget constraint of the first *tâtonnement*, Lange declared that any purchase of goods with money is an act of *supplying money* to the market, and that it is rather *the sale of other goods* that constitutes the demand for money.[17] Similarly, Patinkin contended that in or out equilibrium "the demand for money per unit of time, is identically equal to the *aggregate money value of all goods supplied during the period.*"[18] Since Walras' *encaisse désirée* is clearly defined as the pretrading holdings of cash balances in readiness to make purchases, it naturally does not fit into the so-called Walras' Law, which is no more than an illegitimate extention of the budget constraint for the fictitious preliminary *tâtonnement*. This is of no concern of Walras, because he is specifically arguing that *the encaisse désirée* will play its role only in the second tâtonnement, which will equate the aggregate demand for money to the existing stock of money by adjusting the price of the numeraire in terms of money, and, hence, the general price level.[19]

It is far from my intention to justify or defend Walras' theory of money, which, personally, I regard as still beset with defects.[20] I want only to emphasize here that the so-called Walras' Law is not Walras' own law, and that he would certainly not regard it as applicable to the demand for money, insofar as he would want to treat the excess demand for money entirely differently from all other excess demands, and make it operate alone in a separate *tâtonnement* subsequent to the preliminary one in which only "tickets" (not money) are used for the biddings and askings.

If it is realized that in the real world, where purchases and sales are indeed not all synchronized, and the demand for money consists mostly of pretrading demand for transactions balances (or finance), the so-called Walras' Law cannot, therefore, apply to the excess demand for money, then all Kuska's criticisms on the traditional and Keynesian models of trade can be dismissed as invalid at one stroke. There is really no valid reason at all to believe that the balance of payments of a country is identically equal to the excess demand for money; nor is there any ground to contend that IS-LM model implies implausible assumptions about the form of the demand function for bonds. The entire logical structure of Kuska's arguments would collapse with the realization of the inapplicability of the so-called Walras' Law to the money using real world.

Here readers who are brought up on the Walrasian general equilibrium approach to monetary theory (as taught by Patinkin and his followers) would surely raise the following question; viz., if we dismiss Walras' Law as inapplicable to the excess demand for money, then how could we eliminate the extra market equilibrium equation from the model? The truth is that the so-called Walrasian way of eliminating the otiose equation (*pace* Hicks) has never provided a satisfactory explanation why out of the pair of the supply and demand equations for money and bonds, respectively, one may be suppressed. In Walras' preliminary *tâtonnement,* any good can be chosen arbitrarily as the numeraire, and its excess demand equation can be said to follow from the others. However, no sensible economist has ever thought fit to suppress the excess demand equation for one of the commodities (say, peanuts), and retain instead the excess demand equations for both money and bonds.

It is true that in a money using economy, an effective demand for any good other than money must be a demand in terms of money, and an effective supply of any good other than money must be a supply in exchange for money. Thus, in a sense, when the aggregate demands for all other good are equal to their aggregate supplies, the money offered in purchase must equal the money accepted in sales. This is probably the equality between the supply of and demand for money which the believers in Walras' Law claim to follow from other market equilibrium equations. But this kind of equality between the money offered in purchases and the money accepted in sales—i.e., the "mirror image demand for and supply of money," as aptly called by Valavanis[21]—has nothing to do at all with the determination of the interest rate, or, in other words, with the equilibrium of the "money market" in the sense of common parlance.[22]

It was Keynes who first put forward the proposition in his *General Theory* that the interest rate (or the price of bonds in a simple three goods model) is determined by the supply and demand for money rather than by the supply and demand for bonds. Keynes certainly did not invoke Walras—let alone the so-called Walras' Law—for this switch. The only reference to Walras in the *General Theory* was to the effect that "he is strictly in the classical tradition" in maintaining that "the rate of interest is fixed at the point where saving, which represents the supply of new capital, is equal to the demand for it."[23]

Furthermore, Keynes' later admission (1937) of the finance demand for liquidity, which, as he explicitly pointed out, exists prior to the spending, hence, a "beginning of period" concept as termed by Foley (1975). This fact would clearly make his concept of the demand for money incompatible with the "end of period" concept of the temporary acceptance of money for the sales of other goods, mistakenly identified as the demand for money by Lange and Patinkin. Thus, as has also been pointed out by Foley, the so-called Walras' Law is clearly inapplicable to Keynes' demand and supply equation for money. The explanation why the demand and supply equation for money may be substituted for the demand and supply equation for bonds should never be sought through the so-called Walras' Law. No tears need to be shed for debunking this pseudo law on this score.

Keynes and Keynesians would probably insist that the supply and demand equation for money is the only relevant equilibrium condition for the determination of the interest rate, not just an alternative to supply and demand equation for bonds. It is, however, against our common sense that the price of bonds (i.e., the interest rate) should have nothing to do with the demand and supply for bonds. This is particularly so, if we have to determine a whole structure of interest rates of long, medium, and short terms. How can a single supply and demand equation for money determine a whole structure of interest rates of different terms? The excess demand for money must in some sense be an abbreviated expression for the excess demand for bonds in general, but the connection cannot be the Walrasian budget constraint.[24]

I have, therefore, proposed to establish this connection through what I called the "requirement for finance constraint."[25] In the real world where money is used as the medium of exchange, the possession of ready cash (or acceptable money substitutes) is required to carry out purchases of commodities. Therefore, it we take a period so short that the velocity of circulation of money against commodities is equal to one (i.e., that money can be used only once to buy commodities or services), then we should have the constraint that

$$C^d + M^*(r, W) - M^s \equiv (B^s - B^d).^{26}$$

That is, the finance for C^d, the planned purchases of commodities, plus the demand for idle asset balances M^*, if any, which is probably a function of the interest rate and total wealth, must be adequately covered by money at hand, M^s, supplemented by net borrowing (net sales proceeds of bonds, $B^s > B^d$).[27] If the finance required for the planned purchases of commodities plus the demand for idle balances fall short of the total stock of money at hand, then the excess supply of money would be lended out (or used to buy bonds, $B^s < B^d$). This constraint implies that the excess demand for money identically equals the excess supply of bonds, regardless of whether the markets for commodities and services are in or out of equilibrium. When the excess demand for bonds is reduced to zero, it follows that the excess demand for money will also be zero, and vice versa. There is absolutely no need to invoke the so-called Walras' Law, which is after all an illegitimate extention of the budget constraint for Walras' fictitious preliminary *tâtonnement*.

Thus, when those Keynesian models for the balance of payments analysis make the simplifying assumption that the equilibrium condition for the money market,[28] i.e.,

$$L(Y,\ r,\ W,) = M^s,[29]$$

holds at all times, it certainly does not follow that by implication of the so-called Walras' Law, the balance of payments of the country concerned must necessarily be balanced at all times, which the monetarists treat as one of their newly discovered truths.

Moreover, since there is a similar requirement for finance constraint for each country, the suppression of the bond equations in both countries in a two-country model certainly would not lead to any indeterminancy, as contended by Kuska.[30]

Indeed, Kuska and his fellow monetarists should not be so rash as to criticize at one sweep the traditional and Keynesian economists before they have read any of the literature objecting to the application of the so-called Walras' Law to the real world. It is really scandulous of our education of economists that a whole generation of young economists have been turned out by our universities, who having credulously swallowed the so-called Walras' Law as an incontrovertible axiom of economics without ever pondering over its logical basis or bothering to look up Walras to see what he really said, would simply revel in applying routine mathematical operations to systems of equations capped with the Walras' Law constraint, or in drawing phase diagrams with locii of equilibria for different markets supposed to intersect one another at a single point on account of the so-called Walras' Law. Profound advancements in economic science are actually being expected from this kind of exercises, as witnesses the vast amount of research grants poured out on them. Indeed, Kuska appears to be just one of the Alices, who, having been piped by her mentors into the pseudo-Walrasian Wonderland through the magic looking glass of the so-called Walras' Law, happens to look back through it and finds people who remain outside seemingly doing everything in what now appears to her the topsy-turvey ways.

Notes

*This paper has been circulated for discussion in its preliminary form as Working Paper No. 185 of the Department of Economics, Cornell University, U.S.A.
1. Kuska [1978], p. 669.
2. Tsiang [1977].
3. Tsiang [1966].
4. Tsiang [1977], p. 333.
5. 1978, p. 660. Here Kuska seems to have overlooked the presence of r as the coefficient of M.
6. Kuska [1978], pp. 661–2.
7. Kuska [1978], p. 662.
8. E.g., Valavanis (1955); Clower (1967); Foley (1975), etc.
9. Lange (1942), Patinkin (1949) and (1965).
10. See Kaldor (1934).
11. Keynes (1937).
12. Tsiang (1966) and (1977).
13. Tsiang (1977), p. 335.
14. Walras (1926), Preface to the 4th edition, p. 37, Lesson 20, p. 242, and Lesson 29, p. 316.
15. *Ibid.,* pp. 316–321.
16. *Ibid.,* p. 321.
17. Lange (1942), p. 50.
18. Patinkin (1949), p. 6; and (1965), p. 35.
19. Walras (1926), Lesson 30.
20. E.g., the fact that Walras takes the interest rate as already determined by the preliminary *tâtonnement* together with all the relative prices so that the second *tâtonnement* for the demand and supply of money merely determines the absolute price level; and that he regards the intended purchases of bonds and other financial securities as a source of the demand for cash balances just like the planned purchases of commodities, instead of treating the former differently as an outlet for investing excess holdings of cash; his assumption that the fixed dates of purchases and sales of goods and services are all given exogeneously, etc.
21. Valavanis (1955), p. 353.
22. In common parlance, the "money market" is simply another name for

security market, or, more strictly, the short term sector of the latter.

The sloppy habit of the modern "Walrasian" or rather "Patinkinian" monetary theorists of referring to the "money market" as some nebulous entity separate and different from the bond market, even in a three goods (money, bonds, and commodities) economy is most confusing. For it takes at least two goods to constitute a market. If commodity market is where commodities are traded for money, and bond market is where bonds are traded for money, what remains to be traded for money on the so-called money market? If money is a homogeneous stock, it makes no sense to say that money is traded against money on the money market. The only way to make sense out of that sentence is to interpret it to mean that on the money market present money is traded against future money, which leads us to the common parlance meaning of the term, viz., the synonym of bond market in a broad sense.

23. *General Theory*, pp. 176–177.
24. Foley in (1975) recognized also that because of Keynes' later emphasis on the "finance" demand for liquidity, his demand for money is what may be called a "beginning-of-period" concept. Since the Walras' Law refers only to the "end-of-period" demands and supplies, it cannot be applied to the demand and supply of money in the Keynesian liquidity preference theory.

For some strange reason, however, Foley would regard this freedom from the constraint of Walras' Law as a privilege enjoyed only by the Keynesian liquidity preference theory, and would deny it to the Robertsonian loanable funds. This is surely a mistake based on partisan rather than scientific spirit. See Tsiang (1956) and (1980) for an explanation why what is true for Keynes' finance demand for liquidity must also be true for Robertson's demand for loanable funds.

25. Tsiang (1966), pp. 335–338.
26. Ibid., p. 338, see also Tsiang (1980).
27. Of course, C^d, the planned purchases of commodities, i.e., planned consumption and investment expenditures, are themselves functions of income level and interest rates. See Tsiang (1956), pp. 554–555; Tsiang (1977), pp. 326–327; and also Tsiang (1980).
28. It is to be remembered that here the money market is to be understood as synonymous to the bond market as in common parlance, instead of as an imaginary separate market for money which modern Patinkinian monetary theorist are wont to talk about. See footnote 22 above.
29. The demand for money function, $L(Y, r, W)$, which the Keynesians as well as the Chicago monetarists are accustomed to use, should really be revised to $L(C + I, r, W)$ since the demand for transactions balances (or finance) is meant to finance expenditures. It is true that expenditures are themselves functions of Y and r, perhaps also W. However, the relation between money demand and Y would thus be once removed. As a function of functions of income and interest rates, more exogenous disturbances and stochastic elements could then slip in and makes the demand function for money less stable and less predictable. See Tsiang (1977), pp. 326–327.
30. Kuska, *op. cit.*, p. 662.

References

1. R. W. Clower, "Reconsideration of the Microformulation of Monetary Theory," *Western Economic Journal,* March 1967, **6**, pp. 1–9.
2. D. K. Foley, "On Two Specifications of Asset Equilibrium on Macroeconomic Models," *Journal of Political Economy,* April 1975, **83**, pp. 303–324.
3. Nicholas Kaldor, "A Classificatory Note on the Determinateness of Equilibrium," *Review of Economic Studies,* Feb. 1934, 1. pp. 122–36.
4. J. M. Keynes, "The Ex Ante Theory of the Rate of Interest," *Economic Journal,* Dec. 1937, **47**, pp. 663–69.
5. Edward Kuska, "On the Almost Total Inadequacy of Keynesian Balance of Payments Theory," *American Economic Review,* Sept. 1978, **68**, pp. 659–70.
6. Oscar Lange, "Say's Law: A Restatement and Criticism," *Studies in Mathematical Economics and Econometrics,* ed. O. Lange, F. E. McIntyre and T. O. Yntema (Chicago: University of Chicago Press, 1942), pp. 49–68.
7. Don Patinkin, "The Indeterminacy of Absolute Prices in Classical Economic Theory," *Econometrica,* Jan. 1949, **17**, pp. 1–27.
8. Don Patinkin, "Money, Interest and Prices," 2nd ed., (New York, Harper & Row, 1965).
9. S. C. Tsiang, "Liquidity Preference and Loanable Funds Theories, Multiplier and Velocity Analyses: A Synthesis," *American Economic Review,* Sept. 1956, **46**, pp. 539–64.
10. S. C. Tsiang, "Walras' Law, Say's Law and Liquidity Preference in General Equilibrium Analysis," *International Economic Review,* Sept, 1966, **7**, pp. 326–45.
11. S. C. Tsiang, "The Monetary Theoretic Foundation of the Modern Monetary Approach to the Balance of Payments," *Oxford Economic Papers,* Nov. 1977, **29**, pp. 319–38.
12. S. C. Tsiang, "Keynes's Finance Demand for Liquidity, Robertson's Loanable Funds Theory, and Friedman's Monetarism," *Quarterly Journal of Economics,* May 1980, **94**, pp. 465–91.

CHAPTER 9

The Flow Formulation of the Money Market Equilibrium for an Open Economy and the Determination of the Exchange Rate

S. C. Tsiang*

Since the ascendency of the Keynesian liquidity preference theory, it has come to be widely believed that the right approach to monetary problems should be the so-called stock approach or the portfolio allocation approach. Keynes emphasized that money is an asset to hold. From this observation it seems natural to conclude that monetary equilibrium should imply that the demand to hold money should be equal to the total stock of money.

The stock approach (or portfolio allocation approach) has become so prevalent that even the determination of the exchange rate and the balance of payments have now come to be explained in terms of the stock equilibria of the supply and demand for money and other assets.

In my opinion, the stock approach, however, involves many conceptual difficulties. First of all, it obscures the fact that even though in times of economic depression money is partly held as a store of value, the major bulk of money is normally moving in a continuous circular flow. It is constantly passing out of the hands of one person as the

Reprinted with permission from *Finance Constraints, Expectations, and Macroeconomics*, Oxford University Press, 1988.

means of payment for his expenditures into the hands of others as the embodiment of their incomes and sales proceeds, and in turn will be expended, and so on *ad infinitum*. Thus money is like a body of fluid (or liquid), which is constantly flowing and circulating. To apply the concept of stock equilibrium to such a dynamic body of liquid is hardly appropriate. What we should borrow from physics to apply to the analysis of monetary problems are not the concepts of fluid-statics, where the concept of stock equilibrium may be appropriate, but rather those of fluid-dynamics. The only sort of equilibrium we can meaningfully discuss about a flowing body of liquid is some kinds of flow equilibrium.

Even Professor Tobin, who used to be one of the leading advocates of the stock (or portfolio balance) approach to monetary theory, recently switched quite unheraldedly to the flow approach in his acceptance speech for the Nobel Prize Award in 1981.[1] He has come to recognize that the money market cannot operate within a dimensionless point of time, but must operate in finite time periods, which he called slices of time. Furthermore, he recognized that the equilibrium which can be expected in such a short slice of time can only be that existing between the adjustments in the stock demanded and the stock supplied during the period. Since adjustments in stocks per time period are *ex definitione* flows, Tobin's newly formulated general assets equilibrium theory is, therefore, a sort of flow equilibrium analysis.

Moreover, Tobin at the same time also admitted that, in such a short period as a slice of time, portfolios of individual agents cannot adjust fully to new market information. Lags in response are inevitable and rational in view of the costs of transactions and decisions. Consequently, even when the money market has brought the flow demand for and supply of money (adjustments in stock demand and supply *inter alia*) to equality, the stock demand for and the total existing stock of money need not have reached a mutual equilibrium, which the stock approach economists used to presume as being attainable at every point of time. Indeed, in a dynamic and changing world, the stock equilibrium between aggregate money holdings and the supply of money may never be fully attained.

Furthermore, we should bear in mind that the demand for finance for planned investment expenditure (indeed for planned consumption expenditure as well), which Keynes[2] had admitted he should not have overlooked in his *General Theory*, is really of the nature of a flow generated by a flow decision to invest (or to consume). It is not meant to be held as an asset but is meant to be used in the sense of being expended. Furthermore, the expending of it automatically creates a new disequilibrium in stock holdings. As Keynes himself put it in his second reply to Ohlin, "'Finance' is a revolving fund. . . . As soon as it is used in the sense of being expended, the lack of liquidity is automatically made good and the readiness to be unliquid is available to be used over again."[3] This is essentially a reaffirmation of the traditional conception of the circular flow of money, which flow approach economists had emphasized from the outset, but which Keynes himself had pushed into the obscure background with his emphasis in the *General Theory* that the entire stock of money is being held voluntarily in a general portfolio equilibrium at every moment!

Finally, there is one more difficulty with the stock formulation of the monetary equilibrium which was again recognized by Keynes himself but was neglected by his followers. In his first reply to Ohlin and others, Keynes admitted that "saying that the rate of interest depends on the demand and supply of money.. . . may be *misleading,* because it obscures the answer to the question, demand for money in terms of what?"[4] The correct answer to this question, in Keynes' own opinion, is obviously the one contained in his preceding sentence: "The liquidity preference theory of the rate of interest which I have set forth in my *General Theory of Employment, Interest and Money* makes the rate of interest to depend on the present supply of money and the demand schedule for a present claim on money *in terms of a deferred claim on money*."[5] Thus the money market he has in mind is just the market for deferred claims on money in terms of present money (which other economists are more accustomed to call the market for credit or loans, or bonds, etc.) looked at from the reverse side. The only substantial difference of his new theory with the traditional theory lies in his insistence that the demand for and supply of money, or the supply of and demand for deferred claims on money, should be stated in terms of stocks at each point of time rather than in terms of flows (or changes in stocks) per period of time, and that the equilibrium should be at each point of time rather than for each period of time.

We have already seen above why stock equilibrium at every point of time is not an appropriate concept for studying the circular flow of money in a dynamic world. Now we shall see how *misleading* it has in fact been to say, with Keynes, that the demand and supply of money determine the rate of interest. As Keynes himself had somehow pre-saged, it had indeed obscured the answer to the question "Demand for money in terms of what?" The confusion that ensued was compounded further by the misapplication of the so-called Walras' Law by Lange and Patinkin to the demand for money. Patinkin was known to have said that, on the basis of Walras' Law, every demand for commodities implies a supply of money to the market and every supply of commodities implies a demand for money.[6] Thus an excess supply of peanuts as well as an excess supply of labor may be said to imply an excess demand for money, and presumably would hence exert an influence to push the interest rate up! This is indeed a far cry from Keynes' definition of the demand for money as "the demand schedule for a present claim on money *in terms of a deferred claim on money*," and, needless to say, the conclusion it would lead to is quite contrary to the spirit of Keynes' theory.

I have been on record as a strong objector to the application of Walras' Law to monetary analysis.[7] The basic reason, stated briefly, is that the so-called Walras' Law assumes that all transactions are carried out and cleared against each other at the same time, whereas in the real world large numbers of different transactions are usually carried out at different points of time and in different locations. They are not all cleared against each other, but most of them have to be paid for with money, the generally accepted means of payment. Furthermore, this money must be available and held by the potential buyers before each transaction is executed (unless some substitute for money is used). This imposed a new constraint, which I called the "finance restraint,"[8] using the word "finance" in the sense of Keynes' "finance demand for liquidity."[9] Alternatively it has also been termed very aptly by Clower the "money first constraint."[10] Whatever it is called, it is a much stricter constraint than the "budget constraint" which forms the basis of Walras' Law. Because this much stricter constraint is in force in the real world, the deductions made from the looser constraint are not always valid, and can sometimes be very misleading, as the example given above shows.

Since the "finance constraint" is based on the fundamental observation that money does not circulate with infinite velocity, and since velocity of circulation has no place in stock analysis at points of time where nothing circulates, we must switch from stock analysis to flow analysis, or more specifically to loanable funds analysis. The flow nature of the demand for and supply of loanable funds is based upon the crucial conception that, in a money-using economy, the major bulk of money normally exists in a continuous circular flow. A part of the money in this endless circular flow, however, is observed to be constantly being diverted into a side stream leading to the money market, where it constitutes the supply of loanable funds. From there, borrowers of loanable funds would then take them out and in general would put them back into the main circular stream of expenditures and incomes (receipts).

The emphasis on the flow nature of loanable funds does not imply that the loanable funds theory would be unaware that there are sometimes money balances held inactive, like stagnant puddles lying off the main stream of the money flow. The loanable funds theory, however, would maintain that these stocks of money lying off the main circular flow, as well as the stock of money inside the main circular flow, have no direct impact on the money market except indirectly as arguments of the functions of the flows going into the money market. It is only when people attempt to divert money from the main circular flow into the money market (saving), or into the stagnant puddles (hoarding), or conversely try to withdraw the inactive money from the stagnant puddles for re-injection into the circular flow or into the money market (dishoarding), that the interest rate will be directly affected. In other words, only adjustments in the idle balances (hoarding or dishoarding), together with the regular flows of savings and investment, exert a direct influence on the interest rate.

Since flows mut be measured over time, we must choose a convenient unit to measure time. To take account of the fact that money does not circulate at infinite velocity, it would be more convenient to define the unit period as one "during which the stock of money changes hands once in exchange for commodities and services."[11] In this definition of the unit period I differ from Robertson's definition in that I do not limit the exchanges to final exchanges against the constituents of the community's real income only.[12] The reason for this will become clear later. Based on this definition of the unit period, all gross incomes and sales proceeds from goods and services received during the current period cannot be spent on anything until the next period when they are then said to be "disposable."

This definition of the unit period, however, does not preclude the funds borrowed or realized from sales of liquid financial assets from being expendable during the same period. This differential treatment of the sales proceeds of liquid financial assets as distinguished from the sales proceeds of goods and services is also an attempt to simulate the real situation in our present world; for the velocity of circulation of money against liquid financial assets is in fact observed to be many times faster than that against goods and services. Assuming that there is such a fixed unit period does not necessarily imply that we are *ipso facto* assuming that the velocity of circulation of money is invariable; for variations in the velocity of money can be taken care of in terms of increases or decreases in the idle balances held.

Under this definition of the unit period and the implicit assumptions behind it, each individual therefore faces a financial constraint in that, during a given period he can spend no more than his disposable gross income or sales proceeds and his idle balances (the sum of the two constitutes the entire stock of money he possesses at the beginning of the period), plus the money he can currently raise on the money market. The money market is to be strictly understood as the market where deferred claims on money are traded against present money, as the traditional economists as well as Keynes seem to have understood it. Thus, peanut vendors' demand for money in terms of their excess supply of peanuts would not be counted as effective demand for money if they could not offer any credible deferred claims on money instead of peanuts in exchange for the present money they demand. For that matter, neither would the demand for money of the unemployed laborers be counted as effective demand for money in the money market just on the grounds of the Walras' Law identity.

Thus the effective demands for present money, or loanable funds (when looked at as flows directed at the money market during the current period), may be listed as

D1 funds required to finance current expenditures on gross investment of fixed or working capital, including both maintenance and replacement of existing equipment or working capital as well as new additions.

This requirement may indeed be treated in the net sense, i.e., with the concerned firm's own current savings and depreciation allowances deducted from it, instead of in the gross sense. Since we are going to treat the firm's own savings and depreciation allowances made out of its current disposable revenues as a source of supply of loanable funds, we may therefore treat the entire funds requirement as a demand for loanable funds. Of course, the firms concerned must be solvent and viable enough to be capable of offering credible deferred claims on money in exchange for their demand for present money.

D2 funds to be added to inactive money balances held as liquid reserve assets.

The flow supply of loanable funds to the money market is made up of

S1 current savings defined as disposable income minus planned current consumption expenditure; in the case where current consumption planned is in excess of disposable income, the supply of current savings may be treated as negative

S2 current depreciation and depletion allowances for fixed and working capital taken out of the current disposable gross revenue of the firms concerned

S3 dishoarding withdrawn from previously held inactive balances of money

S4 net creation of additional money by banks during the current period.

The function of the money market is to match the flow demands for loanable funds with the flow supplies. It is not directly concerned with the total existing stock of money nor with the existing stock of deferred claims on money. These total stocks can exert their indirect influences on the money market only in so far as they are the arguments for the determination of the flows of funds supplied to or demanded from the money market.

It is true that the flow equilibrium condition of the money market as conceived by the loanable funds theorists can indeed imply the stock equilibrium condition as conceived by Keynes himself, if only the two necessary conditions mentioned above are satisfied. I have myself demonstrated the equivalence of these two approaches in the past,[13] taking these necessary conditions for granted as the Keynesians generally do.[14]

Recently, however, I have come to doubt this, and this suspicion has led me to abandon the Keynesian approach as a convenient alternative to the loanable funds approach. I have expressed this view in an article[15] criticizing the stock approach of the Keynesian school, and in particular the general asset (stock) equilibrium theory of Tobin, not knowing that he himself has quietly shifted away from the stock approach to a general stock adjustments (flows) approach.[16]

However, I still have some grave misgivings about Tobin's way of treating the flow demand for money entirely as an incomplete and lagged adjustment of the pre-existing stock held at the end of last period towards the new stock demand for money determined by the current values of the arguments and parameters. As we have seen above, the bulk of the current demands for loanable funds are for financing expenditures. They are not meant to be held, but will soon be spent during the same period, and they are determined chiefly by the current flow decisions to spend or not to spend (i.e., to save). To include these as a part of the new stock demand for money would tend to confuse us regarding the sources or the arguments of their demands and supplies.

In fact Tobin's demand for money function[17] is still expressed, as in his earlier paper,[18] as a function of the vector of various rates of asset yields and the level of aggregate income and total wealth, in just the same way as Tobin treats the demand functions for all other assets that may be held. The fact that money is the necessary means for making payments, and that consequently there is a transient demand for money to finance the planned expenditures during the current period, is totally neglected. As a result, the fact that the competition for finance among the planned expenditures before their execution may crowd some out, and thus prevent them from being carried out, is persistently being denied.

In addition to all this, there is always the danger of confusion in saying that the rate of interest is determined by the supply and demand for money in general, because, as presaged by Keynes himself, that might mislead people to think that the excess demands for money in terms of peanuts, labor, and what not may all be considered as jointly determining the interest rate.

With my general objections against the stock-of-money approach to monetary analysis for a closed economy, I naturally view with dismay the new academic vogue of extending the money stock approach to open economies and furthermore ascribing to the stock demand for and supply of money the role of determining either the rate of exchange or the balance of payments in addition to the determination of the domestic interest rate or the domestic price level. The stock demand and supply of money seem to have the magical quality of determining many things at the same time.

Actually, as Keynes himself regretfully pointed out in 1937, the term supply and demand for money should never be used blankly as such: it would give rise to a lot of confusion. The supply and demand for money in terms of what? Since money is the universally accepted means of exchange, it is used as the means of payment for practically every good in every market. An excess demand, say, for peanuts in the peanut market may indeed be said to be an excess supply of money in terms of peanuts in that market. There is no guarantee, however, that the excess supply of money in terms of peanuts in the peanut market will be transferred to the money market, which should be defined specifically as the market for present money in terms of deferred claims on money, or vice versa, and become the excess supply of money in terms of deferred claims on money in the money market.

With our definition of the unit period as one during which the stock of money changes hands once in exchange for all commodities and services, all gross incomes and sales proceeds from goods and services received during the current period cannot be spent on anything until the next period, when they wil then be "disposable." As explained above, however, this definition of unit period does not preclude the funds either borrowed or realized from sales of financial assets from being expendable during the same period. At the beginning of each period, therefore, each individual (or firm) faces a "finance constraint" in that during the period he can spend on goods and services, as well as on additional financial assets, only his disposable gross income and his idle balances carried over from last period (the sum of these two items constitutes the entire stock of money he possesses at the beginning of the period) plus whatever money he can raise currently on the money market.

This constraint differs from the usual budget constraint in that, even though we allow the proceeds from current sales of deferred claims on money to be expendable during the same period, we do not allow the proceeds from sales of other goods and services to be expendable during the same period. To waive this restriction would be equivalent to waiving all restrictions on the velocity of circulation of money.

In algebraic symbols, the "finance constraint," for a private individual (or firm), as well as for the whole private sector in the aggregate, can be written in the following form:

$$Y_{t-1}^p + H_{t-1}^p \equiv C_t^p + I_t^p + \Delta B_t^p + H_t^p \tag{1}$$

where Y_{t-1} is the gross incomes (or revenues) of the last period which become "disposable" this period, H_{t-1}, the idle balances carried over from last period, C_t is the planned consumption expenditures of the current period, I_t, the planned investment expenditures of the current period, ΔB_t, is the net purchases of bonds of the current period, H_t, is the idle balances planned for this period, and the superscript p refers to the private sector.

Next, we assume that there is a banking sector, which is interested only in dealings in the financial market, that is, selling securities (taking in deposits) and buying securities (making loans and investments) at the same time. When an individual bank, or the bank sector as a whole, is a net buyer of securities during the current period, then it must finance its net purchase by either creating more bank money or releasing more cash from its reserves. In either case, there would be a corresponding increase in money supply as defined in monetary statistics. Thus we can say that the finance constraint applicable to the banking sector may be written as

$$\Delta B_t^b \equiv \Delta M_t^s \tag{2}$$

where ΔB_t^b is net purchases of bonds (in the sense of an all-inclusive term for deferred claims on money) and ΔM_t^s is the net current increase in money supply by the banking sector.

We can easily add another sector representing the government here, but we shall refrain from doing it in order to reduce our model to the barest minimum framework.[19]

Adding together the financial constraints for the private and the banking sectors, we get

$$(Y_{t-1}^p - C_t^p) - (H_t^p - H_{t-1}^p) + \Delta M_t^s \equiv I_t^p + (\Delta B_t^p + \Delta B_t^b), \tag{3}$$

or

$$Y_{t-1}^p + H_{t-1}^p + \Delta M_t^s \equiv C_t^p + I_t^p + H_t^p + (\Delta B_t^p + \Delta B_t^b), \tag{3'}$$

where $(Y_{t-1}^p - C_t^p)$ is what Robertson (1940) defined as private savings for the current period and $(H_t^p - H_{t-1}^p)$ is what he called the net hoardings of the current period.

This is still no more than a mere identity based on the finance constraints for the two sectors. It is not an equilibrium condition for any market. The equilibrium condition for the money market, in the sense in which Keynes emphasized in his 1937 articles, should be used (i.e., in the sense of the market for deferred claims in terms of present money), is that

$$\Delta B_t^p + \Delta B_t^b = 0. \tag{4}$$

In words, the aggregate purchases of bonds in terms of present money should be equal to the aggregate sales of bonds in terms of present money by both the private and banking sectors together during each given period.

Substituting this equilibrium into the identity (3) or (3′) we get

$$S_t^p - \Delta H_t^p + \Delta M_t^s = I_t^p \tag{5}$$

where $S_t^p = (Y_t^p - C_t^p)$ is the private savings for the current period and $\Delta H_t^p = (H_t^p - H_{t-1}^p)$ is the net hoardings of the current period; or

$$Y_{t-1}^p + H_{t-1}^p + \Delta M_t^s = C_t^p + I_t^p + H_t^p. \tag{5′}$$

Equation (5) is the loanable funds formulation of the equilibrium of the money market (or the market for deferred claims on money), and equation (5′) is the Keynesian supply- and demand-for-money formulation of the same equilibrium condition.

A word of caution here is necessary with regard to the equilibrium condition (4) and its equivalent (5) in the loanable funds formulation, or (5′) in the supply- and demand-for-money formulation. It merely indicates how the interest rate is determined with or without arbitrary interventions by the banking sector. Therefore, neither (5), the equality between the supply and demand for loanable funds, nor (5′), the equality between the supply and demand for money, necessarily implies any equilibrium or stability in the economy or other markets, because both (5) and (5′) contain the term ΔM_t^s, which indicates the arbitrary intervention by the banking sector (including the central bank) in the money market with injection, or withdrawal, of money into, or out of, circulation. I, therefore, find it very confusing when I hear some modern economists trained in the Patinkinian tradition argue, for instance, that the equality of the supply and demand for money implies equality between the supply and demand for goods and services on account of Walras' Law.

Even when the intervention by banking sector is zero, i.e., $\Delta M_t^s \equiv \Delta B_t^b = 0$, implying that the banking sector merely acts as an intermediary between private savers and borrowers, the equilibrium condition (5′) could at most indicate, with the additional proviso that there should be no net hoarding of idle balances in the current period (i.e., $H_t^p - H_{t-1}^p = 0$), that the aggregate flow expenditures in the current period would be equal to the disposable income inherited from the previous period; i.e., $Y_{t-1}^p = C_t^p + I_t^p \equiv E_t$.

Even that, however, cannot be interpreted as the equality between the supply and demand for goods and services. The reason is that we are not dealing with the Walrasian timeless simultaneous general equilibrium system now, but are trying to probe the process of changes over time with the Robertsonian period analysis. A steady growth of income or expenditure over a period certainly need not imply disequilibrium in the goods and services market. Since we have allowed net investments in capital to take place period after period, it is natural that real output should also increase continuously through the contributions of cumulated past investments. Whether an increase in the flow of money expenditures of the current period over the disposable income of the last period would signify an excess demand for goods and services cannot be determined unless we know the contributions to current output of the past investments.

Many years ago, I attempted to discuss this problem in an article written at the National Univeristy of Peking (Beijing) before its change in political color and spelling.[20] Although I was not then able to do full justice to this subject, I still believe that the nature of the problem and the proper approach to it were quite correctly outlined there. I have no intention of taking up that problem fully now, but I want to emphasize that, in a dynamic world of continuous growth and changes, we cannot say that, according to Walras' Law, which is based upon a static set of timeless simultaneous equations, the excess demand in one market necessarily implies an excess supply in some other market or markets.

I used to think that, properly understood, the loanable funds formulation and the Keynesian demand- and supply-of-money formulation of the money market equilibrium are exactly equivalent, and hence that there is no reason to prefer one to the other except for the sake of convenience as the occasion may demand it. Now I have come to believe that the supply and demand for money formulation of the money market equilibrium condition is misleading in many ways, as we have pointed out above, and that when applied to an open economy, it is particularly likely to lead to many important features of the money market being overlooked.

As we have seen above, the bulk of the total demand for money in (5') is the finance demand for $(C_t^p + I_t^p)$, which far outweighs H_t^p, the demand for idle balances to be held as a store of value. The finance demand for money is not for the express purpose of holding money at all: as Keynes himself pointed out, it is held only for the brief interregnum between the preparations of the finance and the carrying out of the expenditures planned.[21] When these active balances are spent, they do not necessarily set the liquidity positions of their recipients into new stock equilibria, either. Instead, those recipients will be made to feel temporarily overloaded with excess liquidity and will be willing to dispose of at least a part of it, as soon as they have time to do it (i.e., in the next period).

Thus, it definitely seems to me not quite right to treat the finance demand for money as a part of the demands to hold money as a store of wealth, or to say that by the end of the current period the aggregate holdings of money will necessarily be closer to the desired equilibrium aggregate holdings of money than they were at the beginning of the period. In other words, it is not quite appropriate either to say, with Keynes, that the money market equilibrium in each period implies the attainment of the equilibrium stock demand for total money balances, or even to say, with Tobin, that the money market equilibrium implies equality between the net adjustment of the aggregate stock of money held towards the equilibrium stock demand and the net changes in the stock supply of money. To put it in these ways would actually mislead us when faced with the questions as to what the chief arguments for the function of the demand for money are. The formulation of the function of the demand for money as one of the many ways to hold one's wealth tends to mislead people into overlooking the very important element of the flow demand for money to finance the expenditures of the current period. Thus, the demand for money function in modern monetary theory is typically treated as a function of the rate of interest and of the rates of returns of other alternative assets, total wealth and/or total income. The fact that the bulk of the demand for money, namely the finance demand for money, is actually determined by the current flow decisions with respect to investment and consumption expenditures is usually completely overlooked.

When applied to open economies, this type of monetary theory is particularly misleading, because it tends, furthermore, to overlook the fact that in open economies there are additional types of transactions that call for a finance demand for money but that are not fully included in the statistics of final, income, let alone wealth—namely, exports and imports. National income in an open economy is normally defined as

$$Y = C + I + X - Im,$$

where X and Im represent, respectively, exports and imports measured in terms of domestic money; that is, only the net trade balance is included in the final income.

In the matter of financing, however, the entire expenditure on domestic export products must be financed (purchased) with domestic money, just as with any expenditures on investment and consumption. In other words, the total expenditures in the domestic market that need domestic money as the means of finance should be

$$E_t = C_t + I_t + X_t.$$

Correspondingly, the gross disposable revenues carried over from the last period should now be $C_{t-1} + I_{t-1} + X_{t-1} = Y_{t-1} + Im_{t-1}$.

The part of the aggregate expenditures on consumption and investment of the current period that has been directed towards imported goods will in the first instance be received by sellers resident at home, who, however, will not be able to remit the proceeds due to their foreign suppliers abroad until the next period, according to our previous assumption that sales proceeds of goods and services in general will not be disposable until the next period. In the next period, however, just as was pointed out above with respect to the purchases of bonds or deferred claims on domestic money, the purchases of foreign exchange by importers would not tie up the money involved for the whole period, for the sellers of foreign exchange will thereby acquire the money from the organized exchange market quickly enough to use it to make purchases of other goods in the same period.

For the entire private sector, therefore, only its aggregate net purchase of foreign exchange in terms of domestic money, like its aggregate net purchase of bonds, would show up as one of the items that constitute its requirement for finance. Thus the aggregate finance constraint for the private sector in an open economy should be

$$C_t^p + I_t^p + X_t^p + H_t^p + \Delta B_t^p + \pi_t(NPE)_t^p \equiv (Y_{t-1}^p + Im_{t-1}^p) + H_{t-1}^p, \quad (6)$$

where $(NPF)_t^p$ represents the net purchase (or net sales, if negative) of foreign exchange by the private sector, and π_t is the current exchange rate in the sense of the price of foreign exchange in terms of domestic money.

The net purchase of foreign exchange by the private sector is in turn determined by the demand for foreign exchange for planned current imports of foreign products, i.e., by

$$\frac{1}{\pi_t} Im_t^p,$$

which, assuming the nonavailability of import credit, must be paid for in advance in foreign currency minus the aggregate receipts of foreign exchange from exports of the last period,

$$\frac{1}{\pi_{t-1}} X_{t-1},$$

assuming that the disposability of proceeds from exports will be lagged one period, just like domestic sales proceeds of goods and services,[22] plus or minus the desired net adjustments in private holdings of foreign exchange assets on both the domestic and foreign sides, ΔF_t^p, induced by changes in the arguments of the relevant foreign assets holding functions allowing for possible lags in response. That is,

$$(NPF)_t^p = \frac{1}{\pi_t} Im_t^p - \frac{1}{\pi_{t-1}} X_{t-1} + \Delta F_t^p. \tag{7}$$

These terms are all measured in terms of foreign exchange.

The banking sector in an open economy also may be assumed to be interested in the holding of foreign assets as well as domestic bonds. Its net purchase (or sale, when negative) is the desired net adjustments in its holdings induced by changes in the arguments of its demand function for foreign assets, plus the accommodating actions taken to fill in the gap in the supply and demand for foreign exchange of the private sector in order to stabilize the exchange rate.

Its finance constraint should now be changed from (2) to become

$$\Delta B_t^b + \pi_t (NPF)_t^b \equiv \Delta M_t^s, \tag{8}$$

where $(NPF)_t^b$ represents the net purchase of foreign exchange by the banking sector in the current period.

The equilibrium condition for the foreign exchange market is

$$(NPF)_t^p + (NPF)_t^b = 0, \tag{9}$$

while that for the domestic money market in an open economy remains the same as in a closed economy, i.e.,

$$\Delta B_t^p + \Delta B_t^b = 0, \tag{4}$$

as above.

Substituting the finance constraints for the private sector, i.e., (6) into the equilibrium condition (4) for the domestic money market, we get

$$Y_{t-1}^p + Im_{t-1}^p + H_{t-1}^p + \Delta B_t^b = C_t^p + I_t^p + X_t^p + H_t^p + \pi_t(NPF)_t^p, \tag{10}$$

$$= C_t^p + I_t^p + X_t^p + H_t^p + \left(Im_t^p - \frac{\pi_t}{\pi_{t-1}} X_{t-1}^p + \pi_t \Delta F_t^p \right)$$

or alternatively

$$(Y_{t-1}^p - C_t^p) + \Delta B_t^b = I_t^p + \Delta X_t^p - \frac{\Delta \pi_t}{\pi_{t-1}} X_{t-1}^p + \Delta Im_t^p$$

$$+ \Delta H_t^p + \pi_t \Delta F_t^p, \tag{10'}$$

where ΔX_t^p nd ΔIm_t^p may be regarded as the net investments in working capital needed to step up exports and imports, respectively, and

$$\frac{\Delta \pi_t}{\pi_{t-1}} X_{t-1}^p$$

is the gain (or loss, if negative) made on the foreign exchange proceeds of last period's exports that become available currently. The economic meaning of (10') is that the transformed equilibrium condition for the domestic money market in an open economy can be stated as the equilibration of the supply of loanable funds from private savings, plus the capital gain on foreign exchange proceeds of last period's exports, and banks' net purchase of bonds with the demand for loanable funds to finance domestic investment and planned increases in exports as well as in imports, net hoarding (net increase in demand for money to hold) and the net private purchase of foreign exchange assets to hold.

However, it may be observed from (10) that the equilibrium of the domestic money market in an open economy no longer implies the equality of the aggregate demand and supply of money (or vice versa) as Keynes originally maintained. The reason is that in an open economy the increase in money supply is no longer entirely devoted to the purchases of bonds (deferred claims on domestic money) as in a closed economy, part of it may be directed by banks towards the foreign exchange market. It is only when the foreign exchange market is also in equilibrium, i.e., when $NPF_t^p + NPF_t^b = 0$, that the aggregate demand and supply of money are equal, i.e.,

$$Y_{t-1}^p + Im_{t-1}^p + H_{t-1}^p + \Delta M_t^s = C_t^p + I_t^p + X_t^p + H_t^p. \tag{11}$$

Equation (11) is, indeed, the necessary results of the equilibrium in both the domestic money market and the foreign exchange market. It is not, however, sufficient by itself to imply either the equilibrium of the money market or that of the foreign exchange market, for it is consistent with disequilibrium in both the money market and the foreign exchange market, i.e., with both

$$\Delta B_t^p + \Delta B_t^b \neq 0,$$

and

$$(NPF)_t^p + (NPF)_t^b \neq 0,$$

provided that

$$(\Delta B_t^p + \Delta B_t^b) + \pi_t[(NPF)_t^p + (NPF)_t^b] = 0.$$

In order to determine the interest rate or the exchange rate, the demand and supply of money equation (11) must be supplemented by one of the flow market equilibrium conditions of the two markets: with either

$$\Delta B_t^p + \Delta B_t^b = 0, \tag{4}$$

or

$$(NPF)_t^p + (NPF)_t^b = 0. \tag{9}$$

It is therefore rather regretable that the modern monetary theory of the exchange rate should regard the stock demand and supply of money equation as being the sufficient determining force for the exchange rate or the balance of payments.

Anyway, as we have cautioned earlier, the supply and demand for money equation (11), like (5') above, does not have any implication of dynamic equilibrium for the economy, because it can include any arbitrary interventions by the banking sector in the money market and/or the foreign exchange market which add up to ΔM_t^s. Even with the additional condition that the aggregate intervention by monetary authorities, ΔM_t^s, is zero, it can only imply that the total expenditure on goods and services will be equal to the disposable income carried over from the preceding period, provided that net hoarding (the net addition to idle balances) in the current period is also zero. Moreover, the equality between current expenditure and the income of the last period is no guarantee of either the absence of excess demand or supply in the goods and services markets, or the absence of balance of payments deficits or surpluses, for, among other things, the real supply of goods can be changed by the contributions of net investments in past periods that begin to bear fruit in the current period.

The claim of the monetary theory of the balance of payments that the balance of payments deficit or surplus is directly determined by the excess supply or demand for money, respectively, is probably based upon the following argument.

The sum of the finance constraints for the private sector and the banking sector, i.e., the sum of (6) and (8), gives us

$$[Y_{t-1}^p + Im_{t-1}^p + H_{t-1}^p] - [C_t^p + I_t^p + X_t^p + H_t^p] + \Delta M_t^s$$
$$\equiv (\Delta B_t^p + \Delta B_t^b) + \pi_t(NPF_t^p + NPF_t^b), \tag{12}$$

the left-hand side of which may be interpreted as the difference between the total aggregate current supply of money, i.e., $[Y_{t-1}^p + Im_{t-1}^p + H_{t-1}^p] + \Delta M_t^s$, and the total current demand for money, i.e., $[C_t^p + I_t^p + X_t^p + H_t^p]$ and the right-hand side of which is alleged to represent the sum of the excess demand for bonds plus the excess demand for foreign exchange. From this identity, it is deduced that a positive excess supply of money must imply a corresponding excess demand for foreign exchange, if the bonds market (or the market for money in terms of deferred claims on future money) can be assumed to be always cleared. The excess demand for foreign exchange is then identified as the balance of payments deficit. Therefore, it is claimed that an excess supply of money directly and immediately implies an equivalent balance of payments deficit represented by an excess demand for foreign exchange.

This argument hinges upon whether we can identify $(NPF_t^p + NPF_t^b) > 0$ as the balance of payments deficit. $(NPF_t^p + NPF_t^b) > 0$ implies that there are more purchases than sales of foreign exchange in the market. This cannot actually happen in practice; we can only speculate about it as some potentiality under some hypothetical situation. It cannot therefore be used to represent the actual balance of payments deficit in the real world, which can really take place. In actual statistical practice, the balance of payments deficit or surplus is measured by the intervention of the banking sector (or more strictly the intervention of the central bank) in the foreign exchange market; a positive NPF_t^b implying a surplus and a negative NPF_t^b, a deficit. The idea behind this is that the banking sector's (or more specifically, the central bank's) purchase or sales of foreign exchange are largely accommodating actions taken to stabilize the exchange rate. Thus the sales of foreign exchange by the banking sector may be taken as a reflection of the excess demand for foreign exchange by the private sector, which is regarded as the true meaning of the balance of payments deficit.

The net sales of foreign exchange by the banking sector, however, owing to the finance constraint of that sector, i.e. (8), will lead to an equivalent contraction of the domestic money supply unless offset by a net purchase of domestic bonds by the banking sector. Nevertheless, the total money supply after the changes, according to (11), would still be equal to the total demand for money, including both the transactions demand for money and the idle balances (asset demand for money).

The monetarists would probably say that the fact that the supply of money, after its reduction due to the net sales of foreign exchange by the banking sector to the private sector, just equaled the private sector's demand indicates that the demand for money would surely fall short of its supply without the reduction in the latter arising from the net purchase of foreign exchange by the private sector. From this it is then argued that the net purchase of foreign exchange is a deliberate action undertaken by the private sector in order to reduce the excess money supply.

It is dangerous, however, to make such kinds of deductions about causality from identities and market equilibrium conditions, for they do not impart any information as to the direction of causation. To infer cause and effect relationships between the various terms of the identities and equilibrium conditions could often lead to meaningless tautologies.

An attempt to reduce the complex problem of the balance of payments to a single equation of the supply and demand for money is, therefore, not a very helpful approach. In particular, the usual stock formulation of the supply and demand for money equation, as we pointed out above, has the tendency to mislead us into overlooking the flow demand for money for transaction purposes and into concentrating on the asset demand for money alone. Thus the demand for money functions adopted by monetary theorists (e.g., H. G. Johnson (1973) and (1975), or Frenkel and Rodriguez (1975)) usually have the interest rate (or a vector of the rates of return of all alternative assets), real income and wealth, as their chief arguments. Moreover, in their point-of-time stock equilibrium analysis, the flow (income account) variables, including real income, are usually treated as "tentatively exogenous (predetermined) data."[23] Thus any current change in planned expenditures, whether on investment or on consumption cannot exert any direct influence on the money market, since the influence of planned expenditures is never included in the money demand function.

More recently, Pentti J. K. Kouri[24] introduced a slightly modified demand for money function in which the stock of foreign assets (including foreign exchange) is included as an argument. That is,

$$\frac{M^d}{p} = L(\pi, y, A)$$

where A represents the total existing quantity of assets in the domestic country, defined as

$$A = \frac{M}{p} + F$$

where F is the existing amount of foreign assets, π the rate of domestic inflation and y domestic real income. The equilibrium condition for the demand and supply of money, i.e.,

$$L\left(\pi, y, \frac{M}{p} + F\right) = \frac{M}{p},$$

which according to him also implies, through the wealth constraint, the equilibrium condition for foreign exchange, will determine the exchange rate as well as the price level p, which in his model is uniquely linked to the exchange rate through the rigid assumptions of a fixed world price level and a fixed relative price in the world market of the traded goods of the home country. In this all important asset market equilibrium condition, both domestic money and foreign exchange are treated as assets for holding, and their functions as the means of payment in domestic or foreign trade is totally overlooked. Thus, Kouri could claim that the exchange rate is determined to equilibrate the demand for foreign assets with the existing stock of foreign assets, which, because of the wealth constraint, is implied by the equilibration of the demand for money with the stock of money. To relieve the demand and supply of money equilibration of its usual function of determining the rate of interest, he had to simplify his model to such an extent as to assume that non-interest-bearing money is the only domestic asset available, so that there is no interest rate to be determined in the economy. With such a grossly oversimplifed model, Kouri claimed to have successfully constructed a new theory for the determination of the exchange rate, and vindicated the superiority of the fashionable monetary approach.

We may trace the development of such a farfetched academic exercise to the "misleading effect," recognized by Keynes already in 1937,[25] of using the supply and demand for money equation as the equilibrium condition for the money market: namely, the obfuscation of the crucial question "the demand for money in terms of what?"

In the real economy, the demand for domestic money in terms of deferred claims on domestic money (i.e., bonds) is not the same thing as the demand for domestic money in terms of foreign exchange, just as they, in turn, are not the same things as the demand for money in terms of peanuts. Each of them should be equilibrated, respectively, with the supply of money in terms of the same goods, instead of being lumped together to be equilibrated with the total stock of money. There is no special market mechanism that would equilibrate the lumped-together demands for money in terms of different kinds of goods with the total supply of money, however defined, apart from the separate markets for each of the different goods. Besides, as we have pointed out above, the demands for money in terms of different goods in different markets may take on quite different meanings and may refer to different points of time in the period; some may refer to the beginning of the period, and some to the end of the period. For instance, the demand for peanuts in the peanut market is generally treated as a supply of money in terms of peanuts—an end-of-period concept. As a part of the current consumption expenditure, however, it would be treated as a source of the demand for money for finance (transactions) purposes in the money market—a beginning-of-the-period concept. When the demand for money in the money market and that in the peanut market are lumped together indiscriminantly, they would cancel each other out. Similarly, in the present case the net purchase of foreign exchange by the private sector has been treated for the reason elaborated above as an item of demand for money in the domestic money market. However, in the foreign exchange market, if we follow the Lange-Patinkinian tradition, it would generally be treated as an item of the supply of money in terms of foreign exchange. Endless confusions are likely to ensure from this sort of aggregation.

It seems, therefore, far more advisable to stick to the traditional flow approach in dealing with the separate markets, where the price of each good is always determined by the flow demand and supply of the particular good concerned, paying due attention, of course, to interconnections between the markets arising from various constraints. Thus, the rate of interest on domestic loans and bonds is determined first and foremost by the flow demand and. supply of domestic bonds (i.e., of deferred claims on domestic money) in terms of money; viz.,

$$\Delta B_t^p + \Delta B_t^b = 0, \qquad (4)$$

which, owing to the finance constraint for the private sector, we specified for an open economy, i.e., (6), may be written as

$$C_t^p + I_t^p + X_t^p + H_t^p + \pi_t(NPF)_t^p = Y_{t-1}^p + Im_{t-1}^p + H_{t-1}^p + \Delta B_t^b,$$

which can be rearranged as

$$I_t^p + \Delta X_t^p + \Delta Im_t^p + \Delta H_t^p + \pi_t \Delta F_t^p$$

$$= (Y_{t-1}^p - C_t^p) + \frac{\Delta \pi_t}{\pi_{t-1}} X_{t-1}^p + \Delta B_t^b$$

as in (10′) above. The meaning of this is that the equilibrium of the domestic money market in an open economy involves the equilibration of the demand for loanable funds to finance domestic investment and the increase in planned export and import trade, net hoarding and the net private purchase of foreign exchange assets with the supply of loanable funds from gross private savings (including capital gains on foreign exchange proceeds from last period's exports) plus the credit expansion resorted to by the banking sector in order to make the net purchase of domestic bonds. There are obvious links between the domestic money market and the foreign exchange market, since both the planned increases in exports and imports and the net purchase of foreign exchange assets by the private sector depend on the exchange rate and the intervention by the banking sector in the exchange market. If the banking sector intervenes and comes into the exchange market as a net buyer of foreign exchange, then by the equilibrium condition of the exchange market

$$(NPF)_t^p + (NPF)_t^b = 0,$$

the net purchase of the private sector will have to be negative. The $\pi_t(NPF)_t^p$ will be a supply of loanable funds to the domestic money market instead of being an item of demand for loanable funds.

The equilibrium condition $(NPF)_t^p + (NPF)_t^b = 0$ of the exchange market must be analysed by studying its separate flow components individually. As pointed out earlier the net purchase of foreign exchange by the private sector consists of the demand for foreign exchange for planned current imports of foreign products, i.e.,

$$\frac{1}{\pi_t} Im_t^p,$$

minus the supply of foreign exchange from exports of the last period,

$$\frac{1}{\pi_{t-1}} X_{t-1},$$

which becomes disposable only in the current period, plus or minus the net adjustments in private holdings of foreign exchange assets on both the domestic and foreign sides, ΔF_t^p; i.e.,

$$(NPF)_t^p = \frac{1}{\pi} Im_t^p - \frac{1}{\pi_{t-1}} X_{t-1} + \Delta F_t^p. \tag{7}$$

The terms on the right-hand sides are all flows per unit period. The first term

$$\frac{1}{\pi} Im_t^p$$

is probably a function of the current exchange rate, the terms of trade (in the sense of the foreign price level as compared with the domestic price level), and the aggregate domestic expenditures (consumption, investment and planned exports).

Although the second term, the supply of foreign exchange from last period's exports,

$$\frac{1}{\pi_{t-1}} X_{t-1},$$

is a tentatively predetermined magnitude, in the long run it is also an endogenous variable and thus will turn the equilibrium condition (9) into a difference equation. It is likely to be a function of the exchange rate of the relevant period, the terms of trade, domestic productive capacity, and the level of domestic expenditures (including both domestic consumption and investment).

The net adjustments in private holdings of foreign exchange assets, ΔF_t^p, is an even more complex function. It is not merely the desired changes in the private holdings, but the adjustments that the private holders actually find time to carry out in the foreign exchange market. As pointed out by Tobin, who recently switched from being an advocate of the stock approach to being a believer in the flow approach, "in any short period of time, they (private portfolios) will adjust only partially to new information about the financial environment. Lags in response are rational in view of the costs of transactions and decisions."[26] If the private demand for foreign assets is a function of the rates of return on domestic and foreign assets (including interest rates at home and abroad), the expected rate of change in the exchange rate, and the stocks of wealth in the home country and foreign countries, then the net adjustment in private holdings of foreign assets, ΔF_t^p, is likely to be

$$\Delta F_t^p = \lambda [\widetilde{F}_t^p(r_t, r_t^*, \hat{\pi}_t, W_t, W_t^*) - F_{t-1}^p],$$

where $\widetilde{F}_t^p$ is the domestic desired holdings of foreign assets minus foreigners' desired holdings of domestic assets (in terms of their own money) as distinguished from the actual net holdings of foreign assets F_t^p; r_t and r_t^* are the domestic and foreign interest rates, respectively; $\hat{\pi}_t$ is the current expected rate of change in the exchange rate, and W_t and W_t^* are the stocks of wealth in the home country and foreign countries, respectively. This equation assumes a fixed exponential lag pattern for the adjustments in the actual stock of private holdings of foreign assets. Of course, the actual lag pattern could be far more complicated than that and could change abruptly, if big changes in the environment occur. Thus the net adjustment actually carried out is more likely to be influenced by changes in the parameters of the demand function for foreign assets than by the level of those parameters, since if those parameters remain constant at where they are, the private holdings will also gradually come to rest at a given level, and the adjustment of the holdings will taper off to zero.[27] Thus in the long run the importance of stock adjustments is not comparable to that of the regular flow demand and supply of foreign exchange represented by imports and exports. Even though, in the short run, the transient stock adjustments owing to rapid changes in the financial environment and relevant parameters may temporarily overwhelm the regular flows of exports and imports, in the long run the flow variables will assert themselves and dominate the scene. Even the speculators will ultimately base their long-term expected rate upon the relative productive capacities of exports and their abilities to compete in the world markets. Thus even Tobin now deplores the modern tendency to view the exchange rate as merely an asset price and to treat the function of asset markets in general simply as "reconciling wealth-constrained portfolio demands with existing stocks." Instead, he is now of the opinion that "it is more natural to recognize that exchange rates are determined—or held at parities by official intervention—in markets in which the demands and supplies for current and capital accounts are intermingled."[28] The monetarists who think that they are can reach a deeper understanding of the balance of payments and/or the determination of the exchange rate by comparing their usually very crude demand for money function with the stock of money are really deceiving themselves.

Thus, our heritage from Keynes, viz. his liquidity preference theory of interest, which has led the present generation of economists to believe that the money market is where the existing stock of money is equilibrated with the demand for money, unspecified as to what it is in terms of, has indeed had a far reaching and confusing effect upon later developments in monetary and financial theory. Even though Keynes himself later (in 1937) warned about the confusing effect, and reminded us that the demand for money in his liquidity preference theory meant specifically that in terms of deferred claims on money, his warning and reminder have unfortunately largely gone unheeded. With the hero worship and the tendency to conform that prevail among academic economists, it will perhaps take a long time to undo the harm done.

Notes

*President, Chung-Hsa Institution for Economic Research
1. Tobin [1982].

2. Keynes [1937b], p. 667.
3. Keynes [1937b], p. 666.
4. Keynes [1937a], p. 241.
5. Keynes [1937a], p. 241.
6. Patinkin [1965].
7. Tsiang [1966] and [1977].
8. Tsiang [1966].
9. Keynes [1937b].
10. Clower [1967].
11. Tsiang [1956].
12. Roberston [1940].
13. Tsiang [1956] and [1980].
14. In an article in 1958, Patinkin also declared that "the excess demand for money as a flow is identical with the excess demand as a stock. And since for the determination of the rate of interest it is only the excess demand equations which are relevant, the difference between the demand functions (i.e. whether in terms of flows or of stocks) is completely immaterial." (Patinkin 1958, p. 303) What I demonstrated in 1956 and 1980, however, is not merely the identity that exists between the flow excess demand and the stock excess demand for any given asset, but the identity existing between the flow excess demand for loanable funds and the stock excess demand for money as really understood by Keynes himself, i.e., allowing for the demand for money to finance planned expenditures, while excluding those so-called excess demands for money which Patinkin and his followers would deduce from Walras' Law identity.

    In fact, later on in his 1958 article, Patinkin alleged that the excess demand for money (stock or flow) might indicate a direction of movement in the interest rate opposite to that indicated by the excess demand for loans (stock or flow). This is an utterly unfair interpretation of Keynes' liquidity preference theory. It is entirely the result of his misapplication of Walras' Law to the excess demand for money, which inevitably omits the pre-trade demand for finance since Walras' Law deals only with the results of all transactions. Thus on the contrary, Walras' Law would encompass all sorts of post-trade acquisitions of money which Keynes would never include under his definition of the demand for money in terms of deferred claims on money.
15. Tsiang [1982].
16. Tobin [1982].
17. Tobin [1982].
18. Tobin [1969].
19. The finance constraint for the government sector would be

$$T_{t-1} - \Delta B_t^g \equiv E_t^g$$

    where T_{t-1} represents tax revenue received in the preceding period, ΔB_t^g the net purchase (net sales, if negative) of bonds by the government sector, and E_t^g government expenditures planned for the current period.
20. Tsiang [1949].

21. Keynes [1937b], p. 469.
22. Here we are making the tentative assumption that foreign trade credits for both imports and exports are not available. Otherwise, both the requirement for foreign exchange to pay for the planned imports and the receipt of foreign exchange proceeds from exports will be postponed for the durations of credits received or granted. To avoid the complications of having to allow for the different durations of credits for different items of trade, we shall, therefore, adopt the assumption of universal nonavailability of trade credit for the time being. Any trade credits actually received or granted may be tentatively assumed to be included in the net capital flows between the home country and foreign countries.
23. Tobin [1969], pp. 15–16.
24. Kouri [1976].
25. Keynes [1937a], p. 241.
26. Tobin [1982], p. 185.
27. Tsiang [1975], pp. 197–200.
28. Tobin [1982], pp. 188–189.

References

Clower, R. W., "A Reconsideration of the Microfoundations of Monetary Theory," *Western Economic Journal,* **6**, Dec. 1967, pp. 1–9.

Frenkel, J. A., and Rodriguez, C. A., "Portfolio Equilibrium and Balance of Payments: A Monetary Approach," *American Economic Review,* **65**, Sept. 1975, pp. 674–88.

Johnson, H. G., "The Monetary Approach to the Balance of Payments Theory," Connolly, M. B., and Swoboda, A. K., eds., *International Trade and Money–The Geneva Essays,* 1973, pp. 206–25. London: George Allen and Unwin.

Keynes, J. M., a). "Alternative Theories of the Rate of Interest," *Economic Journal,* **47**, June 1937, pp. 241–52.

Keynes, J. M., b). "The Ex-Ante Theory of the Rate of Interest," *Economic Journal,* **47**, Dec. 1937, pp. 663–69.

Kouri, Pentti J. K., "The Exchange Rate and the Balance of Payments in the Short Run and in the Long Run: A Monetary Approach," *Scandinavian Journal of Economics,* **78**, no. 2, 1976, pp. 280–304; reprinted in Herrin, J., Lindbeck, Assar, and Myhrman, Johan, eds., *Flexible Exchange Rates and Stabilization Policy,* ch. 6, same title, pp. 148–72, Westview Press, Boulder, Colorado, 1977.

Patinkin, Don, "Liquidity Preference and Loanable Funds: Stock and Flow Analysis," *Economica,* **25**, Nov. 1958, pp. 300–18.

Patinkin, Don, *Money, Interest and Prices,* 2nd ed., New York: Harper & Row, 1965.

Roberston, D. H., "Mr. Keynes and the Rate of Interest," ch. 1, *Essays in Monetary Theory,* London: P. S. King, 1940.

Tobin, James, "A General Equilibrium Approach to Monetary Theory," *Journal of Money, Credit, and Banking,* **1**, Feb. 1969, pp. 15–29.

Tobin, James, "Money and Finance in the Macroeconomic Process," *Journal of Money, Credit, and Banking,* **14**, May 1982, pp. 171–204.

Tsiang, S. C., "Rehabilitation of Time Dimesion of Investment in Macrodynamic Analysis," *Economica,* **16**, Aug. 1949, pp. 254–88.

Tsiang, S. C., "Liquidity Preference and Loanable Funds Theories, Multiplier and Velocity Analysis: A Synthesis," *American Economic Review,* **46**, Sept. 1956, pp. 539–64.

Tsiang, S. C., "Walras' Law, Say's Law and Liquidity Preference in General Equilibrium Analysis," *International Economic Review,* **7**, Sept. 1966, pp. 329–45.

Tsiang, S. C., "The Dynamics of International Capital Flows and Internal and External Balance," *Quarterly Journal of Economics,* **89**, May 1975, pp. 195–214.

Tsiang, S. C., "The Monetary Theoretic Foundation of the Modern Monetary Approach to the Balance of Payments," *Oxford Economic Papers,* **29**, Nov. 1977, pp. 319–38.

Tsiang, S. C., "Keynes's "Finance" Demand for Liquidity, Robertson's Loanable Funds Theory, and Friedman's Monetarism," *Quarterly Journal of Economics,* **95**, May 1980, pp. 467–91.

Tsiang, S. C., "Stock or Portfolio Approach to Monetary Theory and the Neo-Keynesian School of James Tobin," *IHS Journal,* **6**, 1982, pp. 149–71.

Section III

CHAPTER 10

The Rationale of the Mean-Standard Deviation Analysis, Skewness Preference, and the Demand for Money

S. C. Tsiang*

In the January 1969 issue of the *Review of Economic Studies*, Karl Borch and Martin Feldstein separately criticize the widely used mean-variance analysis of portfolio selection. Borch contends that any system of upward sloping mean-standard deviation (henceforth abbreviated as $E–S$) indifference curves can be shown to be inconsistent with the basic axiom of choice under uncertainty. He points out that one can always pick any two points on an upward sloping indifference curve to represent two Bernoulli distributions with probability $(1 − p)$ of gaining the same amount \$$x$ in both cases and probability p of gaining \$$y_1$ in the case of one distribution and \$$y_2$ in the case of the second distribution; with $y_2 > y_1$, if the second distribution represents the point to the northeast of the other point. Then by the dominance axiom, the second distribution must be preferred to the first, which contradicts the basic meaning of indifference curves. (See Figure 1.)

Feldstein, by using a log utility function and a lognormal distribution for investment outcome has shown that $E–S$ indifference curves for a

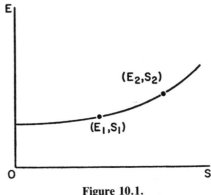

Figure 10.1.

risk-averter need not be convex downwards, though upward sloping. They would change from convex to concave, once the standard deviation of the outcome exceeds the mean multiplied by $1/\sqrt{2}$. On the face of it, this seems to suggest that risk aversion might decrease as risk itself is increased beyond a certain extent. Furthermore, he points out, as Paul Samuelson (1967) did before him, that in general it is not possible to define a preference ordering of portfolios of mixed investments in terms of E and S alone, since a linear combination of several stochastic variables would in general not be a variable of a two-parameter distribution, even if each of the constituent variables is of a two-parameter distribution (except the case where they are all normally distributed.)

This combined assault forced James Tobin, one of the pioneers of the E–S analysis of portfolio choice, to acknowledge that it is applicable only if either the investor's utility function is quadratic, or if he regards the uncertain outcomes as all normally distributed (1969).

It is now generally recognized, however, that a quadratic function is not only limited in its range of applicability as a utility function, but that even within its range of applicability it involves the highly implausible implication of increasing absolute risk-aversion, which both Kenneth Arrow and John Hicks denounced as absurd. On the other hand, the assumption of normal distribution for all outcomes of risky investments and ventures is patently not realistic; for it would rule out all asymmetry or skewness in the probability distributions of returns. The study by Paul Cootner, for instance, suggests that returns of financial investments at least may be more likely to be distributed lognormally, rather than normally, being the cumulative products of random factors rather than their cumulative sums; and thus are likely to positively skewed. Furthermore, progressive taxation, limited liability company organization, and hedging can also change otherwise symmetric distribution of returns of investments into skewed ones in net returns.

If the E–S analysis is restricted to either the case of quadratic utility function or the case of normally distributed investment outcomes, then it would be of very limited application indeed. The purpose of this paper is to point out that there is a justification for the use of E–S analysis beyond the two cases to which Tobin would now confine its application, provided the aggregate risk taken by the individual concerned is small compared with his total wealth, including his physical, financial, as well as human wealth. It is not necessary that risk taken should be infinitesimally small in its absolute magnitude.[1]

However, it will also be pointed out that, because of the constraint on the slopes of E–S indifference curves indicated by our discussion, the E–S analysis would not be capable of rationalizing the demand for idle cash in an investment portfolio, as it was originally called upon to do by Tobin (1958).

1. Justification for Using Moments of Distributions for Preference Ordering of Uncertain Outcomes—Aversion to Dispersion and Preference for Skewness

Borch starts by pointing out that strictly speaking a consistent preference ordering of a set of uncertain outcomes of any different distributions can be established in terms of their respective first n moments only if the utility function of the individual concerned is a polynomial of degree n, as has been shown by Marcel Richter. Unfortunately, it is now generally recognized that polynomials are not suitable as utility function of wealth; for an appropriate utility function $U(y)$ for a risk-avert individual, according to Arrow, should have the following essential properties.

(a) $U'(y) > 0$, i.e., marginal utility of wealth is positive;

(b) $U''(y) < 0$, i.e., marginal utility of wealth decreases with an increase of wealth;

(c) $d[- U''(y)/U'(y)]/dy \leqq 0$, i.e., marginal absolute risk-aversion should, if anything, decrease with an increase in wealth;

(d) $d[- yU''(y)/U'(y)]/dy \geqq 0$, i.e., marginal relative (proportional) risk-aversion should, if anything, increase with an increase in wealth.[2]

Polynomials as utility functions cannot satisfy these requirements at the same time. Utility functions that satisfy these conditions, such as the negative exponential function $U(y) = B(1 - e^{-ay})$, and the family of constant elasticity utility functions: $[1/(1 - a)]y^{1-a}$, $(a > 0)$, and $U(y) = \log y$; etc., are not polynomials. However, nonpolynomials can generally be expanded into Taylor's series provided that they are continuous and have derivatives. That is, if y is a random variable, it can always be written as the sum of its mean plus the deviation from the mean, and, hence,

$$U(y) = U(\bar{y} + h) = U(\bar{y}) + U'(\bar{y})h \qquad (1)$$
$$+ U''(\bar{y})\,\frac{h^2}{2!} + U'''(\bar{y})\,\frac{h^3}{3!}$$
$$+ \ldots + U^{(n-1)}(\bar{y})\,\frac{h^{n-1}}{(n - 1)!}$$
$$+ R_n,$$

where $R_n = U^{(n)}(\bar{y} + \varepsilon h)h^n/(n!)$, $(0 < \varepsilon < 1)$. The utility function thus becomes a polynomial in h (the deviation of y from its mean) with nonstochastic coefficients except for the remainder term. The expected utility is then

$$E[U(y)] = \int_{-\infty}^{\infty} U(\bar{y} + h)f(h)dh \qquad (2)$$
$$= U(\bar{y}) + U''(\bar{y})\,\frac{\bar{m}_2}{2} + U'''(\bar{y})\,\frac{\bar{m}_3}{3!}$$
$$+ \ldots + U^{(n-1)}(\bar{y})\,\frac{\bar{m}_{n-1}}{(n - 1)!}$$
$$+ \frac{1}{n!}\,E[U^{(n)}(\bar{y} + \varepsilon h)h^n], \ (0 < \varepsilon < 1),$$

where $f(h)$ is the density function of h, the deviation of y from $\bar{y}$, and $\bar{m}_2, \bar{m}_3, \ldots, \bar{m}_{n-1}$ are the second, the third, and the successive higher central moments of the distribution. If this series can be shown to be convergent so that the remainder term can be neglected, then the expected utility can be treated as a function of the first $(n - 1)$ central moments of the distribution of y with constant coefficients as if the utility function were a $(n - 1)$th order polynomial of y. The number n is to be varied to ensure sufficient degree of accuracy in approximation.

If the convergence of the series is sufficiently fast, so that, for fairly close approximation, the terms beyond the second moments can be neglected, then indeed the expected utility can be approximately determined by the first two moments, mean and variance, even if the utility function is not quadratic, and the uncertain outcomes not normally distributed. The crucial questions then are under what conditions we can expect the expansion of the utility function to converge quickly, and whether these conditions hold in the usual problems to which the E–S analysis is frequently applied.

Analysis of the expected utility function by its expansion is essentially the approach adopted by both Arrow and John Pratt in establishing the formulae for absolute and relative marginal risk aversion. In their respective works, they both dealt with the case of an individual, who, initially having no risk at all, is confronted with an infinitesimal and actuarially neutral risk. Since risk (variance) is assumed to be infinitesimally small, higher order central moments are assumed to be of even smaller orders and thus all omitted (see Pratt, p. 125). Then obviously expected utility may be approximated by

$$E[U(y)] = U(\bar{y}) + U'' \frac{S^2}{2},\tag{2'}$$

from which it can be readily derived that

$$\left.\frac{d\bar{y}}{dS}\right| = -\frac{SU''}{U' + \dfrac{S^2}{2} U'''}\tag{2''}$$

$$(E[U] = \text{constant})$$

which under the assumption that S is sufficiently small, can be further simplified as

$$\left.\frac{d\bar{y}}{dS}\right| = \frac{-SU''}{U'}.\tag{2'''}$$

$$(E[U] = \text{constant})$$

One cannot, however, trace out a whole indifference map for the mean ($E = \bar{y}$) and the standard deviation S on the assumption that the latter remains very, very small in absolute magnitude all the time. Fortunately, if we plug in some acceptable utility function into equation (2), it becomes clear that it is not really necessary for risk to remain very small in absolute magnitude. What is necessary for the E–S analysis to be a good approximation is merely that risk should remain small *relatively* to the total wealth of the individual concerned.

One of the widely adopted functions for the utility of wealth is the negative exponential function, viz., $U(y) = B(1 - e^{-ay})$. It possesses all the four required properties of an acceptable utility function, except that the required property (c) is satisfied only marginally. With this function, absolute risk-aversion is invariant with an increase or decrease of wealth,[3] whereas it would probably conform more to empirical observations if absolute risk-aversion is decreasing with wealth.

Another widely used type of utility function of wealth is the family of constant elasticity utility functions of the form of $U(y) = K + [1/(1 - a)]y^{1-a}$, $(a > 0)$, or the log function $U(y) = \ln y$. With this type of function, absolute risk-aversion would indeed be decreasing with wealth, but the relative risk-aversion is invariant with wealth. Compared with the former, however, this type of function has a serious defect in that it is generally either undefined or not real (imaginary), or yields negative marginal utility for zero or negative wealth.[4] Thus it should not be used to deal with decisions in face of risk that might involve bankruptcy or negative wealth.

Since the most commonly observed pattern of behavior towards risk of a risk-avert individual is probably decreasing absolute risk-aversion coupled with increasing relative risk-aversion when his wealth increases, the ideal utility function of wealth should lie probably somewhere in between the negative exponential function and the constant elasticity function, and what is found to be true for both the exponential and the constant elasticity utility functions should be valid for most acceptable utility functions.

Let us first plug in the negative exponential utility function into equations (1) and (2) above. Writing y as $(\bar{y} + h)$, equation (1) becomes

$$U(y) = B - Be^{-a\bar{y}} \cdot \left[1 - \alpha h + \frac{\alpha^2 h^2}{2!} - \frac{\alpha^3 h^3}{3!} + \ldots \right] \qquad (3)$$

which converges for all values of h, and the remainder term can always be neglected provided we extend the series to sufficient number of terms. Equation (2) then becomes

$$E[U(y)] = B - Be^{a\bar{y}} \cdot \left[1 + \frac{\alpha^2 S^2}{2!} - \frac{\alpha^3 \bar{m}_3}{3!} + \ldots \right] \qquad (4)$$

which must also converge, provided that the distribution of h has finite moments.[5] If higher order moments are of the order of magnitude of the corresponding powers of S, the series would converge rapidly if αS is a small fraction. The crucial question is, therefore, whether we can reasonably expect that this is the case for most problems of portfolio analysis even though α is here unspecified in magnitude.

I think we can, if we stipulate the plausible speed with which the ultimate bliss, i.e., the upper limit of utility represented by B, is to be approached as wealth increases. That is, if we make the reasonable assumption that a tenfold increase of the total wealth of a normal individual is still unlikely to bring him to within, say, 1 percent (or 0.1 percent) of his ultimate bliss, then we may write

$$B(1 - e^{-10\alpha\bar{y}}) \leqq B(1 - 0.01), \text{ or}$$

$$B(1 - 0.001),$$

$$\therefore \alpha \leqq \frac{\ln 100}{10\bar{y}} = \frac{0.46}{\bar{y}},$$

$$\left(\text{or } \frac{\ln 1000}{10\bar{y}} = \frac{0.69}{\bar{y}}\right).$$

Anyway, it seems safe to maintain that $\alpha = k/\bar{y}$, where $0 < k < 1$. Thus we see that the condition that $\alpha S < 1$ is equivalent to $S < \bar{y}/k$, or that risk be smaller than, say, twice his total wealth, including his human capital (i.e., the capitalized value of his earning capacity) as well as all his financial and physical assets. When we are discussing the behavior of a rational portfolio investor, this condition would undoubtedly hold, for it is extremely unlikely that he would voluntarily assume such enormous risk as would easily make himself bankrupt.

Indeed, if $\alpha S = kS/\bar{y}$ is normally fairly small, then for a fair approximation in many problems, we may safely neglect terms with higher moments than the second or the third, even though, in absolute magnitude, S, i.e., risk, is not infinitesimal. For if we adopt the customary "pure number" measures for skewness and peakedness (kurtosis), viz., $\mu_3 = \bar{m}_3/S^3$ and $\mu_4 = \bar{m}_4/S^4$, respectively, equation (4) may be rewritten as

$$E[U(y)] = \beta - \beta e^{-\alpha\bar{y}} \left[1 + \frac{\alpha^2 S^2}{2!} - \frac{\alpha^3 S^3}{3!} \mu_3 + \frac{\alpha^4 S^4}{4!} \mu_4 - \cdots \right].$$

$$(4')$$

Thus if, for instance, the risk under our consideration (as measured by the standard deviation) ranges only from zero up to, say, 10 percent of the individual's expected value of total wealth, then, assuming $k = 1/2$ roughly, $\alpha S \leqq 1/20$. The coefficient for the pure number measure of skewness in the brackets would be absolutely less than 1/48,000; and that for peakedness would be less than 1/3,840,000. It would seem, therefore, that a fair approximation of the expected utility for most practical purposes can be obtained by considering the mean and the variance only. As the ratio of risk, S, to the mean value of total wealth increases, however, the mean-variance analysis would become less and less accurate, and higher order central moments, in particular $\bar{m}_3$, would have to be taken into consideration.

Equation (4) clearly shows that the influence of skewness $\bar{m}_3/S^3$ on the expected utility is positive. That is to say, a positive skewness of the distribution is a desirable feature, and, other things being equal, a greater skewness would increase the expected utility.[6] This is not a result peculiar to the assumption of a negative exponential utility function, but may be shown to be a general pattern of behavior towards uncertainty on the part of all risk-avert individuals with decreasing or constant absolute risk-aversion with respect to increases in wealth. From equation (2), we may see that the coefficient of $\bar{m}_3$ is $U'''/3!$. For a person with decreasing or constant absolute risk-aversion, U''' must be positive; for absolute risk-aversion is defined as $-U''/U'$, and

$$\frac{d}{dy}\left[\frac{-U''}{U'}\right] = \frac{-U'U''' + (U'')^2}{(U')^2} \leqq 0,$$

only if $U''' \geqq (U'')^2/U' > 0$. Thus if we regard the phenomenon of increasing absolute risk aversion as absurd, we must acknowledge that a normal risk-avert individual would have a preference for skewness, in addition to an aversion to dispersion (variance) of the probability distribution of returns.[7]

It is interesting to note that Harry Markowitz, another pioneer of the E–S analysis, once remarked that

> ... the third moment of the probability distribution of returns from the portfolio may be connected with a propensity to gamble. For example, if the investor maximize utility (U) which depends on E and $V(U = U(E, V)$, $\partial U/\partial E > 0$, $\partial U/\partial V < 0)$, he will never accept an actuarially fair bet. But if $U = U(E, V, M_3)$ and if $\partial U/\partial M_3 \neq 0$, then there are some fair bets which would be accepted. [pp. 90–91]

Nevertheless, as we have shown above, skewness preference $(\partial U/\partial M_3 > 0)$ is certainly not necessarily a mark of an inveterate gambler, but a common trait of a risk-avert person with decreasing or constant absolute risk-aversion. I cannot, therefore, go along with Markowitz in taking the view that since gambling is to be avoided, the third moment needed not be considered in portfolio analysis.

Anyway, skewness preference must be a fairly prevalent pattern of investor's behavior, for modern financial institutions provide a number of devices for investors to increase the positive skewness of the returns of their investments: for example, the organization of limited liability joint stock companies, prearranged stop-loss sales on the stock and commodity markets, puts and calls in stocks etc., which otherwise would perhaps not have been developed.

If we plug in a constant elasticity utility function into (1) and (2), we would reach more or less the same conclusions. In this case, however, we must keep in mind the limitations of constant elasticity utility functions, viz., that they may be undefined, not real, or otherwise inapplicable as a utility function for zero, or negative wealth and that their expansions will not converge unless the deviations from the mean value of wealth remain smaller than the mean itself. That is

$$U(y) = \frac{1}{1-a} (\bar{y} + h)^{1-a} \quad (a > 0) \tag{5}$$

$$= \frac{1}{1-a} (\bar{y})^{1-a} + \frac{h}{(\bar{y})^a} - \frac{a}{2!} \frac{h^2}{(\bar{y})^{1+a}}$$

$$+ \frac{a(1+a)}{3!} \frac{h^3}{(\bar{y})^{2+a}} - \cdots,$$

or, with the logarithm form of constant elasticity utility function,

$$U(y) = \log y = \log \bar{y} \left(1 + \frac{h}{\bar{y}}\right) \tag{5'}$$

$$= \log \bar{y} + \frac{h}{\bar{y}} - \frac{1}{2} \frac{h^2}{(\bar{y})^2} + \frac{1}{3} \frac{h^3}{(\bar{y})^3}$$

$$- \cdots,$$

will not converge unless $|h| < \bar{y}$. As long as this constraint is satisfied, then

$$E[U(y)] = \frac{1}{1-a} (\bar{y})^{1-a} - \frac{a}{2} \frac{S^2}{(\bar{y})^{1+a}} \tag{6}$$

$$+ \frac{a(1+a)}{3!} \frac{\bar{m}_3}{(\bar{y})^{2+a}} - \cdots$$

or, with a log utility function as in (5'),

$$E[U(y)] = \log \bar{y} - \frac{1}{2} \frac{S^2}{(\bar{y})^2} + \frac{1}{3} \frac{\bar{m}_3}{(\bar{y})^3} \tag{6'}$$

$$- \cdots,$$

must also be a convergent series.[8]

In this case, the convergence of the series is slower than in the case of negative exponential utility. Nevertheless, if the risk under consideration remains smaller than, say, 10 percent of the expected value of total wealth, the effects of higher moments might still be fairly safely neglected. For instance, (6′) can be rewritten as

$$E[U(y)] = \log \bar{y} - \frac{1}{2} \cdot \frac{S^2}{(\bar{y})^2} + \frac{1}{3} \frac{S^3}{(\bar{y}^3)} \mu_3 \qquad (6'')$$

$$- \frac{1}{4} \frac{S^4}{(\bar{y})^4} \mu_4 + \ldots$$

where, as before, $\mu_3 = \bar{m}_3/S^3$ and $\mu_4 = \bar{m}_4/S^4$. If $S/\bar{y} < 1/10$, then the coefficient of the pure number measure of skewness is less than $1/3000$, and that of peakedness is absolutely less than $1/40000$.

Again we see that a person with a constant elasticity utility function (hence, risk-avert and with decreasing absolute risk-aversion) must have skewness preference, as the sign of the term with $\bar{m}_3$ in (6) or (6′) is necessarily positive.

Thus we see that the E–S analysis can be justified as a useful approximate method for portfolio selection even when utility function is not quadratic nor are the distributions of investment outcomes always normal. The only condition required is that the risk S assumed by the investor must remain a fairly small fraction of his total wealth, including not only his entire net worth but also his human capital.

The necessity to include human capital as well as nonhuman net worth should be emphasized here; for as long as we recognize that utility function of wealth is nonlinear, and that marginal utility of wealth diminishes with the increase in total wealth, we cannot apply a separate utility (or welfare) function to each separate investment or item of wealth. Since an individual's own personal earning capacity is as much a source of income as his physical and financial assets, his human capital must be included in his utility (or welfare) function with all other items of wealth. Thus the relevant $S/\bar{y}$ ratio in the Taylor's expansion of the expected utility function should not be the ratio of the standard deviation of the returns of risk investment (or portfolio) to the mean of those returns alone, but should always be the ratio of total risk including the former to the mean value of the total wealth of the person concerned. For a normal portfolio investor anyway, this ratio probably can be expected to be a fairly small fraction, and hence the E–S analysis might be a fair approximation with much wider application than its critics are willing to concede.

It might still be objected: if the $E-S$ analysis is only a method of approximation applicable to cases where risk is a small fraction of total wealth, why bother with it at all and not go directly to the general principle of maximizing expected utility. This is indeed the approach favored by many economists and some important works on economic behavior under uncertainty have been achieved without the use of $E-S$ approach or any moments.[9] This approach is quite adequate for theoretical economists who are interested only in the direction of change induced by some hypothetical shift in parameters. For practical investors, who desire a fairly accurate quantitative guidance for action, however, it is not of much help. Since acceptable utility functions are non-linear and non-polynomial, they are generally rather difficult to integrate when multiplied by the density function of random returns of wealth.[10] Generally, it would be more convenient if we should be able to expand the utility function into a Taylor's series and then integrate it term by term. As we have shown above, this approach leads directly to the approximation of the expected utility function by a function of the moments of the distribution, and if convergence warrants it, we might use the terms with the mean and the variance alone for a fair approximation. Furthermore, ordinarily the investor does not know what the exact shapes of the distribution functions of investment returns are. Usually, as in so many problems of applied statistics, one has only some estimates of the locations, dispersions and perhaps some vague idea of the degrees of skewness of the distributions to work on. These facts constitute the basic rationale of the mean-variance analysis.

In a broad sense, the $E-S$ analysis versus the general principle of maximizing expected utility is analogous to the consumers' surplus analysis versus the general equilibrium analysis of welfare gains. For small risk relative to total wealth, the $E-S$ analysis is adequate enough and can be handled quantitatively with much greater facility. Indeed, if the risk is so small that, over the range of random variations of wealth, changes in the marginal utility of wealth (money) can be neglected (which is the equivalent of Marshall's justification for the measurement of consumer' surplus by the triangle under the demand curve), then the increment in expected utility of wealth may be approximated by the utility of the increment of expected wealth. There would be no need to consider even the variance. Surely, as Tobin (1969) claimed in its defense, the $E-S$ analysis represents a major step forward for cases, where, over the range of variations of wealth, decrease or increase in the marginal utility of wealth cannot be neglected.

2. Borch's and Feldstein's Paradoxes and the Impossibility that Slopes of E–S Indifference Curves Equal or Exceed 45°

The above discussion would enable us to give a satisfactory explanation of the paradoxes posed by Borch and Feldstein's criticisms of the E–S analysis.

Borch's criticism, as mentioned in the beginning, is that any system of upward sloping indifference curves in the E–S plane can be shown to be inconsistent with the basic axiom of choice under uncertainty. In Figure 1, (E_1, S_1) and (E_2, S_2) are any two points on a given E–S indifference curve. Borch shows that these two vectors in E and S may be represented by two Bernoulli distributions (x, p, y_1) and (x, p, y_2), where

$$x = \frac{S_1 E_2 - S_2 E_1}{S_1 - S_2} \tag{7}$$

$$p = \frac{(E_2 - E_1)^2}{(E_2 - E_1)^2 + (S_2 - S_1)^2} \tag{8}$$

$$y_1 = E_1 + S_1 \frac{S_2 - S_1}{E_2 - E_2} \tag{9}$$

and

$$y_2 = E_2 + S_2 \frac{S_2 - S_1}{E_2 - E_1} \tag{10}$$

as it may easily verified that the mean and standard deviation of (x, p, y_i) would be E_i and S_i. Since $E_2 > E_1$, and $S_2 > S_i$, y_2 must be $>y_1$. Thus (x, p, y_2) is axiomatically preferable to (x, p, y_1); yet they are supposed to be on the same indifference curve.

This apparent contradiction can be explained as follows. Let us first assume that the relevant section of the indifference curve nowhere has slope equal to or greater than unity (or 45°). The E–S analysis, as we have shown above, is based on the approximation of the expected utility function by its expansion involving no terms higher than the second order. If, however, the third central moment (skewness) of the distribution is known to be positive, its omission would imply a downward bias in the expected utility, as U''' must be positive for a risk-averter (one with upward rising E–S indifference curves), who does not have an increasing absolute risk-aversion (which is generally considered as absurd).

Now on the section of an indifference curve with slope everywhere less than 1, the two Bernoulli distributions, constructed in the above manner to represent any two arbitrary points on the curve, must be positively skewed; and the one representing the point to the northeast of the other must have a greater skewness. For

$$P = \frac{(E_2 - E_1)^2}{(E_2 - E_1)^2 + (S_2 - S_1)^2} < \frac{1}{2}, \tag{11}$$

when $(E_2 - E_1) < (S_2 - S_1)$, as is implied by our assumption that the slope of the relevant section of the $E\text{--}S$ indifference curve is nowhere equal to, or greater than, 1. And $\bar{m}_3$, a measure for skewness, is defined as

$$\bar{m}_3 = [x - py_i - (1 - p)x]^3(1 - p) \tag{12}$$
$$+ [y_i - py_i - (1 - p)x]^3 p$$
$$= p(1 - p)(1 - 2p)(y_i - x)^3 \gtreqless 0,$$

$$\text{as} \quad \begin{cases} 0 < p < \frac{1}{2} \\ p = \frac{1}{2} \\ 1 > p > \frac{1}{2} \end{cases}$$

since it may easily be shown that y_i is always $>x$.[11] The cases where $p = 0$ or 1, being trivial, are excluded. Given that $p < 1/2$ so that both distributions would be positively skewed, the distribution with the probability p of gaining y_2 (represented by the point (E_2, S_2)) must be more positively skewed than the distribution with the probability p of gaining y_1 (represented by the point (E_1, S_1)), as y_2 is $>y_1$.

Thus the contradiction between the implication of the indifference curves and the fact that (x, p, y_2) must be preferred to (x, p, y_1) can be explained by the fact that, in the $E\text{--}S$ analysis, the advantage of the greater skewness of (x, p, y_2) as compared with that of (x, p, y_1) is neglected on the assumption that the influence of skewness is of a smaller order of magnitude than that of variance and mean. So long as this assumption about the order of magnitude is justifiable on the basis of the relative smallness of the standard deviation to total wealth, the treatment of (x, p, y_1) and (x, p, y_2) as approximately indifferent is also justifiable.

This explanation of the paradox, of course, would not be valid if the slope of $E\text{--}S$ indifference curves should rise to 1 or greater. For if so, we can always pick two points (E_1, S_1) and (E_2, S_2) on a given indifference curve such that $E_2 - E_1$ exactly equals $S_2 - S_1$, in which case

$$p = \frac{(E_2 - E_1)^2}{(E_2 - E_1)^2 + (S_2 - S_1)^2} = \frac{1}{2},$$

and hence the two Bernoulli distributions constructed in the manner suggested by Borch would both have zero skewness. Or we may even pick the two points in such way that $(E_2 - E_1) > (S_2 - S_1)$, in which case, $p > 1/2$, and, hence, the two Bernoulli distributions (x, p, y_1) and (x, p, y_2) would both be negatively skewed, and the negative skewness would be absolutely larger in the case of (x, p, y_2), y_2 being $>y_1$, as is obvious from equation (12).

In these cases, we cannot use the neglected influence of skewness to explain why (x, p, y_2) and (x, p, y_1) may be represented by two points (E_2, S_2) and (E_1, S_1) on the same indifference curve, yet, strictly speaking, the former must be preferred to the latter. However, this is not to be regarded as an indication of the inherent inconsistency of E–S indifference map as an approximate representation of the scale of preference for returns and risk. Rather it should be interpreted as an indication that such indifference curves should never be drawn with slope going up to 45° or even greater. This is an important fact which users of E–S indifference curves usually overlook, sometimes with rather absurd results. [12]

In fact, if we go back to the foundation of the E–S analysis, viz., the justifiability of approximating the expected utility function with its quadratic expansion, i.e., equation (2′) above,

$$E[(U(y)] = U(\bar{y}) + U'' \frac{S^2}{2},$$

we could readily see that the slope of the E–S indifference curves,

$$\left. \frac{d\bar{y}}{dS} \right| = \frac{-SU''}{U' + \dfrac{S^2}{2} U'''},$$

$$(E[U] = \text{constant})$$

could not be equal to or greater than 1; for

$$\frac{-SU''}{\dfrac{S^2}{2} U''' + U'} \geqq 1$$

would imply that

$$U' + SU'' + \frac{S^2}{2} U''' \leqq 0$$

which means that, provided the quadratic approximation is a close approximation within this range, the marginal utility of wealth would be brought to zero or to a negative value by a mere deviation of one standard deviation of the actual value of wealth from its mean.

To use the negative exponential utility function as an illustration, if the expected utility of wealth is sufficiently closely approximated by

$$E[U(y)] = B - Be^{-a\bar{y}}\left[1 + \frac{\alpha^2}{2} S^2\right],$$

then

$$\left.\frac{d\bar{y}}{dS}\right| = \frac{\alpha S}{\left(1 + \frac{\alpha^2 S^2}{2}\right)} \tag{13}$$

$$(E[U] = \text{constant})$$

which is necessarily <1. Indeed, it must also be smaller than αS, which must itself be considerably smaller than 1; for otherwise the use of the E–S analysis could not be justified.

Similar conclusions can be obtained with a constant elasticity utility function of either the Cobb-Douglas form or the logarithmic form, so long as the expected utility of wealth can be sufficiently closely approximated by their quadratic expansions, i.e.,

$$E[U(y)] = \frac{1}{1 - a} (\bar{y})^{1-a} - \frac{a}{2} \frac{S^2}{(\bar{y})^{1+a}}$$

or

$$E[U(y)] = \log \bar{y} - \frac{1}{2} \frac{S^2}{(\bar{y})^2}.$$

For then the slope the E–S indifference curves would be

$$\frac{d\bar{y}}{dS} = \frac{\dfrac{aS}{\bar{y}}}{\left[1 + \dfrac{a(1 + a)}{2} \dfrac{S^2}{(\bar{y})^2}\right]}, \tag{14}$$

or

$$\frac{d\bar{y}}{dS} = \frac{\dfrac{S}{\bar{y}}}{\left[1 + \dfrac{S^2}{(\bar{y})^2}\right]}, \tag{14'}$$

respectively. In both cases, $d\bar{y}/dS$ must be smaller than 1. It must also be smaller than $aS/\bar{y}$ or $S/\bar{y}$, as the case may be, which must themselves be considerably smaller than 1 for the use of E–S analysis to be justified.

Even in the cases of quadratic utility function and of normally distributed investment outcomes, where the E–S analysis is considered applicable without restriction, we shall also see that the slope of E–S indifference curves would be smaller than 1 in their relevant range. With a quadratic utility function, the impossibility of the derived E–S indifference curves to be steeper than $45°$ has already been pointed out by Tobin (1958).

In the case where all investment returns are assumed to be normally distributed, Tobin (1958, p. 75) has shown that for each level of $E[U]$,

$$\frac{d\bar{y}}{dS} = \frac{\int_{-\infty}^{\infty} z U'(\bar{y} + Sz)\phi(z; 0, 1)dz}{\int_{-\infty}^{\infty} U'(\bar{y} + Sz)\phi(z; 0,1)dz}, \tag{15}$$

where $\phi(z; 0, 1)$ is the normal density function with zero mean and unity variance. It is not possible to evaluate this expression quantitatively unless the utility function is specified, although it may be demonstrated that for a risk-averter, the indifference curves would be upward sloping and convex downward. It is clear that not every utility function can be employed with untruncated normally distributed returns, as the range of variations reaches from $-\infty$ to ∞. The quadratic utility function and the constant elasticity utility function are clearly ruled out.[13] With a negative exponential utility function $U = B(1 - e^{-\alpha y})$, however, (15) can be evaluated by a different approach; for with this utility function, the expected utility may be expanded into a series of deviations of y from its mean, as shown in (4).

Furthermore, with normal distribution, all odd order central moments vanish, and all even order higher central movements can be expressed as functions of S^2, viz.,[14]

$$\bar{m}_{2k} = \frac{(2k)!}{2^k k!} S^{2k}.$$

Hence

$$\frac{d\bar{m}_{2k}}{dS} = \frac{(2k)!}{2^{k-1}(k - 1)!} S^{2k-1}. \tag{16}$$

Differentiating (4) with respect to $\bar{y}$ and S after eliminating all terms with odd order moments and substituting (16) into the result and then setting both sides to zero, we obtain

Differentiating (4) with respect to $\bar{y}$ and S after eliminating all terms with odd order moments and substituting (16) into the result and then setting both sides to zero, we obtain

$$\frac{d\bar{y}}{dS} = \frac{\alpha S\left(1 + \dfrac{\alpha^2}{2} S^2 + \dfrac{\alpha^4}{8} S^4 + \ldots + \dfrac{\alpha^{2k}}{2^k.k!} S^{2k} + \ldots\right)}{\left(1 + \dfrac{\alpha^2}{2} S^2 + \dfrac{\alpha^4}{8} S^4 + \ldots + \dfrac{\alpha^{2k}}{2^k.k!} S^{2k} + \ldots\right)} = \alpha S. \quad (17)$$

Comparing (17) with (13) above, we can see that the slope of indifference curves computed with the quadratic approximation is a very good approximation indeed, when αS is a smaller fraction.

As we have shown above, the parameter α of a negative exponential utility function must be understood to be of the magnitude of $k/\bar{y}$, where $0 < k < 1$. Thus even though we are not concerned here with the rapidity of convergence, as we were when using quadratic approximation, still for all practical purposes in portfolio analysis, αS should generally be treated as smaller than 1. For αS to be greater than 1 would imply that the investor concerned is assuming a risk (i.e., the standard deviation of the value of his wealth) much larger than the expected value of his total wealth, including his human capital as well as all other nonhuman assets. This must be regarded as a most unlikely situation for a risk-avert investor, and any person with this kind of risk-asset ratio would certainly be considered extremely uncreditworthy. Thus even in this case, slopes of $E-S$ indifference curves should be understood to be normally much smaller than 1 in the range relevant for portfolio investors with risk-aversion, although it is not theoretically impossible for their slope to exceed 1.

It is to be noted, however, that in this case, the indifference curves thus traced out would incorporate all the indirect influences upon the expected utility of S through its linkages with all the even order higher moments, that are peculiar to normal distributions only.[15] Such a system of $E-S$ indifference curves, therefore, cannot be applied to cases where investment outcomes might have any other types of distributions. Certainly, it would be quite senseless to fit, say, two Bernoulli distributions to two points on any indifference curve of this system to try to prove its logical inconsistency.

The paradox posed by Feldstein's criticism can be clarified in the similar manner. He has shown that, with a log utility function and a lognormal distribution for investment outcomes, the $E-S$ indifference curves for a risk-averter need not always be convex downwards but would change from convex to concave, once the standard deviation S exceeds a certain crucial proportion of the mean of total wealth, viz., $\bar{y}/\sqrt{2}$. That is, if the expected utility of wealth is

$$E[U(y)] = \int_{-\infty}^{\infty} \log y f(y) dy \tag{18}$$

$$= \int_{-\infty}^{\infty} x\phi(x) dx = \mu$$

where $f(y)$ is a lognormal distribution and, hence, the logarithm of y, viz., x, has a normal distribution $\phi(x)$ with a mean μ and a variance σ^2, then

$$E[U(y)] = \log \bar{y} - \frac{1}{2}\log\left(\frac{S^2}{\bar{y}^2} + 1\right). \tag{19}$$

This follows readily from the well-known formulae for the mean and variance of a lognormal variable in terms of the mean μ and variance σ^2 of the logarithm of the variable, viz., $\bar{y} = E(y) = \exp(\mu + \sigma^2/2)$, and $S^2 = E(y - \bar{y})^2 = \bar{y}^2 (\exp \sigma^2 - 1)$. Differentiating (19) with respect to $\bar{y}$ and S, and setting both sides to zero we get

$$\frac{d\bar{y}}{dS} = \frac{\dfrac{S}{\bar{y}}}{\left(1 + 2\dfrac{S^2}{\bar{y}^2}\right)} \tag{20}$$

which is >0, but always <1. (See Feldstein, p. 8.)

Comparing this with equation (14′) above, again we see that the slope of E–S indifference curve, which we obtained there by using the quadratic approximation of the log utility function without specifying the probability distribution of investment returns, is indeed a close approximation for this case, provided that $S/\bar{y}$ is a small fraction.

Taking the second derivation along the indifference curve, it is found that

$$\frac{d^2\bar{y}}{dS^2} = \frac{\bar{y}(\bar{y}^2 - 2S^2)(\bar{y}^2 + S^2)}{(2S^2 + \bar{y}^2)^3}, \tag{21}$$

which is positive when $S^2/\bar{y}^2 < 1/2$, but becomes negative when $S^2/\bar{y}^2 > 1/2$, or $S/\bar{y} > 0.707$. (See Feldstein, p. 8.) The indifference curves would look something like the one in Figure 2. On the face of it, it appears that risk-aversion might eventually decrease as risk itself is increased![16]

Such a hasty interpretation, of course, would be quite unwarranted. The reversal of the change in the curvature of E–S indifference curves

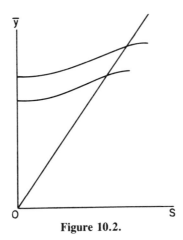

Figure 10.2.

in this case is essentially due to the particular linkages between the mean and variance and higher moments of lognormal distributions. Although lognormal distributions have only two parameters, they are not symmetric but positively skewed. The third central moment such a distribution $f(y)$, where $\log y$ is normally distributed with a mean μ and a variance σ^2, is given by the formula:[17]

$$\bar{m}_3 = \bar{y}^3(e^{3\sigma^2} - 3e^{\sigma^2} + 2). \tag{22}$$

Thus, $\bar{m}_3$ is an increasing function of both $\bar{y}$, the mean, and S^2, the variance, of y. Holding $\bar{y}$ constant, while we increase S, we find[18]

$$\frac{\partial \bar{m}_3}{\partial S} = 6\bar{y}S(e^{2\sigma^2} - 1) > 0. \tag{23}$$

Since a person with a log utility function must have a positive skewness preference, i.e., $\partial E[U]/\partial \bar{m}_3 = 1/3\bar{y}^3 > 0$, and since in Feldstein's derivation of the slope of indifference curves the indirect influences of a change in variance through its linkages with the third and other moments are all taken into account, it is not surprising that the positive influence of the increasing skewness should partly offset the negative influence of increasing dispersion itself.

It is interesting to note that in this case also, E–S indifference curves can never reach a slope of 1; for in this case, indifference curves would attain their maximum slope at their points of inflexion, i.e., at $S/\bar{y} = \sqrt{0.5}$. At the inflexion, the maximum slope is max $(d\bar{y}/dS) = (\sqrt{0.5}/2) = 0.3536$, which is considerably smaller than 1.

It should also be noted that Feldstein's indifference curves are not, strictly speaking, the indifference curves for the expected value of wealth and its standard deviation per se, but for the mean and the standard deviation when they are known to be linked with all other higher moments in the particular ways inherent to the log-normal distribution; viz., through the relationship

$$E(y^k) = \exp\left(k\mu + \frac{\sigma^2 k^2}{2}\right) \tag{24}$$

$$= (\bar{y})^k \exp\left[(k - 1)\,\frac{k\sigma^2}{2}\right]$$

where μ and σ^2 are the mean and variance of $\log y$.[19] They are not derived from knowledge of the investor's utility function alone. They are, therefore, not applicable, unless the terminal value of the investor's total wealth is known to be distributed strictly according to the lognormal distribution.

In general, as Samuelson pointed out (1967), if we want to take into account in the indifference contours all the indirect effects of the mean and variance through their linkages with higher movements, then for a given utility function, we would have a different set of indifference curves for each probability distribution of the terminal value of the total wealth of the investor concerned. We can get a unique set of E–S indifference curves from a given utility function, only if we treat the truncated quadratic expansion of the expected utility function as an adequate approximation and neglect all higher moments. As we have seen, this is justifiable only when $S/\bar{y}$ is fairly small. For small values of $S/\bar{y}$, Feldstein's indifference curves are certainly convex downwards and closely approximated by those derived with the quadratic approximation. It is only when $S/\bar{y}$ is quite large, approaching $\sqrt{0.5} = 0.7071$, that problem of nonconvexity begins to appear. But before that happens, the mean-variance approximation would already have to be supplemented by consideration of the third and higher moments, or even abandoned altogether.

Thus it is clear that while the E–S analysis might be an adequate method of approximation for analyzing the investment behavior of small risk-takers (cautious portfolio investors who normally assume rather small risks relatively to their total wealth), for major risk-takers (entrepreneurs who regularly risk a major proportion of their total wealth), it would have to be supplemented or abandoned.

3. Implications for the Theory of the Demand for Money

One important conclusion of the above discussion is that $E–S$ indifference curves, insofar as their use is warranted, would never attain a slope of 45° or more. Usually, and for cautious portfolio investors in particular, the slopes of $E–S$ indifference curves stay very much less than that. This conclusion has important implications for the theory of the demand for money.

In his pioneering work on the $E–S$ analysis, "Liquidity Preference as Behavior Towards Risk," Tobin employed this analysis to explain why rational people would hold idle cash in their investment portfolios.[20] Although cash yields no income, the risk attached to other income-yielding assets may offset the attraction of their positive yields so that they are no more attractive to hold than cash at the margin of portfolio equilibrium. Diagrammatically, portfolio equilibrium is depicted as a tangency point (except in the case of a "plunger") of a yield-risk opportunity curve with one of the $E–S$ indifference curves, which are usually drawn without much attention to the constraint on their slopes.

If it is realized that the slope of $E–S$ indifference curves usually stay well below 45°, this explanation for the demand for cash in the investment portfolio becomes highly implausible. For if there is any financial asset, the expected yield[21] of which is at least as large as the standard deviation of that yield, then that asset will surely be preferred to cash as investment. If may be shown with the help of Figure 3.

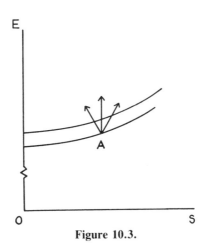

Figure 10.3.

Suppose the existing portfolio of a given investor, the mean and risk of which are represented by the coordinates of the point A on a certain indifference curve, still contains some amount of idle cash holding. If there is any asset, the expected yield (as defined in the preceding footnote) of which is no smaller than it own standard deviation, then by substituting this asset for cash, the investor can move upward from A on the E–S plane at an angle with the horizontal axis at least equal to, but more likely greater than, 45°. See Figure 3. For by substituting that asset for cash, he increases the expected terminal value of his total wealth by the expected yield of that asset, whereas the increment in his total risk would generally be less than the risk of the newly acquired asset itself, so long as the yield of that asset is not perfectly correlated positively with the yield of the existing portfolio. Hence the angle of direction of the move is likely to be greater than 45° with respect to the horizontal, even if the expected yield of the new asset is no greater than its own standard deviation.[22]

If the slope of the E–S indifference curve at A is known to be smaller than 45°, then such a move would certainly carry him to a higher indifference curve. And so long as the slopes of high indifference curves remain smaller than 45°, such moves can be repeated, until the cash holding in the investment portfolio is exhausted.

Thus in order to demonstrate that investment or speculative cash balances really has no place at all in a rational investment portfolio, it is not necessary to show that there is some asset that "dominates" cash (i.e., as riskless as cash, but has in addition some positive yield). Nor is it necessary to show that there is some asset, the expected yield of which is larger than the maximum possible downward deviation from the expected yield. All that is necessary is to demonstrate that there is at least one asset, the expected yield of which is not smaller than its own standard deviation, or at least one asset with a positive expected yield, however small, which is uncorrelated, or negatively correlated, with the yield of the existing portfolio of the investor concerned. The existence of such assets would eliminate all demand for cash for the portfolio balance purpose.[23] Surely, there must be a host of assets in modern financial markets, e.g., savings deposits and Treasury bills, that would satisfy these requirements.

Thus although the E–S analysis was at first introduced by Tobin to explain liquidity preference in the sense of an investment demand for cash, in our defense of it against its critics, we actually find that it is quite incapable of doing what Tobin has expected of it. Rather it seems to indicate that there cannot be any investment demand for money for the so-called portfolio balance purpose. The demand for money must arise from the requirements of anticipated transactions and the precaution against contingencies calling for unplanned cash expenditures. Our discussion should, therefore, cast some strong doubts on the alleged superiority of the modern "wealth approach" or "portfolio balance approach" to monetary theory, which ironically seems to hold sway at present among both the neo-Keynesians and the neo-monetarists.

Incidentally, the importance of skewness preference for major risk-takers should obviously be taken into consideration in problems of investment incentives. For instance, the effects of income tax on risk-taking should be examined not only with respect to its impacts on the mean and variance of investment returns after tax, but also with respect to its impact on the skewness of net returns. A progressive income tax or an income tax without adequate loss offset would certainly have greater adverse effect on the willingness to take risk than a proportional income tax with perfect loss offset that would leave the mean and variance after tax at the same levels.

Notes

*I have benefited from comments by Paul Samuelson, Henry Wan and Leonard Mirman, who have read the draft, and from suggestions of the referee.
1. In this, our justification of the E–S analysis differs from Samuelson's (1970); for Samuelson's defense for the E–S analysis seems to rely upon the risk itself being very small in absolute magnitude.
2. I do not see, however, any compelling reason why utility functions must be bounded both from above and from below. If Arrow's only concern is that "if the utility function is unbounded one can always construct an action with an infinite utility" (p. 25), I fail to see why we should be bothered with such possibilities. Samuelson has indicated to me in a correspondence that he agrees with me on the nonnecessity of the boundedness of utility functions.
3. In this case, the absolute risk aversion = $-U''/U' = \alpha$.
4. The relative risk aversion in the case of constant elasticity utility function of the form $K + [1/(1 - a)]y^{1-a}$ is $yU''/U' = a$. In the case of log utility function, it is unity.

When $a > 1$, $U(y) = K + [1/(1 - a)]y^{1-a}$, like $U(y) = \log y$, approaches $-\infty$, as $y \to 0$. The utility function cannot be continuous when extended to the range of negtive wealth.

When y is negative, $\log y$ is, of course, not real.

When $1 - a > 0$ and is rational, so that y^{1-a} can be written as $y^{p/q}$, where p and q are integers, then if q is even and p odd, $U(y)$ would be imaginary when y is negative. If q is odd but p is even, the utility of negative wealth would be positive and the marginal utility of wealth would be negative. When both p and q are odd, the utility for negative wealth would indeed be negative and the marginal utility positive, but then the marginal utility would increase with wealth, when y is negative.

When $1 - a$ is irrational, y^{1-a} is undefined when y is negative.

5. Lately Benoit Mandlebrot and Eugene Fama (1965, 1971) claim that returns on speculative holdings of commodities or common stocks appear to be distributed according to nonnormal members of stable Paretian distributions with no finite moments. Their claims, however, are open to at least two grave doubts. First, even if it is granted that percentage daily fluctuations of stock or commodity prices do appear to conform well with some nonnormal stable Paretian distribution within the very limited range of observed daily changes, there is no guarantee that fluctuations of stock and commodity prices must conform with such a distribution over its entire range from $-\infty$ to $+\infty$. Indeed, to make such a fantastic claim would clearly run afoul of the obvious constraint that the decline in stock or commodity prices cannot possibly exceed 100 percent. What Mandelbrot and Fama have in mind must be some sort of *truncated* stable Paretian distributions, which, being truncated, would not have infinite moments, nor would be stable under addition.

Secondly, it does not seem to me possible to find an acceptable utility function (in the sense of one that satisfies the above four conditions) that can be applied to a stable Paretian distribution with no finite moments and yet yields a finite possitive expected utility—a necessary condition that investments with returns of such probability distributions would be desired at all. For instance, the negative exponential utility function, which is the only one that I can think of that has the required properties for a risk averter over the full range of wealth variation from $-\infty$ to $+\infty$, would, when applied to a Cauchy distribution (the only nonnormal stable Paretian distribution whose analytical function is known), invariably yields an expected utility of $-\infty$, so long as the mean (or rather median) of the distribution is finite. That is

$$E(U) = B \int_{-\infty}^{\infty} \left\{ 1 - \frac{e^{-y}}{\pi[1 + (y - m)^2]} \right\} dy = -\infty$$

for any finite value of m.

So far Mandlebrot and Fama have failed to show what kind of utility functions investors must have for them to put a finite positive valuation on any prospect of return with an infinite variance, and whether the indicated utililty functions would have the necessary properties for an ordinary risk-avert investor.

6. The connection between decreasing absolute risk aversion and U''' being positive was also pointed out by Joseph Stiglitz (p. 279). But he did not point out that this implies a skewness preference, since he did not operate with moments at all. A note of caution must be entered here; viz., that $\mu_3 = \bar{m}_3/S^3$ is not a perfect measure of skewness. Although a symmetric distribution would necessarily have a zero $\bar{m}_3$ or μ_3, a zero $\bar{m}_3$ or μ_3 does

not imply that the distribution is symmetrical. Nevertheless, μ_3 is usually regarded by applied statisticians as a highly satisfactory measure of skewness.

7. Samuelson in his latest article (1970) has also pointed out that the introduction of the third and higher moments would improve the accuracy of the mean-variance analysis, but he did not say whether the third central moment should have a positive or negative influence on the expected utility.

8. Equations (6) and (6′) are really quite similar, especially since Arrow argues that "the relative risk aversion" (which in the case of (6) is $yU''/U' = a$) "must hover around 1" (p. 37).

9. Stiglitz's contribution on taxation and risk-taking, and David Levhari and T. N. Srivasan and L. J. Mirman on uncertainty and savings are good examples of this approach.

10. The case of a log utility function combined with a lognormal distribution for returns of investment seems to be an exception. See Feldstein's 1969 paper which will be discussed below. However, the peculiar ease of integrating the expected utility function would disappear when one realizes that there might be a certain core in the investor's total wealth, and that the lognormal distribution might apply only to the marginal investment on some risky assets.

11. To show that $(y_i - x) > 0$, it is necessary only to show that $y_1 > x$. From (7) and (9), we may obtain

$$
\begin{aligned}
y_i - x &= \frac{E_1(E_2 - E_1) + S_1(S_2 - S_1)}{(E_2 - E_1)} - \frac{S_2 E_1 - S_1 E_2}{(S_2 - S_1)} \\
&= \frac{S_1(E_2 - E_1)^2 + S_1(S_2 - S_1)^2}{(E_2 - E_1)(S_2 - S_1)} > 0.
\end{aligned}
$$

12. For instance, G. O. Bierwag and Myron Grove by neglecting the constraint on the slopes of E–S indifference curves, were led to the strange conclusion that the indifference curves for any two risky assets (the yield-risk ratios of which are unspecified) are closed curves, which are drawn in their Figure 3 as concentric circles, with the center at some bliss point, apparently not related to the concept of an ultimate bliss in certain types of utility functions such as the negative exponential function. This would imply that a portfolio of, say, 10 shares each of, say, GM and IBM might yield the same expected utility as a portfolio of, say, a million shares each of these two stocks; and that, in the latter situation, the owner could increase his expected utility by destroying some of both assets—a phenomenon which Bierwag and Grove call "contamination by risk," but which is obviously contrary to our common sense.

Now if we realize that the E–S indifference curves would never have slopes greater than unity, then a ray from the origin in the positive E–S space with a slope greater than unity would never cut the same E–S indifference curve twice. Mapped into the two asset space, it means that so long as none of the two assets has a risk greater than its own expected terminal value (which can certainly be said for either GM or IBM stocks, even though they are not riskless), no rays from the origin representing proportionate variations of given portfolios of these two stocks should cut any asset indifference curves more than once. Thus the paradoxical conclusion of Bierwag and Grove can be shown to be incorrect, because they assumed that E–S indifference curves can slope up to be asymptotic to the vertical, so that any rays, with slope of 45° or more, can still cut each E–S indifference curve at two points. Actually the so-called phenomenon of contamination by risk cannot take place unless the risk of the asset involved is greater than its expected terminal value.

13. According to Samuelson (1967, p. 9), an investor with a log utility function would evaluate any normally distributed investment outcome as having an expected utility of $-\infty$. The same can be said of an investor with a constant elasticity utility function with an elasticity greater than unity, since in this case, as in the case of log utility function, utility would approach minus infinity as wealth approaches zero from above.

14. See, e.g., B. W. Lindgren, pp. 87 and 89.

15. As pointed out by Samuelson (1967, p.11), such indifference contours are not drawn from knowledge of the decision maker's risk preferences alone. They must, therefore, be redrawn for each new probability distribution of random outcomes.

16. In fact, if we take the second derivatives of (13), (14) or (14') with respect to S along the respective indifference curves, we would find essentially similar results, viz., that in each case, the indifference curves would be convex downward only when $S/\bar{y}$ is smaller than a certain value, but becomes concave when $S/\bar{y}$ is greater than that value. However, since (13), (14), and (14') are derived from the quadratic approximation of the expected utility functions and such approximation is justified only when $S/\bar{y}$ is very small, only the convex sections of the indifference curves would be meaningful.

17. See e.g., Lindgren, p. 89, where the kth moment about zero of a lognormal distribution is given as $E(y^k) = \exp(k\mu + (1/2)\sigma^2 k^2)$, and $\mathrm{Var}(y) = (\exp\sigma^2 - 1) \cdot (2\mu + \sigma^2)$. From these, it may be worked out that

$$\bar{m}_3 = (\exp 3\sigma^2 - 3\exp\sigma^2 + 2)\bar{y}^3.$$

18. This means that we let σ^2 increase, while reducing μ to keep $\bar{y} = \exp(\mu + \sigma^2/2)$ constant. Since $S^2 = \bar{y}^2 (\exp\sigma^2 - 1)$,

$$\frac{\partial \bar{m}_3}{\partial S} = \frac{\partial \bar{m}_3}{\partial \sigma^2} \cdot \frac{\partial \sigma^2}{\partial S} = 6\bar{y}S(\exp 2\sigma^2 - 1).$$

19. See Lindgren, p. 89.

20. The investment portfolio, or investment balance, is defined by Tobin as funds "that will survive all the expected seasonal excess of cumulative expenditures over cumulative receipts during the year ahead. They are balances which will not have to be turned into cash within the year" (1958, p.66).

21. We define the expected yield of an asset as the expected terminal value (including accrued interest) of a dollar's worth of that asset at current price minus 1.

22. Suppose that the expected terminal value of an investor's total wealth at point A in Figure 3 is $E(W) = W_0[1 + w_p u_p + (1 - w_p)u_c)] = W_0(1 + w_p u_p)$, where W_0 is the initial value of his wealth, $w_p < 1$ is the proportion of his wealth invested in some earning portfolio, the average expected rate of return of which is u_p, and u_c is the rate of return of cash holding, which is assumed to be zero. Since the terminal value of cash holding is supposed to be perfectly certain, the standard deviation of the terminal value of his wealth is simply $S(W) = W_0 w_p \sigma_p$, where σ_p is the standard deviation of the terminal value of his portfolio of earning assets.

    Now suppose that he decides to transfer a small fraction of his wealth x from cash holding on to an asset i with an expected rate of return u_i and a variance σ_i^2, then the expected terminal value of his wealth would be $E(W) = W_0[1 + w_p u_p + x u_i]$, and its standard deviation would be

$$S(W) = W_0[w_p^2 \sigma_p^2 + x^2 \sigma_i^2 + 2w_p x \rho_{pi} \sigma_p \sigma_i]^{1/2},$$

where $\rho_{pi} = \sigma_{pi}/\sigma_p \sigma_i$ is the correlation coefficient between u_p and u_i.

Differentiate both $E(W)$ and $S(W)$ with respect to x, we get $\partial E/\partial x = W_0 u_i$, and

$$\frac{\partial S}{\partial x} = \frac{W_0(x\sigma_i^2 + w_p \rho_{pi} \sigma_p \sigma_i)}{(w_p^2 \sigma_p^2 + x^2 \sigma_i^2 + 2w_p x \rho_{pi} \sigma_p \sigma_i)^{1/2}}$$

$$= W_0 \rho_{pi} \sigma_i, \text{ (at } x = 0).$$

   Therefore, by increasing x at A, where $x = 0$, the (E, S) vector of the investor's total wealth can be moved in the direction of $dE/dS = u_i/\rho_{pi}\sigma_i > u_i/\sigma_i$, so long as $\rho_{pi} < 1$. If $\rho_{pi} = 0$, i.e., if u_i is totally uncorrelated with u_p, then $dE/dS = \infty$. In this case, the arrow drawn from A in Figure 3 would form an angle of 90° with the horizontal, i.e., it would point vertically upward. If u_i is negatively correlated with u_p, then $dE/dS < 0$. In this case, the arrow from A would form an angle greater than 90° with the horizontal, i.e., it would point northwest. In the latter two cases, there is no question but that higher indifference curves would be reached by moving along the arrow (i.e., by increasing x at A).

23. Actually Tobin has already noticed, incidentally to his discussion of the effect of a change in interest rate on liquidity preference, that, with a quadratic utility function, if the rate of interest of bonds r exceeds the risk of bonds σ_g, then tangency solution is impossible (i.e., the investor must hold all bonds no cash). To prove it, he used a rather devious method, suggested to him by Arthur Okun (See (1958) p. 79, especially fn. 1). Actually, the proof should be very simple. If $r > \sigma_g$, then the slope of the opportunity locus $r/\sigma_g > 1$. However, with a quadratic utility function, the slope of mean-standard deviation indifference curves must always be smaller than 1. Hence, tangency solution is impossible. Now we have seen that this is true with all acceptable utility functions for a risk averter. Feldstein also noted that with a lognormal distribution of returns to bonds and a *log* utility function, "the investor will be a 'plunger,' holding only bonds, unless their variance is very high in relation to their expected yield" (p. 9).

References

K. J. Arrow, *Aspects of the Theory of Risk-Bearing, Lectures,* Helsinki 1964.

G. O. Bierwag, and M. A. Grove, "Indifference Curve in Asset Analysis," *Econ. J.,* June 1966, **76**, 337–43.

K. Borch, "A Note on Uncertainty and Indifference Curves," *Rev. Econ. Stud.,* Jan. 1969, **36**, 1–4.

P. H. Cootner, *The Random Character of Stock Market Prices,* Cambridge, Mass. 1964.

E. F. Fama, "The Behavior of Stock Market Prices," *J. Bus. Univ. Chicago,* Jan. 1965, **38**, 34–105.

E. F. Fama, "Risk, Return and Equilibrium," *J. Polit. Econ.,* Jan./Feb. 1971, **79**, 30–35.

M. S. Feldstein, "Mean-Variance Analysis in the Theory of Liquidity Preference and Portfolio Selection," *Rev. Econ. Stud.,* Jan. 1969, **36**, 5–12.

J. Hicks, "Liquidity," *Econ. J.,* Dec. 1962, **72**, 787–802.

D. Levhari, and T. N. Srivasan, "Optimal Savings under Uncertainty," *Rev. Econ. Stud.,* Apr. 1969, **36**, 153–64.

B. W. Lindgren, *Statistical Theory,* New York 1965.

B. Mandelbrot, "The Variation of Certain Speculative Prices," *J. Bus. Univ. Chicago,* Oct. 1963, **36**, 394–419.

H. Markowitz, "Portfolio Selection," *J. Finance,* Mar. 1952, **7**, 77–91.

L. J. Mirman, "Uncertainty and Optimal Consumption Decisions," *Econometrica,* Jan. 1971, **36**, 177–83.

J. W. Pratt, "Risk Aversion in The Small and in The Large," *Econometrica,* Jan. 1964, **32**, 122–36.

M. Richter, "Cardinal Utility, Portfolio Selection and Taxation," *Rev. Econ. Stud.,* Apr. 1960, **27**, 152–66.

P. A. Samuelson, "General Proof that Diversification Pays," *J. Finance Quant. Anal.,* Mar. 1967, **2**, 1–13.

P. A. Samuelson, "The Fundamental Approximation Theorem of Portfolio Analysis in Terms of Means, Variances and Higher Moments," *Rev. Econ. Stud.,* Oct. 1970, **37**, 537–42.

J. E. Stiglitz, "The Effects of Income, Wealth and Capital Gains Taxation on Risk-Taking," *Quart. J. Econ.,* May 1969, **83**, 263–83.

J. Tobin, "Liquidity Preference as Behavior Towards Risk," *Rev. Econ. Stud.,* Feb. 1958, **25**, 65–85.

J. Tobin, "Comment on Borch and Feldstein," *Rev. Econ. Stud.,* Jan. 1969, **36**, 13–14.

CHAPTER 11

The Diffusion of Reserves and the Money Supply Multiplier*

S. C. Tsiang

1. Introduction

The theory of the supply of money has long remained at the stage of mechanistic determination represented by such money supply multiplier equations as

$$M = \frac{Z}{c + r_1(1 - c) + r_2 t},$$
(1)

where M is the total money supply defined as total currency in circulation outside banks plus total demand deposits. Z is the total reserve base in existence, c is the proportion of the total money supply which the public wants to keep in the form of currency, t the amount of time and savings deposits which the public wants to hold as a ratio of the money supply, and r_1 and r_2 are the reserve ratios for the demand and time deposits, respectively. Such an equation is either a tautology if c, t, r_1 and r_2 are understood as the actual ratios between the relevant variables, or an expression of the equilibrium value of money supply, if those ratios are defined as the desired equilibrium relationships between

Finance Constraints and the Theory of Money
ISBN 0-12-701720-8
ISBN 0-12-701721-6 (pbk)

249

Reprinted with permission from *The Economic Journal*, Vol. LXXXVIII, (June 1978) pp. 269–284.

the relevant variables. As a tautology the equation is indeed true at all times, but then it says little more than that the money supply is what it is. As an expression of the equilibrium value for the total money supply, it merely indicates what the money supply would tend to be, if the money supply mechanism is stable, but then how the supposedly fixed coefficients c and t are expected to result from the spending and portfolio decisions of a multitude of individuals needs to be examined in the dynamic context of monetary expansion.

Moreover, such money supply equations seldom allow for more than two types of bank deposits with different reserve requirements, namely, demand deposits and savings or time deposits, apart from currency in circulation. Actually in the United States, at least four types of bank deposits should be distinguished, as the reserve requirement for each type is quite different from those for the others. First, there are the demand deposits of reserve city member banks, for which the reserve requirement is usually the highest. Second come the demand deposits of country member banks with the next highest reserve requirement. Third in the order of reserve requirement are the savings and time deposits. Lastly, we have the deposits of nonmember banks, for which no legal reserve requirement is set, and for which only a minimal amount of reserve of high power money is held in the form of vault cash.[1]

Since November 1972 the distinction in reserve requirements between reserve city member banks and country member banks has been eliminated. New distinctions in marginal reserve requirements, however, have been imposed on the basis of the outstanding volumes of demand liabilities of member banks regardless of their location. The bank reserve regulation in effect since 31 December 1973 stipulates that for net demand deposits of a member bank totalling less than two million dollars, the reserve requirement is 8%; for net demand deposits between two million and ten million dollars, the ratio is $10\frac{1}{2}\%$; for those between ten and a hundred million dollars, $12\frac{1}{2}\%$; for those between a hundred and four hundred million dollars, 18%. Similarly, for time deposits totalling less than five million dollars and for all savings deposits, the required reserve ratio is 3%; while for time deposits over five million dollars the ratio is 5%. Thus to formulate an accurate marginal money supply multiplier, we have to distinguish at least five categories of demand deposits and two categories of savings and time deposits. Furthermore, since the required reserve ratio for a given type of deposit may change abruptly when the amount of those deposits at any given bank reaches certain critical levels, the aggregate reserve requirement of a given bank is no longer a linear function of its deposits. The non-linearity of the reserve requirement function would introduce much complexity into the problem of determining the money supply multiplier. Indeed, it appears as if the Federal Reserve System deliberately wanted to make its own job of controlling the money supply more difficult!

In addition, what would seem to make the determination of the money supply multiplier even more complicated is that these different categories of deposits would most likely be turning over at different velocities. Thus units of high-power money lodged in the reserves for different types of deposits would therefore diffuse to other banks at different speeds. This fact is difficult to take into proper account in the traditional approach which applies a simple converging geometric series to describe the process of money supply expansion. What influences the differing rates of turnover of different types of deposits would have on the equilibrium magnitude of total money supply and on the relative equilibrium volumes of different types of deposits should obviously be of some importance.

Finally, modern banking theory has made it quite clear that the parameters in the money supply equation (1), i.e. c, t, r_1 and r_2, may not be exogenously given but might be subject to the influences of such endogenous factors as the structure of interest rates. Recent developments in money supply theory, therefore, have mostly concentrated on remedying the traditional theory with analysis of bank behaviour in response to changes in market interest rates and the central bank discount rate. The process of diffusion of an injection of reserve base into banks of different types with different reserve requirements, however, has to my knowledge not been adequately investigated.

This paper proposes to deal with this neglected aspect of reserve diffusion by applying a modified Markov chain analysis to the study of the process of money and credit expansion in response to an injection of additional reserve base. The analysis here will be conducted under the simplifying assumption of constant desired as well as required deposit reserve ratios. It would provide a basic framework upon which recent developments in the variability of desired reserve ratios of banks might be superimposed much as the input–output model of the fixed coefficients would form the basis for similar models with variable coefficients. The advantages of this approach are that we shall be able to handle as many banks with as varied reserve requirements as there might be, and that we shall be able to take account of the differing rates of turnover of different types of deposits in our analysis. It will be seen that the traditional money supply multiplier equation is but a simplified description of the steady state of the reserve diffusion process.

It will be shown that the approach to such a steady-state equilibrium may be either asymptotic or oscillating. Indeed, it is even possible that in some extraordinary circumstances, which will be shown to be rather unlikely in reality, the steady state might not be stable so that the system would not approach it, but would diverge from it. As our attempt to determine the stability of the matrix of reserve diffusion and credit expansion by standard analytical methods fails to yield conclusive results, simulation on a small scale is tried to determine within what ranges of values for the crucial parameters involved stability of the system can be reasonably assured.

The influence of the rates of interest on loans, deposits, and other assets, however, will not be dealt with in this analysis, but they can no doubt be introduced into our scheme later, though at some cost of more mathematical complications. The problem of non-linearity of the reserve requirement functions will also be bypassed by assuming that the variations in different kinds of deposits we are considering here would not be big enough to involve crossings of the critical levels, at which the required reserve ratios for deposits abruptly change, and which are fortunately very widely apart anyway.

2. A Markov Chain Approach to the Process of Bank Reserve Diffusion[2]

Let y_{it} = the expected inflow of deposits into a given bank i during period t, and x_{jt} = the expected outflow of deposits from bank j during period t.

Suppose that the outflow of deposits from one bank always ends up in being deposited in some banks including the original bank. Of course part of the outflow may end up as currency in the pockets of some individuals or cash boxes of some firms. However, we may treat currency in pockets as deposits in some special type of banks (say piggy banks or bank n) with special regulations of their own to be specified later.

Let $\mathbf{A}$ be a stochastic matrix, the column elements of which give the probabilities of a given dollar outflow from each bank being redeposited into each of the other banks and itself, so that the expected value of the inflow of deposits to a given bank i would be[3]

$$y_{it} = \sum_j a_{ij} x_{jt} + \Delta z_{it},$$

or

$$\mathbf{y}_t = \mathbf{A}\mathbf{x}_t + \Delta \mathbf{z}_t, \tag{2}$$

where

$$\sum_i a_{ij} = 1, \ \sum_j a_{ij} \text{ not necessarily} = 1.$$

Δz_{it} is the new reserve money created by the open market operations of the central bank during the period that gets deposited by the sellers of bonds into the bank i; and $\Delta \mathbf{z}_t$ is the vector of such deposits of new reserve money at each of the banks.[4]

Let the outflow of deposits of a given bank i be the product of the outstanding balance of its total deposits d_i and their rate of turnover k_i plus the coefficient of utilisation k_i^* (defined as the percentage of the new loans drawn upon during the same period in which they are granted) times the net new loans and investment made by that bank, l_i, i.e.

$$\mathbf{x}_t = \delta[\mathbf{k}]\mathbf{d}_t + \delta[\mathbf{k}^*]l_t, \tag{3}$$

where $\delta[\ ]$ is to be understood as a diagonal matrix with the elements of the column vector inside the square brackets written along its main diagonal. $\mathbf{k}, \mathbf{k}^*$ are vectors, as they may be different for different banks, e.g. the rate of turnover of deposits in savings banks is much lower than that in commercial banks. We may choose the unit period in such a way that $k_i \leqslant 1$. k_i^* is usually also $\leqslant 1$, as most banks implicitly or explicitly require their borrowers to retain a certain portion of their loans as balances in their accounts with the lending banks. For the subsequent periods, the unspent balances of the loans are treated as ordinary deposit balances.

Let $\mathbf{d}_t$ = the balance of total deposits outstanding at the very beginning of period t carried over from the preceding period, and $\mathbf{l}_t$ = net new "loans" granted during the period t. Then

$$\mathbf{d}_t = \mathbf{d}_{t-1} + l_{t-1} + (\mathbf{y}_{t-1} - \mathbf{x}_{t-1}). \tag{4}$$

Substituting for $\mathbf{y}$ and $\mathbf{x}$ by using (2) and (3), we get

$$\mathbf{d}_t = \{\mathbf{I} + (\mathbf{A} - \mathbf{I})\delta[\mathbf{k}]\}\mathbf{d}_{t-1} + \{(\mathbf{A} - \mathbf{I})\delta[\mathbf{k}^*] + \mathbf{I}\}l_{t-1} + \Delta \mathbf{z}_{t-1}. \tag{-5}$$

Here we shall define the term "loans" very broadly to include all earning assets (or nonreserve assets) of the bank. Suppose that the amount of such new "loans" created by a bank is determined by its excess reserves including those coming into its possession during the preceding period. Net addition to (or net reduction in) excess reserves during the period that just ended may be formulated as

$$\Delta e_t = (y_{t-1} - x_{t-1}) - \delta[r](d_t - d_{t-1})$$

where r is the vector of required (or desired) reserve ratios of different banks, and $\delta[r]$ is again a diagonal matrix with the components of the vector r along its diagonal. The reserve ratio for currency in pockets, i.e. r_n, is obviously 1. Thus the amount of excess reserves at the beginning of period t, i.e. e_t, is

$$e_t = (y_{t-1} - x_{t-1}) - \delta[r](d_t - d_{t-1}) + e_{t-1}. \qquad (6)$$

Thus new "loans" creation in period t may be formulated as

$$\begin{aligned} l_t &= \delta[b]e_t \\ &= \delta[b]\{(A - I)x_{t-1} - \delta[r](d_t - d_{t-1})\} + \delta[b](\Delta z_{t-1} + e_{t-1}), \qquad (7) \end{aligned}$$

where b is a vector indicating the response of each bank to its own excess reserves. It might be objected here that this formulation of new loan creation totally ignores the influence of the demand for bank loans (i.e. the supply of loan assets by borrowers). This objection, however, is not as serious as it appears, for we understand here by "loans" all the non-cash earning assets of banks, including bills, bonds, investments, as well as loans in the narrow sense. The acquisition of these earning assets in general by each bank is certainly not restricted by the aggregate supply of these assets. We do ignore, however, the possibility that the loan expansion coefficients [b] and the desired reserve ratios [r] might vary in response to changes in the interest structure, as practically every formulation of the money supply multiplier also does.

It would seem that b_n for bank n, i.e. currency in pockets or cash boxes, should be taken as 0. However, since we have already set $r_n = 1$ above so that there can never be any "excess reserve" in the currency sector (i.e. e_n would always be equal to 0), we can assign an arbitrary value for b_n here, say, 1. This has some computation convenience because we can then write

$$e_t = \delta[b]^{-1}l_t, \qquad (8)$$

which we would not be able to do if some b's have the value of zero.

$[\Delta z_{t-1}]$ is a vector indicating the initial distribution of the newly created reserve money resulting from Federal Reserve bank's open market operation. Δz's are usually heavily concentrated at a few big city banks in New York City, where the open market operations take place. The new addition to the reserve base Z would gradually diffuse throughout the banking system of the country in a process of modified Markov chain with reactions.

Eliminating $\mathbf{x}_{t-1}$, $\mathbf{d}_t$ and $\mathbf{e}_{t-1}$ from (7) by using (2), (3), (4) and (8) we obtain

$$l_t = \delta[\mathbf{w}](\mathbf{A} - \mathbf{I})\delta[\mathbf{k}]\mathbf{d}_{t-1} + \{\delta[\mathbf{w}](\mathbf{A} - \mathbf{I})\delta[\mathbf{k}^*] + \delta[\mathbf{v}]\}l_{t-1}$$
$$+ \delta[\mathbf{w}]\Delta\mathbf{z}_{t-1}, \quad (9)$$

where

$$w_i = b_i(1 - r_i) \text{ and } v_i = (1 - b_i r_i).$$

Thus we have the system

$$\begin{bmatrix} \mathbf{d}_t \\ l_t \end{bmatrix} = Q \begin{bmatrix} \mathbf{d}_{t-1} \\ l_{t-1} \end{bmatrix} + \begin{bmatrix} \Delta\mathbf{z}_{t-1} \\ \delta[\mathbf{w}]\Delta\mathbf{z}_{t-1} \end{bmatrix}, \quad (10)$$

where

$$Q = \begin{bmatrix} \mathbf{I} + (\mathbf{A} - \mathbf{I})\delta[\mathbf{k}] & \vdots & (\mathbf{A} - \mathbf{I})\delta[\mathbf{k}^*] + \mathbf{I} \\ \delta[\mathbf{w}](\mathbf{A} - \mathbf{I})\delta[\mathbf{k}] & \vdots & \delta[\mathbf{w}](\mathbf{A} - \mathbf{I})\delta[\mathbf{k}^*] + \delta[\mathbf{v}] \end{bmatrix}$$

is the matrix of the system.

3. Existence and Uniqueness of the Steady-state Equilibrium of the Diffusion Process

A steady-state equilibrium, with $\Delta\mathbf{z} = \mathbf{0}$, should imply that $\mathbf{d}_t = \mathbf{d}_{t-1} > \mathbf{0}$, and $l_t = l_{t-1} = \mathbf{0}$. It is to be recalled that l has been defined above as net new creation (or contraction, if negative) of loans. Therefore, at any steady-state equilibrium, l_t should be null, since no bank should be constantly expanding or contracting its loans.

Mathematically, it can also be shown that no non-null vector of l would be consistent with any steady-state vector of $\mathbf{d}$ under our system. Take the homogeneous case of equation system (10), i.e. with no reserve injections. At steady state, by the upper partition of (10), we have

$$\bar{\mathbf{d}} = \{\mathbf{I} + (\mathbf{A} - \mathbf{I})\delta[\mathbf{k}]\}\bar{\mathbf{d}} + \{(\mathbf{A} - \mathbf{I})\delta[\mathbf{k}^*] + \mathbf{I}\}\bar{l}, \quad (11)$$

from which we may obtain

$$(\mathbf{A} - \mathbf{I})\delta[\mathbf{k}]\bar{\mathbf{d}} = -(\mathbf{A} - \mathbf{I})\delta[\mathbf{k}^*]\bar{l} - \bar{l} \tag{12}$$

At the same time, by the lower partition of (10) we have

$$\bar{l} = \delta[\mathbf{w}](\mathbf{A} - \mathbf{I})\delta[\mathbf{k}]\bar{\mathbf{d}} + \delta[\mathbf{w}](\mathbf{A} - \mathbf{I})\delta[\mathbf{k}^*]\bar{l} + \delta[\mathbf{v}]\bar{l}.$$

Substituting for $\bar{\mathbf{d}}$ with (12), we get

$$\bar{l} = -\delta[\mathbf{w}]\bar{l} + \delta[\mathbf{v}]\bar{l},$$

which, given that $w_i = b_i(1 - r_i)$ and $v_i = (1 - b_i r_i)$, implies

$$\delta[\mathbf{b}]\bar{l} = \mathbf{0}.$$

Since all b's are >0, therefore, $\bar{l}$ must be a null vector.

Obviously, such a steady state can happen only if the matrix of the system, i.e. $\mathbf{Q}$, has unity as its characteristic root. It is quite clear that unity is definitely one of the characteristic roots of $\mathbf{Q}$; for the matrix $\mathbf{A}$, being a stochastic matrix (or a transition matrix for a Markov chain), must have a maximum root of 1. Furthermore, if $\mathbf{A}$ is irreducible (i.e. indecomposable), then corresponding to the maximum root of unity, there is a unique probability vector $[\bar{\mathbf{a}}]$, all the components of which are positive, such that $(\mathbf{A} - \mathbf{I})\bar{\mathbf{a}} = \mathbf{0}$.[5] Irreducibility of the matrix $\mathbf{A}$ in the present case merely signifies that it is possible for a dollar outflow from any given bank to reach any one of the banks (sectors) after n rounds of circulation, when n is sufficiently large; which fact can certainly be taken for granted.[6]

Then a vector of $\mathbf{d}$ and l with $u_i = \bar{a}_i/k_i$, where $\bar{a}_i$ is the ith component of the fixed probability vector of $\mathbf{A}$, for the ith components of $\mathbf{d}$ and zeros for the components of l (or any scalar multiple of the so-constructed vector) would always yield the same vector as the product when premultiplied by $\mathbf{Q}$, i.e.

$$\mathbf{Q}\begin{bmatrix} \mathbf{u} \\ \mathbf{0} \end{bmatrix} = \begin{bmatrix} \mathbf{u} \\ \mathbf{0} \end{bmatrix}.$$

This can be easily demonstrated, for in the left partition of $\mathbf{Q}$, the terms with $(\mathbf{A} - \mathbf{I})\delta[\mathbf{k}]$ would all disappear when post-multiplied by $\mathbf{u}$. Since not all the components of this vector are zeros, therefore, unity must be one of the characteristic roots of $\mathbf{Q}$.

Furthermore, as the characteristic vector of $\mathbf{Q}$ corresponding to its root of unity, the vector $\{\mathbf{u}, \mathbf{0}\}$ is unique up to a scalar multiplication; for as explained above, $\mathbf{0}$ is the only permissible value for the steady-state vector of the l's and, with $l = \mathbf{0}$, $\mathbf{u}$ which is the unique fixed vector for the upper left submatrix of $\mathbf{Q}$, i.e. $\mathbf{I} + (\mathbf{A} - \mathbf{I})\delta[\mathbf{k}]$, must be the unique steady-state values of the d's apart from a scalar multiplier. Thus we have demonstrated the existence as well as the uniqueness of the steady-state equilibrium for the system (10) regardless of the disturbance vector, $\{\Delta \mathbf{z}_{t-1}, \delta[\mathbf{w}]\Delta \mathbf{z}_{t-1}\}'$.

4. Steady-state Equilibrium of the Reserve Diffusion Process and the Money Supply Multiplier

The steady-state solution given above, however, is unique only up to a multiplication by a scalar-dimensional factor. That is, the steady-state vector of d's would eventually take the value of

$$\bar{\mathbf{d}} = f[\mathbf{u}], \tag{13}$$

where f is the scalar-dimensional factor to be determined, and all l's would tend to zero. Furthermore, at full equilibrium where every bank holds no more excess reserves in excess of its desired (or required) ratio for its deposits, then

$$\sum_{i=1}^{n} r_i \bar{d}_i = \sum z_i = Z \text{ (the total reserve base in existence).} \tag{14}$$

Substituting for $\bar{\mathbf{d}}$ with the steady-state solutions given in (12), we get

$$f \sum_i r_i \bar{a}_i / k_i = Z$$

and hence

$$f = \frac{Z}{\sum_i r_i \bar{a}_i / k_i}. \tag{15}$$

If the total money supply is defined as the sum of the d's exclusive of savings and time deposits (say, the d's of banks g, h, etc.), we may then write

$$M = \sum_j d_j = \frac{Z \sum_j \bar{a}_j / k_j}{\sum_i r_i \bar{a}_i / k_i} \quad (i = 1, 2, \ldots, n; j = 1, 2, \ldots, n, \text{ exclusive of } g, h, \text{ etc.}). \tag{16}$$

Comparing (16) with the traditional money supply equation, i.e. (1) above, it may be observed that they are essentially similar in structure. The traditional money supply equation given above allows only three sectors, namely commercial banks, savings banks, and currency. If we reduce the number of sectors in our own model to three, it can be readily seen that the parameters c, $(1 - c)$, and t in (1) are, respectively,

$$c = \frac{\bar{a}_3/k_3}{\bar{a}_1/k_1 + \bar{a}_3/k_3},$$

$$(1 - c) = \frac{\bar{a}_1/k_1}{\bar{a}_1/k_1 + \bar{a}_3/k_3},$$

$$t = \frac{\bar{a}_2/k_2}{\bar{a}_1/k_1 + \bar{a}_3/k_3},$$

where the common denominator is $\Sigma_{j\neq 2}\,\bar{a}_j/k_j$.

Thus we obtain a generalised money multiplier equation which can include any number of different types of banks with different reserve ratios for their respective deposit liabilities. One thing to be specially noted about this steady-state money multiplier is that its magnitude depends only upon the fixed vector of the diffusion matrix $\mathbf{A}$, i.e. $[\bar{\mathbf{a}}]$, the deposit turnover rate vector $[\mathbf{k}]$ and the reserve ratio vector $[\mathbf{r}]$. The other two vectors that figure also in the matrix $\mathbf{Q}$, i.e. the loan utilisation coefficient vector $[\mathbf{k}^*]$ and the vector of responses to excess reserves $[\mathbf{b}]$ appear to play no role at all. Since the vector $[\mathbf{b}]$ not only figures in the matrix $\mathbf{Q}$, but also enters into the reserve injection vector $\{\Delta\mathbf{z}, \delta[\mathbf{w}]\Delta\mathbf{z}\}'$, $w_i = b_i(1 - r_i)$, it might appear particularly contrary to our intuition that it should have no effect on the steady-state money multiplier.

All this, however, is not merely the conclusions of mathematical deductions, but is also borne out by the simulation we tried. Indeed, so long as the system is stable so that a steady state will eventually be reached, the variations in the vector $[\mathbf{b}]$ are in fact observed to exert no effect on the steady-state equilibrium values of d's and the aggregate money supply, however defined. However, as is to be expected, it is also found that if the vector $[\mathbf{b}]$ becomes too large, the system will fluctuate with increasing amplitude unless otherwise constrained.

The similarity in algebraic structure between our steady-state money supply equation (16) and the traditional money supply equation (1), however, should not be allowed to obscure the basic logical difference between our approach and the traditional approach. The traditional equation such as (1) is usually based upon the assumption that the public desire to keep their total monetary assets in a given fixed combination of different available kinds, namely, demand and savings deposits and currency, in the sense of static (at-the-moment) portfolio allocation. Our approach, however, recognises that monetary assets in general do not lie about in stagnant pools to be consciously allocated into different portfolios. They exist rather in a continuous circular flow. Their temporary lodgings are often not the result of deliberate portfolio decisions, but the result of the directions of expenditures and technical or conventional time lags in their circular transfers from one recipient to another as the medium of exchange. That is to say, the great bulk of the total money supply exists in various channels of circulation rather than lies in the portfolios of economic units.

In our approach, therefore, each "bank" (which term, it is to be remembered, is used to include also currency in pockets) is treated as a "channel" in the general circular flow of monetary assets. The volume of monetary assets in each channel is not simply determined by static at-the-moment portfolio decisions of the public, but, more importantly, by their directions of spending and the speed of flow through each channel (the rate of turnover). A slow down in the speed of flow through a given channel can thus cause the volume of monetary assets contained therein to swell, given the distribution of flows into all the channels. For example, it may be observed from (16) and the formulae for the coefficients equivalent to c, $(1 - c)$, and t of equation (1), the share of deposits of bank i in total money supply is $(\bar{a}_i/k_i)/(\Sigma_j \bar{a}_j/k_j)$, which indicates that this share is governed not only by the fixed vector $[\bar{a}]$ of the diffusion matrix $\mathbf{A}$ (which represents the steady-state distribution of money flows) but also depends inversely on the rate of turnover of the deposits of bank i, i.e., k_i, relative to those of other banks' deposits. It is true that the rate of turnover of monetary assets in each channel reflects in part the portfolio decisions by the owners. Portfolio decisions, however, are not the only factor determining the rate of turnover, let alone the relative volume of monetary assets in each channel.

With the post-Keynesian tendency to overemphasise the store-of-value functions of money more and more under question recently and the means-of-payments function of money once more recognized as the predominant one, the hitherto fashionable portfolio allocation approach to the demand for money also comes to be questioned.[7] Even Hicks, who together with Keynes may properly be regarded as the progenitors of the portfolio allocation approach,[8] has recently expressed his doubt whether we have not overemphasised portfolio choice in explaining the demand for money.[9] Our approach represents an attempt to cut a new path for the determination of the relative shares of different types of money in the dynamic process of money expansion in this new spirit.

It would incidentally enable us to gain a new insight into the nature of the changes in the relative sizes of M_1 and M_2 (in the Friedmanian rather than the Keynesian sense). From our model it is clear that the share of savings bank deposits relative to commercial bank deposits plus currency depends not only on the fixed vector $[\bar{a}]$ of the diffusion matrix $\mathbf{A}$, but also inversely on the rate of turnover of the savings deposits relative to those of the deposits of commercial banks and currency. A decline, say, by one half, of the rate of turnover of the deposits of savings banks, other things being equal, would double the steady-state ratio of those deposits to the deposits of commercial banks plus currency. This is a new aspect which should certainly be explored when we discuss the alleged relative expansion of deposits of nonbank financial intermediaries at the expense of commercial banks, to which Gurley and Shaw had called our attention in the late 1950s.[10]

One clear implication of this possibility is that a relative increase in savings and time deposits, even if it results in an absolute increase in M_2, does not necessarily have an expansionary effect on money income; for the increase in savings and time deposits could itself be the result of a corresponding fall in their rate of turnover. At the same time, the increase in these deposits would necessarily absorb more reserve base away from demand deposits and thus force them to contract if the total reserve base is fixed. Thus the net effect upon money income could be contractionary rather than expansionary.

As an illustration, we may cite the institution of Federal Insurance of Bank Deposits in the United States, which could clearly cause a shift of this nature in favour of deposits at nonbank financial intermediaries. Federal insurance would obviously increase the safety of savings deposits at small nonbank intermediaries relatively more than the safety of deposits at major commercial banks. Thus it would not only change the fixed vector $[\bar{a}]$ of the diffusion matrix $\mathbf{A}$ in favour of deposits at the nonbank intermediaries, but would also tend to lower the rate of turnover of those deposits as they come to be regarded as safer assets to hold. That is, in the formula for the share of deposits of bank i in the total money supply, $(\bar{a}_i/k_i)/(\Sigma_j \bar{a}_j/k_j)$, where the subscript i now refers to nonbank intermediaries, $\bar{a}_i$ would be increased while k_i would be reduced. This would clearly result in a relative increase in the deposits of these intermediaries as compared with the total money supply however defined. The effect upon money income and expenditure of such a relative shift *per se* is clearly contractionary, rather than expansionary, even if it leads to some increase in the sum of currency, demand deposits and deposits at these non-bank intermediaries.

5. Difficulties in Determining the Stability of Money Supply Multiplier

The crucial question now is whether the unique root of unity (the uniqueness of the steady state implies that unity is an unrepeated root of **Q**) is the dominant characteristic root of **Q**. If unity is indeed the unrepeated dominant root, then irrespective of the initial state or the exogenous disturbance applied, the system would always settle down at the same steady state apart from a scalar-dimensional factor to be determined by equation (15).

Analytically, however, it is very difficult to determine whether out of the $2n$ possible roots of the matrix **Q**, 1 is actually the largest in absolute value. Since the elements of **Q** are not all non-negative, there appears to be no standard method to work out the general *necessary* and *sufficient* conditions for stability, although there are some well-known analytical methods, e.g. the Gersgorin Theorem, that would give us the *sufficient* conditions for stability of matrices like **Q**.

The Gersgorin Theorem states that if **A** is a $n \times n$ matrix and

$$\rho_j = \sum_k {}' |a_{jk}|,$$

where $\sum'_k$ denotes the sum from $k = 1$ to n, $k \neq j$, then every eigenvalue of **A** lies in at least one of the discs

$$|\lambda - a_{jj}| \leq \rho_j \ (j = 1, 2, \ldots, n),$$

in the complex λ plane.[11]

In other words, if we plot the diagonal elements of **Q** on the real axis, use each of them in turn as centre and construct a circle around it with the sum of the absolute values of the off-diagonal elements of the corresponding column as radius, then the $2n$ characteristic roots of **Q** must lie within these $2n$ circles or discs. Unfortunately, the $2n$ Gersgorin discs we may construct for the matrix **Q** could clearly cover points outside the unit circle in the complex plane, when realistic values are assigned to such parameters as k's, k^*'s, r's and b's. This implies that not only complex or negative roots but even roots with modulus greater than one cannot be ruled out. However, it does not imply that the system is necessarily unstable either.

If there are complex and/or negative roots that are not quickly damped, then we cannot expect that an injection of reserve, represented by the vector $[\Delta z]$, through open market operation or otherwise, would lead to a smooth expansion of credit and money supply, but should expect it to cause a series of disturbances to the money market. If there are roots with modulus greater than one, then the system would have a tendency to develop cumulative expansion or contraction, which would either crash into the institutional constraints that $d > 0$, or induce some abrupt changes in the parameters that would check the runaway expansion or contraction. It is to be recalled that the deposit level at any bank must be positive, i.e. $d > 0$; for a tendency for the deposits at any bank to drop to zero implies that the bank is going out of business. Then the rank of the A matrix would be reduced and its elements, the columns of which must always sum up to unity, must therefore change. The problem would therefore have to be reset. It would then be rather meaningless to speak of any definite money supply multiplier at all.

6. Simulation with an Illustrative Model

Anyway, available analytical models of determining the stability of a matrix like Q, such as the Gersgorin Theorem or the dominant negative diagonal theorem, merely give us the sufficient conditions for stability, which by definition may not all be necessary for stability. They cannot, therefore, be used to draw any sharp dividing line between the stable and the unstable cases. I have therefore attempted some simulation on a modest scale with the following illustrative model in the hope of finding out within what ranges of values for the parameters involved, stability of the system can be reasonably assured.

I assume that in a closed economy there are only four banks, which together with currency in circulation make five sectors. The first bank is supposed to represent a typical reserve city member bank, which, for the sake of simplicity, is assumed to accept only demand deposits, the reserve ratio is, say, 18%. The second bank is supposed to represent a country member bank, which too shall be assumed to accept only demand deposits, the reserve ratio for which is, say, 13%. The third bank is supposed to represent a non-member bank, which has no legal reserve requirement for its deposits, but which for its own precaution against cash withdrawals does keep a minimum amount of reserves in the form of vault cash, say, 2%. Again for simplicity's sake we assume all its deposit liabilities are demand deposits. The fourth bank is supposed to represent a savings bank, the reserve requirement for its deposits is, say, 5%. The currency sector is designated the fifth sector. The reserve ratio for currency is, of course, 100%, since currency consists entirely of high-power money, which is the reserve base only the monetary authorities can create. Thus the vector of reserve ratios for the five sectors are

$$\{r\}' = \{0.18, 0.13, 0.02, 0.05, 1.00\}'.$$

The rates of turnover of different types of deposits and currency are assumed to be different, such that

$$\{k\}' = \{1.00, 0.90, 0.85, 0.20, 0.90\}',$$

where the rate of turnover of deposits of the reserve city banks is assumed to be the fastest, while that of savings deposits is assumed to be the slowest. The loan utilisation coefficients k^* are also assumed to be different, such that

$$\{k^*\}' = \{0.90, 0.85, 0.85, 1.00, 0\}'.$$

The money diffusion matrix A is assumed to be

$$A = \begin{bmatrix} 0.35 & 0.25 & 0.25 & 0.35 & 0.15 \\ 0.25 & 0.30 & 0.15 & 0.25 & 0.15 \\ 0.10 & 0.10 & 0.25 & 0.10 & 0.10 \\ 0.20 & 0.20 & 0.15 & 0.05 & 0.20 \\ 0.10 & 0.15 & 0.20 & 0.25 & 0.40 \end{bmatrix},$$

the fixed vector of which is calculated to be

$$\{\bar{a}\}' = \{0.273, 0.228, 0.118, 0.169, 0.212\}'.$$

The b vector, indicating the responses of different banks to the presence of excess reserves, is not so easy to specify. Most elementary textbooks on money seem to presume that banks would simply use the amount of excess reserves to make loans, i.e. that the b's are equal to 1. It is easy to show, however, that for a commercial bank, which can normally expect to retain a considerable portion of the loans granted by itself as deposits with itself either in the form of unspent balances of the borrowers or in the form of new deposits by the recipients of loan-financed expenditures who happen to be also depositors at the same bank, it would be more reasonable to expect that it would expand its loans by more than the excess reserves it has on hand.

This may be demonstrated with a very simple model after Tobin.[12] Let the expected value of total deposits of a commercial bank be $E(d) = \phi(L) + \alpha$, where L represents total loans outstanding, $\phi(L)$ the deposit creation function of loans, and α stands for what we might call the non-loan-created part of deposits. Assuming that loans constitute the entire investment portfolio of the bank apart from the reserves it keeps, the basic assets-liabilities balance of the bank may be stated as

$$d + C = L + z, \tag{17}$$

where d stands for deposits, C for capital, L for loans and z for reserves. If the desired reserve ratio for deposits is r, then the condition for no expected excess or deficiency in reserves is

$$\alpha + \phi(L) - L + C = z = r[\phi(L) + \alpha] \tag{18}$$

or

$$(1 - r)[\phi(L) + \alpha] + C - L = 0.$$

Differentiating this equation with respect to α, we get

$$\frac{dL}{d\alpha} = \frac{(1 - r)}{1 - \phi'(1 - r)}, \tag{19}$$

which means that if the bank attempts to maintain neither any excess nor any deficiency in its expected reserves, a unit increase in its non-loan-created deposits would induce it to expand its loans by $(1 - r)/[1 - \phi'(1 - r)]$ units. However, one unit increase in α implies $(1 - r)$ units increase in excess reserves. Therefore, the b coefficient in our model, which signifies the response of the bank to one unit increase in excess reserves would be

$$b = \frac{1}{(1 - r)} \frac{dL}{d\alpha} = \frac{1}{1 - \phi'(1 - r)}, \tag{20}$$

which is obviously greater than 1, since ϕ' is understood to be positive but smaller than unity. Substituting some realistic numerical values into this equation say, $r = 0.12$ and $\phi' = 0.40$, then b would be equal to 1.543.[13]

It is not certain whether all banks actually behave in this way. Clearly the deposit creation function $\phi(L)$ is highly subjective and uncertain. A great deal will depend upon the aggressiveness and risk aversion of the management. We shall not, therefore, assign any definite numerical values to all the elements of the **b** vector, but shall try a series of increasing numerical values (starting from unity) for the **b** coefficients of the three commercial banks, to see how the changes in these coefficients would affect the stability of the system and its final equilibrium.

As explained above, the b coefficient for the currency sector will be assigned the value of unity, even though no loans are expected to be made by that sector. The coefficient for the savings bank will also be assumed to be one, as it is rather implausible that loans granted by a savings bank would create more deposits for itself in a direct way.[14] The series of numerical values for the b vector we tried first are

$$\begin{bmatrix} 1 \\ 1 \\ 1 \\ 1 \\ 1 \end{bmatrix} \begin{bmatrix} 1.5 \\ 1.5 \\ 1.5 \\ 1.0 \\ 1.0 \end{bmatrix} \begin{bmatrix} 2.0 \\ 2.0 \\ 2.0 \\ 1.0 \\ 1.0 \end{bmatrix} \begin{bmatrix} 2.5 \\ 2.5 \\ 2.5 \\ 1.0 \\ 1.0 \end{bmatrix} \begin{bmatrix} 2.6 \\ 2.6 \\ 2.6 \\ 1.0 \\ 1.0 \end{bmatrix} \begin{bmatrix} 2.7 \\ 2.7 \\ 2.7 \\ 1.0 \\ 1.0 \end{bmatrix} \begin{bmatrix} 2.8 \\ 2.8 \\ 2.8 \\ 1.0 \\ 1.0 \end{bmatrix} \begin{bmatrix} 2.9 \\ 2.9 \\ 2.9 \\ 1.0 \\ 1.0 \end{bmatrix}.$$

The vector for reserve injection is postulated to be

$$\{\Delta z_{t-1}, \delta[w]\Delta z_{t-1}\}' = \{1, 0, 0, 0, 0, 0.82b_1, 0, 0, 0, 0\}',$$

which implies that the new reserve money would, in the first instance, all go into the first bank (the reserve city commercial banks) as deposits (presumably by the sellers of securities to the manager of the open market operations of the central bank), and would then diffuse throughout the banking system via the operation of the Q matrix. We shall assume the reserve injection to be a non-repeated single dose.

If the system is stable this reserve injection vector repeatedly multiplied by the Q matrix should approach a fixed characteristic vector of Q, which would be invariant with further multiplication. This implies that the money supply would then have reached a new equilibrium. The resulting fixed characteristic vector would give the cumulated increments of deposits of all banks since the injection of additional reserves, and the final increments of loans by all banks. As explained above, the latter should all be zeros in a steady state.

Since we have shown above that the fixed characteristic vector of Q is independent of the disturbance vector apart from the dimensional factor determined through equation (15), it is obvious that a unit injection of additional reserve would ultimately create the same expansion of deposits in every bank no matter how the reserve injection is initially distributed.

Thus the money multiplier for a one-unit injection of reserves is simply the sum of all the "deposits" in the resultant characteristic vector of Q that we would like to include as the money supply. With a definition of money supply (say, M_1) which excludes the deposits of savings bank, i.e. d_4, we get a money multiplier of approximately 2.48. With a definition of money supply (say, M_2) which includes the savings deposits, the money multiplier would be 4.81 approximately. These results agree entirely with the corresponding steady-state money multipliers calculated with the equation (16) on p. 257, i.e.

$$M_1 = \frac{Z\Sigma_j \bar{a}_j/k_j}{\Sigma_i r_i \bar{a}_i/k_i} \quad (i = 1, 2, 3, 4, 5; j = 1, 2, 3, 5) \quad (21)$$

and

$$M_2 = \frac{Z\Sigma_i \bar{a}_i/k_i}{\Sigma_i r_i \bar{a}_i/k_i} \quad (i = 1, 2, 3, 4, 5), \quad (22)$$

in which, as we noted, the vectors [k*] and [b] do not even appear.[15] In our simulation, as we stepped up the [b] vector through the series given above, the steady-state vectors of d's and l's and the money multipliers would indeed remain the same, so long as the system is approaching a steady state at all.

However, when the **b** coefficients for the three commercial banks are raised to 2.8, the money supply would fluctuate continuously with hardly any tendency to converge. When the **b** coefficients of these three banks are raised to 2.9 and above, the oscillations would become explosive. It is interesting to note that stability would not break down immediately when the commercial banks begin to indulge themselves in multiple loan expansion at a multiple in excess of the steady-state money multiplier, i.e. 2.48, but would break down only when the three commercial banks' loan expansion coefficients are considerably above it, i.e. at 2.80 or higher.

It is noteworthy that in our simulations, the approach to instability inevitably passes through stages of fluctuations and oscillations of increasing violence. In other words, instability appears always to involve complex or negative roots. Since oscillations in deposits are most undesirable to the banks concerned, it may be expected that the latter would quickly learn the lesson that too sanguine a response to excess reserves would lead to excessive losses of reserves in the subsequent periods. Consequently, in the real world, unstable, or even violent, oscillations in deposits following an injection of additional reserves would rarely be observed. Thus, money supply can generally be expected to settle down at its steady-state equilibrium value as described by our generalised multiplier formula, i.e. (16).

It should be remembered, however, that these results are all conditioned upon the basic simplifying assumption of the model, namely that the changes in the structure of interest rates are not supposed to have any effects upon the parameters of the model, i.e. the vectors **k**, **k***, **r** and **b**. In fact, the obtainable rates of interest on loans relative to the rate of interest on borrowing from (or discount at) the central bank (or on the Federal Funds market) and the availability of such federal funds would influence the ratio of reserves against deposits which a bank finds it desirable to hold even though the legally required reserve ratio does not change. And the **b** coefficients are likely to be affected by similar influences too. Moreover, in so far as changes in interest rates can influence the demand for money, the **k** vector (the rates of turnover of deposits and currency) may also be affected. Finally, in so far as banks can compete with each other with interest rates for deposits, gifts for new depositors, advertisements, etc., the elements in the cash diffusion matrix **A** might be changed also, whenever money market conditions induce banks to intensify competition for the reserve base.[16] Thus strictly speaking, all these parameters are not exogenously given, but should be included as endogenous variables in an all-inclusive model.

This is far beyond the intended scope of this paper. The model of money supply expansion presented above is like all linear models in economics, e.g. the multiplier–accelerator model, the input–output model, linear programming model, etc., in that it merely provides a basic framework on which subsequent modifications and embellishments are to be added. Indeed, as Edgeworth has emphasised long before us, "the theorist must not pretend to wisdom, if he knows so little what he is about as to mistake his abstract formulae for rules immediately applicable to policy."[17]

Notes

*I an indebted to Professors William Brock, Simon Levin, Paul A. Samuelson and Henry Wan, Jr., for their valuable suggestions and help with the mathematics; and to two anonymous referees for suggestions for improvements.

1. It is true that non-member banks are usually obliged to hold a fair proportion of reserves for their deposits in the form of demand deposits at other large banks, but since such reserves do not tie up any part of the reserve base, they would not be counted as reserves in the strict sense for our present purpose. The demand deposits at non-member banks are

currently by no means negligible. In recent years they constitute over 20% of total demand deposits of the country.

2. The mathematics used here is similar to that of dynamic input–output analysis. It can also be applied to a multi-sector income multiplier model with the acceleration principle incorporated in the model.

3. Since Markov chains deal with probabilities, the projected future inflows and outflows of deposits are of course all expected values. To save words, the expression "expected" will be omitted in the following.

4. It is implicitly assumed here that the Federal Reserve Bank injects the new reserve money by buying securities from the public who then deposit the money with their own banks. If the Federal Reserve Bank buys directly from the banks, a slight change in the formulation of our model will be necessary, but all the conclusions would remain substantially the same.

5. See, for example, J. G. Kemeny, H, Mirkil, J. L. Snell and G. L. Thompson, *Finite Mathematical Structures* (Prentice-Hall, N.J.), p. 39, 1–3; and also W. Feller, *Introduction to Probability Theory and its Application,* 2nd ed. (Wiley, N.Y.), chapter xv.

6. We shall exclude the freak cases where a dollar outflow from a given bank can reach certain banks only in even numbers of rounds of circulation and others only in odd numbers of rounds. In such freak cases the columns of the matrix **A**, when **A** is raised in power, would not converge to its fixed probability vector [**ā**].

7. E.g. S. C. Tsiang, "The Rationale of Mean-Standard-Deviation Analysis, Skewness Preference and the Demand for Money," *American Economic Review*, vol. 62 (June, 1972), pp. 354–71, esp. §3, pp. 368–70; and B. P. Pesek, "Monetary Theory in the Post-Robertson 'Alice-in-Wonderland' Era," *Journal of Economic Literature,* Sept. 1976, pp. 856–84, esp. pp. 861–3.

8. On account of his seminal paper, "Suggestions for Simplifying the Theory of Money," *Economica,* February 1935.

9. See his "The Two Triads: Lecture I," reprinted in *Critical Essays in Monetary Theory* (Oxford 1967), pp. 14–6.

10. See, for example, J. G. Gurley and E. S. Shaw, "Financial Intermediaries and the Saving-Investment Process," *The Journal of Finance,* vol. 2 (1956), pp. 257–76.

11. See, for example, Peter Lancaster, *Theory of Matrices* (Academic Press, N.Y.), p. 226.

12. See J. Tobin, *Manuscript of Monetary Theory,* chap. 8, "The Theory of Commercial Banking" (unpublished). Some earlier writers, e.g. J. S. Lawrence of Princeton, also believed that the initial expansion of loans by a bank with excess reserves would be a multiple of the initial excess reserves. See J. S. Lawrence, "Borrowed Reserves and Bank Expansion," *Quarterly Journal of Economics,* vol. 42 (Aug. 1928), pp. 593–626, esp. p. 616.

13. Lawrence, in his article quoted above, estimated that the "coefficient of (loan) expansion" on the basis of a unit of excess reserve would be 1.79219. See *op. cit.* p. 616.

14. In other words, ϕ' in this case would be zero. Since the fifties, it has been fashionable for monetary economists to belittle the difference between commercial banks and savings banks. See, e.g. Gurley and Shaw, *op. cit.*, and J. Tobin, "Commercial Banks as Creators of 'Money,'" in Deane Carson (ed.), *Banking and Monetary Studies* (Irwin, Homewood, Ill.), pp. 408–19. There are, however, at least the following two significant differences: (*a*) the deposits of savings banks cannot serve as an acceptable medium of exchange whereas those of commercial banks can; (*b*) savings banks would hardly ever dare to grant loans in excess of their excess reserves on hand, whereas commercial banks, as we have seen above, probably do that fairly regularly.

15. With $\bar{a} = \{0.273, 0.228, 0.118, 0.169, 0.212\}'$, $k = \{1.00, 0.90, 0.85, 0.20, 0.90\}'$, and $r = \{0.18, 0.13, 0.02, 0.05, 1.00\}'$, $\Delta M_1/\Delta Z$ can be easily computed to be 2.48+, and $\Delta M_2/\Delta Z$ can be calculated to be 4.81−.

16. Furthermore, a sort of short circuit might develop supplementary to the operation of the diffusion matrix **A** in that reserve money may be passed from bank to bank through the federal funds market. However, the borrowings and lendings on the federal funds market are probably mostly for very short-term coverings of temporary deficiencies in required reserves rather than for regular operations of the banks. The existence of the facilities of the federal funds market, to which any bank might resort in the contingency of a temporary shortage of reserves, would, however, tend to make the commercial banks less conservative in granting loans with their own excess reserves, i.e. tend to make the *b* coefficient bigger. On the other hand, it might convert part of the fluctuations in deposits and loans, which we have observed as likely to ensue from large *b* coefficients, into fluctuations in the interest rates and tightness or laxity on the federal funds market. Thus the neglect of the federal funds market is part and parcel of the general problem of neglecting all price effects in a linear model.

17. F. Y. Edgeworth, "The Mathematical Theory of Banking," *Journal of Royal Statistical Society,* Mar. 1888, p. 127.

CHAPTER 12

Stock or Portfolio Approach to Monetary Theory and the Neo-Keynesian School of James Tobin

S. C. Tsiang

1. The Ascendancy of the Stock Approach Due to Keynes' and Hicks' Writings, and Hicks' Recent Change of Mind

In classical economics money had traditionally been envisioned as a medium of exchange that circulates through the body economic like its lifeblood in an endless circular flow. Indeed, the analogy between money and blood lies not merely in the fact that they both circulate. Both are durable and can be used again and again. Therefore, both qualify for the title of durable asset. Both are some sort of carrying vehicles. Blood is the carrying vehicle of vital oxygen and other nutrients to supply the various organs of the body, and it also serves as the vehicle to carry away the waste products from the organs for disposal. Money is the vehicle that carries the purchasing power over real goods to each agent in compensation for his service rendered and for goods or assets delivered. When the impounded purchasing power is exercised by the agent in its possession, it necessarily passes out of his

Reprinted with permission from *IHS Journal* (The Journal of the Institute für Hohere Studien, Vienna, Austria). Vol. VI, (1982) pp. 149–171.

hand on to a different agent, carrying the same nominal amount of purchasing power to its next owner.

These circulating media were traditionally not supposed to be held stagnant in any part of the body (physical or economic), though they were known in both cases to circulate sometime faster, sometime slower. Just as the presence of any significant amount of stagnant noncirculating blood in any part of the body is definitely regarded as a pathological or traumatic syndrome, so the presence of any significant amount of stagnant noncirculating money holdings used to be regarded as an irrational and abnormal phenomenon.

During the Great Depression of the 1930s, however, this traditional view was rudely shaken by the observation of fairly widespread phenomena of money held idle as stores of value. Such observations led to Keynes' attempt to explain the demand for money, not merely as the medium of exchange, but also, and in fact chiefly, as the store of value. Since the emphasis is now on the store of value function of money, it is widely believed that the correct approach to money should be to analyse how and why the total existing stock of money is held by the community of individual agents. The most definitive delineation of this new approach to monetary theory was given by Hicks in his seminal article "A Suggestion for Simplifying the Theory of Money,"[1] which preceded the publication of Keynes' *General Theory* by a whole year.[2]

The apparent difficulty in applying the stock approach to a continuous flowing stream is supposed to be overcome by taking a "point of time" view of the situation. As Hicks put it, the "decision to hold money or something else . . . is always made at a point of time."[3] At a point of time, all flows, however rapid, can be transfixed into stationary blocks, and, hence, dealt with as stocks. This is indeed undeniable. However, it is one thing to say that at any particular moment every piece of money must be held somewhere by some one, but it is a totally different thing to say that what money that happens to pass through an individual's hand at any particular moment is precisely the amount of money which he demands to hold on the basis of rational calculation, neither more nor less, in preference to any other assets or goods. At any moment, there must be considerable amounts of money that have just been received by agents who do not really desire to hold these sums in the form of money, but who just had to accept them as legal means of payments for discharging debts owed to them to await proper disposal at later moments. On the other hand, we must also note that at any point of time, there must be money still in the main arteries and veins that is not yet, properly speaking, held by anybody (viz., the so-called "floats").[4] To apply the optimal portfolio allocation analysis to the total stock of money in existence at any particular moment surely could not give an accurate account of the situation.

Hicks certainly did not offer an adequate answer to these questions in his 1935 article, but in his more recent writings he had clearly recognized the importance of these difficulties and consequently declared that the Cambridge school (from Marshall down to Keynes) had "tried to match the whole stock with the voluntary demand, and so interpret the whole stock requirement for money in voluntarist terms. This, I now feel, was confusing; it had sent many of us (myself included) chasing what I now feel to be will-o'-the-wisps."[5]

Nevertheless, with the ascendancy of Keynesian theory, the stock approach (or portfolio approach) has come to be treated as the only respectable approach to monetary theory.[6] Hicks' 1935 article has thus come to be regarded as the guideline for all later studies on monetary theory. Indeed, Tobin, the leader of the Neo-Keynesians in the U.S., once remarked that later developments in monetary theory constitute no more than "dotting the i's and crossing the t's" in Hicks' seminal article.

However, while Tobin and his disciples are still busy at their dotting and crossing, Hicks himself apparently has changed his views. In a joking mood, he has once cautioned his readers not to mistake his "deceased uncle, J. R. Hicks," for himself.[7] (Since he was knighted in 1964, he now signs his name as John Hicks.) In his 1966 lectures at the London School of Economics, he expressed his more recent idea to be that the transactions demand for money, which is quantitatively much the larger part of the total demand for money, should not be regarded as "voluntary."[8] "It is the money that is needed to circulate a certain volume of goods, at a particular level of prices. The old Fisher $MV = PT$ gives a better picture of it than the overvoluntarized 'Cambridge Quantity Equation.' In relation to this part of the money stock, 'Velocity of Circulation' is perfectly appropriate."[9]

2. Tobin's General Asset Equilibrium Approach

Whereas the original pathfinder of the stock approach has thus turned back partially to the Fisherian flow approach, his followers, under the leadership of Tobin, are pressing relentlessly forward along his 1935 "Suggestion" to the bitter end. Their position is set forth uncompromisingly in Tobin's 1969 article "A General Equilibrium Approach to Monetary Theory."[10]

This approach follows faithfully Hicks' 1935 suggestion that "monetary theory needs to be based" upon an analysis, "not of an income account, but of a capital account, a balance sheet. We have to concentrate on the forces which make assets and liabilities what they are."[11] This has merely been paraphrased by Tobin into: "The approach focuses on the capital accounts of economic units, of sectors of the economy, and of the economy as a whole. A model of the capital account of the economy specifies a menu of the assets (and debts) that appear in portfolios and balance sheets, the factors that determine the demands and the supplies of the various assets, and the manner in which asset prices and interest rates clear these interrelated markets."[12]

The fundamental difficulties with the "point of time" stock approach did not even received a slight mention; namely, the nagging questions: How can we treat the money on hand at any particular moment as the optimal portion of wealth we rationally calculated to hold in the form of money on the basis of deliberate portfolio allocation? Are the money sums we have just received as means of payment in any transactions just concluded the deliberate addition to our portfolio demand for cash? And what about the large amount of money still in the arteries and veins that has not yet come into anybody's possession? Tobin just ignored them all and assumed that at any moment each sector is dividing its own total net worth optimally into holdings of different assets. And the sum of the individual demands for each assets is instantly equated to the total available amount of that assets. The demand for each asset is said to be determined by a function of the same general form

$$f_i(\hat{r}, Y/W)W = A_i, \tag{1}$$

where

$$\sum_i A_i = W \text{ (Total wealth constraint)}$$

$$\sum_i f_i = 1$$

$\hat{r}$ = vector of real rates of return ($r_k, r_m, r_s \ldots$),

and where Y is treated as exogenous (i.e., Y is the level of income of the preceding period) and A_i is the total available amount of asset i in the real value.

It should not be forgotten that the continuous circular flows of money is supposed to be transfixed into stocks in hand only by taking a snapshot view at a "point of time" that is supposed to have no time dimension. This would naturally lead to the question how could the adjustment towards the optimal allocation of assets for all the wealth-owners be carried out within such a point of time that by definition could not allow any time for anybody to do anything therein? On the other hand, if we stretch the "point" to allow some time for the carrying out of stock adjustments towards the optimum positions according to the asset-demand functions, how can we at the same time say that during that interval the continuous circular flows of incomes and expenditures could still be taken as at a complete standstill? These flows would surely bring in more money embodying the new incomes into some agents' hand and drain off some money from some agents as the means of payment for their expenditures. This is the fundamental dilemma of the point-of-time stock approach, a dilemma which Tobin and his disciples simply ignored without any explanation.[13]

3. Tobin's Key Behavior Assumption

Moreover, as is likely to happen with eager followers, Tobin went further, at least in one respect, than Hicks of 1935. Namely, whereas Hicks still regarded spending as one of the three displaced alternatives to holding money,[14] Tobin declared as the "key behavioral assumption" of his procedure that "spending decisions and portfolio decisions are independent – specifically that decisions about the accumulation of wealth are separable from decisions about its allocation."[15] This is the so-called "separability assumption." With such an arbitrary assumption Tobin hopes to justify his treatment of the capital account (and the determination of asset prices) separately from all flow decisions, e.g., spending decisions on consumption (hence, saving) and investment, and thus to arrive at his preconceived Keynesian conclusion that saving and investment have no direct effect upon the interest rate except indirectly through the income level they are supposed to establish subsequently.

Such an arbitrary assumption, however, is obviously in contradiction to common sense. It is also contrary to the final opinion on this matter of Keynes himself, whom Tobin still venerates enough to style himself a Neo-Keynesian. Futhermore, it is contradicted even by the implication of his own theory of transactions demand for money, even though he does not seem to realize it for some obscure (possibly subconscious) reasons. [16]

It should be recalled that in 1937, only one year after the publication of the *General Theory,* Keynes had already made a concession to traditional monetary theory in admitting that investment decisions that have not yet been carried out do have a direct effect on the market rate of interest as they necessarily give rise to a sort of "finance" demand for liquidity (money). [17] This is obviously in contradiction to Tobin's "key behavioral assumption" quoted above. It is really surprising how the master's published concession should have been so completely ignored by his disciples for so long.

Even more surprising is the fact that, unaware to himself, Tobin's own significant contribution to the analysis of the transactions demand for money clearly indicated that this type of demand for money would surely be dependent upon the decisions to spend apart from its dependence on the interest rate. [18]

It is true that in that well-known article Tobin never formally introduced the planned expenditure into his model as a determining variable for the demand for transactions money balances. The explanatory variables he employed were income Y, the interest rate r, and the fixed and proportionate costs of asset conversion (transaction) a and b, respectively. However, any reader with a discerning eye can readily tell that the variable Y, viz., periodic income received, could fit in his equations only because he had implicitly assumed that income would be spent fully, neither more nor less, so that the variable Y in his model could be treated indiscriminately as either the income received or the volume of transactions (or expenditures) planned. If part of the income received has been decided to be saved from the beginning, then it is clear from his theory that the part of the income which has been decided not to be spent at all during the period (i.e., to be saved) would be invested on earning assets right at the very beginning of the period. The demand for transactions balances should then be determined in his model with the planned expenditure substituted for income. On the other hand, if the agent concerned should decide to spend more than his income on account of some planned investment project, then it is obvious that it would be the bigger-than-income total expenditure (including both investment and consumption) that should take the place of Y in his equations. These observations would clearly imply that according to his own theory, the chief determinant of the transactions demand for money should be the latter rather the former, as Keynes himself was already on the verge of admitting in 1937. This would in turn imply that flow decisions on consumption as well as investment would have a direct effect upon the transactions demand for money and hence upon the money-holding equilibrium, thus showing up how unrealistic Tobin's own "key behavioral assumption" actually is. It would also contradict the traditional Keynesian tenet, handed down to the postwar generations is all the textbooks on macroeconomics, that savings and investment are not supposed to have any direct influence upon the interest rate except indirectly through the changes in income level they subsequently bring about.

The substitution of an endogenous expenditure term E for the exogenous income term Y in Tobin's system of equations of the demands for different assets may be regarded by some Keynesians as of no substantial significance; for it is claimed that in the steady state equilibrium Y will always be equal to E so that no matter whether Y or E is used in the equation system on p.274, the same steady state solution would be obtained when it is combined with the same submodel of the real sector.

This may be true for the steady state solution, but it is definitely not true for the determination of the path of movement and the speed of movement towards the steady state equilibrium. In a dynamic world we are practically never at a steady state equilibrium. Certainly, if Tobin's general asset equilibrium model is supposed to operate instantaneously for every point of time, we cannot expect the real sector to be at the steady state equilibrium continuously at every point of time. If the asset equilibrium model is to be combined with a model of real sector not in a steady state (I would deliberately refrain from using the term "disequilibrium" here because this term has been much misused nowadays), then income of the preceding period and expenditure planned for the current period cannot be identified with each other and the endogenous nature of the expenditure term cannot be ignored or denied.

Thus it is by an arbitrary, and in fact false, behavioral assumption that Tobin separated the capital accounts and the asset market from flow accounts and flow decisions. Income and production are treated tentatively as exogenous data for the determination of equilibrium on the asset market as a whole. The entire menu of the great variety of assets are supposed to be considered simultaneously, among which money is only one of the great variety of assets in which to hold one's wealth.

One can hardly catch in his model even a glimpse of the old vision that money is the necessary medium of exchange that circulates in a continuous circular flow.

4. Asset Demand for Money Due to Risk Aversion

Tobin evidently thought that his own contribution to the theory of liquidity preference as a behavior towards risk[19] would adequately explain the holding of money balances in investment portfolios at a general asset-market equilibrium. This is, however, an illusion. Although he has correctly perceived that the assumed inelasticity of interest expectation used by Keynes to explain the holding of idle speculative balances is not plausible in the long run, the aversion-to-risk explanation which he proposed as an alternative is not adequate either.

The reason is that the expected return/risk indifference curves (or mean/standard deviation indifference curves), which he employs to explain the holding of money balances in a portfolio equilibrium, are, by the basic underlying assumption of the non-satiability of the demand for wealth, restricted to an upward slope of less than 45%. For an upward slope of such indifference curves greater than (or equal to) 45% would imply that an increment of wealth to its expected value by just one standard deviation would make the marginal utility of wealth drop below (or to) zero, thus violating the basic nonsatiability assumption.

This can be easily demonstrated in the following way. In the case where the expected utility function of wealth can be approximated by its quadratic expansion (which is in fact the only case where the use of mean/standard deviation analysis to the neglect of higher moments is fully justified), the following approximate equation holds:

$$E[U(y)] = U(\bar{y}) + U'' \frac{S^2}{2}, \tag{2}$$

where y is the stochastic wealth, $\bar{y}$ is its expected value and S its standard deviation. From this we can readily see that the slope of the implied mean/standard deviation indifference curves

$$\frac{d\bar{y}}{dS} = \frac{-SU''}{U' + (S^2/2)U'''} \tag{3}$$

$$E[U] = \text{constant}$$

cannot be equal to, or greater than, 1. For if the right hand side of the above equation is equal to, or greater than, 1, then

$$U'(\bar{y}) + SU''(\bar{y}) + \frac{S^2}{2} U'''(\bar{y}) = U'(\bar{y} + S) \leqq 0, \qquad (4)$$

which implies that the marginal utility of wealth would be brought down to zero, or to a negative value, by a mere increase of one standard deviation in wealth from its expected value.[20]

On the other hand, in the asset market, where there are a great variety of assets covering the whole spectrum of long, medium, and short terms, and where the variations of their returns are not all perfectly correlated so that diversification to reduce the total risk of one's portfolio is possible, the market opportunity curve representing the trade-off between expected return and risk confronting an investor with surplus cash left on hand would practically always be of a slope greater than 45%. This implies that so long as there is cash left on hand, the investor can always move to a higher indifference curve by trading cash for some asset with a positive yield but very little risk, or with risk of variation uncorrelated with the risk of variation of other assets of his portfolio thus enabling him to diversify and reduce risk.[21] Thus according to his own return/risk indifference curve analysis, idle cash balances would have no place at all in any investment portfolio.

In a general asset market equilibrium, the demand for money must be overwhelmingly for transactions and precautionary purposes. These demands for money, however, as we argued above and elsewhere,[22] are crucially dependent upon flow decisions on expenditures, rather than upon income received which Tobin treats as exogenously given. Consequently, his arbitrary key behavior assumption that "spending decisions and portfolio decisions are independent" and his interpretation of Hicks' 1935 "Suggestion" to mean that it is for the monetary theory to be concerned only with portfolio decisions would partially deactivate the most vital and dominant part of the demand for money, viz., the transactions demand, by hitching it to a predetermined variable, or what he calls a "tentatively exogenous data" (i.e., income received), instead of hitching it to the currently endogenous variable, planned expenditures, as it should be.[23] The so-called investment demand (or portfolio demand) for money, which Tobin regards as the more crucial and more sensitive part of the total demand for money, is largely illusory and, in fact, is either nonexistent or utterly insignificant in these recent years of very high interest returns on short term assets of very low risk compared with money.

5. Money as One of the Assets of No Particular Significance and the Denial of "Crowding Out" Effect

Perhaps by 1969, Tobin has so convinced himself of the relative insignificance of money that he is no longer interested in the specific nature of the demand for money. In his 1969 article, he simply treats it as just one of the many assets to hold one's wealth in, the demands for which can all be formulated in the same general form, viz.,

$$f_i(\hat{r}, \, Y/W)W = A_i,$$

as stated above. He, therefore, constantly dins into his readers that it is the whole asset market equilibrium that matters, not just the equilibrium between the demand and supply of money; and that there are more important asset prices to look at than the interest rate, the price for parting with money.

Surely, if one shuts one's eyes to the simple fact that money alone can serve as the necessary medium of exchange, and consider it only as one of the many assets to store one's wealth in, then money is by no means an important asset, let alone the most important one, to warrant special attention. Tobin accordingly tells us to pay more attention to what he calls the q ratio, viz., the ratio of the market valuation of reproducible real capital assets to the current replacement cost of those assets. If q is greater than one, it implies that the market valuations of physical capital assets are higher than their current reproduction costs, and hence that it would be profitable to make investment in real capital goods. Thus Tobin and his disciple Brainard would propose to rewrite the investment function for a macroeconomic model in the form of

$$\frac{\Delta k}{k} = \psi(q - \bar{q}) + g, \tag{5}$$

with

$$\psi(q - \bar{q}) \gtreqless 0, \text{ as } (q - \bar{q}) \gtreqless 0,$$

where $\bar{q}$ is the normal value of q, presumably l, and g is the natural growth rate.[24] q is supposed to be determined in the asset market independently of all the flow decisions (including therefore even investment decisions).[25]

In formulating this kind of theory of asset market equilibrium and investment decisions, Tobin and Brainard seem to me to have purged themselves too thoroughly of the traditional idea that money is first and foremost a necessary medium of exchange or means of payments. They, therefore, fail to see that the decision to carry out planned investment in physical capital goods would inevitable give rise to what Keynes in his 1937 article called the finance demand for liquidity before the plan can be executed. This crucial fact is what makes money such an important and special asset. Indeed Keynes admitted in 1937 that this demand for finance is an important point which he himself should not have overlooked previously (i.e., in the *General Theory*).[26]

This interesting as well as instructive change of mind on the part of Keynes, however, appears to have been totally ignored by most Keynesians. Tobin and Brainard, apparently, believed the investment decisions determined according to their equation quoted above by the gap between q and $\bar{q}$, which in turn was determined on the asset market without any reference to the flow decisions, can be carried out forthwith without any further dealings with the money market (or asset market in general).

Keynes, however, after his rediscovery of the demand for finance, apparently had come to believe that even when an entrepreneur has planned a higher level of investment, say, on the basis of a positive $(q - \bar{q})$ as defined by Tobin, he would still not be able to carry it out until he can obtain the finance required for its implementation. Unless the finance (i.e., the additional transactions balances needed) is available at an appropriate rate of interest, the increased willingness to invest may not materialize. Thus Keynes had already recognized in 1937 that "the transition from a lower to a higher scale of activity" would be inhibited by "the growing congestion of the short-term loan market or of the new issue market, as the case may be," if the banks which can create the additional liquidity "refuse to relax." "The investment market can become congested through shortage of cash" (as a result of the increased demand for finance).[27]

The consideration of the requirement for finance, however, is totally excluded in Tobin's model by his own key behavioral assumption and by the use of a predetermined income term instead of an endogenous current expenditure term in the demand functions for money and other assets. This is how Tobin and his disciples could stubbornly deny to this day the possibility of "crowding out" during the transition period, which is so clearly presaged by Keynes in 1937 in the quotations in the preceding paragraph.[28]

If an endogenous current expenditure term E is substituted for the predetermined Y as an argument in the demand functions for money and other assets, Tobin's system of equations represented by Equation (1) above should be rewritten as

$$f_i(\hat{r}, E(\hat{r}, Y)/W)W = A_i, \tag{6}$$

where $E(\;)$ is the expenditure function of the private sector with the vector of real rates of return and the predetermined income as arguments. In particular, his money-securities-capital model[29] should then be reformulated as

$$f_2(R/q, r_m, r_s, E(\hat{r}, Y)/W)W = M/p, \tag{7}$$

and

$$f_3(R/q, r_m, r_s, E(\hat{r}, Y)/W)W = S/p, \tag{8}$$

where $f_2(\;)$ and $f_3(\;)$ are the demand functions for money and securities, respectively, $\hat{r} = (r_k, r_m, r_s)$, $r_k = R/q$, R being the own rate of return of capital goods assumed to be more or less constant in the short run, and r_m is assumed constant or zero.

Here we must interrupt by pointing out that Tobin's wealth constraint,

$$W = qK + \frac{M + S}{p}, \tag{9}$$

is not appropriate to deal with a sudden increase in S due to the government's decision to float an additional amount, say, G, to new securities to finance its deficit spending. For obviously it cannot be assumed that the wealth of the private sector or that of the whole community is instantaneously increased by that amount. Moreover, the government's demand for finance required for its intended spending has obviously not been allowed for in Tobin's equation for the demand and supply of money.

Thus to demonstrate the crowding out effect recognized by Keynes with a hypothetical case of government deficit spending to be financed entirely by floating new securities with no increase in money supply, we must further adapt Tobin's three-asset model to the following form:

$$f_2(r_k, r_m, r_s, E(\hat{r}, Y)/W)W + L_g(G) = M/p \tag{10}$$

and

$$f_3(r_k, r_m, r_s, E(\hat{r}, Y)/W)W = S/p + G, \tag{11}$$

where $L_g(G)$ is the government's new demand for transactions balance required for its additional spending. If we make the convenient assumption that the government would only float as much additional securities as its current requirement for finance, the $L_g(G)$ can simply be assumed as equal to G.

For our instantaneous analysis of the asset markets, W, the wealth of the private sector, must be assumed to be independent of the floating of new securities by the government except in so far as the asset-prices are affected by the floating. Thus the impact of a government decision to carry out deficit spending to be financed by issue of securities can be analysed by differentiting the two equations above with respect to G, subject to

$$W = qK + \frac{M + S}{p} = \frac{R}{r_k} K + \frac{M + S}{p},$$

which implies that

$$\frac{dW}{dG} = \frac{\partial W}{\partial r_k} \cdot \frac{dr_k}{dG} = -\frac{RK}{r_k^2} \cdot \frac{dr_k}{dG}. \quad 30$$

Then we will obtain

$$\left[W\left(\frac{\partial f_2}{\partial r_k} + \frac{\partial f_2}{\partial(E/W)} \cdot \frac{\partial(E/W)}{\partial r_k}\right) - f_2 \cdot \frac{RK}{r_k^2}\right]\frac{dr_k}{dG} +$$

$$+ W\left[\frac{\partial f_2}{\partial r_s} + \frac{\partial f_2}{\partial(E/W)} \cdot \frac{\partial(E/W)}{\partial r_s}\right]\frac{dr_s}{dG} = -1, \quad (12)$$

and

$$\left[W\left(\frac{\partial f_3}{\partial r_k} + \frac{\partial f_3}{\partial(E/W)} \cdot \frac{\partial(E/W)}{\partial r_k}\right) - f_3 \cdot \frac{RK}{r_k^2}\right]\frac{dr_k}{dG} +$$

$$+ W\left[\frac{\partial f_3}{\partial r_s} + \frac{\partial f_3}{\partial(E/W)} \cdot \frac{\partial(E/W)}{\partial r_s}\right]\frac{dr_s}{dG} = 1. \quad (13)$$

Solving for dr_k/dG and dr_s/dG, we get

$$\frac{dr_s}{dG} = \frac{1}{\Delta}\left\{\left[W\left(\frac{\partial f_2}{\partial r_k} + \frac{\partial f_2}{\partial(E/W)} \cdot \frac{\partial(E/W)}{\partial r_k}\right) - f_2 \cdot \frac{RK}{r_k^2}\right] + \right.$$

$$\left. + \left[\left(\frac{\partial f_3}{\partial r_k} + \frac{\partial f_3}{\partial(E/W)} \cdot \frac{\partial(E/W)}{\partial r_k}\right) W - f_3 \cdot \frac{RK}{r_k^2}\right]\right\} \quad (14)$$

and

$$\frac{dr_k}{dG} = \frac{-1}{\Delta}\left[W\left(\frac{\partial f_3}{\partial r_s} + \frac{\partial f_3}{\partial(E/W)} \cdot \frac{\partial(E/W)}{\partial r_s}\right) + \right.$$

$$\left. + W\left(\frac{\partial f_2}{\partial r_s} + \frac{\partial f_2}{\partial(E/W)} \cdot \frac{\partial(E/W)}{\partial r_s}\right)\right], \quad (15)$$

where

$$\Delta = \left[W\left(\frac{\partial f_2}{\partial r_k} + \frac{\partial f_2}{\partial (E/W)} \cdot \frac{\partial (E/W)}{\partial r_k} \right) - f_2 \cdot \frac{RK}{r_k^2} \right]$$

$$\left[W\left(\frac{\partial f_3}{\partial r_s} + \frac{\partial f_3}{\partial (E/W)} \cdot \frac{\partial (E/W)}{\partial r_s} \right) \right]$$

$$- \left[W\left(\frac{\partial f_3}{\partial r_k} + \frac{\partial f_3}{\partial (E/W)} \cdot \frac{\partial (E/W)}{\partial r_k} \right) - f_3 \cdot \frac{RK}{r_k^2} \right] \qquad (16)$$

$$\left[W\left(\frac{\partial f_2}{\partial r_s} + \frac{\partial f_2}{\partial (E/W)} \cdot \frac{\partial (E/W)}{\partial r_s} \right) \right].$$

All the terms in Δ are negative, or nonpositive, except the term

$$-W^2 \cdot \frac{\partial f_3}{\partial (E/W)} \cdot \frac{\partial (E/W)}{\partial r_k} \cdot \left[\frac{\partial f_2}{\partial r_s} + \frac{\partial f_2}{\partial (E/W)} \cdot \frac{\partial (E/W)}{\partial r_s} \right],$$
$$\qquad\qquad - \qquad\qquad - \qquad\quad - \qquad\quad + \qquad\qquad -$$

which is positive (the sign of each derivative is marked underneath). However, comparing it with a similar but negative term in the determinant Δ, viz.,

$$W^2 \cdot \frac{\partial f_2}{\partial (E/W)} \cdot \frac{\partial (E/W)}{\partial r_k} \cdot \left[\frac{\partial f_3}{\partial r_s} + \frac{\partial f_3}{\partial (E/W)} \cdot \frac{\partial (E/W)}{\partial r_s} \right],$$
$$\qquad\qquad + \qquad\qquad - \qquad\quad + \qquad\quad - \qquad\qquad -$$

we can readily see that the second terms in each of the two expressions are identical except with opposite signs and thus cancel each other out. The sum of these two expressions is, therefore, only

$$W^2 \cdot \frac{\partial (E/W)}{\partial r_k} \cdot \left[\frac{\partial f_2}{\partial (E/W)} \cdot \frac{\partial f_3}{\partial r_s} - \frac{\partial f_3}{\partial (E/W)} \cdot \frac{\partial f_2}{\partial r_s} \right].$$
$$\qquad\qquad - \qquad\qquad + \qquad\quad + \qquad\quad - \qquad\quad -$$

Since Tobin has conveniently assumed that

$$0 < \frac{\partial f_2}{\partial (Y/W)} = - \frac{\partial f_3}{\partial (Y/W)}, \text{ and } \frac{\partial f_1}{\partial (Y/W)} = 0$$

which we may assume to hold for similar derivatives with respect to E/W, and that the own derivatives of the f_i are positive, all the cross-derivatives are non-positive, and that $\Sigma_i \partial f_i/\partial r_s = 0$,[31] the above sum must therefore be at least nonpositive. Hence, the determinant Δ must be negative.

This conclusion holds *a fortiori*, if, as is more normally the case,

$$\frac{\partial f_2}{\partial(E/W)} > -\frac{\partial f_3}{\partial(E/W)} > 0, \text{ and } \frac{\partial f_1}{\partial(E/W)} < 0,$$

i.e., if entrepreneurs seek to finance their expenditure plans not only on the short term security market but also on the capital (stock) market.

The numerator of dr_s/dG in (14) has only one positive term, viz., $[\partial f_3/(\partial(E/W))]\cdot[(\partial(E/W))/\partial r_k]\cdot W$. Again this term will be either cancelled out or overwhelmed by a similar negative term $[\partial f_2/(\partial(E/W))]\cdot[(\partial(E/W))/\partial r_k]\cdot W$. Therefore, dr_s/dG is always positive. In other words, the interest rate on short term securities will certainly be forced up by the government's attempt to finance its deficit spending without increasing the money supply even before the spending is carried out.

The numerator of dr_k/dG in (15), however, is quite uncertain in sign. While the two terms inside the first pair of parentheses are both positive, the terms inside the second pair are both negative. Moreover, while $\partial f_3/\partial r_s$ might be numerically bigger than $|\partial f_2/\partial r_s|$, $\partial f_2/(\partial(E/W))$ is likely to be numerically bigger than $|\partial f_3/(\partial(E/W))|$. Thus dr_k/dG is not only uncertain in sign, but also likely to be rather insignificant.

This is, however, obviously the result of our specific assumption that the government will not seek financing in the physical capital market (or the stock market). If instead we are dealing with an increased willingness to invest on the part of private investors, who may seek finance either on the money market (i.e., short term securities market) or on the stock market (the new issue market), then both r_s and r_k would be raised because of the increased demand for finance.

The effect of an increase in government expenditure on private expenditures can then be shown by writing

$$\frac{d(E/W)}{dG} = \frac{\partial(E/W)}{\partial r_s}\cdot\frac{dr_s}{dG} + \frac{\partial(E/W)}{\partial r_k}\cdot\frac{dr_k}{dG},$$

which, after substituting (14) and (15) for dr_s/dG and dr_k/dG, and simplifying, becomes

$$\frac{d(E/W)}{dG} = \frac{W}{\Delta}\left\{\left(\frac{\partial f_2}{\partial r_k} + \frac{\partial f_3}{\partial r_k}\right)\frac{\partial(E/W)}{\partial r_s} - \left(\frac{\partial f_2}{\partial r_s} + \frac{\partial f_3}{\partial r_s}\right)\frac{\partial(E/W)}{\partial r_k}\right\}$$

$$- \frac{1}{\Delta}(f_2 + f_3)\frac{RK}{r_k^2}\frac{\partial(E/W)}{\partial r_s}. \tag{17}$$

This is definitely negative, because both $(\partial(E/W))/\partial r_k$ and $(\partial(E/W))/\partial r_s$ are negative, and $\partial f_3/\partial r_s + \partial f_2/\partial r_s \geq 0$.

$$\frac{dE}{dG} = W \cdot \frac{d(E/W)}{dG} + EW \cdot \frac{dW}{dG}$$

$$= W \cdot \frac{d(E/W)}{dG} - EW \cdot \frac{RK}{r_k^2} \cdot \frac{dr_k}{dG}. \qquad (18)$$

Since, as is shown above, dr_k/dG is likely to be insignificant in magnitude though uncertain in sign, dE/dG can be quite safely taken as being negative. If the market value of the total net worth of the private sector W depends negatively on r_s as well as it is here assumed to depend upon r_k, then the conclusion holds *a fortiori*.

We have thus demonstrated the crowding-out effect with a modified model of instantaneous general asset equilibrium of Tobin's type. We can now understand why once Keynes had made the concession of the demand for finance, he was forced also to recognize the phenomenon of crowding-out on the money and capital markets right at the stage of financing. Of course, he could still wriggle out of this recognition by asserting that the speculative (or asset) demand for money is infinitely interest-elastic (i.e., $\partial f_3/\partial r_s \to \infty$ and $\partial f_2/\partial r_s \to \infty$), which would make dr_s/dG as well as dr_k/dG approach 0. Apparently, however, Keynes' confidence in the infinite elasticity of liquidity preference in 1937 was already not as strong as in 1936. Hence his ready admission that "the investment market can become congested through shortage of cash."[32]

Unfortunately, however, he failed to see the other side of the demand for finance, viz., that since consumption as well as investment require finance, and since saving implies abstention from consumption, an increase in saving would, therefore, imply a release of finance formerly required for consumption expenditures. It is thus a tarnish on Keynes' accomplishment that he should deny vehemently that saving could ever provide the finance required for investment, until his sudden *volte-face* in *How to Pay for the War*.[33]

How disappointing it is to find that forty years later the Neo-Keynesian should still fail to recognize the requirement for finance even on the part of investment, which Keynes had already so explicitly conceded.

6. The Stock Approach versus the Flow Approach

The question remains whether the modern stock approach rather than the traditional flow approach is indeed more appropriate for money market analysis and interest determination. In two previous articles,[34] I have repeatedly shown that the liquidity preference theory with its stock approach and the loanable funds theory with its flow approach can be shown to be identical, provided that the former is correctly interpreted to take into consideration the finance demand for liquidity for consumption as well as investment expenditures and that the stock equilibrium is indeed achieved for every point of time.

This is not at all surprising; for flows are after all nothing but changes and adjustments in stocks. If the stocks were originally at equilibrium to start with, then an equilibrium in their changes and adjustments should lead to a new equilibrium in stocks. This does not, however, necessarily imply that it is therefore a matter of indifference whether one approach is to be adopted instead of the other. In my opinion, there are good reasons for us to prefer the traditional flow approach to the modern stock approach in the dynamic world we live in.

First of all, although the stock approach is claimed to be applicable to instantaneous point-of-time analysis as in Tobin's theory, it is nevertheless implausible to presume that every economic agent can achieve instantaneously a rationally decided portfolio equilibrium with respect to all his assets in immediate response to any changes in market conditions.[35] What can at the best be claimed for such general asset equilibrium approach is that it might point to the equilibrium interest rates and asset prices at some remote steady state that might be reached ultimately in the long run. It cannot be expected to determine the day to day interest rates on the market in a dynamic world of frequent changes.

Once it is conceded that stock demands for money or other assets cannot be instantaneously adjusted completely, then inevitably we have to fall back upon a flow analysis; for partial adjustments of the stocks over time are flows, and while the stocks are undergoing partial adjustments in a dynamic situation, the stock equilibrium conditions obviously do not hold. We must then analyse how the market equilibrates the flows in order to be able to determine any asset prices at all.[36]

Secondly, as already pointed out above, the transactions demands for money, which constitute by far the major portion of the total demand for money, are not demands for money to hold, but are demands for money to spend. As such, they are really not of the nature of nonrecurrent and once-for-all stock demands, but rather of the nature of recurrent flows; for they must be continuously disbursed and then replenished. They are like an industrial firm's recurring demands for raw materials used for current operation rather than its demands for capital equipment and precautionary stockpiles. Or if we may be allowed to use the analogy of the circulation of blood once more, the transactions demands for money are to be likened to our body organs' demands for blood, which are not for certain stocks of blood to be held here and there all the times, but for continuous flows of blood of certain *volumes per minute* to flow through the organs concerned.

To apply a stock approach to such flow demands by taking only a point-of-time view (or a balance-sheet view) will surely not do them justice. A few ready examples of the misunderstandings that the application of a stock approach to flow demands is likely to engender are the inabilities on the part of modern monetary theorists brought up on the stock approach to make the distinction between an increase in demands for money to spend and an increase in demands for money to hoard,[37] and their failure to recognize that the direct structural determinant of the demands for transaction balances is the planned expenditures rather than total wealth or income received.

The flow approach, on the other hand, takes a rather commonsense view of the money market as the market where the amount of loanable funds, embodied in money, which people are willing to put on the market during an interval of time, is matched with and equated to the amount people are willing to take off the market during the same period.[38] Other asset markets are to be viewed similarly as operating in terms of flows if we are to obtain a dynamic view.

In the very short run, the equilibrium of total stock holdings does not concern the money market and other asset markets except in so far as the holders seek to adjust their holdings felt to be out of equilibrium with their desires through these markets. These adjustments in stock holdings, whether they are instantaneous full adjustments or lagged partial adjustments, are to be dealt with together with other regular flow demands and supplies to achieve the period by period equilibrium. Thus, lagged and incomplete adjustments of stocks in the short run would have no reason to cause indeterminacy in interest rates and asset prices.

The regular flow demands for money to finance investment expenditures and the flow supply of savings (i.e., money that can be spared from financing the savers' own consumption expenditures out of their income received) would of course be dealt with honestly as flows instead of being artificially transfixed into stocks by taking only a snapshot view of them. In this way, we shall be able to visualize money not as lying about here and there in stationary stocks, or stagnant puddles, but as moving in continuous circular flows: say, first issuing from the firms (as a collective group) in the forms of wages and profits going to the households (the other collective group), from which they emerge again partly as flows of consumption expenditures which go back directly to the firms, and partly as savings which go into the money market (including banks and other intermediaries), out of which the inflows of savings would reemerge either enlarged or reduced as net new loans to the firms to finance their investment expenditures (or, to a much minor extent, to some households to finance their expenditures on durable goods). All these expenditures on goods (investment or consumption) go back to the firms as their sales revenues, thus completing the circuit (Figure 1). It is then clear that this circular flow would get bigger and bigger (or smaller and smaller), if the flow of savings from the households become enlarged (or reduced) in their passage through the money market to come out as net new loans to finance investment expenditures. In this way, we can easily visualize why the excess of investment over savings (which must be defined in the Robertsonian sense) leads to an expansion of nominal income flow, and the shortfall of investment below savings leads to a contraction. The chief means of the banking system to finance more investment than the inflow of savings is to create additional money, and the additional money thus created is directly injected into the expenditure streams instead of going first into some investment portfolios.

Of course, this simplified image of money circulation in the economy has omitted many complicating factors, among which the possibility that the flow of savings from households might branch off into pools and puddles of stagnant liquidity, or inactive balances, and get trapped there (i.e., the phenomenon of hoarding), or that, conversely, the stagnant liquidity of these pools and puddles might drain into the flows of expenditures or the flows of savings into the money market and thus enlarge them (i.e., the phenomenon of dishoarding). The former phenomenon was what Keynes had observed during the Great Depression, which he tried to rationalize and explain with his liquidity preference theory.

To analyse the factors that determine the levels of these stagnant pools and puddles of inactive balances, and the causes that induce them to suck in from, or to disgorge into, the main stream of expenditures and savings would surely require a sort of dynamic analysis of portfolio adjustments. But it is quite a different matter to maintain that, just

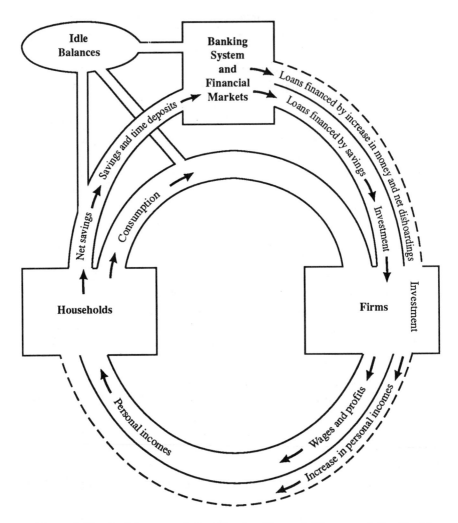

Figure 1 Simple Diagram of the Circular Flow of Money and the Banking System Cum Financial Markets

because of the existence of some stagnant pools of inactive balances off the main circular flows, the entire stock of money must be subject to a stock analysis in a stationary general equilibrium framework of the asset market, artificially constructed by excluding all flow decisions from consideration. That is surely to go to a dogmatic extreme in order to conform with the prevalent academic fashion.

The general portfolio equilibrium approach of Tobin and other Keynesians would present instead a mental picture of a large number of stagnant noncirculating pools and puddles linked by channels to a central asset market, which totally blocks out the vision that money actually circulates in an endless circular flow (Figure 2). In particular, the upper loop of the circular flow in Figure 1, which depicts how the intermediation of the money market (including banks) between savings and investment could expand or contract the circular flow of money, is totally obliterated (compare Figure 1 and Figure 2).

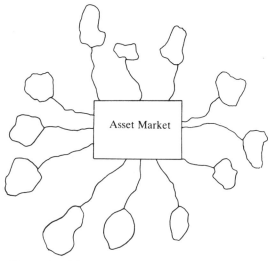

Figure 2 Neo-Keynesian Mental Picture of Portfolio Demands for Money and the Asset Market

The relation between an increase in money supply, which is always imagined by the Keynesians as going directly to all these stagnant puddles but never injected directly into the expenditure flows,[39] and the subsequently expansion of income would appear to them very tenuous and remote indeed. This kind of mental picture seems to provide the rationization for their penchant for increasing the money supply and lowering the interest rate, which is shared by practically all Keynesians. And Tobin is certainly no exception, as we shall presently see.

It seems to me much more sensible therefore, to deal with the money involved in the main circular flows of expenditures and receipts with a honest flow analysis and to combine this with a dynamic stock-adjustment analysis of the inactive puddles of liquidity. Since the adjustments (increases or decreases) in stocks per unit of time are of the same dimension as flows, there should be no fundamental difficulties in this eclectic approach of combining stock adjustments with flows. This is the essence of the loanable funds approach, which I have tried repeatedly to recommend to the economic profession.[40] In my latest attempt, I believe I have shown that this common sense approach seems to be at least capable of explaining the effects of changes in the expectation of price inflation upon the interest rate in a much more satisfactory way than either the Keynesian liquidity preference theory or Friedman's Monetarist approach.[41]

7. Appraisal of the Positive Contributions of Tobin's General Equilibrium Approach

What then is the positive contribution of Tobin's general equilibrium stock approach to monetary theory? I would not say that it is without merits just because it started with the inappropriate assumption that spending decisions and portfolio decisions are independent, and capital accounts can be treated separately from production and income. The effort to bring the whole menu of assets into the analysis does yield some return in clarifying the fact that the existence of more low-risk or riskless assets in the total asset menu would probably make investors more willing to take on more risky assets, such as physical capital assets (or their financial counterpart, industrial shares). Thus it implies that the q ratio might increase even though the pure interest rate (the price of parting with money) has not declined. This clue might lead one to expect that an increase in relatively less risky assets other than money, e.g., short term bills, might also have some expansionary effect on investment activity by raising q. However, the result of total differentiation which Tobin carried out on his equation system for a three assets (money-securities-capital) model in his 1969 paper indicates that the effect on q of an increase of short term securities, supposed to be less risky than capital, (i.e., an increase in S in Tobin's model), is quite ambiguous with indeterminate sign, because, as might be expected intuitively, the increased willingness to undertake risk may be offset by the rise in interest rate brought about simultaneously by the increase in securities. After all the fuss, only an increase in the quantity of money (among all the three assets) turned out to have a definitely expansionary effect by causing both the interest rate to fall and the q ratio to rise (or

$r_k = R/q$ to fall, R being exogenously given).[42] So after all, the general equilibrium approach covering all the assets presented as a new approach by Tobin did not bring any definite new results. Rather it imparts to the readers an impression of a lot of thunders yielding but few drops of rain.

In a subsequent joint article with Brainard, Tobin and his coauthor explained further that q is affected not only by the relative supplies of different assets but also by many other factors, among which inflation seems to me most important and most relevant to our time. They have very astutely pointed out that the inflation rate has very damaging effects on q for several reasons. First, current taxation system in the United States would tax away part of the nominal profits, which really reflect increased costs of replacing depreciated capital stocks. Secondly, inflationary news is likely to be considered by entrepreneurs the harbinger of anti-inflationary policies – bringing recession, stagflation, or price controls, all damaging to the future streams of their real earnings.

To these, we might add the omitted fact that inflation is most likely to cause very frequent and haphazard changes in relative prices of different products, because inflation is not likely to push all prices up evenly and proportionately in step with each other. This fact would greatly increase the risk of production, since the real profits to be made from productive enterprises depend crucially upon relative prices.

Recent experiences of the stock markets in the United States fully bear out the damaging effects of inflation upon entrepreneurs' expectation of their future streams of earnings.

Yet in spite of these astute observations about the damaging effects of inflation on q, Tobin and Brainard would nevertheless confidently assert that if q is low, and we do not know what are the causes, "the appropriate remedial action – and the only remedial action available to the monetary authority – is to expand the supply of bank reserves."[43] This unconditional recommendation seems to me to involve a serious inconsistency if there is a possibility that q is low because of, say, persistent inflation for the reasons given above. If persistent inflation is the cause, as is now the case in the United States, would the appropriate remedial action stilll be a further speed-up of the monetary expansion to lower the nominal interest rate? This deeply ingrained penchant for increasing the money supply and lowering the interest rate is, indeed, as the late Sir Dennis Robertson put it, "the canker at the heart of the Keynesian theory,"[44] and the Keynesian faithful in the United States have surely been seeing to it that it would come to roost in their own country as in Great Britain.

No one can deny that Tobin is one of the brightest economists of our generation. This is fully attested to by his important and sophisticated contributions to the theories of the demand for money, portfolio allocation, and macroeconomics in general. Yet one is constantly surprised that he should repeatedly overlook or disregard some obvious and crucial facts – omissions that make his theory and policy recommendations biased in a partisan way. Perhaps one might suggest that he should endeavor to exorcise from his mind the Baconian "idols" [*Bacon*], that seem to be playing tricks on him: in particular, the idols of the tribe (*idola tribus*) which generate a tendency to support a preconceived opinion by affirmative evidences while neglecting all negative or opposed ones, and the idols of the theater (*idola theatri*) that generate a proneness to fallacious models of thinking as a result of an accepted system of philosophy, in this case, the so-called "new economics" and the exclusive stock approach that seem to have preempted his brilliant mind.

Acknowledgment

I am deeply indebted to Professors Milton Friedman, Gottfried Harberler, Sir John Hicks, Fritz Machlup, and Lord Robbins for reading the manuscript at different stages and for valuable suggestions and encouragements. Needless to say, I am alone responsible for whatever errors that remain in this paper.

Notes

1. Hicks [1935].
2. Hicks himself acknowledges that the basic idea in his 1935 article was already contained in Keynes' *Treatise* [Hicks 1973].

   In the *General Theory*, however, Keynes concentrated almost exclusively on the stock demand and supply of money instead of dealing simultaneously with an entire menu of different assets, even though in Chapter 17 of the *General Theory* there was a discussion of the equilibrium condition for the holding of any asset in general.

   It was definitely Hicks who first clearly outlined the three basic principles of the modern stock approach to monetary theory, viz., (1) that one has to work in terms of a balance sheet and hence to deal with all assets and liabilities at the same time; (2) that choice between assets is choice between probability distributions; and (3) that the cost of making transactions is vital.

Thus Tobin's description of Hicks' "Suggestion" as the guideline of the modern stock approach is literally true.

3. Hicks [1935], p. 4.
4. Such floats have been estimated at as much as around 50% of the total money supply. See Liang [1980], a Ph.D. thesis written at Harvard University under the supervision of Profs. James S. Duesenberry and Benjamin M. Friedman.
5. Hicks [1967], p. 16.
6. It seems that the stock approach to monetary theory is favored also by the monetarists of the Chicago School. According to a personal conversation I had recently with Prof. M. Friedman, however, the stock approach of the Chicago School owes its inspiration not to Keynes or Hicks, but to Frank Knight, who used to teach that all durable goods should be treated as capital goods and dealt with as stocks.

    Furthermore, the Chicago School tends to use the stock demand and supply equation for money to determine the price level rather than the interest rate. For the latter, they tend to emphasize the marginal rate of return on investment and the supply of investible funds, and, therefore, seem to have greater affinity with the classical flow approach.
7. Hicks [1975], p. 365.
8. The characterization of the transactions demand for money as not being voluntary, however, is rather unfortunate; for surely Hicks could not have meant that the transactions demand for money is totally beyond the control of the agent concerned.

    I venture to suggest that what Hicks really wanted to say is that the demand for transactions balances is inevitably linked with the decision to spend (on consumption as well as on investment) even though the quantitative relation between the two might be flexible to some extent. This, however, implies a total denial of the validity of the usual Keynesian separability assumption discussed below.
9. Hicks [1967], pp. 15–16.
10. Tobin [1969].
11. Hicks [1935], p. 12.
12. Tobin [1969], p. 15.
13. A Keynesian reader commented that here I have ignored their implicit assumption that there is no cost of transactions in assets. This assumption is supposed to ensure that portfolio adjustments can be achieved instantaneously.

    This is equivalent to saying that if only the luncheon is assumed to be free, it would be, and could be, gulped down instantaneously. Furthermore, we must not forget that Tobin's explanation of the demand for transactions balances is entirely predicated on the presence of costs of transaction in assets [Tobin, 1956] – one of the ideas which he took over from Hicks' 1935 "Suggestion." If Tobin really assumed here that there is no cost of transactions in assets, he would have at the same stroke eliminated all transactions demand for money in his general equilibrium approach to money.

Anyway, this Keynesian reader soon relented enough to admit that the nonexistence of transactions costs and instantaneous portfolio adjustments are, of course, not strictly true in the real world.

14. Hicks [1935], p. 65.
15. Tobin [1969].
16. Tobin [1956].
17. Keynes [1937].
18. Tobin [1956].
19. Tobin [1958].
20. Tsiang [1972], p. 364, and [1974], pp. 447, 450.
21. Tsiang [1972], pp. 269–270, and [1974], p. 450.
22. Tsiang [1969], pp. 110–113.
23. The differences in theoretical implications brought about by formulating the demand for transactions balances with planned expenditure as its chief explanatory variable instead of income received are discussed at some length in Tsiang [1980].
24. Tobin/Brainard.
25. To say that q is greater than 1, or $\bar{q}$, is only an another way of saying that the marginal efficiency of capital assets is greater than the interest rate applicable to investments on capital assets. For Tobin's q, the demand price for existing capital assets, is related to R and r_k according to his rate of return equation

$$r_k q = R$$

where R is defined as "the perpetual real return obtainable by purchasing a unit of capital at its cost for production p," [Tobin, 1969, p. 20] and, therefore, is roughly the same as what Keynes defined as the marginal efficiency of capital. r_k, therefore, must be the rate of return which the owners of the existing capital goods are willing to put up with from their investments in capital goods. Thus it is obvious that if $q > 1$, $R > r_k$.

This had already been pointed out clearly in the *General Theory:*

"Now those assets of which the normal supply-price is less the demand-price will be newly produced; and these will be those assets of which the marginal efficiency would be greater (on the basis of their normal-supply price) than the rate of interest (both being measured in the same standard of value whatever it is)" [Keynes, 1936, p. 228].

The only innovation which Tobin introduced is that the existing market yield of capital assets r_k is substituted for the pure rate of interest on monetary securities, which he designated as r_s. The gap between r_k and r_s may be interpreted as the extra risk premium for holding assets of more uncertain returns, such as capital assets, as compared with assets with more certain returns, such as short run government securities. However, if the risk of uncertain returns is already subsumed under the definition of the marginal efficiency of capital goods and properly discounted for, as is presumably done in Keynes' formulation, then it should certainly be r_s that is to be compared with the marginal efficiency as in the *General Theory*.

The only advantage of introducing r_k as the special rate applicable to capital assets as distinguished from the rate of interest on government securities is to separate out the extra risk premium for holding assets of uncertain returns such as capital goods. Indeed, Tobin's only contribution in his "General Equilibrium Approach" [Tobin, 1969] seems to me to consist in pointing out that this extra risk premium, i.e., the gap between r_k and r_s, may be narrowed if the amount of relatively riskless assets such as government securities are increased relatively to the more risky assets such as capital goods.

It must be noticed that Tobin and Brainard treat q as well as r_k as invariant with respect to the rate of investment, which was hardly Keynes' final view on the matter.

26. Keynes [1937], p. 667.
27. Keynes [1937], pp. 668–669.
28. Tobin/Buiter.
29. Tobin [1969], p. 24, equations (II.7) and (II.8).
30. In Tobin's model, S represents short term securities, the prices of which is apparently assumed to be independent of r_s.
31. Tobin [1969], pp. 24–25.
32. Keynes [1937], p. 669.
33. Keynes [1940],
34. Tsiang [1956] and [1980].
35. See footnote 13 above.
36. Suppose stock adjustments are not instantaneous and complete but only partial per unit of time, i.e.

$$\frac{dL}{dt} = \lambda[L(E_t, r_t, \pi_t, W_t, \ldots) - M_t],$$

or

$$\Delta L_t = \lambda \Delta t[L(E_t, r_t, \pi_t, W_t, \ldots) - M_{t-1}].$$

Then the stock equilibrium condition for the money market

$$L_t(E_t, r_t, \pi_t, W_t, \ldots) = M_t$$

obviously does not hold while adjustments are being made and we cannot therefore determine the interest rate or anything with this unsatisfied equilibrium condition. We must resort to some sort of flow equilibrium condition in the money market (or other asset markets), e.g.

$$\Delta L_t = \lambda \Delta t[L(\ ) - M_{t-1}] = \Delta M_t^s,$$

to determine the interest rate and other asset prices. This flow equilibrium condition is obviously not contained in the stock equilibrium condition given above.

37. It is most unfortunate that the term "hoarding" or "dishoarding" has come to be used indiscriminately by modern economists in the sense of any increase, or any decrease, in the aggregate demand for money, respectively.

An increase in demand for money due to a decision to increase expenditures (i.e., an increase in transactions demand for money) is totally different in effects on economic activities from an increase in demand for inactive balances [see Tsiang, 1977, 328–331].

38. Robertson [1966a], p. 151.
39. Tobin seems always to think in terms of an open market purchase by the central bank when he talks about an increase in money supply. It is true that when the central bank makes an open market purchase, the additional high-power reserve money would generally go in the first instance into the reserves of banks and other financial houses (i.e., into their portfolios). However, by the ordinary definition of money supply, money in the reserves of banks are not included in the aggregate money supply.

When banks seek to expand their loans on the basis of their excess reserves, i.e., when the real increase in money supply takes place, the additional money will then predominately get injected into the expediture streams of the borrowers as we depicted in the top loop of Figure 1.

40. Tsiang [1956] and [1980]. Although we have quoted extensively from Hicks' "Two Triads" lectures above to show up the fundamental difficulties with the exclusive stock approach to the demand for money, it does not necessarily imply that we are going to take those lectures as our new guideline and to follow it to the letter, as Tobin did with the 1935 "Suggestion." One may reasonably take exception to Hicks' new opinion that the demand for transactions balances should be regarded as entirely involuntary.

All we want to emphasize here is that we should not hitch it to the predetermined data, the income received, but should relate it to the current flow decision variable, expenditure plans. This would still allow the demand for transactions balances to be optimally determined in relation to the costs of asset conversions, and the opportunity costs of holding money. In other words, the loanable funds approach does not imply that we have to assume constant velocity of circulation even for the transactions balances alone.

41. Tsiang [1980], esp. 488–490.
42. Tobin [1969], p. 25.
43. Tobin/Brainard, p. 247.
44. Robertson [1966b], p. 212.

References

Bacon, F., *Novum Organum*. Ed. by T. Fowler. Reprint of 1889 ed. Darby, PA, 1979.

Friedman, M., "The Quantity Theory of Money – A Restatement," *Studies in the Quantity Theory of Money*. Ed. by M. Friedman. Chicago 1956.

Hicks, J. R., "A Suggestion for Simplifying the Theory of Money," *Economica*, 2, 1935, 1–19.

Hicks, J. R., *Critical Essays in Monetary Theory*, London 1967.

Hicks, J. R., "Recollections and Documents", *Economica*, February, 1973.

Hicks, J. R., "Revival of Political Economy The Old and the New," *Economic Record*, September, 1975, 365–367.

Keynes, J. M., *The General Theory of Employment, Interest, and Money*, London 1936.

Keynes, J. M., "The Ex-ante Theory of the Rate of Interest," *Economic Journal* 47, 1937, 663–669.

Keynes, J. M., *How to Pay for the War*, London 1940.

Liang, M.-Y., *The Involuntary Demand for Money and the Case of Missing Money*, Ph.D. Dissertation, Harvard University, 1979, published as Monograph Series, No. 17, The Institute of Economics, Academia Sinica. Taipei 1980.

Robertson, D. H., "Mr. Keynes and the Rate of Interest," A lecture given in 1939; reprinted in Sir D. Robertson, *Essays in Money and Interest*. Ed. by Sir J. Hicks. Manchester 1966a.

Roberston, D. H., "Some Notes on the Theory of Interest," Sir D. Robertson, *Essays in Money and Interest*. Ed. by Sir J. Hicks. Manchester 1966b, 203–222.

Tobin, J., "The Interest Elasticity of Transactions Demand for Cash," *Review of Economics and Statistics* 38, 1956, 241–247.

Tobin, J., "Liquidity Preference as Behavior Towards Risks," *Review of Economic Studies* 25, 1958, 65–86.

Tobin, J., "A General Equilibrium Approach to Monetary Theory," *Journal of Money, Credit, and Banking* 1, 1969, 15–29.

Tobin, J., and W. C. Brainard, "Assets Markets and the Cost of Capital," *Economic Progress, Private Values and Public Policy*, Essays in Honor of W. Fellner. Ed. by B. Balassa and R. Nelson. Amsterdam 1977, Ch. 11, 235–262.

Tobin, J., and W. Buiter, "Long-run Effects of Fiscal and Monetary Policy on Aggregate Demand," *Monetarism*. Ed. by J. L. Stein. Amsterdam 1976, 273–309.

Tsiang, S. C., "Liquidity Preference and Loanable Funds Theories Multiplier and Velocity Analyis A Synthesis," *American Economic Review* 46, 1956, 539–564.

Tsiang, S. C., "The Precautionary Demand for Money: An Inventory Theoretical Analysis," *Journal of Political Economy* 77, 1969, 99–117.

Tsiang, S. C., "The Rationale of the Mean-Standard Deviation Analysis, Skewness Preference, and the Demand for Money," *American Economic Review* 62, 1972, 254–271.

Tsiang, S. C., "The Rationale of the Mean-Standard Deviation Analysis: Reply and Errata for Original Article," *American Economic Review* 64, 1974, 442–455.

Tsiang, S. C., "The Monetary Theoretic Foundation of the Modern Monetary Approach to the Balance of Payments," *Oxford Economic Papers* 1977, 319–338.

Tsiang, S. C., "Keynes' 'Finance' Demand for Liquidity, Robertson's Loanable Funds Theory, and Friedman's Monetarism," *Quarterly Journal of Economics* 95, 1980, 467–491.

Section IV

CHAPTER 13

Keynes' "Finance" Demand for Liquidity, Robertson's Loanable Funds Theory, and Friedman's Monetarism*

S. C. Tsiang

Students of monetary theory might sometimes wonder why Great Britain, which had been the cradle of the science of economics and the home of so many eminent economists, should have been plagued by persistent inflation and balance of payments crises after the Second World War, much more so than some other countries that had suffered even more severe devastation than she did, e.g., West Germany and Japan.[1] It would, therefore, seem useful to take stock of the development of prevailing British monetary theories in order to trace whether and where a wrong turn might have been taken that could be responsible for the postwar policy that got her repeatedly into inflationary and balance of payments troubles.

I think we do not have to go back any farther than the so-called Keynesian Revolution, which from the point of view of monetary theory is really not much of a revolution. In fact, in the post-*General Theory* writings of Keynes, he had already made an important concession to traditional monetary theory, which, if carried to its logical conclusion,

Reprinted by permission of John Wiley & Sons, Inc. from the *Quarterly Journal of Economics*, Vol. XCVI, 3 (May 1980), pp. 467–491. © 1980 by John Wiley & Sons, Inc.

would completely erode away his original revolutionary stand.[2] Unfortunately, few people managed to press this concession to its logical conclusion. As a result, certain mistaken ideas have been retained in the Keynesian theory that have come to be firmly established in most postwar textbooks and classrooms. On the other hand, traditional monetary theory, as expounded by Robertson in particular, who more than anybody else correctly perceived the wrong turn taken by Keynes, and who had strenuously tried to call attention to it, was practically banished from all textbooks and classrooms in the United Kingdom as well as in the United States.

The crucial concession made by Keynes to the critics of his liquidity preference theory of interest rate is his acknowledgment of the so-called "finance" demand for liquidity, or the demand for "finance" for planned investment yet to be carried out. This concession was made by Keynes in his reply to the criticism by Bertil Ohlin.[3]

Ohlin espoused a Swedish variant of the neoclassical theory and contended that the rate of interest depends on the interaction at the margin between the supply of new credit due chiefly to *ex ante* savings and the demand for it arising chiefly out of *ex ante* investment. Ex ante investment is understood to be investment expenditures that are being planned but not yet carried out. Somewhat symmetrically, *ex ante* savings are defined as planned savings out of income that is expected to accrue subsequently.[4]

Now Keynes was a man with enough business experience to know that an entrepreneur, having decided upon an investment project, does need to obtain finance for it before it is carried out. Since the need for finance takes place before the execution of the investment project, *ex post* savings, which he claimed in the *General Theory* would be created automatically by the investment, cannot be available yet to meet the demand. He knew, therefore, that it would be in vain to deny that *ex ante* investment would have a direct impact on the interest rate before the multiplier effect on income has time to work out. Here he realized that he must retreat a step from his position taken in the *General Theory*. He made the concession, however, in a face-saving way by arguing that the demand for "finance" in preparation for investment plans is really a special kind of demand for money or liquidity, which, he admitted, is an additional factor he should not have overlooked previously, "since it is the coping stone of the liquidity theory of the rate of interest."[5]

In Keynes' own words, "during the interregnum—during that period only—between the date when the entrepreneur arranges his finance and the date when he actually makes his investment, there is an additional demand for liquidity without, as yet, any additional supply of it necessarily arising. In order that the entrepreneur may feel himself sufficiently liquid to be able to embark on the transaction, someone else has to agree to become, for the time being at least, more unliquid than before."[6]

Having made the concession graciously, he launched into a counter-attack on Ohlin, choosing the right weak spot as the target for his thrust. Ohlin suggested that the demand for credit (or finance) for the *ex ante* investment could be met by the supply of credit provided by *ex ante* savings. Unfortunately, in order to make the concept of *ex ante* savings symmetric to the concept of *ex ante* investment, Ohlin and his Swedish colleagues defined the former as planned savings out of incomes that are expected to accrue in the future. But how could savings yet to materialize at some future date provide the ready finance currently needed by the investors? Keynes was certainly right in saying that the supply of finance must come out of existing cash balances or banks' credit creation. So after all, the interest rate must still be determined by the demand for liquidity (of money), including the newly recognized demand for finance, and the supply of liquidity, including new liquidity created by banks.

Thus, a forced concession was turned into at least a partial victory. Actually, in a monetary economy, where loans are perforce given and taken in money, it should not make much difference to say that the rate of interest (i.e., the price of loans) is determined by the supply and demand for loans, or that it is determined by the supply and demand for money, in which these loans are given and taken. The crucial question is how one formulates or specifies the function of the demand for money, and what kind of answers one would get to certain specific questions, such as whether an increase in planned investment, or a decline in the propensity to save, would have a direct impact in raising the rate of interest given the supply of money. In the *General Theory*, Keynes merely allowed the value of income, or output produced Y and the rate of interest r as the main arguments of the demand for money function (or functions, as Keynes in the *General Theory* formulated the demand for money in two separate functions, $M^d = L_1(Y) + L_2(r)$). With the demand for money function specified either as $M^d = L(Y, r)$ or as $L_1(Y) + L_2(r)$, and the equilibrium condition $M^d = M^s$ assumed as the determining mechanism for the interest rate, it necessarily follows that the changes in the marginal efficiency of investment and the propensity to save cannot have a direct impact on the interest rate given the supply of liquidity. The effects on the interest rate must operate indirectly through their possible effects on Y.

Yet only one year after the publication of the *General Theory*, Keynes had already conceded that an increase in planned investment due, say, to a rise in the marginal efficiency schedule of investment would exert a direct impact on the rate of interest through the increase in the "finance" demand for liquidity, which he acknowledged as having been overlooked in the *General Theory*. It is very unfortunate that the Second World War soon intervened. Keynes immediately became preoccupied with momentous national affairs, and therefore perhaps never had time to figure out how the demand for money function should be reformulated to allow for the finance demand for liquidity. Since the war, most of his disciples in the United Kingdom as well as in the United States appear to have kept a sort of discreet silence about the "finance" demand for liquidity, which the master had declared to be the "coping stone of the liquidity theory of the rate of interest," at least until I pointed out that it provides a crucial clue for the reconciliation of the liquidity preference theory of interest with the loanable funds theory.[7] Indeed, not only the Keynesians and Neo-Keynesians, but even the Chicago monetarists continue to formulate the money demand function as $L(Y, r)$, or $PL(y, r)$, with various attempts to make it more sophisticated by adding more arguments to it, e.g., expected rate of inflation, expected normal rate of interest, the value of total wealth, etc., and in the case of Milton Friedman and his disciples, by interpreting the real income y as the expected permanent real income rather than current income. None of these sophistications, however, would make the money demand function reflect any more sensitively the "finance demand for liquidity"; indeed they might make the money demand function even less sensitive to it.

Although Keynes made this important concession about planned investment, he remained absolutely adamant with respect to his position on the effect of a change in savings. In the same article, he wrote: "If there is no change in the liquidity position, the public can save *ex-ante* and *ex-post* and ex-anything-else until they are blue in the face, without alleviating the problem in the least—unless, indeed, the result of their efforts is to lower the scale of activity."[8] There is great defiance in the tone, which suggests that, come what may, he is not going to abandon this position.

Nevertheless, his concession on the demand for finance for planned investment actually made his position on savings also untenable, and we shall see that in his counterattack on Ohlin he had actually maneuvered himself right into Robertson's position without realizing it at the time.

In stressing the importance of the demand for finance for planned activity and the ineffectiveness of savings in exerting any influence on the interest rate, Keynes wrote: "The higher scale of planned activity increases, so long as it lasts, the demand for liquidity altogether irrespective of the scale of savings. *Exactly the same is true whether the planned activity by the entrepreneur or the planned expenditure by the public is directed towards investment or towards consumption.*"[9] This clearly indicates that the logic, which made Keynes admit that there is a demand for finance for planned investment, now made him realize that there is also a demand for finance for planned consumption expenditures as well. This is not surprising at all. After all, in a money economy all expenditures have to be conducted with acceptable means of payment, i.e., money, and therefore, all expenditure plans must be provided with the wherewithal to make the expenditures. It is, therefore, total planned expenditure that should be regarded as the primary determinant of the transactions demand for money, not income produced or received, transitory or permanent. If we simply substitute aggregate planned expenditure (for investment as well as for consumption) for income as the chief argument for the money demand function, it would be easy to show that the liquidity preference theory of interest really comes to the same thing as the traditional loanable funds theory. And what Robertson had been saying all along is perfectly right either in terms of the supply and demand for money or in terms of the supply and demand for loanable funds. It is rather Keynes and his followers that were in the wrong when they were insistent against the traditional theory that savings exert no direct influence on the interest rate until they cause the level of activity to decline.

Let me demonstrate this assertion with some very simple mathematics. Suppose we can agree that the demand for money (or liquidity preference) function can be written as $M_t^d = L(C_t^p + I_t^p, r_t, \pi_t, W_t, \ldots)$, where C_t^p and I_t^p are current planned consumption and investment expenditures, respectively, at the beginning of the current decision-making period, r_t the current rate of interest to be determined by the market, π_t the current expected rate of price inflation, and W_t the current value of total wealth.[10] The dots following these variables indicate that we shall keep our mind open as to the question whether more arguments should be introduced into the demand for money function. Then the liquidity preference theory of the interest rate may be summarized by the stock equilibrium condition.[11]

$$M_t^s = L(C_t^p + I_t^p, r_t, \pi_t, W_t, \ldots), \tag{1}$$

which must be established at the beginning of each decision-making period for the determination of the current interest rate. Let us compare this equilibrium condition, which is to be established for the current period, with the equilibrium condition that had already been established in the preceding period; i.e.,

$$M_{t-1}^s = L(C_{t-1} + I_{t-1}, r_{t-1}, \pi_{t-1}, W_{t-1}, \ldots), \tag{2}$$

where the planned expenditures have already been carried out and become actual expenditures of the period. The sum $C_{t-1} + I_{t-1}$ is therefore the income received of the preceding period, i.e., Y_{t-1}. But first let us expand the right-hand side of equation (1) around $r_{t-1}, \pi_{t-1}, W_{t-1}$, so that (1) becomes

$$M_t^s = L(C_t^p + I_t^p, r_{t-1}, \pi_{t-1}, W_{t-1}, \ldots) + L_r(r_t - r_{t-1}) \tag{1a}$$
$$+ L_\pi(\pi_t - \pi_{t-1}) + L_w(W_t - W_{t-1})$$

$$+ \text{ terms in higher orders of differentials and derivatives.}$$

Next let us make the reasonable assumption that the demand for money function is linear (but not necessarily homogeneous) in planned expenditures so that

$$L(C^p + I^p, r, \pi, W, \ldots) \tag{3}$$
$$= k(r, \pi, W, \ldots)(C^p + I^p) + \bar{L}(r, \pi, W, \ldots).$$

Substituting (3), with appropriate time subscripts added, into (1a) and (2) respectively, and taking the difference, we get

$$\Delta M_t^s = k(r_{t-1}, \pi_{t-1}, W_{t-1}, \ldots)(C_t^p + I_t^p - C_{t-1} - I_{t-1}) \tag{4}$$
$$+ L_r \Delta r_t + L_\pi \Delta \pi_t + L_w \Delta W_t$$

$$+ \text{ terms in higher orders of differentials and derivatives, or}$$

$$\Delta M_t^s = k_{t-1} I_t^p - k_{t-1} I(Y_{t-1} - C_t^p) \tag{4a}$$
$$+ L_r \Delta r_t + L_\pi \Delta \pi_t + L_w \Delta W_t + \ldots,$$

where $k(r_{t-1}, \pi_{t-1}, W_{t-1}, \ldots)$ is abbreviated as k_{t-1} and $(C_{t-1} + I_{t-1})$ is written as Y_{t-1}.

It can be immediately recognized that (4a) is nothing but the equilibrium condition for the loanable funds market as stipulated by Robertson. $(Y_{t-1} - C_t^p)$ is exactly what he defined as planned saving, which is not what is expected to be saved out of income accruing in the future, but what is planned to be saved out of disposable income (i.e., income received in the preceding period). All the terms in differentials and derivatives constitute net hoarding (if positive) or dishoarding (if negative). [12] Everything that Robertson tried to tell us is quite right. In particular, what has become the central issue of contention, viz, the question whether a change in thrift (or propensity to save) will have a direct effect on the rate of interest, should clearly be decided in favor of Robertson. From equation (4a) it is clear that an increase in thrift, which lowers the schedule of planned consumption, will certainly bring about a decline in interest rate in order to redress the current money market equilibrium without operating indirectly through the multiplier effect, Pigou effect, the real balance effect, and whatnot, which modern economists find necessary to invoke to reconcile the classical view with the Keynesian doctrine. All the scorn and ridicule that Keynes and his followers heaped upon Robertson and the loanable funds theory of interest are totally unjustified. [13]

One point to which a Keynesian economist might raise objection in this connection is that Keynes appears to believe that apart from the demand for finance there is yet another component of the transactions demand (or the active demand) for liquidity. In his 1938 reply to Robertson, he wrote

> The total demand (for liquidity) falls in two parts: the inactive demand due to the state of confidence and expectation on the part of the owners of wealth, and the active demand due to the level of activity established by the decisions of the entrepreneurs. The active demand in its turn falls in two parts: the demand due to the time-lag between the inception and execution of the entrepreneurs' decisions, and the part due to the time-lags between the receipt and disposal of income by the public and also between the receipt by entrepreneurs of their sale-proceeds and the payment by them of wages, etc. [14]

Now the second element of what he classifies as the active demand really does not deserve this title. It should rather be called the "passive acceptance of money," for these sums are not what the public or entrepreneurs plan to keep in the form of money, but are merely what they passively accept for services rendered or goods sold pending rational disposal later on at a more appropriate time. All transactions balances start out as demand for finance either for investment or for consumption expenditures, and end up as passive acceptance of cash toward the end of a cycle of money circulation to await reallocation at the beginning of a new cycle either as finance required for new expenditure plans again or as inactive hoards (asset balances).[15]

In the analysis of interest determination, only the active demand for finance and the idle balances deliberately held should be set against the available supply of money, for only they are the objects of rational decisions of the agents concerned at the beginning of the period; i.e., the moment when decisions are supposed to be made.[16]

Once the liquidity preference theory is reformulated in the way we suggested (i.e., in terms of first differences), many of the most baffling remarks in Keynes' two notes on "finance" demand for liquidity[17] become quite understandable to us.

For instance, in the 1937 note Keynes asserted that "'Finance' is a revolving fund. . . . As soon as it is used in the sense of being expended, the lack of liquidity is automatically made good and the readiness to become temporarily unliquid is available to be used over again."[18] A page later he continued: "Consumption is just as effective in liquidating the short term finance as savings is. There is no difference between the two." In his 1938 reply to Robertson, he again wrote

> The finance or cash, which is tied up in the interval between planning and execution, is released in due course after it has been paid out in the shape of income, whether the recipients save it or spend it. There is, therefore, just as much reason for adding current consumption to the rate of increase of new bank-money in reckoning the flow of cash becoming available to provide new finance as there is for adding current savings.

In the end he added rather contemptuously

> Until Mr. Robertson understands that, he will not grasp what I am driving at, however carefully I attempt to rewrite it.[19]

As things turned out, Robertson failed completely to understand Keynes' strange logic that would make both consumption and savings equally the components of the supply of finance. He was instead utterly flabbergasted. With his characteristic irony, he thrust home:

> "The comforting doctrine that an act of investment necessarily breeds equivalent acts of saving by other persons becomes for the moment transmuted into the even more comforting doctrine that it doesn't matter whether it does or not."[20]

How Keynes could have arrived at such an amazing conclusion is indeed a historical puzzle. Robertson, following the lead of Shaw[21] suggested that perhaps the confusion was due to the fact that Keynes had mixed up "maintaining intact a given aggregate stock of capital without a rise in the rate of interest" with "maintaining a given rate of increase in the aggregate stock of capital without a rise in the rate of interest."[22] This explanation, however, seems to me rather farfetched, for it is most unlikely that an economist of Keynes' calibre would ever fail to make such an obvious distinction. When we reformulate the liquidity preference theory into the first difference form, i.e., equation (4), it becomes clearer where the confusion could have crept into his mind.

It may be observed from the first term of equation (4) that consumption and investment expenditures actually carried out, i.e., C_{t-1} and I_{t-1}, have a sign opposite to that of planned consumption and investment still requiring "finance," i.e., C_t and I_t, and thus appear to serve as a sort of countervailing force to the demand for "finance." This is perhaps what Keynes had in mind when he wrote: "Finance is a revolving fund. . . . As soon as it is used in the sense of being expended, the lack of liquidity is automatically made good. . . ." That is, consumption and investment expenditures actually carried out, C_{t-1} and I_{t-1}, appear to provide the finance for the new consumption and investment expenditures planned, C_t and I_t. Only when aggregate planned expenditures, $(C_t + I_t)$, exceed aggregate expenditures previously carried out, $(C_{t-1} + I_{t-1})$, will there be an upward pressure on the interest rate.

So far, it seems to be all right. However, when Keynes went on to assert with equanimity that "consumption is just as effective in liquidating short-term finance as saving is," he was clearly wrong about timing. In dynamic analysis, timing is vitally important. Keynes, however, was perhaps most at home with equilibrium analysis, where economic variables do not need time subscripts. When timing and time subscripts are taken into consideration, the above remark is surely wrong; for Keynes must have confused C_t with C_{t-1}. The latter does carry a sign opposite that of I_t and C_t in the demand for and supply of finance equation, (4). At the moment of decision for the current period, however, C_{t-1} is already a given datum of the past. It is no longer a decision variable. Only current consumption C_t, or its complement, saving $(Y_{t-1} - C_t)$, is still to be decided together with the current investment plans. From equations (4) and (4a), it is obvious that C_t would be competing with current investment, I_t for available finance. It is only $(Y_{t-1} - C_t) = S_t$ that can properly be said to provide the finance for investment apart from dishoarding or money creation. It is true that an increase in current consumption adds to nominal disposable income for the next period, but that will not be available until the next period, and even then whether it will be available as finance for investment of the next period depends entirely upon whether anything will be saved out of it.[23]

It is most unfortunate that modern economists hardly bother to examine the controversy between Keynes and Robertson in their own writings any more. And the myth that the Keynesian liquidity preference theory had completely vanquished the Robertsonian loanable funds theory has been lightly accepted in academic circles, even though among the practical banking circles there remains a tenacious skepticism about it. Thus, the triumphant Keynesian theory of interest handed down to an adoring postwar generation of economists a body of doctrines according to which saving does nothing to finance investment that consumption cannot do equally well; all saving does is to lower the level of activity and employment, and, hence, it is a selfish, antisocial act; investment can always generate an equal amount of saving automatically to finance itself; the rate of interest should, therefore, be kept low at all times even in the face of inflation to stimulate investment; the money supply is a matter of no concern, since the elasticity of speculative demand for liquidity is believed always to be so great as to eliminate all its influences, etc. As early as 1951, Robertson already warned: "This is, indeed, I think, the canker at the heart of the Keynesian theory of interest—a canker which has since (if cankers can so act) abundantly come home to roost."[24] When we look back at the postwar history of Great Britain, with its persistent inflation, recurrent balance of payments difficulties, disappearing private savings and low efficiency of investments that actually managed to get carried out in the inflationary scramble for resources, can any fair-minded economist help but recognize that the so-called Keynesian doctrines should bear no small share of responsibilities for the postwar malaise of Great Britain?

Nowadays a reaction against Keynesian economics has apparently set in. The new challenge to Keynes, however, seems all to come under the banner of new monetarism with Friedman as the leader. Robertson, the chief critic of Keynes during his lifetime, is hardly remebered by the new generation of economists. It is natural for us to ask ourselves whether the teachings of the new monetarism really represent a much more advanced state of development of monetary theory that renders everything said by Robertson obsolete. My answer to this question is an emphatic "no."

Although one must admit that Friedman has made important contributions to economic theory, and, in particular, to policy matters, e.g., in advocating flexible exchange rates and in persuading central bankers to pay more attention to money supply—for these he well deserved the recent award of the Nobel Prize—his monetary theory is a rather incongruous mixture of Keynes and Irving Fisher and is obviously still in a stage of *tâtonnement*, to use a word made familiar by Walras in a different connection. It is particularly unsatisfactory in explaining the short-run determination and adjustment of the interest rate on the money market. This is apparent in his latest attempts to synthesize his own theory in two articles published successively in 1970 and 1971.

In these articles he first presents a model of six equations, in seven variables, rather similar to the model of Modigliani[25] but with the equations for the aggregate production function, the aggregate employment function, and the wage reaction function omitted.

Specifically, Friedman writes

$$M^D = P \cdot l(Y/P, r) \tag{F1}$$

$$M^S = h(r) \tag{F2}$$

$$M^D = M^S \tag{F3}$$

$$C/P = f(Y/P, r) \tag{F4}$$

$$I/P = g(r) \tag{F5}$$

$$Y/P = C/P + I/P. \tag{F6}$$

With M^D, M^S, Y, P, r, C, and I as the seven variables to be determined but only six equations, it is not surprising that the system is indeterminate. He then asserts that the traditional quantity theory would add the equation

$$Y/P = Y_0 \tag{F7a}$$

to close the system. Equations (F4) and (F5) can then be solved for the interest rate r, and equations (F1) to (F3) then yield an equation relating the price level to the nominal quantity of money.

The simply Keynesian income-expenditure theory is alleged to close off the system by adding the equation

$$P = P_0, \tag{F7b}$$

which enables equations (F1) to (F3) to define the Hicksian LM curve and equations (4) to (6) to define the Hicksian IS curves.[26] The intersection of these two curves then determines the equilibrium Y/P_0 and r and thus the whole system.

This is essentially Hicks' IS–LM model. In fact, Modigliani's 1944 article had presented a more comprehensive model, which included the production function, employment function, and the wage reaction function, and which is capable of demonstrating that the additional equations of the quantity theorists and the Keynesians, i.e., (F7a) and (F7b), are not, as Friedman alleges, just arbitrary assumptions to close off the system, but the consequences of the particular forms of the wage-reaction function that the two camps, respectively, regard as correctly reflecting the real situation of their times.

We shall not, however, dwell on this here, but shall proceed to examine what Friedman himself presents as the third alternative approach. This turns out to be merely the addition of an extra equation for the determination of the nominal interest rate quite apart from equation (F3) for the supply and demand for money, or the savings-investment equation (F6). Namely, he now adds

$$r = \rho^* + \left(\frac{1}{P}\frac{dP}{dt}\right)^* \tag{F8}$$

$$r = \rho^* + \left(\frac{1}{Y}\frac{dY}{dt}\right)^* - \left(\frac{1}{y}\frac{dy}{dt}\right)^* = k_0 + \left(\frac{1}{Y}\frac{dY}{dt}\right)^*, \tag{F9}$$

where ρ^* is the "permanent" or "anticipated" real rate of interest, $(1/P)(dP/dt)^*$ is likewise the "permanent" or "anticipated" rate of price change, and $(1/Y)(dY/dt)^*$ and $(1/y)(dy/dt)^*$ the "anticipated" rates of growth of nominal and real income, respectively. It is further conveniently assumed here that the anticipated real rate of interest minus the anticipated rate of growth of real income is somehow invariant and equal to a constant known to every asset-owner or speculator. Thus, the nominal rate of interest is no longer one of the endogenous variables to be determined by the equilibrium conditions of the market, but is specially determined by an exogenous constant k_0 plus a predetermined variable $(1/Y)(dY/dt)^*$, which is supposed to depend only on past history, viz., $Y(T)$ or $M(T)$, $T < t$, in his notation.[27]

This rather dubious procedure is claimed to be a combination of key ideas taken from Keynes and Fisher. From Keynes he borrows the idea that "a substantial body of asset-owners who have firmly held views about the rate of interest" can "force the current rate into conformity with their anticipations." The idea he takes over from Fisher is that in equilibrium the nominal interest rate should equal the real rate plus the rate of increase of prices. Thus, what Friedman in effect assumed is that a powerful body of wealthy "speculators," as Keynes would call these asset-owners, would virtually peg the nominal rate of interest at a level equal to a known constant plus their unanimous and firmly held anticipated rate of increase of nominal income.

The big question here is how a multitude of asset-owners or speculators can reach a consensus of firmly held opinions on the future rate of increase of nominal income. Sir Roy Harrod, who was one of the discussants of Friedman's paper at the Sheffield seminar, was quick in pointing out that "I do not think that we can accept an asterisked term for the future rate of increase of prices or the future rate of increase of nominal income. Surely they must depend in part on policy decisions, which cannot be anticipated."[28] To this we may add that even if we grant that asset-owners do form some sort of rough guess about what the government, monetary authorities, and trade unions will do, how can such rough guesses be held with firm conviction without any shred of uncertainty? And furthermore how can there ever be a consensus of such individual guesses among all the asset-owners?

For the sake of argument, however, let us grant for the moment that such a unanimous and firmly held anticipation of the future rate of increase of nominal income is indeed possible. Nevertheless, the next step of argument that Friedman takes from this assumption still involves a serious logical error. He first transforms his money demand function into nominal terms,

$$M^D = Y \cdot l(r), \qquad (F1a)$$

on the assumption that the elasticity of the demand for money with respect to real income is unity (or that the demand function for real balances is homogeneous of degree one with respect to real income). This is rather surprising in view of Friedman's usual emphasis that this demand function must be defined in terms of real magnitudes and that the elasticity of demand for money with respect to real income is generally larger than unity. Now he claims that "the present theory is for short-term fluctuations during which the variation in per capita real income is fairly small. Given that the elasticity is unlikely to exceed 2.0, no great error can be introduced for such moderate variations in income by approximating it by unity."[29] Combining this equation with (F2) and (F3) above, he gets

$$Y(t) = M(t)/l(r) = V(r) \cdot M(t), \tag{F10}$$

where V, the velocity of circulation, is simply the inverse of $l(r)$. Equation (F10), together with (F9), is said to constitute a two-equation system for determining the level of nominal income at any point of time. Equation (F9) is supposed to determine the nominal interest rate by an exogenous constant plus a variable depending entirely on predetermined data. With the nominal interest rate determined, the velocity of circulation is supposed to be determined also. Equation (F10) will then determine nominal income by the current money supply. This is essentially the gist of Friedman's new monetary theory of nominal income, which he claims to be based on a synthesis of Keynes and Fisher.

However, if we recall the implications of the Keynesian assumption that he made in equations (F8) and (F9) above, it should be clear that it is logically impossible to make this kind of deduction. By now Friedman seems to have forgotten that the Keynesian assumption of the nominal interest rate being pegged by speculators (or asset-owners) at a predetermined level necessarily implies perfectly elastic liquidity preference on their part at that level. That is, in order to peg effectively the nominal rate at a predetermined level, the speculators must be ready to buy an infinite amount of bonds with money balances whenever the nominal rate of interest tends to rise ever so little above the level, and to sell an infinite amount of bonds for money whenever the nominal rate tends to drop ever so little below that level. Thus, $l'(r)$ at the predetermined level of interest rate, say r^*, must be $-\infty$, and

$$V'(r)|_{r=r^*} = \frac{-l'(r)}{l^2}\bigg|_{r=r^*} = +\infty. \tag{F11}$$

This in effect implies that $V(r^*)$ is quite indeterminate and can be any finite number. Equation (F10), therefore, has no predictive value at all either in the short run or in the long run. In the short run, when there is no change in expectation (i.e., r^* is given), any exogenous change in M due to government policy would cause nominal income to change according to

$$\frac{dY}{dM} = M \cdot V'(r)|_{r=r^*} \cdot \frac{dr}{dM} + V(r^*). \tag{F12}$$

Friedman apparently thinks that the first term on the right-hand side can simply be neglected because his Keynesian-Fisherian assumption has taken care that $dr/dM \to 0$ from the negative side. He forgets, however, that the very same assumption implies also that

$$V'(r)|_{r=r^*} \to \infty.$$

Thus, the first term constitutes an indeterminate form of $\infty \cdot (-0)$, which can take any negative value. This is in essence the traditional Keynesian ground for disregarding altogether the influence of any changes in money supply. Thus, the forgotten implication of the idea he borrowed from Keynes would completely foil his hope of obtaining a monetarist result from an artificial liaison between Keynes and Fisher.

For a long-run dynamic path, Friedman simply takes the logarithmic derivation of equation (F10) to get

$$\frac{1}{Y}\frac{dY}{dt} = \frac{1}{V}\frac{dV}{dr}\frac{dr}{dt} + \frac{1}{M}\frac{dM}{dt}, \tag{F13}$$

and then argues that since his Keynesian assumption underlying equations (F8) and (F9) would peg the nominal rate of interest at the expected rate of asset-owner, dr/dt would in effect be the rate of change of their expected rate, i.e., $dr^*/dt = d/dt(1/Y)(dY/dt)^*$. Furthermore, $1/V \, dV/dr$ is simply treated as a finite positive magnitude s. This might be justified by arguing that since dr/dt would in effect be only dr^*/dt, the adjustment in the demand for money, or in the velocity of circulation, to be taken into account is the adjustment of the nonspeculative demand for money, i.e., that for transactions or precautionary purposes, which is certainly finite in magnitude.[30] This is again logically not permissible; for dr/dt should be split into the change due to the change in the expectation of the speculators and the change due to the exogenous and unexpected change in money supply, i.e.,

$$\frac{dr}{dt} = \frac{dr^*}{dt} + \frac{d(r - r^*)}{dM} \cdot \frac{dM}{dt}. \tag{F14}$$

And we must point out that in the context of Friedman's theoretical framework the response of the velocity of circulation to a change in the rate of interest differs entirely according to whether the change in rate is due to a change in the expected rate of all asset-owners or due to a deviation of the market rate from the expected rate of asset-owners. In the former case, no speculative activity on the part of asset-owners will be induced. The response would consist entirely of the usual adjustments in the demands for transactions and precautionary balances. In the latter cases, the response would be overwhelmingly dominated by the speculative activities of asset-owners who, according to Friedman's

assumption borrowed from Keynes, would be prepared to buy with cash
(or sell for cash) an infinite amount of interest-bearing assets to peg the
market rate of interest at their own expected rate. Thus, strictly
speaking, velocity should be regarded as a function of two separate
variables, i.e.,

$$V = V(r^*, r - r^*),$$

of which $\partial V/\partial r^*$ is a finite positive magnitude, whereas $\partial V/\partial(r - r^*)$
approaches $+\infty$. Thus,

$$\frac{1}{V}\frac{dV}{dt} = \frac{1}{V}\frac{\partial V}{\partial r^*}\frac{dr^*}{dt} + \frac{1}{V}\frac{\partial V}{\partial(r - r^*)} \cdot \frac{d(r - r^*)}{dt}, \qquad \text{(F15)}$$

and Friedman's equation (F13) should really be written as

$$\frac{1}{Y}\frac{dY}{dt} = \frac{1}{V}\frac{\partial V}{\partial r^*}\frac{dr^*}{dt} + \frac{1}{V}\frac{\partial V}{\partial(r - r^*)}\frac{d(r - r^*)}{dM}\frac{dM}{dt} + \frac{1}{M}\frac{dM}{dt}.$$

$$\text{(F13a)}$$

Again the right-hand side would be indeterminate; for even though
Friedman can claim that his assumption would make $d(r - r^*)/dM$
approach zero, he cannot dismiss the whole second term as negligible,
because the very assumption that makes $\partial(r - r^*)/\partial M$ approach -0
would at the same time make $\partial V/\partial(r - r^*)$ approach $+ \infty$. Their
product, therefore, can be any finite negative magnitude. Equations
(F13) and (F13a) are, therefore, totally unable to determine a definite
dynamic path of the nominal income.

Thus, Friedman's attempt to bring forth a hybrid new monetary
theory of nominal income out of an artificial liaison between Keynes
and Fisher must be declared a failure. The issue of this alliance will
inevitably bear the dominant Keynesian characteristics of infinitely
elastic liquidity preference, which totally disqualifies it for the monetarist designs that Friedman has planned for it.

What a pity that Friedman had so lightly rejected the Robertsonian
loanable funds approach in favor of the demand and supply of money
approach, and that, furthermore, Keynes' concession on the finance
demand for liquidity, which Ohlin and Robertson had forced out of him,
seems to have escaped his notice also![31] For the only way to salvage his
position is to abandon the supposedly Keynesian assumption that
speculative asset-owners have a firmly held expectation that the nominal
interest rate will be at a predetermined level, $r^* = \rho^* + (1/P)(dP/dt)^*$,
but to adopt instead a rather un-Keynesian assumption that the investing
entrepreneurs have a perfectly elastic marginal efficiency of investment

schedule at the rate r^*. Then, if he takes the loanable funds approach, he will be able to say that the nominal interest rate will be directly pegged at r^*, because the entrepreneurs' demand for loanable funds for investment purposes is perfectly elastic at that rate. Moreover, since the additional loanable funds demanded by the entrepreneurs, in cases when the market rate tends to drop below r^*, will be used on investment expenditures, they will not result in any decline in the velocity of circulation of money as the absorption of money supply by speculating asset-owners would. *Mutatis mutandis* for the case where the market rate tends to rise above r^*.

Unfortunately, however, Friedman's model is formulated in the prevailing Keynesian fashion, namely, the money market equilibrium condition is stated in terms of equality between the demand and supply of money, which is incapable of showing the direct influence of the demand for loanable funds on the market rate. It can, indeed, show that the IS curve would be horizontal in this case, and, hence, fix the market rate at r^*. But in this case, the influence of a change in inflation-expectation on the market rate will be indirect, for it must operate through the expansion or contraction of income.

To show that the alternative assumption would be able to fix the nominal interest rate directly at r^* in a Keynesian model, we must invoke Keynes' conceded concept of the finance demand for liquidity. In other words, we must say that the entrepreneurs, who have infinitely elastic marginal efficiency of investment at the rate r^*, would necessarily also have infinitely elastic demand for "finance" at that rate. The additional money supply absorbed by these entrepreneurs, would be put into active circulation to finance investment expenditures and, hence, would not by itself decrease the velocity of circulation, as the absorption of money supply by the speculating asset-owners would. (*Mutatis mutandis* for a release of money supply by the investing entrepreneurs.)

As we have argued above, to reflect the transactions demand for money properly, the money demand function should have as its main argument the aggregate planned expenditure rather than income produced or permanent income. That is, the money demand function should be written as

$$M^D = Pl(C/P + I/P, r),$$

instead of Friedman's (F1). If it is further assumed that the elasticity of the demand for money with respect to planned expenditure is unity, this function could be transformed, similarly to Friedman's (F1a), into

$$M^D/P = (C/P + I/P)l(r),$$

where $l(r)$ is the inverse of the velocity of money. With the money demand function thus reformulated, then the assumption that the marginal efficiency of investment is perfectly elastic at r^*, i.e.,

$$I/P = g(r), \text{ and } g_r|_{r=r^*} = -\infty,$$

would necessarily imply a perfect elastic demand for money at r^*, i.e.,

$$\frac{d(MD/P)}{dr} = \left(\frac{C}{p} + \frac{I}{p}\right)l_r + (f_r + g_r)l(r) = -\infty, \text{ at } r = r^*.$$

The nominal rate of interest would then be successfully pegged at r^*, yet the velocity of circulation would remain constant at $1/l(r^*)$. This would then satisfy precisely the desiderata of Friedman's theory of nominal income.

Nevertheless, I cannot help wondering why it is at all necessary for Friedman to go to the length of making such an extreme assumption that the nominal interest rate is somehow rigidly fixed at the level of $r^* = \rho^* + (1/p)(dP/dt)^*$, which seems to fly in the face of reality. With Robertson' loanable funds theory, or our revised liquidity preference theory shown above, we should be able to get a reasonably accurate explanation of the short-run movements of nominal income without resorting to such an unrealistic assumption. Equation (4) clearly shows that the excess of planned expenditure over disposable nominal income $(Y_t^p - Y_{t-1})$ is due partly to an increase in money supply and partly to dishoarding, i.e.,

$$\Delta Y_t = Y_t^p - Y_{t-1} = \frac{1}{k_{t-1}} \{\Delta M_t^s - (L_r\Delta r_t + L_\pi\Delta\pi_t + \ldots)\}. \quad (5)$$

Dividing both sides by Y_{t-1}, we obtain

$$\frac{\Delta Y_t}{Y_{t-1}} = \frac{M_{t-1}}{k_{t-1}Y_{t-1}} \cdot \left\{ \frac{\Delta M_t^s}{M_{t-1}} - \frac{r_{t-1}L_r}{M_{t-1}} \frac{\Delta r_t}{r_{t-1}} - \frac{\pi_{t-1}L_\pi}{M_{t-1}} \cdot \frac{\Delta\pi_t}{\pi_{t-1}} - \ldots \right\}$$
(5a)

$$= \frac{1}{\eta_t^Y} \cdot \frac{\Delta M_t^s}{M_{t-1}} + \eta_t^r \cdot \frac{\Delta r_t}{r_{t-1}} + \eta_t^\pi \cdot \frac{\Delta\pi_t}{\pi_{t-1}} - \ldots,$$

if we define

$$\eta_t^Y = \frac{Y_{t-1}}{M_{t-1}} k_{t-1}, \qquad \eta_t^r = -\frac{r_{t-1}}{M_{t-1}} L_r,$$

and

$$\eta_t^\pi = - \frac{\pi_{t-1}}{M_{t-1}} L_\pi.$$

η_t^Y, η_t^r and η_t^π may be called the elasticities of demand for money with respect to expenditure, interest rate, and expected rate of inflation, respectively, for period t. For short-run analysis, they may reasonably be assumed to be fairly stable in magnitude. Thus, we obtain a dynamic adjustment equation for the rate of change of nominal income as a function of the rates of change of interest rate and expected price inflation, etc. If we follow Friedman in assuming that current anticipation of price inflation depends entirely on predetermined data and that other influences on the demand for money are relatively unimportant, then we need only one more equation to close the system. That equation is provided by the definition that $Y_t^p = C_t^p + I_t^p$ and the consumption and investment functions; i.e.,

$$Y_t^p = C^p(Y_{t-1}, r_t, \pi_t, \ldots) + I^p(Y_{t-1}, r_t, \pi_t, \ldots), \qquad (6)$$

which makes the current planned expenditure dependent upon current interest rate and predetermined data including disposable income.

Thus, we have a determinate short-run dynamic system for both nominal income and the nominal interest rate, where both variables are to be determined by the money market mechanism. This is totally unlike Friedman's two-equation system (F9) and (F10), where the nominal interest rate is arbitrarily assumed to be fixed by speculative asset-owners' anticipation of a price increase. This Robertsonian loanable funds approach certainly does not rely either upon the assumption of constant real output or upon the assumption of constant price or wage level, any more than Friedman's own theory of money income. It can be applied, therefore, to a dynamic world where real output and prices are constantly changing. Indeed, we shall see below that it can cope with expected price inflation more satisfactorily than Friedman's own new approach. Of course, like Friedman's own new approach, it only tries to explain the short-run movement of money income and expenditure. It cannot explain the movements of real output and prices. That task must wait until we have specified the production function, employment function, and the wage-reaction function.

The astonishing Fisher-Keynesian assumption invoked by Friedman, namely, that the nominal rate of interest must (or normatively should) reflect fully and instantly the anticipated rate of increase of prices, would not have been sanctioned either by Keynes or by Fisher, even though Friedman makes it in their names. Keynes in his *General Theory*[32] actually denounced Fisher's proposition that the anticipation of a price increase will directly cause the nominal interest rate to rise. Fisher[33] on his part only asserted that the money rate of interest will rise somewhat as a result of an expected increase in prices, but he was cautious enough to add that it "does not usually change enough to fully compensate for the appreciation or depreciation."

At the Sheffield Seminar, Sir Roy Harrod, one of Keynes' original disciples, brought up Keynes' objection to Fisher, and solemnly declared that "the idea that a new found expectation (of price rise) can alter the relative value of two money-denominated assets is logically impossible, and must not be accepted into the corpus of economic theory."[34] Indeed, if the function of the demand for money is to be specified in the way Friedman insists it should be, namely,

$$M/P = L(y^*, r, \pi, \ldots),$$

where y^* stands for expected permanent real income rather than current income, then an increase in the expected rate of inflation π would seem more likely to lower the nominal interest rate than to raise it, for an increase in the expected rate of inflation will lower the attractiveness of money as a store of value (i.e., L_π is likely to be negative), and there is certainly no reason to expect permanent real income to change immediately in the offsetting direction.

I have, therefore, looked with great anticipation for Friedman's answer to this challenge. I was very disappointed indeed to find in the summary of the general discussion only a rather garbled description of an anonymous argument advanced against Harrod, which goes somewhat as follows. A change in the expected rate of inflation would upset the equilibrium relation between the return of bonds and the yield of equities, the dividends of which can presumably be expected to rise by approximately the same proportion as the rise in prices. It is admitted that in principle the balance can be restored either by a jump in the nominal prices of equities that lowers the yield on equities down to the level of the interest rate on bonds, or by a rise in the nominal interest rate to the level of elevated expected yield on equities. For some obscure reason, the former is considered to be ruled out, and it is claimed to be "more rational to suppose that the balance between bonds and equities would be maintained by a rise in the money rate of interest relative to the yield of equities."[35]

What a feeble argument against Harrod's challenge this is! The reason why the first alternative, i.e., that the money value of equities should rise enough to lower the expected yield on equities to the level of the money rate of interest, can be ruled out is not convincingly stated. Furthermore, if it can be granted that an increase in the expected rate of inflation will reduce the attractiveness of money as an asset to hold, a rise in the nominal rate of interest that is supposed to follow as a direct consequence would further reduce the demand for money to hold. Where would the resulting excess supply of money be absorbed? Friedman's demand for the money function certainly gives no answer to this question. The surprising thing is that he does not seem to be even bothered by this question.

Here one is again prompted to exclaim, what a pity that Friedman seems to be so unfamiliar with Robertson's writings! For Robertson, as one anonymous discussant at the Sheffield seminar pointed out, had already put his finger on the spot where Keynes went wrong in "his curious misunderstanding of Professor Fisher's celebrated proposition about the influence of price movements on the rate of interest." The answer to this question, as Robertson[36] indicated, can be provided in terms of the "finance" demand for liquidity, which Keynes confessed to have overlooked in his *General Theory*. A rise in the expected rate of inflation increases the profitability of investment at the original money rate of interest and thus will stimulate planned investment expenditures. At the same time, the public's expenditure on consumption goods, especially on the durable and storable kinds, will also increase because of the expected rise in their future prices. Thus, the "finance" demand for money (for planned investment as well as consumption) will increase. This increase in the demand for finance will generally outweigh the decrease in the demand for money as an asset to hold, which in normal circumstances is of very minor magnitude to begin with. In terms of the notation used in our loanable funds equation, i.e., equation (4) above,

$$k_{t-1}\left(\frac{\partial I^p}{\partial \pi} + \frac{\partial C^p}{\partial \pi}\right)\Delta\pi + L_\pi\Delta\pi > 0, \text{ when } \Delta\pi > 0. \tag{7}$$

If there is no accommodating increase in the money supply by the monetary authorities, the rate of interest must rise to restore the equilibrium of the money market. Thus, Fisher is certainly right in saying that a rise (or decline) in the expected rate of price inflation will directly push the money rate of interest up (or down) instead of first causing the level of activity to rise (or fall) and then exerting its influence on the interest rate indirectly through the changes in the level of activity, as the Keynesians insist to be the case.

Moveover, Fisher[37] is also right in adding that "the money rate of interest, while it does change somewhat, does not usually change enough to compensate fully for the appreciation or depreciation" (of money). This can be demonstrated with our equation for the demand for and supply of loanable funds, i.e., equation (4). Differentiating equation (4) with respect to both r_t and π_t, we get

$$\frac{dM^s}{dr} \Delta r_t = \left[k_{t-1}\left(\frac{\partial I^p}{\partial \pi} + \frac{\partial C^p}{\partial \pi}\right) + L_\pi \right]\Delta\pi_t$$
$$+ \left[k_{t-1}\left(\frac{\partial I^p}{\partial r} + \frac{\partial C^p}{\partial r}\right) + L_r \right]\Delta r_t.$$

Hence

$$\frac{\Delta r_t}{\Delta\pi_t} = \left[k_{t-1}\left(\frac{\partial I^p}{\partial \pi} + \frac{\partial C^p}{\partial \pi}\right) + L_\pi \right] \Big/ \left[\frac{dM^s}{dr} - k_{t-1}\left(\frac{\partial I^p}{\partial r} + \frac{\partial C^p}{\partial r}\right) - L_r \right],$$
$$(8)$$

which is positive, because, as we pointed out above, the numerator is generally positive and every term of the denominator is also positive. There is, however, reason to believe that this ratio is generally smaller than unity. For if it can be assumed that planned investment and consumption expenditures are functions of the real rate of interest rather than the money rate of interest, then

$$\frac{\partial I^p}{\partial \pi} + \frac{\partial C^p}{\partial \pi} = -\left(\frac{\partial I^p}{\partial r} + \frac{\partial C^p}{\partial r}\right) > 0.$$

Moreover, since $L_\pi < 0$ and $(dM^s/dr - L_r) > 0$, therefore, $\Delta r_t/\Delta\pi_t < 1$.

This is fully borne out by the recent experience of inflation both in the United Kingdom and the United States. College bursars or investment officers in both countries as well as other private asset-owners generally find it very hard merely to maintain the real value of the assets under their management, let alone to be sure of getting their anticipated real rate of return. Friedman's assumption that the money rate of interest will always be equal to asset-owners' anticipated real returns, plus their expected rate of price inflation seems to fly directly in the face of actual experience. It would certainly be disowned by Fisher as well as Keynes, even though Friedman claims lineage from them both.

Thus, Robertson's loanable funds theory (or Keynes' liquidity preference theory revised for its neglect of the finance demand for liquidity, which we have demonstrated comes to the same thing) has certainly not been made obsolete by the new monetarism. Indeed, it is the latter that should have a lot to learn from Robertson.[38]

Notes

*This paper is a revised version of a talk given to a seminar at Nuffield College, Oxford, and again to a seminar at York University, England. I am indebted to Sir John Hicks, Fritz Machlup, Paul Samuelson, Maurice Scott, and Michael Sullivan for reading the manuscript and for valuable suggestions for improvement.

1. At least until Prime Minister Callaghan had firmly renounced the economic principle that had guided the postwar British government policy up to that time.

   On 29 September, 1976 *The Times* of London carried on its front pages a report of the Prime Minister's speech to the Labor Party Conference, which contained the following excerpt:

   "It used to be thought that a nation could just spend its way out of recession and increase employment by cutting taxes and boosting government spending. 'I tell you in all candor that that option no longer exists.' Insofar as it existed in the past, it had always led to a bigger dose of inflation followed by a higher level of unemployment."

2. Another "revolutionary" feature of the Keynes theory is in the theory of employment, where the classical assumption that the supply of labor is a function of the real wage rate is replaced by a new assumption that workers would be content with a fixed money wage rate until full employment is reached. This has proved untrue also. Trade unions nowadays not only are deeply concerned with the real wage rate but would even seek to raise it periodically regardless of the increase in productivity.

3. Ohlin [1937a] and [1937b].

4. Ohlin [1937a], p. 61–66.

5. Keynes [1937], p. 667.

6. Keynes [1937], p. 665.

7. Tsiang [1956]. The importance of the concept of the "finance" demand for liquidity, however, remained for many years unappreciated by economists even after the publication of my 1956 paper. Nine long years had to elapse before Davidson [1965] brought it up again in his discussion of Keynes' theory of interest.

   Davidson's approach differs from mine in one very important respect. Namely, he formulates the consumption function and the income identity in the Keynesian, rather than the Robertsonian, fashion, i.e., he neglects the time lags entirely and writes

   $$C_t = a_1 + b_1 Y_t$$

and

$$Y_t \equiv C_t + I_t.$$

These equations naturally imply the Keynesian conclusion that

$$Y_t = \frac{I_t + a_1}{1 - b_1}$$

for every t, viz., the instantaneous multiplier principle totally independent of the money market [Davidson, 1965, pp. 52 and 57]. While this kind of formulation might be excusable for comparative static analysis, to combine this with a money demand function that is supposed to incorporate Keynes' finance demand for money, however, would involve a gross logical inconsistency. For the finance demand for liquidity, as Keynes himself put it, exists "during the interregnum—*and during that period only*—between the date when the entrepreneur arranges his finance and the date when he actually makes his investment" [1937, p. 665]. If the unit period is defined short enough to capture such ephemeral demands for finance in their action on the money market, how can the period be long enough for the income multiplier to be worked out completely during the same period? Recent econometric studies invariably indicated that it will take at least one to two years for the income multiplier to work out reasonably fully. Furthermore, the multiplier process itself must operate through the mechanism of the money market, and, therefore, should not be taken for granted as an exogenously determined magnitude in formulating the demand for money in a dynamic analysis of the money market, as Davidson did in his equations (5) and (8) [1965, pp. 52 and 58]. (Cf. Tsiang [1956], pp. 555–63.)

Thus, Davidson's article was not able to point out the fundamental shortcomings of the Keynesian theory of interest.

8. Keynes [1937], p. 668.
9. Keynes [1937], p. 667.
10. In his obituary on Robertson, Samuleson [1963] suggested that, in view of Roberston's insistence that savings have a direct influence on the rate of interest, maybe he would want to replace $r = L(M, Y)$ with $r = L(M, Y, S(Y))$ as the money market equilibrium equation, which would imply a demand for money function something like $M^d = L(Y, r, S(Y))$.

This, however, will not do; for such a demand function for money would be incapable of reflecting the finance demand for liquidity on the part of planned investment expenditures, which Keynes himself had already conceded. An increase in planned investment expenditures would still have to result in an actual increase in the income level after they are carried out before they can exert any influence on the interest rate; whereas, in fact, planned expenditures should exert an upward pressure on the interest rate already in their financing stage.

I think, therefore, the above formulation represents more correctly the essence of the loanable funds theory as well as the liquidity preference theory revised for the recognition of the finance demand for liquidity.

11. Where C_t^p and I_t^p are, of course, schedules or functions, i.e., $C_t^p(Y_{t-1}, r_t, \pi_t,$

$W_t, \ldots)$ and $I_t^p(Y_{t-1}, r_t, \pi_t, W_t, \ldots)$, rather than given magnitudes.

12. Robertson would further simplify the equilibrium condition (4a) by setting k_{t-1} equal to unity. This simplification can be justified on the ground that the average decision period which we have taken as the unit time period is in fact the average length of the time between the procuring or allocation of a unit of money as the finance for a certain planned expenditure and the time when it becomes ready to be allocated again as finance for new expenditure or as idle balance. It is in fact the full cycle length of circulation of an average unit of the transactions balance. During such a unit time period, k, the inverse of the velocity of circulation of active balance, should be unity.

If the new equilibrium interest rate and other current relevant arguments are different from those of the last period so that k_t is different from k_{t-1}, this means only that for the start of the next period (i.e., period $t + 1$) the unit decision period has to be adjusted appropriately such that k_t, is again equal to unity.

In order to avoid unnecessary controversy with fastidious readers, however, I shall leave k_{t-1} in equations (4) and (4a) as they are.

13. The essence of the above argument had already been presented in my September 1956 article. Although I wrote it without any prior consultation with Robertson, it must have met his general approval. Within a month of its publication, I received an unsolicited letter from him dated 22 October, 1956, written in longhand, which started by saying:

"I have just read your article in *AER* with great interest and appreciation. So far as I can judge, it really clears these matters up completely. . . . Whether your article will relieve Mrs. Robinson from the orgy of expectoration and self-stigmatization to which she is reduced by any mention of the concept of loanable funds, I cannot tell. . . ."

At the end, he added:

"Again many compliments, and—if I may be so egotistical—warm thanks for the rigorous demonstration that I have not been talking utter rot all these years."

Unfortunately, Robertson's hope that I might have helped in convincing his detractors that what he taught was right and that his warnings should be heeded was far from being fulfilled during his lifetime.

14. Keynes [1938], p. 319.

15. The length of such cycles is implied in the length of our chosen unit time period, which we called the decision-making period previously. It is not necessarily fixed but, as we have postulated above in equations (3) and (4), might vary according to the k function. It is certainly not true that the loanable funds theory has to assume a constant k, let alone a constant velocity of circulation.

Because we have allowed for the possibility of nonhomogeneity of the demand for money function L with respect to planned expenditures as in equation (3), even a constant k would not necessarily imply a constant average velocity of circulation.

16. It should be noted, therefore, that my reconciliation of the liquidity

preference theory with the loanable funds theory is quite different from Hicks' attempt by means of Walras' Law [Hicks, 1939, pp. 155–59]. I have specifically rejected the so-called Walras' law as inapplicable to the demand for money, as the major part of it, i.e., the transactions (or finance) demand for money, is a pre-trading demand, whereas the identity that is now known as Walras' Law holds only for the post-trading acquisition of (or parting with) traded goods.

This point was elaborated on in Tsiang [1966 and 1977].

17. Keynes [1937] and [1938].
18. Keynes [1937], p. 666.
19. Keynes [1938], p. 332.
20. Robertson [1940], p. 15.
21. Shaw [1938].
22. Roberston [1940], p. 16.
23. Professor Mirrlees of Oxford, however, told me that he thinks that Keynes' position is perfectly defensible. He suggests that what Keynes tried to say is merely that whether the public spends on consumers' goods (consume) or spends on financial assets (save), the money expended would eventually reach the hands of entrepreneurs and become available to finance investment in the same way. This argument contains a major flaw, which has already been pointed out by Robertson himself [Robertson, 1940, p. 5]. That is, apart from the difference in timing of the availability of proceeds, the proceeds of the sales of consumers' goods would normally be earmarked to finance the reproduction of the consumers' good sold. It will not be available to finance new investment, unless the entrepreneur concerned decides not to replace the reduced stock. In the latter case, it is the deliberate disinvestment of inventory on the part of the entrepreneur, not the consumption of the public itself, that provides the finance for new investment.
24. Robertson [1966], p. 212.
25. Modigliani [1944].
26. In a footnote on p. 43, however, Friedman [1971] corrected himself by admitting that Keynes did not really assume that the price level is constant but only that the money wage rate is constant.
27. Friedman [1971], p. 50.
28. Harrod [1971], p. 60.
29. Friedman [1971], p. 43.
30. Friedman [1971], pp. 50–51.
31. In Friedman [1970], there was some brief mention of loanable funds in connection with the adjustment of interest rates in a single paragraph (p. 227). In his 1971 paper, however, there is no more reference to loanable funds. Indeed, when Davidson criticized Friedman for having neglected the "finance" demand for money [1972, pp. 875–76], the latter simply brushed aside this valid criticism with a single sentence to the effect that "Davidson makes no case for attaching particular significance to the simplification in the (money) demand function that he singles out (i.e., the omission of

planned expenditures as an argument of the function)" [Friedman, 1972, p. 929], without more ado.

I hope I have made a much stronger case for the finance demand for liquidity, or rather for the loanable funds theory, than Davidson did.

32. Keynes [1936], pp. 142–43.
33. Fisher [1955], p. 491.
34. Harrod [1971], p. 62.
35. Friedman [1971], p. 70.
36. Robertson [1940], pp. 21–23.
37. Fisher [1955], p. 491.
38. Elsewhere, I have written a paper commenting on the new monetarism as applied to the balance of payments theory. See Tsiang [1977].

References

Davidson, P., "Keynes's Finance Motive," *Oxford Economic Papers,* XVII (March 1976), 47–65.

Davidson, P., "A Keynesian View of Friedman's Theoretical Framework for Monetary Analysis," *Journal of Political Economy,* LXXX (Sept./Oct. 1972), 864–82.

Fisher, Irving, *Theory of Interest* (New York: Kelly, 1955).

Friedman, M., "A Theoretical Framework for Monetary Analysis," *Journal of Political Economy,* LXXVII (March/April 1970), 193–238.

Friedman, M., "A Monetary Theory of Nominal Income," Ch. III, *Monetary Theory and Monetary Policy in the 1970's, Proceedings of the 1970 Sheffield Money Seminar,* G. Clayton, J. C. Gilbert, and R. Sedzwick, eds. (Oxford: 1971), pp. 41–57: also published in *Journal of Political Economy,* LXXIX (March/April 1971), 323–37.

Friedman, M., "Comments on the Critics," *Journal of Political Economy,* LXXX (Sept./Oct. 1972), 906–50.

Harrod, R., "Discussion Papers (a)," Ch. III, *Monetary Theory and Monetary Policy in the 1970's, Proceedings of the 1970 Sheffield Money Seminar,* G. Clayton, J. C. Gilbert and R. Sedzwick, eds. (Oxford: 1971), pp. 58–68.

Hicks, J. R., *Value and Capital* (Oxford: 1939).

Keynes, J. M., *The General Theory of Employment, Interest and Money* (London: Macmillian, 1936).

Keynes, J. M., "The Ex-Ante Theory of the Rate of Interest," *Economic Journal,* XLVII (Dec. 1937), 663–69.

Keynes, J. M., "D. H. Robertson on 'Mr. Keynes and Finance,' Comments," *Economic Journal,* XLVIII (June 1938), 318–22.

Modigliani, F., "Liquidity Preference and the Theory of Interest and Money," *Econometrica,* XII (Jan. 1944), 45–88.

Ohlin, B., "Some Notes on the Stockholm Theory of Savings and Investment, I," *Economic Journal,* XLVII (March 1937a), 53–69.

Ohlin, B., "Some Notes on the Stockholm Theory of Savings and Investment, II," *Economic Journal,* XLVII (June 1937b), 221–40.

Robertson, D. H., "Mr. Keynes and 'Finance,'" *Economic Journal,* XLVIII (June 1938), 314–18.

Robertson, D. H., "Mr. Keynes and the Rate of Interest," Ch. 1, *Essays in Monetary Theory* (London: P. S. King, 1940).

Robertson, D. H., "Some Notes on the Theory of Interest," a contribution to *Money, Trade and Economic Growth,* Essays in Honor of Professor J. H. William (New York: Macmillan, 1951); reprinted in Sir Dennis Robertson, *Essays in Money and Interest* (Manchester: Collins, 1966), pp. 203–22.

Samuelson, P. A., "D. H. Robertson (1890–1963)," this *Journal,* LXXVII (Nov. 1963), 517–36.

Shaw, E. S., "False Issues in the Interest Theory Controversy," *Journal of Political Economy,* XLVI (Dec. 1938), 838–56.

Tsiang, S. C., "Liquidity Preference and Loanable Funds Theories, Multiplier and Velocity Analysis: A Synthesis," *American Economic Review,* XLVI (Sept. 1956), 539–64.

Tsiang, S. C., "Liquidity Preference and Loanable Funds Theories of Interest: Reply," *American Economic Review,* XLVII (Sept. 1957), 673–78.

Tsiang, S. C., "Walras' Law, Say's Law and Liquidity Preference in General Equilibrium Analysis," *International Economic Review,* VII (Sept. 1966), 329–45.

Tsiang, S. C., "The Monetary Theoretic Foundation of the Modern Monetary Approach to the Balance of Payments," *Oxford Economic Papers,* XXIX (Nov. 1977), 319–38.

CHAPTER 14

A Critical Note on the Optimum Supply of Money

S. C. Tsiang

One of the widely current ideas about the optimal management of the money supply is that money is essentially costless for the society to create and that, therefore, the community's demand for money balances should be satisfied to the full. To achieve this purpose, it is suggested that the opportunity cost of holding money balances should be reduced to zero to match the zero cost of creating money supply.

This idea originated from Chicago[1] but appears to have penetrated as far down to the east coast as New Haven and Cambridge, where people usually are not so readily swayed by the winds blown from the Windy City.[2] The purpose of this paper is to raise a lone cry of warning against the hidden dangers involved in this now widely accepted idea, and to point out its theoretical flaws.

To reduce the opportunity cost of holding money to zero so as to induce each individual not to waste effort or real sources to economize on the holding of money balances, essentially the following method has been suggested: to let money, i.e., means of payments, bear a nominal interest rate not lower than that on any other financial securities denominated in money units and to make this nominal rate on money

Finance Constraints and the Theory of Money
ISBN 0-12-701720-8
ISBN 0-12-701721-6 (pbk)

331

Reprinted with permission from the *Journal of Money, Credit, and Banking*, Ohio State University Press, Vol. I, 2 (May 1969), pp. 266–280.

plus the rate of price deflation (or minus the rate of price inflation) equal to the real rate of return on physical assets (presumably net of rewards for entrepreneurial risk taking). We shall proceed by examining first the profound effects which this seemingly sensible proposal would have upon the financial and monetary mechanism of the economy.

Since in any modern economy, there are inevitably many diverse kinds of financial assets with different nominal yields, the proponents of this theory of optimal management of money supply are not always specific as to the yield of which financial assets they want to equate the nominal yield to be put on the means of payments. Judging from the basic idea that the opportunity cost of holding money balances should be reduced to zero, however, it seems only logical that the nominal yield on money should be made equal to that of the highest yielding financial assets; for, otherwise, holding cash balances would still involve an opportunity cost of thereby not being able to hold some assets with higher yields. The fact that assets with higher yields are also the more risky or the less liquid is not a sufficient counter argument. For the whole idea is that the extra liquidity of money compared with other assets is costless to produce. Why not then use this free supply of extra liquidity to satiate the demands for liquidity on the part of all asset holders?

It is important to realize what profound changes in the financial market mechanism this kind of monetary management would bring about. When money bears nominal interest rate equal to that on any non-monetary assets, all nonmonetary assets would be dominated by "money" and, hence, would be completely displaced by money as stores of value. When the nominal rate on money minus (plus) the rate of price inflation (deflation) is further equated to the real yield of physical assets (net of entrepreneurial incomes), then physical assets also would no longer be held as pure investment either. They would not, however, be completely displaced by money, as they would still be held by entrepreneurs who derive entrepreneurial incomes in combining other factors with physical assets in productive activities, or by consumers who derive direct services from them.

Money, however, would become the only financial assets. Since money by definition is also the means of payment, there cannot be a market for "money as financial assets" in terms of "money as means of payment." In other words, the financial market (or money market, in the sense of this term as used in real world) would disappear with the complete displacement of nonmonetary financial assets by money. If we start with an economy with three types of goods—commodities, securities, and money—where two markets are operative, the market for commodities in exchange for money and the market for securities in exchange for money, we would end up with only two types of goods: commodities and money. In such an economy, only one market is possible, viz., the market for commodities in exchange for money or vice versa. Thus the Chicago proposal for the satiation of the demand for money as an asset to hold would imply the elimination of the market for securities and hence the mechanism for the determination of the money rate of interest. After the satiation of the demand for money balances, the nominal rate of interest rate on money must become an exogenous parameter to be determined at the discretion of the monetary authorities.

Before we embrace this proposal for the optimal management of money supply, therefore, we must take some time to examine first whether the state of economy after the adoption of such a proposal would be stable, and, secondly, how the functions now performed by the financial market (however imperfectly) would be taken over by other mechanisms that might still be left in an economy with satiated demand for money balances.

Let us first examine the stability question. When there is no market for the automatic adjustment of the nominal rate of interest, the nominal rate on money can be brought into equilibrium with the marginal real rate of return on physical capital goods only through the adjustment of the expected rate of price inflation or deflation. Would the price mechanism be able to achieve this adjustment automatically? To put it more concretely, if there is some accidental deviation from equilibrium, would the rate of price inflation (or deflation) change to restore equilibrium or to aggravate the disequilibrium? These are questions of vital importance, which the advocates of the satiation of the demand for money balances have not satisfactorily answered. It is my opinion that the price mechanism is likely to be unstable with a super-abundant supply of money, and therefore, I think that Professor Friedman's proposal for what he calls the optimal supply of money is highly dangerous.

I shall try to demonstrate this with a simple model, based chiefly upon that of Professor Stein's,[3] but with some necessary modifications. Suppose that the rate of price change is determined by the rate of excess demand for commodities in the following manner:

$$\pi = \lambda[I(r(k) + \pi^* - \bar{\imath}) - S(y(k), \bar{\imath} - \pi^*, \theta v)];$$

$$I' > 0;\ S_1 > 0,\ S_2 \geq 0,\ S_3 \leq 0, \quad (1)$$

where $\pi = \dot{P}/P$ is rate of price increase, π^* the expected rate of price increase, and y the real output per unit of effective labor, which for simplicity we shall assume to be a function of the amount of capital per unit of effective labor k only (which implies constant full employment an flexible wage rate); I and S are, respectively, the planned investment and saving in real terms per unit of labor; r the rate of return on physical capital; $\bar{\imath}$ the nominal rate of interest on money which is not determined on the market but fixed by the monetary authorities, and which could be zero; $v = (M/PN)$ is the real cash balancees per unit of labor; θ the proportion of total money supply that consists of "outside money"; and λ the speed of price adjustment in response to excess demand. We shall assume further that the expected rate of price inflation depends upon the actual rate of price inflation in the following form

$$\pi^* = g(\pi). \quad (2)$$

In addition to this equation for the dynamic process of price adjustment we still have the demand and supply equation for money, viz.,

$$v = L(E,\ r + \pi^* - \bar{\imath},\ \theta v);\quad L_1 > 0_1\ L_2 \leq 0,\ L_3 \geq 0; \quad (3)$$

where the demand for money L is supposed to be a function of real planned expenditures $E \equiv I + y - S$, the difference between the expected real yields of physical capital and money balances, and the amount of outside money that might generate a real balance effect when price level changes. This formulation differs from the commonly accepted form in that E is substituted for $y(k)$ as the first argument. This is, I believe, a matter of some importance in dynamic analysis; for the demand for transactions balances, i.e., "money to spend" is primarily a function of our planned spending, and planned spending, even when expressed in real terms, need not be identical to real output, as we have already recognized in permitting *ex ante* investment to diverge from *ex ante* saving. We shall point out later the practical significance of making this modification.

Since there is only one market in existence, this equation cannot be treated as another equilibrium condition for the determination of another price. Rather should it be regarded as a constraint that the total money supply available must always be divided between "money to spend" and "money to hold," and that total expenditure E must be somehow financed out of the existing money supply. Equation (3) is, therefore, really an identity rather than an equilibrium condition.[4] Thus the forms of the investment and saving functions postulated in equation (1) must conform to the form of the liquidity preference function in equation (3), which acts as a constraint on total expenditure. In particular, investment I must be defined to include the substitution of commodities or physical assets for money due to changed expectation of price inflation. We shall see whether in such a one-market economy, short run price stability is ensured.

Let us suppose that we start from an equilibrium state in which the rate of price inflation is constant and equal to $\pi_0 = u - n$ where

$$u = \frac{1}{M}\frac{dM}{dt} \quad \text{and} \quad n = \frac{1}{N}\frac{dN}{dt}.$$

Then suppose that there are some exogenous disturbances, in the form of a sudden change in the rate of return to physical capital due to innovation, or a jolt to price expectation, or shifts in the investment or saving functions, which cause the rate of price inflation to change. The time rate of change of π in the neighborhood of the disturbed equilibrium may be approximated by the following linearized differential equation, if, for such short-run reaction of prices, we assume k to be constant.

$$(d\pi/dt) = \lambda[(I' + S_2)g' + S_3\theta v](\pi - \pi_0) \tag{4}$$

where $(\pi - \pi_0)$ is the displacement of π from its initial equilibrium value π_0. The stability of price movement clearly requires that

$$[(I' + S_2)g' + S_3\theta v] < 0. \tag{5}$$

Here I', S_2 and g' are all positive. Only S_3 is negative, as an increase (decrease) in the real value of cash balances (when they consist of outside money) is likely somewhat to reduce (increase) the eagerness for further saving and thus to stimulate (discourage) consumption. Stability therefore requires that the discouraging effect on consumption of the shrinking real balances (to the extent that they consist of outside money) should outweigh the stimulating effect on the increased rate of price inflation upon investment, (which should be interpreted to include hoarding of commodities as well as physical capital assets as hedge against inflation) and the discouraging effect on saving of the reduced real yield of money as assets.

This appears to me very unlikely to happen, for the very observation of the fact that because of inflation the real value of one's money balances is shrinking, which observation is supposed to discourage his consumption spending on account of the so-called real balance effect, would also alert him to shift out of money balances to physical assets. On balance, his net demand for physical goods is likely to be increased rather than reduced, i.e., $[(I' + S_2)g' + S_3\theta v]$ is likely to be greater than zero. Thus price movement is likely to be unstable in such an economy. With the financial market eliminated, there is no other market mechanism to check the unstable price movement.

We would get a similar picture if we look at the supply and demand equation for money, instead of the excess demand equation for commodities. Differentiating (3) with respect to time, we get

$$-v(\pi - \pi_0) = L_1 \frac{dE}{dt} + L_2 g' \frac{d\pi}{dt} - L_v \theta v(\pi - \pi_0). \tag{6}$$

Since E is defined as $I + y - S$ and $y(k)$ is assumed to be constant in the short run, thus, using (1), we may write

$$\frac{dE}{dt} = \frac{d}{dt}(I - S) = \frac{1}{\lambda} \frac{d\pi}{dt}.$$

Substituting this into (6), we get

$$\frac{d\pi}{dt} = -\frac{(1 - \theta L_v)v}{\frac{1}{\lambda} L_1 + g' L_2}(\pi - \pi_0). \tag{7}$$

The stability condition is then[5]

$$-\frac{(1 - \theta L_v)v}{\frac{1}{\lambda} L_1 + g' L_2} < 0. \tag{8}$$

Here the numerator $(1 - \theta L_v)v$ is clearly positive; for L_v, though positive, is necessarily smaller than 1. That is to say, an increase in one's wealth embodied in money balances would generally induce some increase in one's demand for money balances, but the induced increase in demand for money balances would normally be smaller than the initial increase in wealth. Thus the stability of price movement depends essentially on whether the denominator is positive. If $(L_1 + \lambda g' L_2) < 0$, the price movement would be unstable.

The first term of the denominator represents the rate of interest in transactions balances in real terms required to sustain a given rate of increase of price inflation (which requires an ever widening gap of excess demand). The second term $g'L_2$, which is negative, represents the substitution of commodities for money, or dishoarding, induced by a given rate of increase of price inflation. If the attempted rate of dishoarding induced by a given rate of increase of price inflation exceeds the rate of increase in transactions balances required to sustain that given rate of increase of price inflation, price inflation would proceed at a faster and faster rate.[6]

Looking at the dynamics of price movement from this angle, again stability does not appear very likely. Indeed, when we make money so abundant as to displace all non-monetary financial assets in existence, and satiate all demands to hold money, then the absolute magnitude of the substitution effect on the demand for money of a change in expected price inflation, i.e., $|L_2|$, is likely to be so large as to overwhelm L_1. And because of the superabundance of money supply in the economy, the substitution of commodities for money (or dishoarding) once started would become a tremendous avalanche, which could rampage for a long time before it would spend itself.

It is true that the cumulative price inflation or deflation can be checked by an appropriate adjustment of the nominal interest rate on money by the monetary authorities, i.e., by applying an appropriate counter shock to offset the initial shock. But if the system is inherently unstable, a counter shock sufficient to stop the cumulative deviation in one direction would inevitably send prices moving cumulatively in the opposite direction. The best one can hope for under such an economy is that the monetary authorities, with great vigilance, foresight, and quick response, would be able to keep prices moving back and forth within reasonably narrow bounds (a kind of perpetual stop-and-go situation). I would not expect that Professor Friedman would normally attribute a high degree of foresight and vigilence to the officials constituting our monetary authorities, but his proposal for the optimal supply of money would make such foresight and vigilence on the parts of monetary authorities absolutely necessary.

Let us now examine the next question: how the functions now performed by the financial market could be discharged when the financial market is eliminated with the displacement by money of all nonmonetary financial assets. The financial market in a modern economy performs, in a perhaps rather imperfect manner, the functions of channeling saving to investment and to satisfy the demands to borrow on the part of deficit spenders with the supply of lending on the part of surplus spenders. How would these functions be discharged in an economy where money constitutes the only financial assets in existence? In such an economy, the savers who are not simultaneously investors would certainly not offer their savings to the market but would simply add their savings to their money balances. If there is, say, a decrease in propensity to save, the only signal investors would get would be a rise in the excess demand for commodities and in the rate of price inflation. This signal is likely to induce investors to step up their investment activities rather than to reduce them. The result is, as we have seen above, a cumulative upward price movement. Conversely, an increase in the propensity to save would lead to a cumulative downward price movement much in the same manner as described in the fable to the bees.

Nor would the monetary authorities be able to step in and perform the functions of the financial market even as imperfectly as they are performed now. For the monetary authorities would have no way to detect changes in propensity to save or in the inducement to invest either. The most they can do is probably to reverse the already started cumulative price movement by an appropriately big adjustment of the nominal interest rate on money as we have described above.

It is, indeed, an irony of the history of economic thoughts that Keynes, in quest of the euthanasia of the rentiers, and Friedman, in quest of the maximization of the aggregate utility of money balances, should both come to advocate the flooding of the economy with liquidity or real balances. Whatever the goals the advocates have in mind, the outcomes would have one thing in common, viz., an economy of monetary instability, where direct control of private expenditures would ultimately become necessary to prevent the price system from breaking down or getting into perpetual fluctuations.

Where the modern theory of the optimal supply of money goes wrong is that it regards the aggregate utility, which the community as a whole derives from the total money supply, as merely the sum total of the utility which individual holders of money balances might be expected to derive from their own holdings. The truth is, however, that one should not merely look at the sum of the utility of each individual which he might be expected to obtain from his real money balance, if his real balance is to be increased alone. For when the real balances of the whole economy are increased together, there would arise considerable diseconomies to the economy, which are not taken into account in the areas under the individual demand curves for real balances. The "external diseconomies" generally take the form of the gradual break-down of the stability of the price system and the impairment of the efficiency of the financial market in channeling savings toward invest-ment. Moreover, these diseconomies would begin to appear long before we reach the so-called optimal state of complete satiation of the demand for real money balances.

This we shall demonstrate with a simple model that has both a commodity market and a financial market (or a bond market) in operation. First we write as above

$$\pi = \lambda[I(r + \pi^* - i) - S(y, i - \pi^*, \theta v)], \tag{9}$$

which is similar to (1) except that i here represents the market interest rate on bonds (assumed to be the only kind of nonmonetary financial assets), which is now an endogenous variable to be determined by the money (or bond) market equilibrium condition,

$$v = L[E, r + \pi^* - \bar{i}, i - \bar{i}, \theta v], \tag{10}$$

where again we have replaced $E \equiv I + y - S$ for y as the chief argument for the determination of transactions demand for money.[7] $\bar{i}$ is the nominal interest rate which the monetary authorities has imposed on money as inducement for people to hold more real money balances (i.e., as inducement for them not to economize on holding money balances) and which, we shall assume, is not yet raised as high as the market rate on bonds. So long as this is the case, bonds will not be completely dominated by money and there will be a market for bonds in exchange for money and vice versa. With the existence of a bond market, it is now possible to get rid of the excess supply of money by offering it to the bond market, or to make up the deficiency in money balances by borrowing (or selling bonds) on the bond market. Equation (10) is, therefore, an equilibrium condition for the bond market, instead of being a constraint for total expenditure as equation (3).[8]

The dynamic adjustment of the market rate on bonds is supposed to follow the following differential equation:

$$\frac{di}{dt} = \phi[L - v], \tag{11}$$

where ϕ is the speed of adjustment of the market rate of interest and $0 \leq \phi \leq \infty$. If the adjustment of interest rate is instantaneous, $\phi = \infty$.

Again, let us now start from equilibrium state in which the rate of price inflation is constant and equal to $\pi_0 = u - n$ and the market interest rate has reached its equilibrium level i_0 which is constant. Suppose there is some exogenous shock to the I or S function, which temporarily causes π to deviate from π_0 and i from i_0. Then the movement of π and i may be approximated to the following linearized differential equations:

$$d\pi/dt = \lambda[(I' + S_2)g' + S_3\theta v](\pi - \pi_0) - \lambda(I' + S_2)(i - i_0) \quad (12)$$

$$di/dt = \phi\{L_1[(I' + S_2)g' + S_3\theta v] + L_2g' + (1 - \theta L_v)\}(\pi - \pi_0)$$
$$+ \phi[L_3 - L_1(I' + S_2)](i - i_0). \quad (13)$$

The system is locally stable if and only if

$$\lambda[(I' + S_2)g' + S_3\theta v] + \phi[L_3 - L_1(I' + S_2)] < 0, \quad (14)$$

$$L_3[(I' + S_2)g' + S_3\theta v] + (I' + S_2)[L_2g' + (1 - \theta L_v)v] > 0. \quad (15)$$

Condition (14) is simply that the sum of the characteristic roots of the coefficient matrix of (12) and (13) must be negative, and condition (15) states that the determinant of the matrix (or the products of the characteristic roots) must be positive.

On the left-hand side of condition (14), the terms inside the first pair of square brackets are very likely to be on balance positive; for from equation (12) it is easy to see that $[(I' + S_2)g' + S_3\theta v]$ is the net change in excess demand for commodities induced by an acceleration of price inflation, which therefore is likely to be positive. The terms inside the second pair of square brackets are both negative. Thus, whether this stability condition can be satisfied or not depends chiefly upon the relative speed of adjustment of the commodity and the money (or bond) markets.[9] It is obvious that if the market rate of interest is extremely sluggish in adjustment, as when it is pegged by the monetary authorities, the price system cannot be stable, in so far as an acceleration of price inflation would always increase the excess demand for commodities.[10]

In condition (15), the first term is likely to be negative as L_3 is negative. Thus, whether this stability condition can be satisfied or not depends upon whether the second term is sufficiently larger than zero to offset the negative first term. Inside the second pair of square brackets $v(1 - \theta L_v)$ is indeed positive as we have explained above, but L_2g' is again negative. It is crucial for the stability of the prices, therefore, that the absolute values of both L_2 and L_3, the two substitution effects on the demand for real money balances, must be sufficiently small. In other words, the stability condition (15) may be rearranged as

$$\frac{1}{v} \cdot |L_3| \cdot \left[g' + \frac{S_3 \theta v}{(I' + S_2)} \right] + \frac{g'}{v} \cdot |L_2| < (1 - \theta L_v). \qquad (16)$$

Now, if we follow Friedman's suggestion of inducing people to hold more and more real money balances relatively to other less liquid nonmonetary assets, these two crucial coefficients L_2 and L_3 are both likely to increase in their absolute values. For provided that the indifference curves for risk and yield of most individuals are of the normal, concave, downward-sloping shape (the type of indifference curves for risk-averters and diversifiers), and that people's absolute risk aversion does not normally increase with an increase in his real wealth,[11] the substitution effect (in relation to the money balance held) of a given change in the yield of risky assets relative to that of the riskless asset (money) is likely to become greater and greater as the proportion in the portfolio of the holding of riskless assets increases. Thus it is quite possible that the stability of the system could be destroyed long before we reach the so-called optimal state, in which money balances replace all nonmonetary financial assets as store of value.

As to the impairment of the efficiency of the financial market, I shall propose the following criterion of efficiency as the basis for our discussion. When the whole system is unstable, the financial market is, of course, unable to perform its function of channeling saving towards investment or to finance investment with saving. An increase in thrift would start a cumulative downward price movement with investment activities discouraged rather than stimulated. Only when the system is stable can we talk about the efficiency of the financial market. A shift in the saving or the investment function can then be expected to lead a new equilibrium situation. The efficiency of the financial market may then be tested by the following criterion. If under one set of circumstances, an upward (downward) shift of the saving function results, at the new equilibrium, in more increase (decrease) in investment and less change in price movement than under another set of circumstances, then we may say that the financial market is performing more efficiently under the former set of circumstances than under the latter. This criterion is substantially unchanged if we substitute a shift in the investment function for a shift in the saving function. In that case, this criterion is to be reformulated to read: if an upward (downward) shift in the investment function results, at the new equilibrium, in more increase (decrease) in saving and less change in price movement, the financial market is to be judged as to have performed its function more efficiently.

In applying this criterion, let us turn back to the simple model represented by equations (9) and (10), which we rewrite here, for convenience of reference,

$$\pi = \lambda[I(r + \pi^* - i) - S(y, i - \pi^*, \theta v) - \alpha], \qquad (9^*)$$

$$v = L[E, r + \pi^*, i - \bar{i}, \theta v]. \qquad (10)$$

It is to be noted that a shift variable α has been inserted in equation (9^*). An α with a negative sign may be interpreted either as an upward shift of the saving function or a downward shift of the investment function, and an α with a positive sign as an upward shift of the investment function or a downward shift of the saving function. Thus we see that whether we apply the test criterion on the basis of a shift of the saving function or that of the investment function should not make any substantial difference.

We shall for the moment interpret α as an upward shift of the saving function and differentiate (9^*) and (10) with respect to α to obtain a comparative static system of changes in the equilibrium values of the variables. For the sake of simplification here, we shall assume that real money balances v is somehow kept constant by the monetary authorities even in face of changing rate of price inflation, as the relative efficiency of the financial market is unlikely to be altered by the adoption of this particular monetary policy. Thus we get from (9^*) and (10)

$$[\lambda g'(I' + S_2) - 1] \frac{d\pi}{d\alpha} - \lambda(I' + S_2) \frac{di}{d\alpha} = \lambda \qquad (17)$$

$$[L_1(I' + S_2) + L_2]g' \frac{d\pi}{d\alpha} + [L_3 - L_1(I' + S_2)] \frac{di}{d\alpha} = L_1. \qquad (18)$$

Solving these equations, we obtain

$$\frac{d\pi}{d\alpha} = \frac{\lambda L_3}{(I' + S_2)[L_1 + \lambda g'(L_2 + L_3)] - L_3} \qquad (19)$$

and

$$\frac{di}{d\alpha} = \frac{-(L_1 + \lambda g'L_2)}{(I' + S_2)[L_1 + \lambda g'(L_2 + L_3)] - L_3}. \qquad (20)$$

Since the denominator of these expressions is the determinant of the coefficient matrix of this system, we may invoke the correspondence principle and regard its positiveness as a necessary condition for stability. As it is meaningless to discuss the efficiency of the financial market when the whole system is unstable, we shall therefore presume that the denominator of (19) and (20) is positive for our problem at hand.

Thus, so long as the equilibrium is stable, $d\pi/d\alpha$ is negative since L_3 is generally negative. It will become zero only when $L_3 = 0$. In other words, the ideal fuctioning of the financial market, i.e., the capability to cope with shifts in the saving or investment functions without causing any disturbances to price level, can be achieved only when the interest elasticity of substitution between money balances and other assets is zero. The partial derivative of $d\pi/d\alpha$ with respect to L_3 is

$$\frac{\partial}{\partial L_3}\left(\frac{d\pi}{d\alpha}\right) = \frac{\lambda(I' + S_2)(L_1 + \lambda g' L_2)}{\Delta^2}, \tag{21}$$

where Δ is the denominator of (19) or (20). Since we know that so long as the system is stable, $d\pi/d\alpha$ would increase from some negative value to zero, as L_3 increases from some negative value to zero, $(\partial/\partial L_3)(d\pi/d\alpha)$ must then be positive, and, therefore, $(L_1 + \lambda g' L_2)$, about the sign of which we would otherwise be uncertain, must be positive within the bounds of stability.[12]

Applying this information to (20), we may conclude that $di/d\alpha$ is, like $d\pi/d\alpha$, also negative.

The change in investment activities as a result of the upward shift in saving function can be obtained from (9*), (19), and (20).[13]

$$\frac{dI}{d\alpha} = I'g'\frac{d\pi}{d\alpha} - I'\frac{di}{d\alpha} = \frac{I'}{\Delta}[L_1 + \lambda_{g'}(L_2 + L_3)]. \tag{22}$$

It may be observed that if the absolute values of L_2 and L_3 are sufficiently large (but not large enough to destroy the stability of the system by turning the determinant of the coefficient matrix Δ negative), $dI/d\alpha$ can be negative. In other words, if the substitution effects on the demand for money balances are sufficiently large, they may cause planned investment activities to respond perversely to an increase in propensity to save, even if they are not yet large enough to break down the stability of the system.

Taking the partial derivatives of $dI/d\alpha$ with respect to L_2 and L_3, we get

$$\frac{\partial}{\partial L_2}\left(\frac{dI}{d\alpha}\right) = \frac{-\lambda_{g'} I' L_3}{\Delta^2} > 0 \tag{23}$$

$$\frac{\partial}{\partial L_3}\left(\frac{dI}{d\alpha}\right) = \frac{I'(L_1 + \lambda_{g'} L_2)}{\Delta^2} > 0. \tag{24}$$

The latter derivative is judged to be positive on the basis of the information we obtained from (21), i.e., the partial derivative of $d\pi/d\alpha$ with respect to L_3.

Thus the maximum response of investment activities to an increase in propensity to save is obtained when $|L_2|$ and $|L_3|$ are reduced to zero, in which case

$$\frac{dI}{d\alpha} = \frac{I'}{I' + S_2}, \ (L_2 = L_3 = 0).$$

From these observations, we may conclude that, so long as the increase in the proportion of money balances in the portfolios tends to increase the substitution effects on the demand for money of a change in the yields of riskier assets, increasing the supply of money relatively to other assets of the community would first impair the efficiency of the financial market and then break down the stability of the system. These external diseconomies may far outweigh the extra marginal utility under the tail ends of individual demand curves for real balances supposed to be acquirable if only we remove the incentive to economize money.

Indeed, in my opinion, if the aggregate demand for money of the community can be represented by an L-shaped curve with the yield differential between non-monetary assets and money measured on the vertical axis (as most statistical studies of the demand curve for money seem to indicate), then, for the sake of stability and efficiency of the financial market, we should keep this yield differential sufficiently high, or keep the supply of money sufficiently scarce relative to the supply of other assests, so as to hold back the demand for money balances to the fairly vertical part of the demand curve, rather than push it down to the nearly horizontal part of the curve. When the yield differential between nonmonetary assets and money is already dangerously low in the above sense, then, should any need to stimulate employment or growth arise, fiscal policy that does not increase the supply of money should always be preferred to expansionary monetary policy that would further increase the money supply and lower this interest differential.

It is rather unfortunate that latest theoretical discussions of money and economic growth should concentrate so heavily on the case of a smooth balanced growth. In fact, the growth of any economy, especially, its technical progress, inevitably proceeds with plenty of jolts and jerks. It is, therefore, vitally important for us to see to it that our monetary and price system should be stable enough to stand these shocks in our search for the optimum monetary management.

Notes

1. I first came across this idea in Professor Friedman's Fordham University lectures. (Friedman [2], pp. 72–74) This idea was further elaborated in his yet unpublished manuscript, "The Optimum Quantity of Money." [3]
2. See for instance Tobin [8] and Samuelson [5].
3. Jerome L. Stein, "Neoclassical and Keynes–Wicksell Monetary Growth Models" [6]; see also [7].
4. In any case any reader should worry about the apparent inconsistency, in view of the so-called Walras' law, between a nonzero excess demand for commodities in equation (1) and the equality of supply and demand for money in equation (3), I would like to refer him to my article on "Walras' Law, Say's Law and Liquidity Preference in General Equilibrium Analysis." [9] There I have pointed out that the accounting identity of Walras' Law refers to the excess demand for (or supply of) goods other than money and its mirror image excess supply of (or demand for) money, which latter should really be called the net loss (or acquistion) of money by trading (*op. cit.*, esp. pp. 334 and 344).

   The demand for money on the right hand side of equation (3) here, however, consists of the pretrading demand for transactions balances plus the demand for money to hold. There is no reason why these pretrading demands for money should fall short of (or exceed) the supply of money according as there is an excess demand for (or supply of) commodities (*op. cit.*, esp. p. 341).

   In an economy in which there are no financial assets other than money, the pretrading demand for money must always be equal to the supply of money. For in such an economy, the only way to get rid of money is to spend it on commodities. Before the spending takes place, however, the money is held as the transactions balance of the potential spender, required to finance his intended expenditures. After his spending, the money will become the transactions balance of somebody else, unless the other person wants to add to his money to hold. Thus, for each individual as well as for the community as a whole, as soon as there is an excess supply of (or excess demand for) the "money to hold," the excess would automatically be absorbed into (or taken out of) the "money to spend."

   Equation (3) above thus corresponds to equation (7), the "requirement for finance restraint," in my 1966 article with the demand and supply for bonds, which are non-existent in this model, eliminated. (See *op. cit.*, §4, esp. 338.)
5. Since equation (3) is a constraint on aggregate expenditures $E = I + y - S$,

the parameters of the I and S functions in equation (1) must be consistent with the parameters of the L function in equation (3), such that

$$- \frac{(1 - \theta L_v)v}{\frac{1}{\lambda} L_1 + g' L_2} = (I' + S_2)g' + S_3 \theta v.$$

Thus we are merely looking at the same problem from a different angle. This new angle of viewing, however, may give additional insight on the likelihood of stability.

6. If we follow the prevailing practice of formulating the demand for money function as $L[y(k), r + \pi^* - \bar{i}, \theta v]$ instead of the right hand side of our equation (3), then, with y assumed as constant in the short run equation (7) would become

$$\frac{d\pi}{dt} = - \frac{(1 - \theta L_v)v}{g' L_2} (\pi - \pi_0), \qquad (7')$$

which would always be unstable, as the denominator is unquestionably negative. With our formulation, there is still hope for stability, if dishoarding is not very sensitive to the rate of price inflation or if price adjustment is slow enough (i.e., if λ is small enough).

7. The reason for replacing real income y with planned expenditures E is given briefly on p. 334. With the market rate of interest introduced as an endogenous variable to be determined by the equation, there are more grounds for rejecting $L[y(k), r + \pi^*, i - \bar{i}, \theta v]$ as the appropriate formulation of the demand function for money.

    If the right-hand side of our equation (10) is written in this way, then a new technological innovation, which raises the expected rate of returns of physical capital r, would first of all bring abut a fall in the market rate of interest, at least until additional output y has come about through more investment and the adoption of the new technique; for the only influence on the demand for money in the immediate short run would be $L_2 \Delta r$, which is negative. This seems to me highly plausible; for surely even if real output is yet unchanged by the innovation, the increased expected rate of returns of physical capital, given the market rate of interest, would have stimulated planned investment expenditures, which, even before they are carried out, would have created additional demand for finance and thus exerted an upward pressure on the market rate of interest. This *modus operandi* of the financial market can be truthfully represented in our model, only if we revise the demand function for money to $L[E, r + \pi^*, i - \bar{i}, \theta v]$ as we did in the text; for then E would include all the planned investment expenditures stimulated by the technological innovation and the increase in r.

    Another strange result that one would get, if we are to adopt here the widely accepted formulation of the demnad function for money is shown in footnote 9.

8. What I called the "requirement for finance restraint" in my 1966 article would, in terms of symbols used here, take the form of $v - L \equiv B^d - B^s$, where B^d and B^s represent the demand and supply of bonds (cf. equation

(7) on p. 338 of that article). Thus the excess supply of money is identically equal to the excess demand for bonds, regardless of whether there is equilibrium or disequilibrium on the commodity market.

9. We have already shown in equation (5) that $[(I' + S_2)g' + S_3\theta v] < 0$, is the stability condition for the model with no financial market, which condition is much more stringent and much less likely to be satisfied than condition (14) given here for the model with a financial market.

10. Here again, I found that writing the demand and supply equation for money in the widely accepted form of $v = L[y,\ r + \pi^*,\ i - \bar{i},\ \theta v]$, instead of (10) above, we would get rather queer results. For instead of (13), we would now have $di/dt = \phi[L_2g' + (1 - \theta L_v)v](\pi - \pi_0) + \phi L_3(i - i_0)$, and the stability condition (14), would become $\lambda[(I' + S_2)g' + S_3\theta v] + \phi L_3 < 0$, while the stability condition (15) would remain the same. This new stability condition (14) implies that, assuming as we did that the terms inside the square brackets sum up greater than zero, stability is impossible, unless L_3 is a sufficiently large negative magnitude. This implies in particular that the system is unstable when L_3 is either zero or quite small in absolute magnitude, as classical economists and Professor Friedman presume it to be under the quantity theory of money. This seems to be definitely unreasonable. With our revised formulation of the demand and supply equation for money, the stability condition (14) does not depend on L_3 being sufficiently smaller than zero; for $-L_1(I' + S_2)$ is always negative.

11. Here we use the term absolute risk aversion in the sense as defined by K. Arrow, i.e., $-U''(x)/U'(x)$, where x is wealth and $U(x)$ is the utility function [1]. It is true that with a quadratic utility function of wealth, an increase in an individual's wealth necessarily leads to an increase in his absolute risk aversion, but that is to be regarded as a reason for the rejection of the hypothesis of a quadratic utility function rather than as a reason for the belief that people's absolute risk aversion should increase with wealth, which is empircally highly implausible ([1], p. 26; also [4], p. 802).

12. We have already shown above (on pp. 334–336) that $(L_1 + \lambda_{g'}L_2) < 0$ would imply instability for the model with no financial market.

13. Here I shall examine the response of planned investment activities only, even though, in the case of price deflation, some unintentional investment might occur. Since unintended investment usually takes the form of unintended accumulation of stock, they are not very productive and hence should not be taken on the same basis as planned investment in our examination of the efficiency of the financial market.

References

1. Arrow, Kenneth, J. "The Portfolio Approach to the Demand for Money and other Assets: Comment," *Review of Economics and Statistics*, **45**, (supplement, February, 1963), 24–27.

2. Friedman, Milton. *A Program for Monetary Stability*, New York, 1959.
3. Friedman, Milton. "The Optimum Quantity of Money," an unpublished manuscript, 1967.
4. Hicks, John, R. "Liquidity," *Economic Journal*, **72** (1962), 787–802.
5. Samuelson, Paul. "What Classical and Neoclassical Monetary Theory Really Was," *Canadian Journal of Economics*, **1**, No. 1, 1968.
6. Stein, Jerome L. "Money and Capacity Growth," *Journal of Political Economy*, **74** (1966), 451–65.
7. Stein, Jerome L. "Neoclassical and Keynes-Wicksell Monetary Growth Models," *Journal of Money, Credit, and Banking*, **1** (1969), 151–71.
8. Tobin, James. "Notes on Optimal Monetary Growth," *Journal of Political Economy*, **76** (1968), 833–59.
9. Tsiang, S. C. "Walras' Law, Say's Law and Liquidity Preference in General Equilibrium Analysis," *International Economic Review*, **7** (1966), 329–45.

Section V

CHAPTER 15

LF and LP

John Hicks

I am grateful to Professor Tsiang for taking me back to this old dispute—between the two theories of interest, loanable funds (LF) and liquidity preference (LP)—and for reminding me that what I said about it in the thirties should not be left as my last (explicit) word on the subject. I still think that there was some truth in what the LF party (Robertson, following Marshall, and Tsiang, following Robertson) have said about it; there was also some truth in the LP theory of Keynes. But I am now quite convinced that my first attempt at a reconciliation was superficial. Certainly what I said in *Value and Capital* (1939) did not get to the heart of the matter. It is not enough to proceed in a Walrasian manner, pointing out that in an *n* goods model, with *n* − 1 *relative* prices to be determined, it is arbitrary which of the *n* supply–demand equations one chooses to eliminate, taking it as following from the others. There was indeed a little more to be done in that direction, which does clear some things up[1]; it is not without uses, but I am sure it would not have satisfied either Robertson or Keynes.[2] Perhaps, at long last, I can find something which might have been acceptable to each of them.

Finance Constraints and the Theory of Money
ISBN 0-12-701720-8
ISBN 0-12-701721-6 (pbk)

351

1.

The issue is often presented as one of stocks and flows, and it is true that LF is a flow condition, while LP relates to stocks. This, I accept, is part of the problem, but it is by no means the whole.

It is nevertheless a step towards finding a solution if one begins by insisting that stock and flow relations *both* require attention. One must put the argument in a proper accounting framework. Neither side in the thirties was very good at that, for social accounting was only in the process of being worked out. But the translation is not difficult and does, I think, remove some differences, although by no means all as we shall see.

Let us look accordingly at the simplest possible model in which the issue comes up. It is a model of a closed economy in which there are just two things which are exchangeable for money—one being goods (including services), the other bonds, which are (reliable) promises to pay a regular income, fixed in money terms, to whoever is the holder. The bonds are homogeneous, and we can make the goods homogeneous by supposing that their *relative* prices are fixed exogenously. So there are just two prices to be determined, the price of goods and the price of bonds, the latter being (arithmetically) expressible as a *current* rate of interest.

So as to give the flow aspect due attention, let us consider the working of the model during a period. A period must have a start and it must have a finish. If we consider the start by itself, we must look at stocks. There will be, in this initial position, a certain stock of bonds and a certain stock of money. The price of the bond must be such that there are holders who are willing to hold that particular stock of bonds, neither more nor less. A change in their holdings of bonds must, in the first place, imply a purchase or sale of bonds for money. So if we just look at that by itself, it is a change which must be affected by people who have a choice between holding money or holding bonds. The clearest case in which there is such a choice is when the holding of money and the holding of bonds are directed to much the same purpose. It is hard to see that this can be anything else than that which figures in Keynes' LP, a requirement for liquidity, the need to have a "precautionary" reserve, a reserve against emergencies.

It would thus appear that if we just look at the start of the period, what happens there must be determined by stock equilibrium relations, which lead to LP in the Keynesian manner. But the "flow" party will rightly say that we must not stop at that point; we must go on to see what happens during the period.

The period indeed has a finish as well as a start, and there seems to be no reason why the finish, if taken by itself, should not be treated in the same way as appeared to be appropriate for the start. But the *difference* between the position at the end from what it was at the beginning must be a matter of what has happened during the period. If new bonds have been issued during the period, the stock of bonds at the end will be different from what it was at the beginning. The *change* in the rate of interest during the period must then be a matter of what is needed for this additional stock to be held.

It would have to be said by a pure LP (or Keynesian) theorist that these extra bonds would have to be taken up by people who were willing to add them to their reserves, holding them in place of the "precautionary" money reserves which they would otherwise have been holding. Thus, unless there were new supplies of money coming in (from outside) during the period, the change in the rate of interest would be a matter of the elasticity of a liquidity preference curve.

A quite consistent stock-flow theory could be constructed on these lines, but I am sure that a good LF theorist, such as Robertson, would have refused to accept it. For he would have refused to accept that the holding of bonds as a *reserve asset* is the only reason for holding bonds.

Keynes himself (in his *General Theory*) had granted, indeed had emphasized, that the holding of money itself as a reserve asset (his "precautionary" and "speculative" motives) is not the only motive for holding money. There is also what he called the transactions motive. So a pure LP theory, which confines attention to the choice between money and bonds as *reserve assets*, is incomplete even on the side of money. But if it is incomplete on that side, is it not incomplete on the other side also? Is there not another motive for holding bonds—just to get a regular, steady income from them?

If one is just looking at the (initial) stock equilibrium, the introduction of these other motives may seem unnecessary. They seem to come in as no more than background. But when we pass on to consider the change *over* our period, they become more important. For it cannot then be denied that the extra bonds might be held not as reserve assets but as sources of income, accumulated out of savings. If the new bonds, issued during the period, were matched by new savings, made during the period, there need be no additional bonds to be held by those who were holding bonds as a reserve. The change in the rate of interest during the period would then, as the LF party said, be such as would generate a flow of savings to match the new investment (issue of bonds).

A model in which *all* these things were taken into account could not, I think, have failed acceptance, at least in principle, by both Robertson and Keynes. But having got so far in agreement, they would still have had their differences. These could not have been theoretical differences; in a narrow sense they would have been differences of judgement on which the choice-margins that had been identified were of practical importance. This, being an empirical question, could have been answered quite properly in different ways at different times. It could be that it would have been proper to answer it in one way in the 1880s (Marshall), one way in the 1920s and 1930s (Keynes and Robertson) and one way in the 1980s, and again, it would be possible to answer it in different ways in different countries.

2.

Such empirical questions are beyond the scope of this paper; there is nevertheless some preparatory work that could be useful in dealing with them and with which a theorist should be able to cope. It is convenient to set it out by considering some special cases.

(i) Take first the working of our model as it would have been in a primitive condition, before the bonds (and the rate of interest on them) were introduced. The only exchanges which would then have been practicable would have been between goods and money. Even so, some of the distinctions we have been making would have applied, for it would already have been possible for some of the existing supply of money to be held as a reserve asset ("hoarded"); only the remainder, after these hoards had been subtracted, would have been used as means of payment for the purchase of the current (flow) supply of goods. So if adopting Keynes' notation, M_1 is the money which circulates and M_2 is hoarded (money supply = $M_1 + M_2$), it makes for clarity to give M_1 the *velocity* so that M_1V is current expenditure on goods and services. (It should be emphasised that if the "quantity equation" is written in this form, it is a *stock* equilibrium condition; it is a statement of the quantity of money left over after M_2 has been subtracted, which is needed to support or to finance the current *rate* of money expenditure.)

If it has to be granted, even in this primitive form of our model, that not all of the money supply will be circulating, should not the same be true for the *goods*? Why should there not also be goods, stocks of which are held off the market? It could be that they are held as reserves against emergencies (like M_2). But it could indeed also be that they were held for the "psychic" or invisible income that was obtained from them, houses and their contents being a leading example. Thus on the side of goods we need a three-way classification, G_1 corresponding to M_1, G_2 to M_2, and G_3 which so far has no M to match it. All of these should figure on a combined balance sheet, or stock account, of our economy.

Is it, however, correct to take M_3 to be missing? If we are thinking about a commodity money, which for our primitive economy might well seem to be appropriate, surely it is not missing. For this is where the gold that was used for ornaments (or for filling teeth) would fit in. It is only when the money is pure credit money, nothing but a promise to pay, that there may be doubts about M_3. But there is no room for that in our primitive economy.

There is just one more thing to be said before passing on. We need names for the classes of G's and M's that have been distinguished. I have been in the habit[3] of describing G_1 and M_1 on the balance sheet as *running assests* and G_2 and M_2 as *reserve assests*, and I do not think that these names can be bettered. To find a good name for the third of the classes has been harder.[4] I now think that it is best to be bold and to call them *income assets*—assets which are held for the sake of the income (psychic or otherwise) which is expected to be *directly* derivable from them. (It is, of course, accepted that an income is *indirectly* derivable from the running assets, an income which they yield through the part which they play in the process of production.)

(ii) Now let us reintroduce our bonds. They will evidently need to be given a corresponding classification, B_1, B_2, B_3. Here it is B_1 which is a bit mysterious; I shall come to it later. But B_2 is clearly the bonds that are held for Keynes' LP motive and B_3 those held for an income motive which Robertson warned us not to forget. Indeed, in terms of our model, it is B_3 which is easier to understand, for what the bond offers is a regular income, which is just what is wanted under B_3. The problem is rather in what way a long bond, such as we are assuming, can serve as a reserve asset, as B_2.

A necessary condition is that the bond should be resellable. If there were no market in previously issued bonds, a bond could only be held under B_3. Anyone who had subscribed for a bond would have to keep it.

The introduction of long-term borrowing, so long as this restriction held, would not prevent the model from working in what would readily be recognized as a "classical" manner. The bond would not replace the money which was being held as a reserve asset (M_2); it would make no difference to what was needed as that reserve asset, so the only source from which the purchase of the bonds could be financed would be M_1. The money that was withdrawn from that would presumably be spent by the borrower; so expenditure of money, both taken together, would appear to be unchanged. No doubt it would be difficult for a large issue to be financed at once in this manner, but a flow of borrowings (for investment) could readily be financed in this way by a flow of savings. So the rate of interest could be determined, over a period, by what was needed to make these flows of savings and "investments" match.

This, on the classification here adopted, is no more than an extreme case; at the other extreme is that in which the bonds can easily be resold, so they fall into the B_2 category. They would then replace at least some of the money held under M_2; so, quite apart from the spending of the funds which had been raised, there would, in terms of M_2, be dishoarding. The borrowing in itself would be a cause of monetary expansion. The (current) rate of interest would be determined, by what was necessary to induce a substitution of M_2 for B_2—liquidity preference!

Thus, the one extreme gives us a "classical" model and the other extreme one which is *purely* Keynesian. But I doubt whether Robertson or even Keynes were really thinking in terms of such extreme cases. There is plenty of room in between for something quite a bit more realistic.

There is obviously no reason why the bonds that are held should not include some B_2 and some B_3, but the people who are holding them in the one way or the other could be different people. The B_2 bonds would be held by professionals,[5] who had good contacts with a market (indeed they themselves would constitute the market), while the B_3 bonds would be held by "outsiders." The rate of interest, or current price of bonds, would be determined by the sum of demands from these two sources; it would nevertheless be the case that potential sales and purchases of B_2 would be likely to be large in relation to the purchases (they could only be purchases) of B_3.

The National Debt of the British Government, which a British economist writing in the twenties or thirties could hardly have failed to have in mind, was a war debt which, when it was issued, must surely have been mainly taken up by the financial sector, our "market." The current rate of interest upon it would have been determined by what that sector charged to take it up, and that would have been a matter of LP and the supply of money. Since the M_2 that was available to that sector would not have been unlimited, the rate of interest would rise very high if the supply of money were not increased. If the rate were kept down, prices of goods would rise rather freely. When the abnormal war expenditure stopped, the debt could gradually pass into the hands of "solid" savers (B_3), and their willingness to hold the debt would become more important. That is indeed what seems to have happened, after more than one of Britain's wars.[6]

I must not go further in that direction; in any serious discussion of such historical experiences there would be many more things to be considered. I will just make two points in conclusion. One is that when the model is extended in this manner, so as to admit an "inside" and an "outside" sector, room can readily be found for other credit instruments, "shorts" in particular, which we shall naturally expect to be largely held "inside," so that an LP theory, of some kind, will apply to them.[7] The other is that the older economists, including Keynes and Robertson, were thinking of a world in which expectations of long-term rates were rather stable and in which expectations of the long-term level of the prices of goods were also fairly stable. That is a condition that in more recent years has often been absent. Its absence makes the execution of monetary policy more difficult, and it is not easy to see that monetary policy alone can bring it back.

Notes

1. "ISLM — An Explanation" (*Collected Essays II*, p. 318–31).
2. As I have indeed been told by those whom I may fairly regard as their modern representatives – S. C. Tsiang on the one side, Richard Kahn on the other.
3. See the third of my "Two Triads" papers (*Critical Essays*, 1967, pp. 38–59) and also, what is largely a continuation of that, "Solidity, Fluidity and Liquidity," first published in my *Collected Essays II*, pp. 255–69. I myself rank these, together with "Simplification" of 1935, as my major contributions to monetary theory.
4. In these earlier papers I called them *investment assets*, but this, quite apart from the horrible overuse of the word *investment*, does not quite get the point. I am now convinced that *income assets* is better.

5. One may think of the professionals as needing to hold some amount of bonds in order to stay in business, so that is where we find B_1.
6. Certainly after the Napoleonic War and after World War I.
7. If they are used as a means of payment, they would appear as B_1.

CHAPTER 16

The Context of S. C. Tsiang's Monetary Economics

David Laidler

1.

It is often argued that, in comparison with the pattern of steady change, some would say progress, which may be discerned in the history of the theories of value and distribution, the development of monetary economics has been rather haphazard. But monetary economics does change. Thus, anyone comparing the state of the subdiscipline in, say, the mid-1960s with that prevailing a century earlier would be more struck by differences than similarities.[1] In part the differences in question reflect a change (for good or ill is not in question here) in economists' views on just what are the important policy questions and reflect a change in the preconceptions about the appropriate background against which such questions might be framed. In the 1960s the central issues seemed to revolve around the influences running between monetary factors and such real variables as income and employment; in the 1860s the link between money and prices was at the forefront—even, be it noted, in the context of what would now be called the business cycle. Moreover, in the 1960s the combined influence of the Keynesian

ISBN 0-12-701720-8
ISBN 0-12-701721-6 (pbk)
359

Revolution and postwar American dominance of economics had made the typical textbook monetary model one of a closed economy. A century earlier, the openness of the economy was taken for granted, and balance of payments theory was an important and integral component of monetary theory.

But the change that took place in monetary economics over the century we are considering involved a fundamental change in the tools of monetary economics, too. Not just the Quantity Theory of Money but what would now be called its "transactions" version completely dominated classical monetary economics. Closely associated, though the exponents of that monetary economics deployed "supply and demand" analysis to elucidate the relationship between money and prices, the analysis to which that label was attached was very different from anything to which we would now apply it. In those pre-Marshallian days, the importance of conceiving of supply and demand as *schedules*, as opposed to simple *quantities*, was by no means fully appreciated, nor was the stock-flow distinction clearly understood. Even so, when we cut through their semantic imprecision, we find that when classical monetary economists spoke of the "supply of money" they usually meant the nominal value of a flow of money expenditures, while by "demand for money" they meant a flow of real goods and services offered in exchange for it. The price level was then determined by the interaction of these two flows because of the accounting necessity that the values of nominal outlays and receipts must be equal for the economy as a whole.

By the 1960s, in contrast, the analysis of the "supply and demand" for money was cast firmly in terms of stocks. Moreover, such analysis was treated not as a piece of theory sufficient by itself to tackle any interesting problem but as a component of some more complex general equilibrium system, of which the Hicks–Hansen IS–LM model is the archetype. This, be it noted, is as true of work in the tradition of Friedman's "New Quantity Theory" as anything to which the Keynesian label could be attached.[2] In the 1960s economists could, and did, disagree about whether the "supply and demand for money" was more important for explaining the behavior of prices, output, or the rate of interest, but they (almost) all agreed that the "supply and demand" in question should be conceived of as schedules—or rather multivariate functions—determining supply and demand for a stock of money and that such functions needed to be embedded in a general equilibrium model of the economy as a whole if their analysis was to be a fruitful exercise.

2.

The above mentioned radical change in the nature of monetary theory was not simply the outcome of the so-called "Keynesian Revolution." The publication of Keynes' *General Theory* in 1936 was, to be sure, a crucial event in the development of monetary thought, but it was nevertheless only one step, albeit a giant step, among many in an untidy process of intellectual evolution. The beginning of that process can indeed be traced back to the 1860s, at least, when John Cairnes and John Stuart Mill, influenced by the empirical example of Britain's monetary experience in the wake of the gold discoveries of the 1840s and 1850s, began to explore the role played by the level of interest rates in what we would now call the transmission mechanism of the effects of changes in the quantity of money. They supplemented the by then well established view that the rate of interest was an essentially "real" phenomenon determined by the interaction of the forces of productivity and thrift with the vital qualification that, in the short run, when the quantity of money was in the process of changing, that variable would become in part a monetary phenomenon.[3]

Specifically Cairnes and Mill envisaged new money coming into circulation through the lending activities of the banking system and, in so doing, adding to the supply of credit available to firms in just the same way as would an increase in real saving. Hence, the process of money creation, while it continued, would push the rate of interest to a level below its "natural" (the adjective was used by Mill long before Wicksell) value. The view that productivity and thrift determined the interest rate thus became a special case of a more general theory that had it determined by the supply and demand for "loanable funds"—a special case true only in the long run when the rate of money creation by the banking system was zero so that the supply of loanable funds became identical to the economy's supply of savings.[4]

At first this theory of the interest rate was used solely as a component of an account of the mechanism linking secular changes in the quantity of money to secular changes in the price level. In Wicksell's (1898) substantial elaboration of the Cairnes-Mill analysis, the deviation of the market interest rate from its natural level was seen as creating an excess demand for goods—of investment over saving to put it in later vocabulary—but this in turn was viewed as a proximate cause of nothing more than a rising price level. In due course, however, and in different ways in different hands, the loanable funds approach to the theory of the rate of interest became an important ingredient of the body of business cycle analysis which, before the publication of the *General Theory*, attempted, with differing degrees of success (typically low), to explain the recurrence of economic crises associated not just with falling prices but with depressions in the level of real economic activity, too. The idea of a marginal efficiency of capital schedule, linking firms' planned expenditure on investment to the rate of interest—a central concept of the model developed by Keynes in the *General Theory*—is to be found underlying in one form or another the demand side of the market for "loanable funds" in much pre-*General Theory* literature in the business cycle.[5]

The link between the monetary and real sectors of the economy forged by the loanable funds approach to interest rate theory was one important factor forcing monetary economics away from reliance on simple supply and demand mechanisms. If the interaction of money with the real economy was of the essence in bringing about price level (and perhaps output level) variations, then a more general analytic framework enabling multimarket interactions to be dealt with was required. However this step was not enough, in and of itself, to bring about the whole of the change in the nature of monetary theory described earlier. It was also necessary to reformulate statements about the supply and demand for money in terms of stocks instead of flows. Here again we must go back to the later 19th century to find the origins of this idea and, in particular, to the work of Alfred Marshall and his pupils—though we must not overlook the fact that Walras was also a pioneer of what has come to be called the "cash balance" approach to monetary theory.[6] Marshall sought to reformulate monetary economics in terms of the same individual choice-theoretic analysis which he employed elsewhere in his work. Hence, instead of focusing upon the *market* phenomenon of money's circulation, he concentrated upon the *individual* phenomenon of its being held.

Though Marshall and his pupils (not least the younger Keynes) wished to transform the method of analysis used in monetary theory, their view of money's role in the economy, of the problems which monetary theory should address, and indeed of the results which they believed it should obtain, were the same as those of conventional quantity theorists. For the Cambridge economists, as much as for any classical monetary theorist, money was a means of exchange, the central problem to be addressed by monetary theory was the interaction between the quantity of money and the general price level, and the central result to be obtained was the *ceteris paribus* prediction of strict proportionality of movements in the price level to those of the quantity of nominal money. That is why posterity has labelled their work "the Cambridge version of the quantity theory" without doing any great violence to it, though Marshall and his pupils did not characterise themselves as quantity theorists.

Their central analytic concept was not some transaction velocity idea but rather an income velocity concept that in turn derived from the notion that the representative economic agent would seek to hold a stock of *real balances* (the phrase is Keynes') which bore a determinate relationship to real income. Keynes was clearer than other Cambridge economists about income being the relevant variable here. Marshall wrote sometimes of wealth, sometimes of income, and, along with Pigou and Lavington, often used the ambiguous term "resources." Nevertheless to formulate monetary theory in terms of the demand function for a *stock of money* was to take the first, though only the first, step towards placing it in the context of a theory of portfolio choice in which money became viewed as an asset, the "price" of holding which was the income to be had from holding other assets. This later development was, of course. the work of Hicks and the Keynes of the *Treatise* and *General Theory*.

3.

In Keynes' *General Theory*, the rate of interest played the central role in linking the monetary and real sectors of the economy, as it had in the work of virtually all his important predecessors since J. S. Mill. However once the supply and demand for money was formulated in stock terms, and the rate of interest identified as the "price" of holding money, the status of "loanable funds" analysis as an explanation of the interest rate became unclear. Was it perhaps the case that, with the advent of the liquidity preference idea, monetary theory had acquired one too many explanations of the determination of the interest rate?

Keynes' own answer to this question was affirmative. As is by now well understood, his habits of thought were Marshallian rather than Walrasian. His vision of the macroeconomy involved a series of essentially partial equilibrium market experiments operating in sequence rather than some kind of simultaneous determination of all the economy's endogenous variables.[7] Any simplification of Keynes' views involves an element of caricature, but the caricature that has him thinking of the stock supply and demand for money determining the interest rate, the interest rate then determining the level of investment, and the level of investment, through the multiplier process, in turn generating the volume of saving necessary to match it, is surely more recognisable than most. Keynes had an uncertain grasp of the feedback effects of income changes on the demand for money and often took the position that "liquidity preference" (i.e. the stock demand for money interacting with a stock supply) as opposed to "loanable funds" (i.e. the flow supply and demand of credit) was the factor determining the rate of interest.

Not everyone, even at Cambridge, agreed, and Sir Dennis Robertson in particular who had, perhaps not coincidentally, been the slowest of all the Cambridge economists to find room for the "Cambridge version" of the quantity theory in his work, was the most visible defender of the "loanable funds" view. There is no need here to enter into a detailed discussion of Keynes' and Robertson's exchange on this issue (not least because Tsiang deals with it himself, particularly in his 1956 *AER* article. Chapter 3 in this volume).[8] It will suffice to note that, as far as mainstream monetary economics was concerned, the issue was settled, perhaps it would be better to say defined away, by the reformulation of Keynes' ideas in terms of an explicitly general equilibrium model in which all the economy's endogenous variables were simultaneously determined.

Walras' law, as it has come to be known, tells us that, in an economy whose equilibrium may be characterised by the solution to a set of simultaneous equations, one market may always be eliminated from explicit analysis. The excess demand for whatever is traded in it will always be exactly matched by excess supplies elsewhere, and if these sum to zero, then excess demand in this former market too must be zero. Stock-flow problems can be sidestepped by dividing time into discrete intervals, as Patinkin (1965 Mathematical Appendix II) conclusively shows. The validity of Walras's law for a barter economy is not controversial, but it is for an economy characterised by monetary exchange. However, if *the conventional general equilibrium framework is accepted as appropriate to monetary analysis*, it implies that one can eliminate the "money market" and appear to have a "loanable funds" theory of interest, or one can eliminate the market for "loanable funds" and appear to have a "liquidity preference theory," and nothing of any substantive analytic significance hinges upon this choice.

To the question attributed to Abba Lerner—suppose we eliminated the market for peanuts?—the exponent of general equilibrium theory will reply not that we then have one too many theories of the rate of interest again but that in general equilibrium each endogenous variable is determined by the interaction of all markets and that the habit of identifying a specific market with the determination of a particular price (such as the rate of interest) is a bad one, inculcated by thinking in partial equilibrium terms about a problem that requires a general equilibrium approach.

Arguments such as these seemed to settle the matter for the majority of economists, and the theoretical research agenda in monetary economics in the 1940s and 50s whose crowning achievement was of course Don Patinkin's magnificent *Money, Interest and Prices*, largely involved seeking ever more rigorous general equilibrium formulations of the properties of a monetary economy. Note however, that I here refer to the majority of economists; by the 1950s a small group of dissenters from the idea that general equilibrium techniques are appropriately applied to monetary problems, prominent among who was S. C. Tsiang, began to make itself heard (if not widely understood!). The main purpose of this book is to make the papers in which Tsiang expressed his dissent readily accessible, and it would be redundant, therefore, for this commentator simply to paraphrase him. Let me instead offer my own interpretation of his concerns (without, let it explicitly be said, thereby committing myself to agreement with him on all scores).

4.

The fundamental point of Tsiang's dissent, one that is much more widely accepted now than it was twenty or thirty years ago, was that somehow, in the process of reformulating the theory of money in explicitly Walrasian terms, mainstream monetary economists had purged their analysis of any references to money's role as a means of exchange in the economy. Somewhere along the line between Marshall and Patinkin, the demand for a stock of the means of exchange had become the demand for a store of value, for an asset pure and simple. Thus, though general equilibrium analysis is useful for understanding the properties of an artificial barter economy in which, among other things, a nominal asset could be traded and held, it is not useful for understanding a real world economy in which trade is carried on not by barter but by monetary exchange.[9]

Now to be sure, the Hicks–Keynes analysis of liquidity preference did concentrate upon the demand for money as a pure store of value and showed how such a demand could arise where the expected return on other assets was subject to uncertainty. But to show that such a factor *can* lead to a demand for money as an asset is a far cry from showing that, in an *actual* economy, it *will* be the dominant factor underlying and explaining agents' money holding. Indeed, nominal capital value certain, but interest bearing assets, such as savings deposits, unambiguously dominate money as hedges against interest rate uncertainty, while high quality short term paper, Treasury Bills for example, will usually do so. Hence, as Tsiang often notes, a theory of the demand for money which treats it as a pure store of value cannot account for money holdings on the scale we observe them in the real world, and a theoretical framework which requires that money be so treated is unlikely to be satisfactory.[10]

Now it is *not quite* true that money's means of exchange role cannot be reconciled with the application of Walrasian analysis. In Patinkin's work, time is divided into periods—"Hicksian Weeks." Prices are formed at the beginning of the period by *tâtonnement*, and the "demand for money" which underlies price formation is a demand for a stock of real balances to be held over the interval from the end of this week to the beginning of the next. Such a demand *could* be motivated by treating money as a pure store of value, but Patinkin does not do so. Instead, he separates the process of price formation from that of exchange and, after prices are set *at the beginning* of the week, he has exchange *during* the week mediated by money. By introducing a stochastic element into the timing of trades, and a cost of being unable to engage in them for want of cash, a precautionary demand for money during the week is generated which implies a positive holding of cash when all trades have been completed. Through this indirect route Patinkin justifies the inclusion of end of week cash balances in agents beginning of week utility functions.

How satisfactory Patinkin's justification for putting real balances into the utility function of the representative agent inhabiting his general equilibrium model is regarded is perhaps a matter of taste. To a generation of economists mainly concerned with empirical predictions, and armed with the phrase "as if" as a first (and sometimes last) line of defence against *a priori* criticism of their models' premises, its artificial nature presented no problems. However, the intellectual fashion nowadays has swung against what Robert E. Lucas, Jr. and his associates term "implicit theorising," and their demands—that if money is to be introduced into a model as an object of choice, the demand for it should spring naturally and essentially from the tastes and technology specified as underlying the model—are not so easily satisfied. The exchange technology which Patinkin postulates to justify money holding plays no role at all in determining the way in which his model behaves. Some would call it an *ad hoc* appendage used to justify referring to a non-interest-bearing nominal asset as money, because as far as the model's behaviour is concerned, it is the existence of an end of period demand for this asset and its appearance in the budget constraint which agents face at the beginning of the next period, that are important.

Though the rhetoric of Patinkin's analysis characterises money as a means of exchange, the logical properties of his model require only that it be a pure store of value. In criticising the general equilibrium monetary theory of the 1950s and 1960s along such lines. Tsiang and others were forerunners of contemporary critics of implicit theorising about money; though I hasten to add that they would certainly not have found satisfactory attempts, such as Sargent and Wallace (1982), to rectify matters by explicitly deriving a store of value role for "money" from the tastes and technology that might characterise an economy in which trade between overlapping generations is nevertheless carried on by barter. On the contrary, the essential "technological" characteristic of the economy that Tsiang, et al., emphasised was the institution of monetary exchange. Their objection to the general equilibrium monetary theory that dominated the discipline in the 1950s and 60s was, as we have already seen, that it did not deal with the consequences of this institutional fact.

5.

The work of these critics, not least Tsiang, was not just a matter of negative commentary. They also offered positive suggestions about alternative ways to proceed, suggestions that may be summarised as follows. First, they preferred to think of decisions being taken and implemented in a monetary economy following a definite sequence, rather than being simultaneous. In this respect they committed themselves to a method of analysis that, in the 1930s and 40s was probably most fully developed by the Stockholm school but which, in English economics, had found its most consistent advocate in Sir Dennis Robertson.[11] Moreover, they argued that money's role as a means of exchange implied that the decision to hold money must be implemented before expenditure plans were executed. To put it in Tsiang's terms, Keynes' (1937a) "fourth motive" for holding money, the "finance" motive, is an alternative and correct specification of his first, the transaction motive, not, as Keynes himself argued, a supplement to it. However, correctly understood, this view implied that (unless there existed some genuine asset demand for money) money holding would be strictly complementary to and derived from the demand for goods, rather than money being an alternative object of choice.[12]

But, if the demand for money is an *ex ante*, beginning of period phenomenon, what determines (i) the quantity of money that agents actually end up with at the end of a trading period, (ii) the amount that they carry over to the next, and (iii) the amount that the general equilibrium approach to monetary theory would interpret as a realisation of agents' demand for money? According to Tsiang this amount is realised from sales that are made during the period and is no more than the involuntary side effect of selling goods and services in a monetary economy.

The problems on which Tsiang brought these insights to bear are numerous, as the reader of his collected works will see. Notable among them is the liquidity preference/loanable funds issue in interest theory, for in terms of Tsiang's vision of a monetary economy, the liquidity preference approach boils down to a rather odd way of restating the traditional loanable funds theory. Also of considerable interest are his forays into balance of payments analysis. The elasticities approach supplemented by an assumption of unemployed resources never seemed to him to be an adequate framework for dealing with balance of payments issues, because unlike so many of his contemporaries, Tsiang never lost sight of the essential monetary element in balance of payments flows. He may thus be referred to as one of the pioneers of the reestablishment of *a* monetary approach to balance of payments theory. However, the use of the indefinite article here rather than the definite is quite deliberate and, as the reader will see, appropriate too, for Tsiang's balance of payments theory is far from being a carbon copy of that of Frenkel and Johnson (1976) and their associates.

In the history of economic analysis we frequently find ideas taking on a significance that their early protagonists neither intended nor even foresaw, and so it is in this case. For the contemporary reader, two of

Tsiang's ideas stand out, namely the notion that the demand for money stems from the social convention that before one can buy goods one must have or be able to obtain money to do it with, and the closely related idea that agents' actual money holdings often represent the unintended outcome of trading activities, rather than the conscious implementation of a plan to hold cash *per se*. The first of these ideas is nowadays known as the "finance constraint," and the second underlies the "buffer-stock" or "shock-absorber" view of money.[13]

The two ideas are, as I have already remarked, closely related, both stemming from an insistence that money's principal function is that of a means of exchange. In this respect, neither idea can claim to have found its first expression in the works of Tsiang, Clower (1967), Hicks (1967), Lejonhufvud (1968), Jonson (1976), Kohn (1984), Carr and Darby (1981), Laidler (1984), or anyone else whose name is associated with recent analysis based on them. Current efforts to analyse money's means of exchange role are attempts to *reestablish* monetary economics in terms that would have been, in broad outline at least, familiar to pre-Keynesian Quantity Theorists, not to take it along a brand new path which it has never followed before. Nevertheless, there are differences aplenty between modern analysis and the traditional quantity theory, and indeed between the efforts of the last few years, and those of Tsiang. It is worth drawing attention to some of the latter before closing this essay.

6.

Tsiang's work, as the reader of the following pages will see, usually concentrates on carefully describing the sequence of events which takes place within a single "week," a time period short enough so that spending decisions are constrained by cash inherited from the past because proceeds from current sales arrive too late to be spent until next period. It does not, as does modern work based on the "cash-in-advance" constraint (which is, if only for the sake of semantic clarity, best thought of as a special case of the finance constraint), make the connection between *future* consumption plans, *future* sales plans, and *current* activities. As soon as this is done, end of period cash holdings cease to be a mere residual from this period's activities but become the result of implementing the first step in a planned sequence of trades, a step explicitly designed to ensure, among other things, that this week's end-of-period cash holdings will satisfy next week's beginning of period demand for money. In short, though the finance constraint, and the idea that there is an involuntary element to observed money holdings, are both related to the idea of money as a means of exchange, the former does not inevitably imply the latter as Tsiang sometimes seemed to argue.

If agents have *costless* access to a capital market (and a capital market always appears in Tsiang's discussions) then the link between end-of-period realised cash holdings and planned money balances for the beginning of the next period may be broken by movements in and out of bonds, and Tsiang's insistence on the involuntary nature of the former may then be justified. However, the typical simple cash-in-advance constraint model does not permit agents access to the capital market (that is the sense in which it is a special case of the finance constraint), and end-of-period money holdings are an object of choice in such a system. Indeed the existence of any meaningful transactions costs in the capital market gives agents an incentive to direct this period's trading activities towards realising a stock of cash that will satisfy next period's requirements.

However, even in this latter case, it is not hard to explain why realised end-of-period money holdings might have an involuntary element to them. Only if the current period's plans are both totally dominated by next period's cash needs, and completely satisfied, will the money holdings observed at the end of the period be exactly equal to those needed to begin the next one. If not, then an involuntary element will reappear in observed money holdings in the sense that these will fluctuate around a long-run planned time path. Once one leaves single period analysis and gives up costless access to a capital market, there is a breakdown in Tsiang's sharp distinctions among the demand for money conceived of as a sum desired at the beginning of the period, as an average held over time, and as an end of period target. [14] The demand for money becomes an *average* of beginning of period *targets*, which partially determine the cash holdings which agents will seek to *realise* at the end of each preceding period.

Now all this amounts to saying that modern extensions of the cash-in-advance-buffer-stock ideas appear in the context of explicitly multiperiod models that have a stochastic element to their structure. The analytic techniques needed to model the economy in this way are largely products of the last twenty years, stemming from the work of Miguel Sidrauski (1967) on intertemporal maximising behaviour as a basis for monetary theory and Robert E. Lucas, Jr. (e.g. 1972) on modelling expectations formation in an explicitly stochastic environment. Small wonder then that Tsiang, whose major contributions were made before 1970, took only a first step, albeit a critically important one, in turning monetary economics (or at least a segment of it) back to its traditional task of explicitly analysing monetary exchange. Nor will the reader miss the irony that the techniques needed to realise Tsiang's vision were produced by economists interested in developing the very general equilibrium approach to monetary economics of which he was so skeptical—indeed sometimes downright scornful. [15]

7.

Essays on topics in the history of economic thought can sometimes be brought to a neat conclusion to the effect that new ideas have been established, debates have had clear outcomes, fallacies have been revealed, and so on. So it would always be if the story of the development of economic analysis was a straightforward one about the progress of knowledge. This model of the history of knowledge, as I noted at the outset of this paper, fits (or perhaps may be forced to fit) the history of theories of value and distribution more readily than that of monetary economics. To be sure, new ideas do appear in monetary economics, new techniques are employed, and new results are generated. But the subject's capacity to help us think about the world we live in, to organise our knowledge of it, and to make useful predictions about the outcome of potential monetary experiments is not always unambiguously enhanced. Good ideas in monetary economics are lost as well as found, and much work over the years has been devoted to the recovery and reestablishment of useful insights that have been prematurely and often inadvertently discarded. Nor is such intellectual archaeology mainly the task of historians; monetary theorists, with varying degrees of self-consciousness about what they are up to, play the major role.

All this is, I believe, amply illustrated by the developments discussed in this essay and by the collected writings on monetary economics of S. C. Tsiang which this essay intended to place in historical context. It was surely a good idea to try to apply to monetary economics the same analytic tools that seemed so successful in dealing with "real" economics, and so long as the tools in question were those of Marshallian partial equilibrium analysis, there seems to have been no cost to doing so. But when the tools became those of Walrasian general equilibrium theory it was a different matter. As Frank Hahn (e.g. 1984) has frequently reminded us, the Walrasian world has no room for a means of exchange; money in that role is a substitute institution for the Walrasian market, not a complement to it. Hence, whether its exponents were conscious of it or not—and often they were not—monetary theory making explicit use of the Walrasian framework could not help but reduce money to being a pure store of value.

A few monetary theorists, including the author of these collected works were, as we have seen, acutely aware of this problem from the outset, and their dissent is now beginning to bear fruit. Money's role as a means of exchange is once again an important and explicit foundation for much research in monetary economics. This crucial idea, inadvertently mislaid for thirty years or more, has been rediscovered. Does this mean that monetary economics is now on the right track to advance our understanding of the world we live in? This author would be inclined to say yes. But the reader should be reminded that everyone involved on all sides of the debates I have outlined in this essay also thought that their work was on the right track; so perhaps my own optimism on this score should be qualified with a little skepticism on the part of the reader. The skepticism should be informed skepticism though, and not least among the knowledge that should inform it is some familiarity with the papers that form the raison d'être of this volume. Whether they agree or disagree with Tsiang, monetary economists should read him.

Acknowledgements

I am grateful to Meir Kohn for helpful comments on an earlier draft of this paper, which draws heavily on research on the history of monetary economics being carried out with the much appreciated financial aid of the Social Science and Humanities Research Council of Canada.

Notes

1. For a survey of the state of monetary economics, at least in Britain at the beginning of the 1870s, see Laidler (1988).
2. As S. C. Tsiang notes in his 1980 *QJE* paper. Chapter 13 of this volume.

3. I am well aware of Henry Thornton's (1802) analysis of these issues, in many respects more thorough than that of Cairnes and Mill. However, nowadays, Thornton has many more readers among monetary economists than do his contemporaries and, when these monetary economists read his work in isolation, they are left with the impression that monetary economics as a whole was far more developed than, in fact, it was at the beginning of the 19th century. Moreover, they frequently fail to realise that Thornton's work faded into obscurity with its quality unappreciated until Viner (1937) and Hayek (1939) rediscovered its importance in the 1930s. Anyone doubting this should look at Hollander (1911), the standard source for a long time on the monetary economics of the "Bullionist debate," to see how poorly Thornton there comes off, not least in having his personal identity confused with that of his brother Samuel!

4. On all this, see Cairnes (1873) and Mill (1865).

5. See, among other sources, Fisher (1910) whose "rate of return over cost" concept is identical to Keynes' marginal efficiency notion, or Myrdal (1932, 1939). Not all important business cycle theorists emphasised this aspect of the savings investment mechanism, however. Hawtrey for one put the influence of short interest rates on inventory accumulation at the centre of the picture. On Hawtrey, see Deutsher (1984).

6. Marshall's first exposition of this approach occurs as one of his earliest surviving unpublished notes, dating from 1871. See Whitaker (ed.) (1975). Accessible accounts of Walras' (1886) contribution are Marget (1931) and Patinkin (1965 Supplementary Note C).

7. This aspect of Keynes' work is particularly, and, in my view, appropriately, emphasised by Chick (1981).

8. But the interested reader may consult Robertson (1937) and Keynes (1937b).

9. Tsiang of course was not the only dissenter here. The contributions of Robert Clower (see (1985) for a collection of his essays on these matters), Axel Leijonhuvfud (1968) and indeed Sir John Hicks (See particularly 1967, Chapter 1) should also be explicitly mentioned.

10. Tsiang takes these issues up in his (1982) *IHS Journal* article, Chapter 12 in this volume.

11. And which finds its most eloquent defense in the writings of Sir John Hicks (e.g. 1956, reprinted as Chapter 18 of Hicks 1982).

12. The "finance motive" is introduced by Keynes in (1937a).

13. The "cash-in-advance" constraint is usually attributed to Clower (1967), and he did indeed fully and independently articulate the idea in that paper. Nevertheless the concept underlies Tsiang's (1956) *AER* paper, reprinted here as Chapter 3, and is well developed in his 1966 *IER* piece, Chapter 6 of this volume.

14. See in particular Tsiang's 1966 *IER* paper, Chapter 6 in this volume, for a discussion of this distinction.

15. This is not the only instance in which ideas and techniques that stem from the "New Classical" revolution have been instrumental in strengthening the very ideas which that revolution sought to overthrow. For a penetrating (and entertaining) account of these matters, see Howitt (1986).

References

Cairnes. J. E. (1873), "Essays Towards a Solution of the Gold Question" in *Essays in Political Economy*. London, Macmillan (reprinted Kelley 1965).

Carr, J. and Darby, M. (1981) "The Role of Money Supply Shocks in the Short-run Demand for Money," *Journal of Monetary Economics*. **8** (September) 183–200.

Chick (1981), *Macroeconomics after Keynes*, Oxford. Philip Allan, Cambridge, Massachusetts, MIT Press.

Clower, R. W. (1967) "A Reconsideration of the Microfoundation of Monetary Theory." *Western Economic Journal*. **6** (December) 1–8 (reprinted in Clower (1985)).

Clower, R. W. (1985), *Money and Markets*. (ed. D. Walker). Cambridge, Cambridge University Press.

Deutscher. P. R. (1984), *R. G. Hawtrey and the Development of Macroeconomics in the Interwar Period*. Unpublished Ph.D. thesis, University of Toronto.

Fisher, I. (1910), *The Rate of Interest, Its Nature, Determination and Relation to Economic Phenomena*. New York, Macmillan.

Frenkel J. and Johnson. H. G. (1976), *The Monetary Approach to the Balance of Payments*. London, Allan and Unwin.

Hahn. F. H. (1984), *Equilibrium and Macroeconomics*. Cambridge, Massachusetts, MIT Press.

Hayek, F. A. von (1939), "Introduction" to H. Thornton *Paper Credit...*

Hicks. J. (1967), *Critical Essays in Monetary Theory*. London, Oxford University Press.

Hicks, J. (1982), *Money Interest and Wages Collected Essays in Economic Theory*. Vol. II. Cambridge, Massachusetts, Harvard University Press.

Hollander. J. (1911), "The Development of Monetary Theory from Adam Smith to Ricardo," *Quarterly Journal of Economics*. **25** (May) 429–470.

Howitt. P. W. (1986), "The Keynesian Recovery," *Canadian Journal of Economics*. **19** (Nov.) 626–641.

Jonson. P. D. (1976), "Money, Prices and Output, An Integrative Essay," *Kredit und Kapital*. (4) 499–518.

Keynes. J.M. (1930) *A Treatise on Money* (2 vols.), London, Macmillan.

Keynes, J. M. (1936), *The General Theory of Employment, Interest and Money*. London, Macmillan.

Keynes, J. M. (1937a), "The General Theory of Employment," *Quarterly Journal of Economics*. **51** (February) 209–233.

Keynes, J. M. (1937b), "Alternative Theories of the Rate of Interest," *Economic Journal*. **47** (June) 241–252.

Kohn, M. (1984), "The Finance (Cash in Advance) Constraint Comes of Age: A Survey of Some Recent Developments in the Theory of Money," Dartmouth College (mimeo).

Laidler, D. (1984), "The Buffer Stock Notion in Monetary Economics," *Conference Papers* supplement to the *Economic Journal*. **94** (March) 17–34.

Laidler, D. (1988), "British Monetary Orthodoxy in the 1870s" *Oxford Economic Papers* **40** (March) 74–109.

Leijonhufvud. A. (1968), *On Keynesian Economics and the Economics of Keynes*. London, Oxford University Press.

Lucas. R. E., Jr. (1972), "Expectations and the Neutrality of Money," *Journal of Economic Theory*. 4 (2) 115–138.

Marget. A. (1931), "Léon Walras and the 'Cash Balance Approach' to the Problem of the Value of Money," *Journal of Political Economy*. 39 (October) 569–600.

Marshall, A. (1871), "Money" [item 11-2-1 of J. Whitaker (ed.) *Early Economic Writings of Alfred Marshall*. Vol. I. London. Macmillan (1975)].

Mill. J. S. (1865), *Principles of Political Economy...* (6th ed.) London.

Myrdal. G. (1932), *Monetary Equilibrium*. English Translation, with minor emendations, London, W. Hodge. (1939).

Patinkin. D. (1965), *Money, Interest and Prices*. (2nd ed.) New York, Harper Row.

Robertson. D. H. (1937), "Alternative Theories of the Rate of Interest: Three Rejoinders II," *Economic Journal*. 47 (September) 428–436.

Sargent. T. J. and Wallace (1982), "The Real Bills Doctrine Versus the Quantity Theory," *Journal of Political Economy*. 90 (December) 1212–1236.

Sidrauski. M. (1967), "Rational Choice and Patterns of Growth in a Monetary Economy," *American Economic Revew*. 67 (May, papers and proceedings) 534–544.

Thornton. H. (1802), *An Inquiry into the Nature and Effects of the Paper Credit of Great Britain*. Reprinted with an Introduction by F. A. von Hayek, London. 1939.

Viner J. (1937), *Studies in the Theory of International Trade*, New York, Harper.

Walras. L. (1886), *Théorie de la Monnaie*, Lausanne, Corbaz.

Wicksell. K. (1898), *Interest and Prices*. (Tr. R. F. Kahn for the Royal Economic Society) London, 1936.

CHAPTER 17

The Cash-in-Advance Constraint in International Economics

Alan C. Stockman

For money, unlike other goods, is not merely wanted for its services or utilities as an assest to hold *after* all the transactions in the current period are settled, though this would be the case with the asset demand for money for which the function of money as a liquid store of value is the primary consideration. Money, however, is not merely a store of value, but also a necessary medium of exchange; money is demanded to finance the planned transactions yet to be carried out. This is what Keynes called the demands for "finance" which he regarded as some peculiar kind of demand for money, but which is really nothing but the transactions demand for money proper.

S. C. Tsiang (1966)

1. Introduction

The "finance constraint" formulated by S. C. Tsiang (1966) (in a paper written at the University of Rochester) and Robert Clower (1967) has been used extensively in recent years, particularly in models of international monetary economics. This essay summarizes some of this recent work and explains the role of the "money first" or "cash-in-

Finance Constraints and the Theory of Money
ISBN 0-12-701720-8
ISBN 0-12-701721-6 (pbk)

advance" constraint in these models. In particular, this essay addresses several criticisms of the cash-in-advance formulation that are frequently repeated by macroeconomists.

2. The Cash-in-Advance Constraint Formalizes the Transactions Demand for Money

As is clear from Tsiang's statement quoted above, the cash-in-advance constraint is intended simply as a formal representation of the transactions demand for money. The classic transactions demand models of Baumol (1952) and Tobin (1958) make the implicit assumption that money is required for transactions and add a cost of "going to the bank" so that almost all expenditure is financed by cash held in advance. The Baumol-Tobin model of money demand is more sophisticated in some ways than the cash-in-advance approach: it allows variation in the frequency with which households exchange money and other assets and in the payments period (the frequency of income receipts). But the Baumol-Tobin model, as usually formulated, is partial rather than general-equilibrium. The cash-in-advance approach can usefully be thought of as a simplification of the Baumol-Tobin model to make its application to general equilibrium easier. In particular, in a discrete time model, it can be thought of as postulating that the costs of "going to the bank" in the Baumol-Tobin model are zero if the household goes only once per "period" and infinite (or prohibitively high) for trips of greater frequency.

3. Alternative Models of Money: Why Cash-in-Advance?

There are several ways of introducing money into optimization models; why use the cash-in-advance model? Consider a discrete time model of an economy with a representative price-taking household. (The choice of discrete rather than continuous time is irrelevant for most of the issues discussed here.) Assume households have a time-separable utility function with a fixed rate of time preference. Households are assumed to maximize discounted expected utility,

$$E_0 \sum_{t=1}^{\infty} \beta^{t-1} U(c_t) \tag{1}$$

where $0 < \beta < 1$, subject to the sequence of budget constraints

$$y_t + z_t/p_t + \alpha_{t-1} r_t = c_t + (m_t - m_{t-1})/p_t + q_t(\alpha_t - \alpha_{t-1}), \quad (2)$$

where $\{y\}_t$ is an exogenous stochastic process representing endowments $\{z\}_t$ is an exogenous stochastic process representing lump-sum nominal transfer payments from the government; p_t is the price of goods in terms of money at date t; α_t is a vector of quantities of other assets (i.e. all assets except money) held by the household at the end of date t; r_t is the vector of returns paid by those assets as interest or dividends at date t; c_t is consumption at date t; m_t is the nominal quantity of money held by the household at the end of date t, and q_t is the price vector of assets α in terms of consumption goods. Households have initial stocks of money m_0 and assets α_0.

Assume that there are no limitations on the types of assets that can be traded in this model, so asset markets can be treated as complete. All households are identical by assumption, so m_t is the per capita money supply at date t and α_t is zero unless there are some assets in the economy, such as government bonds, that are not (directly) liabilities of households. For simplicity, assume that the government's only activity is to supply fiat money and change its quantity via lump-sum taxes or transfer payments, so α is identically zero. (Nothing crucial in this discussion hinges on this assumption.)

It is obvious that money has zero value in the equilibrium of this economy. To model a monetary equilibrium, one must modify the model so that money provides some services. One way to do this is to modify the utility function so that the household maximizes

$$E_0 \sum_{t=0}^{\infty} \beta^t U(c_t, m_t/p_t). \quad (1')$$

The usual timing convention is that end-of-period money holdings enter the utility function, but this is not necessary. This "money-in-utility" formulation can be very useful for certain problems, as McCallum (1985) has argued. Feenstra (1988) has argued that, by varying the form of the function $u(\ )$ above, including the cross-derivative u_{12}, one can reproduce many alternative stories about the role of money.

An alternative method of introducing money is by assuming that money is a factor of production (of output). Assume that y_t is produced with real money balances and an inelastic supply of other factors (nonreproducible, nondepreciating capital, and fixed labour supply). Then (2) becomes

$$y(m_{t+1}/p_t) - z_t + \alpha_t r_t$$
$$= c_t + (m_{t+1} - m_t)/p_t + q_t(\alpha_{t+1} - \alpha_t). \quad (2')$$

A third method of introducing money into the optimization problem is to postulate that there are transactions costs of exchange and that money reduces those costs. One way to formulate this is to replace (2) by

$$y_t - z_t + \alpha_t r_t = c_t[1 + \theta(m_t/p_t)] + (m_{t+1} - m_t)/p_t$$
$$+ q_t(\alpha_{t+1} - \alpha_t), \qquad\qquad (2'')$$

where $\theta(m_t/p_t)$ is the level of transactions costs that are paid by the household per unit of consumption purchased and $\theta(\ )$ is a decreasing function. In this formulation, the household must buy the gross amount $c_t[1 + \theta(m_t/p_t)]$ of the consumption good in order to consume the net amount c_t.

Finally, money can be introduced into the optimization problem through a cash-in-advance constraint. In addition to (1) and (2), the household faces the constraint

$$c_t \leq (m_{t+1} + z_t)/p_t, \qquad\qquad (3)$$

where $m_{t-1} + z_t$ is the household's nominal money stock at the beginning of period t. This constraint is sometimes relaxed so that some fraction of consumption goods can be purchased without the use of money. Alternatively, the model can be reinterpreted so that c is a vector of consumption goods, and the constraint (3) can be applied to only a subvector of the consumption vector (as in Lucas and Stokey, 1983, who call one set of goods "cash goods" and the other goods—not requiring money for purchase—"credit goods.").

There are other methods of introducing money into optimization problems; one prominent method involves use of overlapping generations models. McCallum (1982) provides a critical discussion of this method.

4. On the Equivalence of Cash-in-Advance and Money-in-Utility Models

Feenstra (1986) demonstrates that the money-in-utility formulation includes many other models as special cases. In particular, the cash-in-advance model discussed above can be replicated with a Leontief utility function so that households maximize

$$E_0 \sum_{t=0}^{\infty} \beta^t U\{\min[c_t, (m_{t-1} + z_t)/p_t]\}. \tag{1''}$$

Feenstra argues that the utility function in (1'') can be approximated by a concave utility function with a positive cross derivative between money and consumption, so that households would maximize

$$E_0 \sum_{t=0}^{\infty} \beta^t U[c_t, (m_{t-1} + z_t)/p_t],$$

where $U_{12} > 0$.

As Feenstra notes, however, not all cash-in-advance models can be rewritten as models with money in the utility function in this way. The key point is that restrictions on the utility function can capture relations between money holdings and consumption or other variables that enter utility directly, but they cannot capture relations between money holdings and variables that do not appear separately in the utility function. Consider, for example, the model in Stockman (1981). Physical capital is used as an input in the production of consumption goods with the technology

$$y_t = f(k_{t-1}),$$

where k_{t-1} is capital installed at date t. (The function f could be random without changing anything important.) For simplicity, suppose capital depreciates fully after one period. Output can be consumed or invested:

$$y_t = c_t + k_t.$$

Finally, adopt the (key) assumption that households must use money held at the beginning of the period to buy goods regardless of whether those goods are consumed of invested:

$$c_t + k_t \le (m_{t-1} + z_t)/p_t. \tag{3'}$$

This model cannot be written in terms of a utility function of consumption and real money balances alone. Instead, investment would enter the utility function as well; following Feenstra's reasoning, households would have to maximize

$$E_0 \sum_{t=0}^{\infty} \beta^t U\{\min[c_t, ((m_{t-1} + z_t)/p_t - k_t)]\}.$$

Similarly, the usual money-in-utility formulation will not replicate a cash-in-advance formulation if households must use money to purchase financial assets. If, in the cash-in-advance model above, "firms" do the investing by retaining output for use as capital, and if firms sell financial assets to households which must buy them with money, then the cash-in-advance constraint is again (3′) and the model cannot be replicated with a money-in-utility model. Similar comments apply to the model of Helpman and Razin (1985) in which money must be used to buy financial assets as well as consumption goods.

The usual money-in-utility formulation would also be unable to replicate the cash-in-advance model if output is exogenous and *durable*, even if money is used only to purchase goods and not assests. Obviously, this interpretation can be given to the model above if (e.g. with costless storage) $f(k) = k + x$, where k is stock of inventories of goods held by households and x is an exogenous level of output each period.

5. Timing in Cash-in-Advance Models

Issues of timing of transactions arise in cash-in-advance models because goods purchased during some time interval must be paid for with money held at the beginning of that interval. (If money acquired by selling goods at one point in time could then be *instantly* used to buy goods, then there would be no finite demand for the stock of money.) Most cash-in-advance models make the assumption that goods and financial assets are alternately traded. As time passes, the asset market (AM) is open for an interval of time, where assets are bartered, followed by a product market (PM) where goods and money are exchanged, followed by another asset market, and so on as in the following diagram.

A "period" is usually defined as an adjacent pair of AM and PM intervals; whether a period is defined so that the AM or PM comes first is irrelevant to the model. But the timing assumed for the arrival of information to households, the accrual of transfer payments or payments of taxes, and so on, can be important elements of a model. Stockman (1980) assumed that information about the realization of random variables is available at the beginning of a PM interval, and that actual payments of transfers occur at this time (with a "period" defined as a PM interval followed by an AM interval). Lucas (1982) assumed that all information regarding realizations of random variables is available at the beginning of the AM interval, and that all transfer payments are made at this time. (He also defines a "period" as an AM interval followed by a PM interval.)

With Lucas' (1982) timing assumptions, it is easy to see that *if* the nominal interest rate is strictly positive rather than zero, then the equilibrium of this model with the cash-in-advance constraint (3) implies that nominal income equals the nominal quantity of money. A strictly positive nominal interest rate implies that households would never choose, during AM trade, to hold more money than is required for purchasing goods at PM trade because money is dominated by nominal bonds. Otherwise a household would sacrifice interest earnings without getting any compensating benefits. Every household, then, spends all the money it holds on goods, so equation (3) holds as an equality for each household. Aggregation of (3) over households and substitution of the equilibrium conditions ($c_t = y_t$ and $m_{t-1} + z_t = M_t$, the per capita nominal money supply after transfers at the beginning of period t) then implies that the price level is given by

$$p_t = M_t/y_t. \tag{4}$$

This result implies that the velocity of money is insensitive to variations in the nominal interest rate, as long as it is positive. This "unit velocity" result has been cited by critics as a reason not to use the cash-in-advance method for introducing money. However, this result is not inherent in the cash-in-advance approach.

The condition that (3) hold as an equality, which requires a strictly positive nominal interest rate, is required for the result (4). The interest rate will be strictly positive only for certain restricted stochastic processes or for certain realizations of random variables. To see this most clearly, consider a version of the cash-in-advance model with Lucas' (1982) timing. Suppose

$$\beta E_t U'(c_{t+1})/p_{t+1} > U'(M_t/p_t)/p_t. \tag{5}$$

Inequality (5) says the following: if the household is spending all of its money today (at data t), then the expected discounted utility from a reduction in current spending in order to *hold* a unit of money—at zero interest—and spend it *next* period is larger than the current marginal utility cost of spending one less unit of money today. So it is better for the (representative) household *not* to spend all of the money it is holding at the beginning of the period than to spend it all. That is, the household can benefit by saving some of this money for next period, even if the nominal interest rate on this savings is zero. Of course, it would be even better for the household to lend the money and obtain positive interest receipts. But, because all households are alike and want to lend at *any* positive interest rate, the equilibrium nominal interest rate must be zero. This situation can occur in one of two cases: (i) if output at date t is particularly high (relative to expected output next period) and U'' is not sufficiently large in absolute value—so that the high equilibrium consumption does not lower U' very much but reduces p_t (with a unit elasticity if all money were spent) and so raises the right-hand side of (5), or (ii) if output is particularly low and U'' is very negative, so that the right-hand side of (5) is high.

So the cash-in-advance model predicts that, for certain realizations of random variables, not all money will be spent. Instead, some money that could have been spent will simply be held. Consequently, the velocity of money is endogenous (and is affected by the expected rate of monetary growth). As explained above, this "precautionary demand for money" exists only when the nominal interest rate is zero. However, Svensson (1985a) showed that there is an alternative interpretation of this same model in which velocity is endogenous *and* the nominal interest rate is strictly positive. Suppose there is an "early-morning asset market," an additional AM interval that occurs each period before the information about the current state of nature is available. Consider the equilibrium interest rate on loans in this "early AM." It is strictly positive because it is a weighted average of a strictly positive nominal interest rate (with strictly positive probability) and a zero nominal interest rate. So the pre-information nominal interest rate will always be positive. Nevertheless, the post-information nominal interest rate will be zero in exactly those states of the world in which households do not spend all of their money. So the velocity of money will be endogenous and the (pre-information) nominal interest rate is strictly positive.

In *any* model with representative households that do not spend all of their money in some periods (so that velocity is less than one per period), households would find that the equilibrium nominal interest rate they can obtain on short-term loans—for the duration of the time that they are holding money—is zero. So the properties of the "money demand function" in the cash-in-advance model turn out not to differ from other models of money nearly as much as most critics of the approach have claimed. The velocity of money is variable and can, in fact, be written as a decreasing function of the nominal interest rate.

However, the cash-in-advance model also has the advantage that, when the economic issues being investigated do not turn on variable velocity, exogenous stochastic processes can be restricted so that—for simplicity in the model—velocity would be fixed at unity.

There are also other versions of cash-in-advance models in which the demand for money depends on the nominal interest rate, so that velocity is variable. This is the case in the model developed by Lucas and Stokey with "cash goods" and "credit goods" where the cash-in-advance constraint applies only to the former class of consumption goods. Even if the velocity of money for cash goods were fixed at one, the velocity with respect to total income or expenditure would be variable. Similarly, if there are differentiated goods and households must use money only for goods that they are net buyers of, as in ongoing work by the author and Harold Cole (1987), the demand for money depends on the nominal interest rate. Other cash-in-advance models with variable velocity, due to an endogenous length of period, include Fried (1973) and Leach (1983).

6. Cash-in-Advance in International Monetary Models

The cash-in-advance constraint has been used more widely in international macroeconomic models than in closed economy models. One reason for this is the problem of introducing two different moneys into a model. With a money-in-utility model, one could either place both moneys in the utility function or make utility functions of domestic and foreign households differ, with only domestic money in the representative domestic household's utility function, and so on. The cash-in-advance model is useful in international models because it provides a clear method of connecting the use of moneys to expenditures and incomes. Although the assumption that green money is used for one set of goods (e.g. those sold in Greenland) while blue money is used for another set of goods (e.g. those sold in Blueland) is auxiliary to the cash-in-advance model, this clear method of connecting moneys and goods provides an advantage over other approaches to the introduction of money in an optimizing model.

In most work it has been assumed that the money used in any transaction is the seller's country's currency, though Helpman and Razin (1984) have investigated consequences of the opposite assumption, namely that the buyer's country's money is used in all transactions. The cash-in-advance model can also be used to illustrate clearly the Karaken-Wallace (1981) result on exchange rates when moneys are perfect substitutes; one can construct a model in which either of two currencies can be used for any transaction, making the nominal exchange rate indeterminate and its expected rate of change equal to zero. (See also King, Wallace, and Weber, 1986.)

The usual assumptions regarding the use of sellers' currencies in international models incorporating the cash-in-advance constraint are frequently justified by citing a study by Grassman (1973) which showed that a large fraction of international transactions are denominated in the seller's currency. This, of course, is not a clear justification for the sellers' currencies assumption, because the currency of denomination of a contract can easily differ from the currency used to complete the transaction by extinguishing the debt. Nevertheless, it provides a good starting point for research. The sellers' currency assumption also ignores domestic resale of imported products, but this could be introduced at the cost of trying to model heterogeneity of importers and consumers.

An important result from international models incorporating the cash-in-advance approach involves a rehabilitation of flow approach to exchange rates, but this time justified in a rigorous general equilibrium setting (see Stockman, 1987; Tsiang, 1986, has also contributed recently to this growing literature). This flow approach can be contrasted with the stock or asset-market approach that followed from the monetary approach to the balance of payments.

The development of the modern equilibrium flow approach to exchange rates has been important for several reasons. First, it has integrated exchange rate theory into general equilibrium asset-pricing models. This has permitted greater understanding of the connections between exchange rate behavior and asset price behavior in general equilibrium models. It has also assisted the development of monetary models in which the formal analogies between the pricing of money and the pricing of other assets becomes apparent, as in Svensson (1985a). Second, these models have been useful for developing rigorous comparisons of alternative exchange rate systems. Helpman (1981) explored rigorously the differences between these systems in a perfect foresight model, and Lucas (1982) did the same in a stochastic model. The importance of this approach does not necessarily lie in the conclusions of those papers but in the issues on which they focused and the contribution to clear and rigorous thought about the sources of any differences between equilibria under alternative exchange rate systems.

Third, the equilibrium models of exchanges rate have provided an alternative explanation for observed exchange rate behavior that does not suffer from some of the empirical failures that previous models of exchange rates had, such as predicting far more intrinsic dynamics in real and nominal exchange rates than is observed in the data. Finally, these models have permitted rigorous analysis of the connections between exchange rates, money growth rates, and real output (e.g. Svensson 1985b); exchange rates and the current account or international capital flows (e.g. Stockman and Svensson, 1987); exchange rate behavior and variations of risk premia (e.g. Hodrick, 1987); exchange rates and nontraded goods (e.g. Helpman and Razin, 1982, and Stockman and Dellas, 1986); the effects of capital controls and exchange controls (Stockman and Hernandez, 1988); and so on.

None of these developments in international monetary economics *requires* the cash-in-advance model as a part of its argument; virtually all of the important economic points made in these papers could have been made in models using some other method of introducing money. But the fact that these developments have come so rapidly, almost always using the cash-in-advance formulation, is a testimony to the method as a modeling technique that has elicited substantive progress on economic issues.

The cash-in-advance approach has usually been a part of models in an "equilibrium" or flexible-price tradition. But this is not a necessary part of the approach. Svensson (1986) and Svensson and Wijnbergen (1987) have developed models incorporating the cash-in-advance constraint that assume that nominal prices must be set by sellers before they observe the state of demand. The reason that sluggish price-adjustment models have not used the cash-in-advance approach as much as the equilibrium models is primarily due to the fact that they have not used optimizing models as much as have equilibrium models. The papers by Svensson and Wijnbergen, and related work by others, may be changing that fact in the near future.

7. Criticisms of the Cash-in-Advance Approach; Conclusions

One of the main criticisms heard by proponents of the cash-in-advance approach is that the "distortions" (relative to a barter economy) introduced by that approach are too small to be important empirically. This criticism, as far as I know, has not been made in print, but economists who use the cash-in-advance model will recognize that they have heard it repeated frequently at conferences and in discussions. The distortion at issue is, of course, the wedge that has been discussed in the papers by Wilson, Stockman, Aschauer and Greenwood, Stockman, Abel, and others. This distortion involves the cost, paid implicitly by a person who uses money to purchase something, of holding the money prior to the purchase. When applied to labor supply, the point is that leisure time need not be purchased with money while market goods must be, consequently people can avoid paying an "inflation tax" (or paying seigniorage) by buying leisure time rather than market goods (which leads labor supply to be lower in periods of higher inflation). When applied to capital, there are two points. First, if capital must be purchased with money just as any consumption good must be, then the net return from capital equals the gross return minus the cost of holding money before buying the capital (which leads the capital stock to be lower in the presence of higher inflation). Second, even if capital can be obtained without going through an exchange involving money, antici- pated changes in the rate of inflation affect the capital stock. This occurs because the future income generated by an increase in capital will be used to purchase future consumption goods, and these purchases will involve the future payment of an inflation tax with a magnitude that depends on the inflation rate in the future. The alternative to using current output for investment is to use it for consumption, which involves paying an inflation tax with a magnitude determined by the current inflation rate. So the investment choice is affected by the rate of inflation expected in the future relative to the current inflation rate. When applied to different types of goods—e.g. what Lucas and Stokey call "credit goods," which can be purchased on credit without ever holding money, and "cash goods," which must be purchased with money—the point is that goods that require a greater holding of money prior to their purchase (the Lucas-Stokey "cash goods") have a gross relative price to consumers that rises in the inflation rate (leading consumers to substitute away from cash goods toward credit goods when inflation rises).

Are these distortions "too small"? The obvious question is "too small for what?" If the nominal interest rate is 12% per year and a person holds cash for one month prior to buying a good, he pays roughly a 1% "tax" on the purchase, as compared with buying leisure time or "credit goods." The magnitude of the distortion to rate of return to capital is of similar magnitude. This is clearly too small an effect to postulate as the main source of effects from the money supply to aggregate output and employment. But no one, as far as I know, has proposed these wedges as major forces in business cycles. (Similar considerations have led most macroeconomists to reject models that rely heavily on a Mundell-Tobin effect to generate business cycles.) If the elasticity of the steady-state capital stock with respect to the rate of return is about unity, this distortion would lead to a 1% lower capital stock in the presence of 12% inflation (and a zero real interest rate) than with zero inflation. On the other hand, if inflation were 120% per year, then the magnitude of the distortion rises tenfold, and the magnitude of the effect could be important. While this distortion might be mitigated by a rise in the frequency of payments, it might be reinforced by other distortions in the economy (cf. Kohn, 1984).

The fact that the cash-in-advance model generates these distortions should not count against the model even if they are of negligible empirical importance under normal circumstances in advanced countries. Instead, the fact that the model has called attention to connections between the use of money for transactions and relative prices, real factor allocations, and households' allocative decisions should be considered a success for the model. There may be other connections that have not yet been discovered or modeled rigorously, but these initial rigorous attempts have at least begun the task of integrating the theory of money with nontrivial allocation decisions in general equilibrium theory.

A second set of criticisms of the cash-in-advance approach that is frequently heard—particularly by proponents of the overlapping generations approach to money—is that the cash-in-advance model does not help us determine either why money is used at all (rather than barter) or which good will be used as money (and why fiat money has any value at all). These are clearly difficult issues that no one has adequately resolved. One answer that proponents of the cash-in-advance approach sometimes give is that they are not attempting to answer these questions but are restricting themselves to other questions and using a model in which—realistically—money (and fiat money at that) *is* used. This, however, is not necessarily an adequate response. We know from other examples that *why* something is done—rather than the fact *that* it is done—can frequently matter for its effects. For example, we know that the effects of sluggish nominal wage or price adjustment does not necessarily imply the results postulated by Keynesian models; if the sluggishness is the result of some optimal risk-sharing arrangement then it need not affect real allocations at all—or, if it does, it improves real allocations (by improving the allocation of risk) rather than creating situations of excess demand or supply.

It might be that, when someone finally develops a satisfactory model to explain why money is used, and what is accepted as a means of payment, and so on, the model will have implications that are quite different from existing models of money. But that fact is not guaranteed, either. Meanwhile, alternative models of money do no better on this score than the cash-in-advance models do. Clearly, models that put money in the utility or production functions face these same problems. But so do overlapping generations models of money. Usually there is only one asset in overlapping generations models, and the economists who write down the models simply choose to call that asset "money." But that name does not mean that the asset has many of the properties that we usually attribute to money. When OG models are written with "money" and "nominal bonds," there are usually *ad hoc* restrictions implied that prevent certain people from holding nominal bonds, e.g. it is sometimes assumed that nominal bonds come only in large denominations that poorer people cannot afford. Then bonds and money can coexist, with the rich holding bonds and the poor holding money. But the assumption that interest-bearing assets like bonds cannot be broken down by financial intermediaries into smaller denominations (something that would clearly provide positive private returns in those models) is as *ad hoc* as assumptions made in cash-in-advance models that only a certain thing may be used as money, e.g. because vending machines have been built only to recognize that kind of thing in exchange for goods. Each is a "technological" assumption that is blatantly *ad hoc*.

Cash-in-advance models *do* fail to answer some important questions, but—on the same level—so do all other existing models of money. This simply means that the theory of money is not "done." The cash-in-advance approach, pioneered by S. C. Tsiang and Robert Clower, has been a key component of many advances in monetary economics and international finance in recent years, and it is likely to remain a useful tool for some time to come.

Acknowledgements

I would like to thank Meir Kohn for comments. This research has been supported by the National Science Foundation.

References

Abel, Andrew (1985), "Dynamic Behavior of Capital Accumulation in a Cash-in-Advance Model," *Journal of Monetary Economics.* **16**, 55–72.

Aschauer, David and Greenwood, Jeremy (1983), "A Further Exploration in the Theory of Exchange Rate Regimes," *Journal of Political Economy.* **91**, October, 868–75.

Baumol, William (1952), "The Transactions Demand for Cash: An Inventory-Theoretic Approach," *Quarterly Journal of Economics.* **66**, November, 545–56.

Clower, Robert W. (1967), "A Reconstruction of the Microfoundations of Monetary Theory," *Western Economic Journal.* **6**, December, 1–9.

Cole, Harold and Stockman, Alan C. (1987), "Specialization, Transactions Technologies, and Money Growth," University of Rochester, March.

Feenstra, Robert C. (1986), "Functional Equivalence between Liquidity Costs and the Utility of Money," *Journal of Monetary Economics.* **17**, no. 2, March, 271–92.

Fried, Joel S. (1973), "Money, Exchange, and Growth," *Western Economic Journal.* **11**, 285–301.

Grassman, Sven (1973), "A Fundamental Symmetry in International Payments Patterns," *Journal of International Economics.* **3**, May, 105–16.

Helpman, Elhanan (1981), "An Exploration in the Theory of Exchange Rate Regimes," *Journal of Political Economy.* **89**, October, 865–890.

Helpman, Elhanan and Razin, Assaf (1982), "Dynamics of a Floating Exchange Rate Regime," *Journal of Political Economy.* **90**, 728–54.

Helpman, Elhanan (1984), "The Roles of Savings and Investment in Exchange Rate Determination under Alternative Monetary Mechanisms," *Journal of Monetary Economics.* **13**, May, 307–26.

Helpman, Elhanan (1985), "Floating Exchange Rates with Liquidity Constraints in Financial Markets," *Journal of International Economics.* **19**, August, 99–118.

Helpman, Elhanan (1985), "Exchange Rate Management: Intertemporal Tradeoffs," NBER working paper #1590.

Jovanovic, Boyan (1982), "Inflation and Welfare in the Steady State," *Journal of Political Economy.* **90**, June, 561–77.

Karaken, John and Wallace, Neil (1981), "On the Indeterminacy of Equilibrium Exchange Rates," *Quarterly Journal of Economics.* **96**, May, 207–222.

Kimbrough, Kent (1987), "International Linkages, Exchange Rate Regimes and the International Transmission Process: Perspectives from Optimizing Models," forthcoming in L. H. Officer (ed.) *International Economics.* Boston: Kluner-Nijhold.

King, Robert; Wallace, Neil and Weber, Warren (1986), "Extrinsic-Uncertainty Exchange Rate Equilibria," working paper, Federal Reserve Bank of Minneapolis.

Kohn, Meir (1981), "In Defense of the Finance Constraint," *Economic Inquiry.* **19**, April, 177–95.

Kohn, Meir (1984), "The Inflation Tax and the Value of Equity," *Canadian Journal of Economics*. **XVII**, May, 312–26.

Kohn, Meir (1985), "The Finance (Cash-in-Advance) Constraint Comes of Age: A Survey of Some Recent Developments in the Theory of Money," Dartmouth College.

Leach, J. (1983), "Inflation as a Commodity Tax," *Canadian Journal of Economics*. **16**, August.

Lucas, Robert E. (1980), "Equilibrium in a Pure Currency Economy," *Economic Inquiry*. **28**, April, 203–20.

Lucas, Robert, E. (1982), "Interest Rates and Currency Prices in a Two-Country World," *Journal of Monetary Economics*. **10**, 335–60.

Lucas, Robert E. and Stokey, Nancy (1982), "Optimal Fiscal and Monetary Policy in an Economy without Capital," *Journal of Monetary Economics*. **12**, July, 55–93.

Persson, Torsten (1984), "Real Transfers in Fixed Exchange Rate Systems and the International Adjustment Mechanism," *Journal of Monetary Economics*. **13**, May, 349–70.

Salyer, Keven (1985), "Cash-in-Advance Economies: A Study of Inflation and the Timing of Markets," Vanderbilt University.

Stockman, Alan C. (1980), "A Theory of Exchange Rate Determination," *Journal of Political Economy*. **88**, 673–98.

Stockman, Alan C. (1981), "Anticipated Inflation and the Capital Stock in a Cash-in-Advance Economy," *Journal of Monetary Economics*. **8**, October, 387–93.

Stockman, Alan C. (1985) "Effects of Inflation on the Pattern of International Trade," *Canadian Journal of Economics*. **XVIII**, no. 3, August, 587–601.

Stockman, Alan C. (1987), "The Equilibrium Approach to Exchange Rates." *Economic Review*, Federal Reserve Bank of Richmond, March-April, 12–31.

Stockman, Alan C. and Dellas, Harris (1986), "International Portfolio Non-diversification and Exchange Rate Variability," University of Rochester, 1986.

Stockman, Alan C. and Svensson, Lars E. O. (1987), "Capital Flows, Investment, and Exchange Rates," *Journal of Monetary Economics*. **19**, no. 2, March, 171–202.

Stockman, Alan C. and Cole, Harold (1987), "Specialization, Transaction Technologies, and Money Growth," University of Rochester.

Stockman, Alan C. and Hernandez, Alejandro (1988), "Exchange Controls Capital Controls, and International Financial Markets," forthcoming, *American Economic Review*.

Svensson, Lars E. O. (1985a), "Money and Asset Prices in a Cash-in-Advance Economy," *Journal of Political Economy*. **93**, 919–44.

Svensson, Lars E. O. (1985b), "Currency Prices, Terms of Trade, and Interest Rates: A General Equilibrium Asset-Pricing, Cash-in-Advance Approach," *Journal of International Economics*.

Svensson Lars E. O. (1986), "Sticky Goods Prices, Flexible Asset Prices, Monopolistic Competition, and Monetary Policy," Institute for International Economic Studies, Stockholm.

Svensson, Lars E. O. and van Wijnbergen, Sweder (1987), "International Transmission of Monetary Policy," Institute for International Economic Studies, Stockholm.

Tobin, James (1956), "The Interest-Elasticity of the Transactions Demand for Cash," *Review of Economics and Statistics*. **39**, August, 241–47.

Tsiang, S. C. (1966), "Walras' Law, Say's Law, and Liquidity Preference in General Equilibrium," *International Economic Review*. **7**, September, 329–45.

Tsiang, S. C. (1986), "The Flow Formulation of the Money Market Equilibrium for an Open Economy and the Determination of the Exchange Rate," *Symposium on Monetary Theory*. Taipei.

Wilson, Charles, (1979), "An Infinite Horizon Model with Money," in J. Green and J. Scheinkman (eds.), *General Equilibrium, Growth, and Trade: Essays in Honor of Lionel McKenzie*. New York: Academic Press.

Author Index

Subject Index

Economic Theory, Econometrics, and Mathematical Economics

Edited by Karl Shell, *Cornell University*

Recent titles